WOMEN'S
CHANGING ROLES

ISSN 1538-666X

WOMEN'S CHANGING ROLES

Margaret Alic

INFORMATION PLUS® REFERENCE SERIES
Formerly published by Information Plus, Wylie, Texas

GALE GROUP

THOMSON LEARNING

*Detroit • New York • San Diego • San Francisco
Boston • New Haven, Conn. • Waterville, Maine
London • Munich*

WOMEN'S CHANGING ROLES

Margaret Alic, *Author*

The Gale Group Staff:
Coordinating Editors: Ellice Engdahl, *Series Editor*; Charles B. Montney, *Series Graphics Editor*
Managing Editor: Debra M. Kirby
Contributing Editors: Elizabeth Manar, Kathleen Meek
Contributing Associate Editors: Paula Cutcher-Jackson, Prindle LaBarge, Heather Price, Michael T. Reade
Imaging and Multimedia Content: Barbara J. Yarrow, *Manager, Imaging and Multimedia Content*; Dean Dauphinais, *Imaging and Multimedia Content Editor*; Kelly A. Quin, *Imaging and Multimedia Content Editor*; Robyn Young, *Imaging and Multimedia Content Editor*; Leitha Etheridge-Sims, *Image Cataloger*; Mary K. Grimes, *Image Cataloger*; David G. Oblender, *Image Cataloger*; Lezlie Light, *Imaging Coordinator*; Randy Bassett, *Imaging Supervisor*; Robert Duncan, *Imaging Specialist*; Dan Newell, *Imaging Specialist*; Luke Rademacher, *Imaging Specialist*; Christine O'Bryan, *Graphic Specialist*
Indexing: Amy R. Suchowski, *Indexing Specialist*
Permissions: Lori Hines, *Permissions Assistant*; Maria Franklin, *Permissions Manager*
Product Design: Michelle DiMercurio, *Senior Art Director and Product Design Manager*; Michael Logusz, *Graphic Artist*
Production: Evi Seoud, *Assistant Manager, Composition Purchasing and Electronic Prepress*; Keith Helmling, *Buyer*; Dorothy Maki, *Manufacturing Manager*
Cover photo © PhotoDisc.

TABLE OF CONTENTS

Most of the more than 143 million women in America are white and between the ages of 18 and 64, according to the data in this chapter. More than ever before are also single (divorced, widowed, or never-married). The effect of this and other demographic trends on living arrangements and household types and sizes is analyzed.

Women are obtaining more education in fields of study more varied than did previous generations. School attendance and achievement (from test scores to degrees earned) are discussed, along with the topics of single-sex vs. co-ed schools and female participation in school-sponsored athletic programs.

A history of women's participation in the American workforce starts this chapter, which investigates contemporary female workers by occupation, age, race, marital status, education, and children. Information on work-related issues of interest to women—such as welfare reform, part-time jobs, flextime schedules, and telecommuting—is included, along with rates of and reasons for unemployment among women.

Though most women still work in traditionally "female" jobs, more are moving into such fields as construction, law, and business. This chapter contains information on women in the corporate world; in the fields of science, engineering, and technology; in academia; and in the military. Women-owned businesses and prospects for women's progress in previously male-dominated professions are also considered.

Women's incomes have been rising in comparison with men's. Still, as this chapter makes clear, there is a substantial earnings gap between the sexes, influenced by factors of race, marital status, motherhood, occupation, and education. Single-mother families, welfare reform, lack of child support, and a shortage of pensions are explained as reasons that more women than men hold poverty status.

A look at birth rates by mothers' age, race, ethnicity, education, income, and marital status begins this chapter. Unmarried childbearing and births to teenagers are also examined, along with health issues related to pregnancy and motherhood. The focus then shifts to childbearing alternatives, such as contraception, abortion, childlessness, and adoption. Last, the chapter addresses family and work arrangements for single mothers, grandmothers, and working mothers.

This chapter details various kinds of child care available, including home-based care by relatives and non-relatives, child care centers, and preschools. An account of employee benefits and government laws that assist working parents touches on family leave, flexible scheduling, on-site facilities, backup programs, resource and referral services, the Child Care and Development Fund, and Head Start. Shifting to elder care issues, this chapter looks at the lack of programs for the elderly outside the home, dilemmas of the "sandwich generation" and working women, and business responses to these problems.

What role do women voters and elected officials play in American politics? This chapter indicates that women exert growing influence but are less politically active than men. Women's patterns of registration and voter turnout, positions on issues, and party affiliation are described; and information about women serving in Congress and in state and municipal government is also presented. The chapter ends with a discussion of women in the federal government's executive branch.

Women are less likely than men to be victims of violent crime, but they outnumber men as victims of rape, sexual assault, and domestic violence, according to data in this chapter. Domestic violence and sexual harassment (in business, prison, and the military, as well as on college campuses) are discussed in depth.

Women commit only about 20 percent of crimes, but their arrest rates are rising in most categories except property crime. This chapter presents and interprets statistics on violent crimes by women, female prisoners, and the death sentence as applied to women.

CHAPTER 11

Women's health issues are the focus of this chapter, which begins by surveying access to health care. Cardiovascular disease, cancer, and other leading causes of death in women are discussed, along with AIDS, additional sexually transmitted diseases, and osteoporosis. The chapter examines mental depression and eating disorders and also considers preventive measures like smoking cessation, substance abuse control, diet, nutrition, and exercise.

PREFACE

Women's Changing Roles is one of the latest volumes in the Information Plus Reference Series. Previously published by the Information Plus company of Wylie, Texas, the Information Plus Reference Series (and its companion set, the Information Plus Compact Series) became a Gale Group product when Gale and Information Plus merged in early 2000. Those of you familiar with the series as published by Information Plus will notice a few changes from the 2000 edition. Gale has adopted a new layout and style that we hope you will find easy to use. Other improvements include greatly expanded indexes in each book, and more descriptive tables of contents.

While some changes have been made to the design, the purpose of the Information Plus Reference Series remains the same. Each volume of the series presents the latest facts on a topic of pressing concern in modern American life. These topics include today's most controversial and most studied social issues: abortion, capital punishment, care for the elderly, crime, health care, the environment, immigration, minorities, social welfare, women, youth, and many more. Although written especially for the high school and undergraduate student, this series is an excellent resource for anyone in need of factual information on current affairs.

By presenting the facts, it is Gale's intention to provide its readers with everything they need to reach an informed opinion on current issues. To that end, there is a particular emphasis in this series on the presentation of scientific studies, surveys, and statistics. These data are generally presented in the form of tables, charts, and other graphics placed within the text of each book. Every graphic is directly referred to and carefully explained in the text. The source of each graphic is presented within the graphic itself. The data used in these graphics are drawn from the most reputable and reliable sources, in particular the various branches of the U.S. government and major independent polling organizations. Every effort

has been made to secure the most recent information available. The reader should bear in mind that many major studies take years to conduct, and that additional years often pass before the data from these studies is made available to the public. Therefore, in many cases the most recent information available in 2002 dated from 1999 or 2000. Older statistics are sometimes presented as well, if they are of particular interest and no more recent information exists.

Although statistics are a major focus of the Information Plus Reference Series, they are by no means its only content. Each book also presents the widely held positions and important ideas that shape how the book's subject is discussed in the United States. These positions are explained in detail and, where possible, in the words of their proponents. Some of the other material to be found in these books includes: historical background; descriptions of major events related to the subject; relevant laws and court cases; and examples of how these issues play out in American life. Some books also feature primary documents, or have pro and con debate sections giving the words and opinions of prominent Americans on both sides of a controversial topic. All material is presented in an even-handed and unbiased manner; the reader will never be encouraged to accept one view of an issue over another.

HOW TO USE THIS BOOK

As they marry later in life, have fewer children, get more education, and participate in the labor force in growing numbers, the roles American women play are changing. However, in terms of caregiving responsibility, earnings and assets, and gender-linked jobs, many women have experienced little change in their roles. These conflicting developments are illustrated by information on demographic trends, educational achievement, employment, financial status, parental responsibilities, political roles, victimization, and health issues that is presented and explained in this book.

Women's Changing Roles consists of eleven chapters and three appendices. Each of the chapters is devoted to a particular aspect of women's changing roles. For a summary of the information covered in each chapter, please see the synopses provided in the Table of Contents at the front of the book. Chapters generally begin with an overview of the basic facts and background information on the chapter's topic, then proceed to examine sub-topics of particular interest. For example, Chapter Seven: Child Care and Elder Care begins with a discussion of caregiving in general, emphasizing that women still bear the major responsibility for this task even though rising workforce participation rates mean they spend less time in the home. It then details various kinds of child care available, including home-based care by relatives and nonrelatives, child care centers, and preschools. Means by which business and government assist in providing child care (from flexible scheduling, on-site facilities, and resource and referral services to family leave, the Child Care and Development Fund, and Head Start) are listed and explained. Problems specific to elder care and employers' responses to them are also included. Readers can find their way through a chapter by looking for the section and sub-section headings, which are clearly set off from the text. Or, they can refer to the book's extensive index if they already know what they are looking for.

Statistical Information

The tables and figures featured throughout *Women's Changing Roles* will be of particular use to the reader in learning about this issue. These tables and figures represent an extensive collection of the most recent and important statistics on women, as well as related issues—for example, graphics in the book cover estimated median age at first marriage; educational attainment by race and sex; civilian labor force participation rates by sex and age; twenty leading occupations of employed women; women's earnings as a percentage of men's; birth rates by age of mother; percent of children by type of child care arrangement; reported rates of voting and registration by race and sex; number of victimizations by race, gender,

and age; sentenced prisoners under state jurisdiction, by offense and gender; and estimates of AIDS in women. Gale believes that making this information available to the reader is the most important way in which we fulfill the goal of this book: to help readers understand the issues and controversies surrounding women's changing roles in the United States and reach their own conclusions.

Each table or figure has a unique identifier appearing above it, for ease of identification and reference. Titles for the tables and figures explain their purpose. At the end of each table or figure, the original source of the data is provided.

In order to help readers understand these often complicated statistics, all tables and figures are explained in the text. References in the text direct the reader to the relevant statistics. Furthermore, the contents of all tables and figures are fully indexed. Please see the opening section of the index at the back of this volume for a description of how to find tables and figures within it.

In addition to the main body text and images, *Women's Changing Roles* has three appendices. The first is the Important Names and Addresses directory. Here the reader will find contact information for a number of government and private organizations that can provide information on women's roles. The second appendix is the Resources section, which can also assist the reader in conducting his or her own research. In this section, the author and editors of *Women's Changing Roles* describe some of the sources that were most useful during the compilation of this book. The final appendix is the index. It has been greatly expanded from previous editions, and should make finding specific topics in this book even easier.

COMMENTS AND SUGGESTIONS

The editors of the Information Plus Reference Series welcome your feedback on *Women's Changing Roles.* Please direct all correspondence to:

Editors
Information Plus Reference Series
27500 Drake Rd.
Farmington Hills, MI 48331-3535

ACKNOWLEDGEMENTS

The editors wish to thank the copyright holders of material included in this volume and the permissions managers of many book and magazine publishing companies for assisting us in securing reproduction rights. We are also grateful to the staffs of the Detroit Public Library, the Library of Congress, the University of Detroit Mercy Library, Wayne State University Purdy/Kresge Library Complex, and the University of Michigan Libraries for making their resources available to us.

Following is a list of the copyright holders who have granted us permission to reproduce material in Information Plus: Women's Changing Roles. Every effort has been made to trace copyright, but if omissions have been made, please let us know.

Acknowledgements are listed in the order the tables and figures appear in the text of Women's Changing Roles. For more detailed citations, please see the sources listed under each table and figure.

Figure 1.1. Smith, Denise I. and Renee E. Spraggins. "Figure 2. The Male-Female Ratio: 1900 to 2000," in *Gender: 2000*, September 2001. U.S. Census Bureau.

Table 1.1. "Table 3. Female Population by Age, Race and Hispanic or Latino Origin for the United States: 2000," in *Census 2000 Summary File 1* [Online], October 3, 2001. http://www.census.gov/population/cen2000/phc-t9/tab03.pdf. [Accessed October 6, 2001]. U.S. Census Bureau.

Table 1.2. "Table 1. Male-Female Ratio by Race Alone or in Combination and Hispanic or Latino Origin in the United States: 2000," in *Census 2000 Summary File 1* [Online], September 10, 2001. http://www.census.gov/population/www/cen2000/phc-t11.html. [Accessed September 18, 2001]. U.S. Census Bureau.

Table 1.3. Hollmann, Frederick W., Tammany J. Mulder, and Jeffrey E. Kallan. "Pro-jected Life Expectancy at birth by Race and Hispanic Origin, 1999 to 2100," in *Methodology and Assumptions for the Population Projections of the United States: 1999 to 2100*, Population Division Working Paper No. 38, 2000. U.S. Census Bureau.

Table 1.4. "Table 8. Foreign-Born Population by Citizenship Status, Year of Entry, and Sex: March 2000," in *Current Population Survey, March 2000* [Online], March 15, 2001. http://www.census.gov/population/socdemo/gender/ppl-121/tab08.txt. [Accessed October 11, 2001]. U.S. Census Bureau.

Table 1.5. Fields, Jason and Lynne M. Casper. "Table 5. Marital Status of People 15 Years and Over: March 1970 and March 2000," in *America's Families and Living Arrangements: March 2000*, Current Population Reports P20-537, June 2001. U.S. Census Bureau.

Table 1.6. "Table MS-2. Estimated Median Age at First Marriage, by Sex: 1890 to the Present," in *Families and Living Arrangements* [Online], June 29, 2001. http://www.census.gov/population/socdemo/hh-fam/tabMS-2.txt. [Accessed September 18, 2001]. U.S. Census Bureau.

Table 1.7. Fields, Jason and Lynne M. Casper. "Table 7. Characteristics of Unmarried Partners and Married Spouses by Sex: March 2000," in *America's Families and Living Arrangements: March 2000*, Current Population Reports P20-537, June 2001. U.S. Census Bureau.

Table 1.8. Fields, Jason and Lynne M. Casper. "Table 8. Characteristics of Unmarried and Married Male-Female Couples: March 2000," in *America's Families and Living Arrangements: March 2000*, Current Population Reports P20-537, June 2001. U.S. Census Bureau.

Figure 1.2. Fields, Jason and Lynne M. Casper. "Figure 1. Households by Type: Selected Years, 1970 to 2000," in *America's Families and Living Arrangements: March 2000*, Current Population Reports P20-537, June 2001. U.S. Census Bureau.

Table 1.9. Fields, Jason and Lynne M. Casper. "Table 1. Households by Type and Selected Characteristics: March 2000," in *America's Families and Living Arrangements: March 2000*, Current Population Reports P20-537, June 2001. U.S. Census Bureau.

Table 1.10. Fields, Jason and Lynne M. Casper. "Table 6. Living Arrangements of Younger and Older Adults: March 2000," in *America's Families and Living Arrangements: March 2000*, Current Population Reports P20-537, June 2001. U.S. Census Bureau.

Table 1.11. "No. 1213. Homeownership Rates by Age of Householder and Family Status: 1985 to 1999," in *Statistical Abstract of the United States: 2000*, 2001. U.S. Census Bureau.

Table 2.1. "No. 250. Educational Attainment by Race, Hispanic Origin, and Sex: 1960 to 1999," in *Statistical Abstract of the United States: 2000*, 2001. U.S. Census Bureau.

Table 2.2. "Table 7. Percent of the Population 3 to 34 Years Old Enrolled in School, by Race/Ethnicity, Sex, and Age: October 1975 to October 1999," in *Digest of Educational Statistics 2000*, January 2001. National Center for Education Statistics.

Table 2.3. "Table 10-3. Average Reading Scale Scores, by Sex and Age: 1971-99," in *The Condition of Education 2001*, July 2001. National Center for Education Statistics.

Table 2.4. "Table 12-3. Average Mathematics Scale Scores, by Sex and Age: 1973-99," in *The Condition of Education 2001*, July 2001. National Center for Education Statistics.

Table 2.5. "Table 13-3. Average Science Scale Scores, by Sex and Age: 1970-99," in *The Condition of Education 2001*, July 2001. National Center for Education Statistics.

Table 2.6. "Table 185. College Enrollment Rates of High School Graduates, by Sex: 1960 to 1999," in *Digest of Education Statistics 2000*, January 2001. National Center for Education Statistics.

Table 2.7. "Table 248. Earned Degrees Conferred by Degree-Granting Institutions, by Level of Degree and Sex of Student: 1869-70 to 2009-10," in *Digest of Education Statistics 2000*, January 2001. National Center for Education Statistics.

Table 2.8. "Table 266. Bachelor's Degrees Conferred by Degree-Granting Institutions, by Racial/Ethnic Group, Major Field of Study, and Sex of Student: 1997-98," in *Digest of Education Statistics 2000*, January 2001. National Center for Education Statistics.

Table 2.9. "Table 269. Master's Degrees Conferred by Degree-Granting Institutions, by Racial/Ethnic Group, Major Field of Study, and Sex of Student: 1997-98," in *Digest of Education Statistics 2000*, January 2001. National Center for Education Statistics.

Figure 2.1. Pratt, Megan. "Percent of Female Doctorate Recipients by Broad Field, 1969, 1979, 1989, 1999," in *Association for Women in Science* [Online]. http://www.awis.org/statistics/science_human.JPG. [Accessed October 11, 2001]. National Science Foundation's Division of Science Resources Statistics.

Table 2.10. "Table 275. First-Professional Degrees Conferred by Degree-Granting Institutions, by Racial/Ethnic Group, Major Field of Study, and Sex of Student: 1997-98," in *Digest of Education Statistics 2000*, January 2001. National Center for Education Statistics.

Table 2.11. "No. 431. High School Students Engaged in Organized Physical Activity: 1999," in *Statistical Abstract of the United States: 2000*, 2001. U.S. Census Bureau.

Table 2.12. "Table 1. Change in Number of Women Participants for NAIA and NCAA Schools," in *Intercollegiate Athletics: Four-Year Colleges' Experiences Adding and Discontinuing Teams*, March 2001. U.S. General Accounting Office.

Table 3.1. Fullerton, Howard N., Jr. "Table 1. Civilian Labor Force Participation Rates by Sex and Age, 1950 to 1998 and Projected, 2015 to 2025," in "Labor Force Participation: 75 Years of Change, 1950-98 and 1998-2025." *Monthly Labor Review*, v. 122, n. 12, December 1999. Bureau of Labor Statistics.

Table 3.2. "2. Employment Status of the Civilian Noninstitutional Population 16 Years and Over, by Sex, 1969 to Date," from "Average Annual Tables," in *Employment and Earnings*, v. 48, n. 1, January 2001.

Table 3.3. "Table A-2. Employment Status of the Civilian Population by Race, Sex, Age, and Hispanic Origin," in "The Employment Situation: August 2001." *BLS News*, September 7, 2001. Bureau of Labor Statistics.

Table 3.4. "Table 2. Families by Presence and Relationship of Employed Members and Family Type, 1999-2000," in *Employment Characteristics of Families in 2000* [Online], April 19, 2001. ftp://146.142.4.23/pub/news.release/famee.txt. [Accessed September 23, 2001]. Bureau of Labor Statistics.

Table 3.5. "Table 4. Families With Own Children: Employment Status of Parents by Age of Youngest Child and Family Type, 1999-2000 Annual Averages," in *Employment Characteristics of Families in 2000* [Online], April 19, 2001. ftp://146.142.4.23/pub/news.release/famee.txt. [Accessed September 23, 2001]. Bureau of Labor Statistics.

Table 3.6. "15. Employed Persons in Agriculture and Nonagricultural Industries by Age, Sex, and Class of Worker," from "Average Annual Tables," in *Employment and Earnings*, v. 48, n. 1, January 2001.

Table 3.7. "22. Persons at Work in Nonagricultural Industries by Age, Sex, Race, Marital Status, and Usual Full- or Part-time Status," from "Average Annual Tables," in *Employment and Earnings*, v. 48, n. 1, January 2001.

Figure 3.1. "Chart 1. Flexible work schedule, by age bracket," in "Flexible Work Schedules: What Are We Trading Off to Get Them?" *Monthly Labor Review*, v. 124, n. 3, March 2001. Bureau of Labor Statistics.

Table 3.8. "Table 6. Employed Workers with Alternative and Traditional Work Arrangements by Selected Characteristics, February 2001," in *Contingent and Alternative Employment Arrangements* [Online]. http://www.bls.gov/news.release/conemp.t06.htm. [Accessed September 25, 2001]. Bureau of Labor Statistics.

Table 3.9. "36. Multiple Jobholders by Selected Demographic and Economic Characteristics," from "Average Annual Tables," in *Employment and Earnings*, v. 48, n. 1, January 2001.

Table 3.10. "24. Unemployed Persons by Marital Status, Race, Age, and Sex," from "Average Annual Tables," in *Employment and Earnings*, v. 48, n. 1, January 2001.

Table 3.11. "29. Unemployed Persons by Reason for Unemployment, Sex, Age, and Duration of Unemployment," from "Average Annual Tables," in *Employment and Earnings*, v. 48, n. 1, January 2001.

Table 3.12. "7. Employment Status of the Civilian Noninstitutional Population 25 Years and Over by Educational Attainment, Sex, Race, and Hispanic Origin," from "Average Annual Tables," in *Employment and Earnings*, v. 48, n. 1, January 2001.

Table 3.13. "Table 4. Employment and Total Job Openings, 1998-2008, by Education and Training Category," in *BLS Releases New 1998-2008 Employment Projections* [Online], November 30, 1999. ftp://146.142.4.23/pub/news.release/ecopro.txt. [Accessed September 23, 2001]. Bureau of Labor Statistics.

Table 4.1. "20 Leading Occupations of Employed Women 2000 Annual Averages," in *Statistics and Data* [Online]. http://www.dol.gov/dol/wb/public/wb_pubs/20lead2000.htm. [Accessed September 21, 2001]. U.S. Department of Labor.

Table 4.2. "9. Employed Persons by Occupation, Sex, and Age," from "Average Annual Tables," in *Employment and Earnings*, v. 48, n. 1, January 2001.

Table 4.3. "10. Employed Persons by Occupation, Race, and Sex," from "Average Annual Tables," in *Employment and Earnings*, v. 48, n. 1, January 2001.

Table 4.4. "Appendix table 5-3. Scientists and Engineers in the U.S. Labor Force, by Occupation, Race/Ethnicity, and Sex: 1997," in *Women, Minorities, and Persons with Disabilities in Science and Engineering: 2000*, 2000. National Science Foundation's Division of Science Resources Statistics.

Figure 4.1. Pratt, Megan. "Women as a percentage of employed doctoral scientists and engineers in universities and 4-year colleges, by broad field of doctorate and academic rank: 1999," in *Women in Science Statistics* [Online]. http://www.awis.org/statistics/statistics.html. [Accessed October 2001]. National Science Foundation's Division of Science Resources Statistics.

Table 4.5. Manning, Lory and Vanessa R. Wright. "Table 7-1: Active Duty Servicewomen by Branch of Service, Rank, Race, and Hispanic Origin, May 31, 1999," in *Women in the Military: Where They Stand*, Third Edition, 2000. Women's Research and Education Institute. Reproduced by permission.

Figure 4.2. Manning, Lory and Vanessa R. Wright. "Figure 7-1: Active Duty Servicewomen in the Department of Defense Services by Officer/Enlisted Status, 1972–1999 (in percentages)," in *Women in the Military: Where They Stand*, Third Edition, 2000. Women's Research and Education Institute. Reproduced by permission.

Figure 4.3. "Figure 7-5: Occupational Profile of Active Duty Officers in the Department of Defense Services by Sex, 1999 (percent distributions)," in *The American Woman 2001–2002: Getting to the Top*, Third Edition, 2000. Women's Research and Education Institute. Reproduced by permission.

Table 4.6. "Women-Owned Firms in the United States: 1987-1999," 1999. U.S. Census Bureau and Center for Women's Business Research.

Figure 4.4. "Figure 1. Fastest Growing Occupations: 1998-2008," in *Land of Plenty: Diversity as America's Competitive Edge in Science, Engineering and Technology*, September 2000. Congressional Commission on the Advancement of Women and Minorities in Science, Engineering, and Technology Development. Data courtesy of the National Science Foundation. Reproduced by permission of the Congressional Commission on the Advancement of Women and Minorities in Science, Engineering, and Technology Development.

Table 5.1. "Table 7. Median Income of People by Selected Characteristics: 2000, 1999, and 1998," in *Income 2000* [Online]. http://www.census.gov/hhes/income/income00/inctab7.html. [Accessed November 7, 2001]. U.S. Census Bureau.

Table 5.2. Field, Jason and Lynne M. Casper. "Table 2. Family Groups by Type and Selected Characteristics of the Family: March 2000," in *America's Families and Living Arrangements: March 2000*, June 2001. U.S. Census Bureau.

Figure 5.1. DeNavas-Walt, Carmen, Robert W. Cleveland, and Marc I. Roemer. "Figure 3. Median Earnings of Workers 15 Years Old and Over by Work Experience and Sex: 1967 to 2000," in *Money Income in the United States: 2000*. Current Population Reports, P60-213, September 2001. U.S. Census Bureau.

Table 5.3. "Table p-40. Women's Earnings as a Percentage of Men's Earnings by Race and Hispanic Origin: 1960 to 1999," in *Historical Income Tables - People* [Online]. http://www.census.gov/hhes/income/histinc/p40.html. [Accessed September 23, 2001]. U.S. Census Bureau.

Table 5.4. "Table 1. Median Usual Weekly Earnings of Full-Time Wage and Salary Workers by Selected Characteristics, 2000 Annual Averages," in *Highlights of Women's Earnings in 2000*, Report 952, August 2001. Bureau of Labor Statistics.

Figure 5.2. "Women's Earnings as a Percent of Men's, Median Usual Weekly Earnings of Full-Time Wage and Salary Workers, by Age, 2000," in *MLR: The Editor's Desk* [Online], September 5, 2001. http://www.bls.gov/opub/ted/2001/Sept/wk1/art02.htm. [Accessed September 23, 2001]. Bureau of Labor Statistics.

Table 5.5. "Table 9. Median Usual Weekly Earnings of Full-Time Wage and Salary Workers by Sex, Marital Status, and Presence and Age of Own Children Under 18 Years Old, 2000 Annual Averages," in *Highlights of Women's Earnings in 2000*, Report 952, August 2001. Bureau of Labor Statistics.

Table 5.6. "Table 2. Median Usual Weekly Earnings of Full-Time Wage and Salary Workers by Occupation and Sex, 1983 and 2000 Annual Averages," in *Highlights of Women's Earnings in 2000*, Report 952, August 2001. Bureau of Labor Statistics.

Figure 5.3. "Chart 3. Percent Change Between 1979 and 2000 Median Usual Weekly Earnings by Educational Attainment and Sex," in *Highlights of Women's Earnings in 2000*, Report 952, August 2001. Bureau of Labor Statistics.

Table 5.7. "Table 10. Median Hourly Earnings of Wage and Salary Workers Paid Hourly Rates by Selected Characteristics, 2000 Annual Averages," in *Highlights of Women's Earnings in 2000*, Report 952, August 2001. Bureau of Labor Statistics.

Table 5.8. "Table 44. Wage and Salary Workers Paid Hourly Rates with Earnings At or Below the Prevailing Federal Minimum Wage by Selected Characteristics," from "Average Annual Tables," in *Employment and Earnings*, v. 48, n. 1, January 2001.

Table 5.9. Dalaker, Joseph. "Poverty Thresholds in 2000 by Size of Family and Number of Related Children Under 18 Years," in *Poverty in the United States: 2000*, Current Population Reports, P60-214, September 2001. U.S. Census Bureau.

Table 5.10. "Table 16. Poverty Status of the Population in 1999 by Age and Sex: March 2000," in *Women in the United States: March 2000*, Current Population Survey Supplement, PPL-121, March 15, 2001. U.S. Census Bureau.

Figure 5.4. Dalaker, Joseph. "Figure 6. Poverty Rates of People in Families by Family Type and Presence of Workers: 2000," in *Poverty in the United States: 2000*, Current Population Reports, P60-214, September 2001. U.S. Census Bureau.

Table 5.11. Dalaker, Joseph. "Table F. Income Deficit or Surplus of Families and Unrelated Individuals by Poverty Status: 2000," in *Poverty in the United States: 2000*, Current Population Reports, P60-214, September 2001. U.S. Census Bureau.

Table 5.12. Porter, Kathryn H. and Allen Dupree. "Table 2: Poverty Rates for People in Families with Children," in "Poverty Trends for Families Headed by Working Single Mothers: 1993 to 1999," August 2001. Center on Budget and Policy Priorities. Reproduced by permission.

Table 5.13. Porter, Kathryn H. and Allen Dupree. "Table 6. People in Working Single-Mother Families Lifted out of Poverty by Government Benefits," in "Poverty Trends for Families Headed by Working Single Mothers: 1993 to 1999," August 2001. Center on Budget and Policy Priorities. Reproduced by permission.

Table 5.14. Oliveira, Victor. "Table 1. Real Expenditures for the Food Stamp Program Were Lower in Fiscal 1999 Than in Fiscal 1990, While Other Nutrition Assistance Programs Grew," from "Food Assistance Expanded, Then Contracted in the 1990's," in *FoodReview*, v. 23, n. 3, September-December 2000.

Table 5.15. Nord, Mark. "Table 2. Food Insecurity Among Low-Income Households Not Receiving Food Stamps Rose Between 1995 and 1999," from "Food Stamp Participation and Food Security," in *FoodReview*, v. 24, n. 1, January-April 2001.

Figure 5.5. Oliveira, Victor and Craig Gundersen. "Figure 1. Participation in WIC Increased During Most of the 1990's," from "WIC Increases the Nutrient Intake of Children," in *FoodReview*, v. 24, n. 1, January-April 2001.

Figure 6.1. Ventura, Stephanie, et al. "Live Births and Fertility Rates: United States, 1930-99," from "Births: Final Data for 1999," in *National Vital Statistics Reports*, v. 49, n. 1, April 17, 2001.

Table 6.1. Martin, Joyce A., et al. "Birth Rates by Age of Mother, Live-Birth Order, and Race and Hispanic Origin of Mother: United States, Preliminary 2000," from "Births: Preliminary Data for 2000" in *National Vital Statistics Reports*, v. 49, n. 5, July 24, 2001.

Figure 6.2. Ventura, Stephanie, et al. "Birth Rates by Age of Mother: United States, 1960-99," from "Births: Final Data for 1999," in *National Vital Statistics Reports*, v. 49, n. 5, July 24, 2001.

Table 6.2. Ventura, Stephanie, et al. "Table A. Birth and Birth Rates for Teenagers by Age: United States, 1991-2000," from "Births to Teenagers in the United States, 1940-2000," in *National Vital Statistics Reports*, v. 49, n. 10, September 25, 2001.

Figure 6.3. Ventura, Stephanie, et al. "Figure 1. Birth Rate for Teenagers 15-19 Years and Percent of Teenage Births to Unmarried Teenagers: United States, 1950-2000," from "Births to Teenagers in the United States, 1940-2000," in *National Vital Statistics Reports*, v. 49, n. 10, September 25, 2001.

Figure 6.4. Ventura, Stephanie, et al. "Figure 4. Birth Rate for Teenagers 15-17 Years by Race and Hispanic Origin: United States, 1980-2000," from "Births to Teenagers in the United States, 1940-2000," in *National Vital Statistics Reports,* v. 49, n. 10, September 25, 2001.

Table 6.3. "Table 9. Nonmarital Childbearing According to Detailed Race and Hispanic Origin of Mother, and Maternal Age and Birth Rates for Unmarried Women by Race and Hispanic Origin of Mother: United States, Selected Years 1970-99," in *Health, United States, 2001,* 2001. National Center for Health Statistics.

Table 6.4. Ventura, Stephanie, et al. "Table J. Numbers of Twin, Triplet, Quadruplet, and Quintuplet and Other Higher Order Multiple Births: United States, 1989-99," from "Births: Final Data for 1999," in *National Vital Statistics Reports,* v. 49, n. 1, April 17, 2001.

Figure 6.5. Ventura, Stephanie, et al. "Figure 10. Twin Birth Rates by Age of Mother: United States, 1990 and 1999," from "Births: Final Data for 1999," in *National Vital Statistics Reports,* v. 49, n. 1, April 17, 2001.

Figure 6.6. "Figure POP6.B. Percentage of all births that are to unmarried women by age of mother, 1980 and 1999," in *America's Children: Key National Indicators of Well-Being 2001,* July 2001. Federal Interagency Forum on Child and Family Statistics.

Figure 6.7. Ventura, Stephanie, et al. "Figure 7. Selected Characteristics for Teenage Mothers and Mothers Aged 20 Years and Over: United States, 1999," from "Births to Teenagers in the United States, 1940-2000," in *National Vital Statistics Reports,* v. 49, n. 10, September 25, 2001.

Table 6.5. "Table 62. Current Cigarette Smoking by Adults, according to Sex, Race, Hispanic Origin, Age, and Education: United States, Average Annual 1990-92, 1993-95, and 1997-99," in *Health, United States, 2001,* 2001. National Center for Health Statistics.

Table 6.6. Joyce A. Martin, et al. "Table A. Total Births and Percent of Births with Selected Demographic and Health Characteristics, by Race and Hispanic Origin of Mother: United States, Final 1999 and Preliminary 2000," from "Births: Preliminary Data for 2000" in *National Vital Statistics Reports,* v. 49, n. 5, July 24, 2001.

Table 6.7. "Table 12. Low-Birthweight Live Births, According to Mother's Detailed Race, Hispanic Origin, and Smoking Status: United States, Selected Years 1970-99," in *Health, United States, 2001,* 2001. National Center for Health Statistics.

Table 6.8. "Box 3. Racial and Ethnic Disparities in Breastfeeding Rates and Healthy People 2010 Breastfeeding Objectives for the Nation," in *HHS Blueprint for Action on Breastfeeding,* Fall 2000. Office on Women's Health, U.S. Department of Health and Human Services.

Table 6.9. "Contraceptive Use among Women," in *Contraceptive Use: Facts in Brief,* March 1998. Reproduced by permission of The Alan Guttmacher Institute.

Table 6.10. "Table 16. Legal Abortion Ratios, according to Selected Patient Characteristics: United States, Selected Years 1973-98," in *Health, United States, 2001,* 2001. National Center for Health Statistics.

Table 6.11. "Table 4. Women 15-44 Years of Age Who Have Not Had at least 1 Live Birth, by Age: United States, Selected Years 1960-2000," in *Health, United States, 2001,* 2001. National Center for Health Statistics.

Table 6.12. Fields, Jason and Lynne M. Casper. "Table 4. Single Parents by Sex and Selected Characteristics: March 2000," in *America's Families and Living Arrangements: March 2000,* Current Population Reports, P20-537, June 2001. U.S. Census Bureau.

Table 6.13. "Table POP5.A. Family Structure and Children's Living Arrangements: Percentage of Children under Age 18 by Presence of Parents in Household, Race, and Hispanic Origin, Selected Years 1980-2000," in *America's Children: Key National Indicators of Well-Being 2001,* July 2001. Federal Interagency Forum on Child and Family Statistics.

Figure 6.8. "Figure 4-12: Labor Force Participation Rates of Mothers with Children under 18 by Children's Age, 1978-1998," in *The American Woman 2001-2002: Getting to the Top,* 2001. Women's Research and Education Institute. Reproduced by permission.

Table 6.14. "Employment Status of Mothers with Own Children Under 3 Years Old by Single Year of Age of Youngest Child and by Marital Status, 1999-2000 Annual Averages," in *Employment Characteristics of Families in 2000* [Online]. ftp:// 146.142.4.23/pub.news.release.famee.txt. [Accessed September 29, 2001].

Table 6.15. "Table F. Labor Force Participation Among Mothers 15 to 44 Years Old by Fertility Status and Selected Characteristics: June 1998," in *Fertility of American Women June 1998: Population Characteristics,* Current Population Reports, P20-526, September 2000. U.S. Census Bureau.

Table 7.1. "Table 5. Employment status of the population by sex, marital status, and presence and age of own children under 18, 1999-2000 annual averages," in *Employment Characteristics of Families in 2000,* [Online], April 19, 2001. http://stats.bls.gov/news.release/famee.nr0.htm. [Accessed October 11, 2001]. Bureau of Labor Statistics.

Table 7.2. "Table POP7. Child Care: Percentage of Children by Type of Care Arrangement for Children from Birth through Third Grade by Child and Family Characteristics, 1995 and 1999," in *Ameri-*

ca's Children: Key National Indicators of Well-Being 2001, July 2001. Federal Interagency Forum on Child and Family Statistics.

Figure 7.1. Wirt, John, et al. "Before and After School Care: Percentage of children in grades K-8 who received various types of care before and after school: 1999," in *The Condition of Education 2001,* June 2001. U.S. Department of Education, National Center for Education Statistics.

Table 7.3. "Table 1. Incidence of Child Care Resource and Referral Services by Industry, Establishment Size, and Region, June 2000," in *Pilot Survey on the Incidence of Child Care Resource and Referral Services in June 2000* [Online], November 2000. http://www. bls.gov/ncs2/ncrp0002.pdf. [Accessed October 2, 2001]. Bureau of Labor Statistics.

Table 7.4. "Table 2: Selected States' Child Care Expenditures of Federal and State Funds, Fiscal Years 1995 to 2000," in *Child Care: States Increased Spending on Low-Income Families,* February 2001. U.S. General Accounting Office.

Table 8.1. "Table 1. Projections of the Population by Voting Age, for States, by Race, Hispanic Origin, Sex, and Selected Ages: November 7, 2000," in *Projections of the Voting-Age Population for States: November 2000 Tables* [Online]. http://www.census. gov/population/socdemo/voting/proj00/ tab01.txt. [Accessed October 7, 2001].

Table 8.2. Day, Jennifer C. and Avalaura L. Gaither. "Table C. Reported Rates of Voting and Registration by Selected Characteristics: November 1998," in *Voting and Registration in the Election of November 1998,* Current Population Reports, P20-523RV, August 2000. U.S. Census Bureau.

Table 8.3. "Voter Turnout in Non-Presidential Elections," in *Sex Differences in Voter Turnout* [Online], 2000. http://www. cawp.rutgers.edu/pdf/sexdiff.pdf. [Accessed October 7, 2001]. Center for American Women and Politics, Eagleton Institute of Politics, Rutgers, The State University of New Jersey. Reproduced by permission.

Table 8.4. *Gender Gap Evident in Numerous 1998 Races,* 1999. Center for American Women and Politics, Eagleton Institute of Politics, Rutgers, The State University of New Jersey. Reproduced by permission.

Table 8.5. "Percentage of Women in Elective Offices," in *Women in Elective Office 2001* [Online], 2001. http://www.cawp.rutgers.edu/pdf/elective.pdf. [Accessed October 7, 2001]. Center for American Women and Politics, Eagleton Institute of Politics, Rutgers, The State University of New Jersey. Reproduced by permission.

Table 8.6. "Women in the U.S. Congress 1917-2001," in *Women in the U.S. Congress*

2001 [Online], 2001. http://www.cawp.rutgers.edu/pdf/cong.pdf. [Accessed October 7, 2001]. Center for American Women and Politics, Eagleton Institute of Politics, Rutgers, The State University of New Jersey. Reproduced by permission.

Table 8.7. "Statewide Elective Executive Offices," in *Women in Elective Office 2001* [Online], 2001. http://www.cawp.rutgers.edu/pdf/elective.pdf. [Accessed October 7, 2001]. Center for American Women and Politics, Eagleton Institute of Politics, Rutgers, The State University of New Jersey. Reproduced by permission.

Table 8.8. "Women in State Legislatures 2001," in *Women in State Legislative Office* [Online], 2001. http://www.cawp.rutgers.edu/pdf/stleg.pdf. [Accessed October 7, 2001]. Center for American Women and Politics, Eagleton Institute of Politics, Rutgers, The State University of New Jersey. Reproduced by permission.

Table 8.9. "Municipal Officials," in *Women in Elective Office 2001* [Online], 2001. http://www.cawp.rutgers.edu/pdf/elective.pdf. [Accessed October 7, 2001]. Center for American Women and Politics, Eagleton Institute of Politics, Rutgers, The State University of New Jersey. Reproduced by permission.

Figure 9.1. "Rate of Violent Victimization per 1,000 Persons Age 12 or Over," in *Criminal Victimization 2000: Changes 1999-2000 with Trends 1993-2000,* June 2001. Bureau of Justice Statistics.

Table 9.1. "Table 2. Rates of Violent Crime and Personal Theft, by Gender, Age, Race, and Hispanic Origin, 2000" in *Criminal Victimization 2000: Changes 1999-2000 with Trends 1993-2000,* June 2001. Bureau of Justice Statistics.

Table 9.2. "Table 10. Number of Victimizations and Victimization Rates for Persons Age 12 and Over, by Race, Gender, and Age of Victims and Type of Crime," in *Criminal Victimization in United States, 1999 Statistical Tables* [Online]. http://www.ojp.usdoj.gov/bjs/pub/pdf/cvus99.pdf. [Accessed October 12, 2001].

Table 9.3. "Table 4. Victim and Offender Relationship, 2000," in *Criminal Victimization 2000: Changes 1999-2000 with Trends 1993-2000,* June 2001. Bureau of Justice Statistics.

Table 9.4. "Table 29. Percent of Victimizations Involving Strangers, by Gender and Age of Victims and Type of Crime," in *Criminal Victimization in United States, 1999 Statistical Tables* [Online]. http://www.ojp.usdoj.gov/bjs/pub/pdf/cvus99.pdf. [Accessed October 12, 2001].

Table 9.5. "Table 93. Percent of Victimizations Reported to the Police, by Type of Crime, Victim-Offender Relationship and Gender of Victims," in *Criminal Victimization in United States, 1999 Statistical Tables* [Online]. http://www.ojp.usdoj.gov/bjs/pub/pdf/cvus99.pdf. [Accessed October 12, 2001].

Figure 9.2. "Figure 2.8. Forcible Rape: Percent Change from 1995," in *Crime in the United States—1999* [Online]. http://www.fbi.gov/ucr/Cius_99/99crime/99c2_01.pdf. [Accessed November 2001]. Federal Bureau of Investigation.

Figure 9.3. Fisher, Bonnie S. et al. "Exhibit 8. Victim-Offender Relationship for Rape Victimizations Committed by Single Offenders," in *The Sexual Victimization of College Women,* December 2000. National Institute of Justice and Bureau of Justice Statistics.

Table 9.6. "Table 2.5. Murder Victims, by Age, Sex, and Race, 1999," in *Crime in the United States—1999* [Online]. http://www.fbi.gov/ucr/Cius_99/99crime/99c2_01.pdf. [Accessed November 2001]. Federal Bureau of Investigation.

Table 9.7. "Table 2.15. Murder Circumstances by Victim Sex, 1999," in *Crime in the United States—1999* [Online]. http://www.fbi.gov/ucr/Cius_99/99crime/99c2_01.pdf. [Accessed November 2001]. Federal Bureau of Investigation.

Figure 9.4. Rennison, Callie Marie and Sarah Welchans. "Figure 1. Rate of Violence by an Intimate Partner, by Gender, 1993-98," in *Intimate Partner Violence,* May 2000. Bureau of Justice Statistics.

Figure 9.5. Rennison, Callie Marie and Sarah Welchans. "Figure 10. Percent of intimate partner victimization reported to police, by gender, race, and ethnicity, 1993-1998," in *Intimate Partner Violence,* May 2000. Bureau of Justice Statistics.

Table 9.8. Rennison, Callie Marie and Sarah Welchans. "Table 8. Reasons Intimate Partner Violence Was Not Reported to the Police, by Gender of Victim, 1993-98," in *Intimate Partner Violence,* May 2000. Bureau of Justice Statistics.

Table 9.9. Fisher, Bonnie S., et al. "Exhibit 14. The Extent of Verbal and Visual Victimization," in *The Sexual Victimization of College Women,* December 2000. National Institute of Justice and Bureau of Justice Statistics.

Table 10.1. "Table 40. Arrests, Females, by Age, 1999," in *Crime in the United States—1999* [Online]. http://www.fbi.gov/ucr/Cius_99/99crime/99c2_01.pdf. [Accessed January 18, 2002]. Federal Bureau of Investigation.

Table 10.2. "Table 33. Ten-Year Arrest Trends by Sex, 1990-1999," *Crime in the United States—1999* [Online]. http://www.fbi.gov/ucr/Cius_99/99crime/99c2_01.pdf. [Accessed November 2001]. Federal Bureau of Investigation.

Table 10.3. "Table 8. Offender Characteristics, by Most Serious Offense Type, 1997-99," in *Hate Crimes Reported in NIBRS, 1997-99,* September 2001. Bureau of Justice Statistics.

Table 10.4. Beck, Allen J. and Jennifer C. Karberg. "Table 12. Number of inmates in State or Federal prisons and local jails, by gender, race, Hispanic origin, and age, June 30, 2000," in *Prison and Jail Inmates at Midyear 2000,* March 2001. Bureau of Justice Statistics.

Table 10.5. Beck, Allen J. and Jennifer C. Karberg. "Table 4. Prisoners under the jurisdiction of State or Federal correctional authorities, by gender, 1990, 1999, and 2000," in *Prison and Jail Inmates at Midyear 2000,* March 2001. Bureau of Justice Statistics.

Table 10.6. Beck, Allen J. and Jennifer C. Karberg. "Table 6. Number of inmates under age 18 held in State and Federal prisons, by gender, June 30, 1990, 1995, and 1998-2000," in *Prison and Jail Inmates at Midyear 2000,* March 2001. Bureau of Justice Statistics.

Table 10.7. Beck, Allen J. and Paige M. Harrison. "Table 17. Partitioning the Total Growth of Sentenced Prisoners under State Jurisdiction, by Offense and Gender, 1990-99," in *Prisoners in 2000,* August 2001. Bureau of Justice Statistics.

Table 10.8. Greenfeld, Lawrence A. and Tracy L. Snell. "Children of women under correctional supervision, 1998," in *Women Offenders,* 1999. Bureau of Justice Statistics.

Table 10.9. Snell, Tracy L. "Women under sentence of death, 12/31/99," in *Capital Punishment 1999,* December 2000. Bureau of Justice Statistics.

Figure 11.1. "Figure 11.2. Percent Distribution of Respondent-Assessed Health Status, by Sex: All Ages, United States, 2000," in *National Health Interview Survey* [Online]. http://www.cdc.gov/nchs/data/nhis/measure11.pdf. [Accessed October 8, 2001].

Figure 11.2. "Figure 1.2. Percentage of Persons Aged Under 65 Years without Health Insurance Coverage, by Age Group and Sex: United States, 2000," in *National Health Interview Survey* [Online]. http://www.cdc.gov/nchs/data/nhis/measure01.pdf. [Accessed October 8, 2001].

Figure 11.3. Dailard, Cynthia. "Women uninsured and Medicaid recipients, Age 15-44, 1994-99," from "Challenges Facing Family Planning Clinics and Title X," in *The Guttmacher Report,* v. 4, n.2, pp. 8-11, April

2001. Reproduced by permission of The Alan Guttmacher Institute.

Figure 11.4. "Figure 3.2. Percentage of Persons Who Failed to Obtain Needed Medical Care during the Past 12 Months due to Financial Barriers, by Sex and Age Group: All Ages, United States, 2000," in *National Health Interview Survey* [Online]. http://www.cdc.gov/nchs/data/nhis/measure03.pdf. [Accessed October 8, 2001].

Figure 11.5. "Cardiovascular Disease Mortality Trends for Males and Females United States: 1979-1998," in *2001 Heart and Stroke Statistical Update,* 2000. Copyright American Heart Association. Reproduced by permission of the American Heart Association.

Table 11.1. "Estimated Inpatient Cardiovascular Operations, Procedures and Patient Data by Sex, Age and Region," in *2001 Heart and Stroke Statistical Update,* 2000. Copyright American Heart Association. Reproduced by permission of the American Heart Association.

Table 11.2. "Table 32. Leading Causes of Death and Numbers of Deaths, According to Sex, Race, and Hispanic Origin: United States, 1980 and 1999," in *Health, United States, 2001,* 2001. National Center for Health Statistics.

Figure 11.6. "Leading Sites of New Cancer Cases* and Deaths—2001 Estimates," in *Cancer Facts and Figures 2001,* 2001. American Cancer Society, Inc. Reproduced by permission.

Table 11.3. "Table 82. Use of Mammography for Women 40 Years of Age and Over according to Selected Characteristics: United States, Selected Years 1987-98," in *Health, United States, 2001,* 2001. National Center for Health Statistics.

Table 11.4. "Table 44. Maternal Mortality for Complications of Pregnancy, Childbirth, and the Puerperium, according to Race, Hispanic Origin, and Age: United States, Selected Years 1950-98," in *Health, United States, 2001,* 2001. National Center for Health Statistics.

Figure 11.7. "AIDS Incidence* for Women and Percentage of AIDS Cases, January 1986-June 2000, United States," in *HIV/AIDS Surveillance in Women L264 Slide Series through 2000* [Online]. http://www.cdc.gov/hiv/graphics/images/l264/l264-1.htm. [Accessed October 10, 2001].

Table 11.5. "AIDS Cases and Rates in Adult/Adolescent Women, by Race/Ethnicity, Reported in 2000, United States," in *HIV/AIDS Surveillance in Women L264 Slide Series through 2000* [Online]. http://www.cdc.gov/hiv/graphics/images/l264/l264-2.htm. [Accessed October 10, 2001].

Figure 11.8. "Estimates* of AIDS in Women, by Exposure Category Diagnosed July 1999-June 2000, United States," in *HIV/AIDS Surveillance in Women L264 Slide Series through 2000* [Online]. http://www.cdc.gov/hiv/graphics/images/l264/l264-4.htm. [Accessed October 10, 2001].

Table 11.6. "Table 2. Reported cases of sexually transmitted disease by gender and reporting source: United States, 1999," in *Sexually Transmitted Disease Surveillance 1999,* September 2000. Centers for Disease Control and Prevention.

Table 11.7. Strock, Margaret. "Symptoms of Depression and Mania," in *Depression,* 2000. National Institute of Mental Health.

Figure 11.9. "Figure 8.2. Percent Distribution of Smoking Status Among Adults Aged 18 Years and Older, by Sex: United States, 2000," in *National Health Interview Survey* [Online]. http://www.cdc.gov/nchs/data/nhis/measure08.pdf. [Accessed October 8, 2001].

Table 11.8. "Table 66. Alcohol Consumption by Persons 18 Years of Age and Over, According to Sex, Race, Hispanic Origin, and Age: United States, 1997-99," in *Health, United States, 2001,* 2001. National Center for Health Statistics.

Table 11.9. "Table 1. Prevalence of Obesity by Gender and Demographic and Behavioral Characteristics, 1994 and 1998," in *Cancer Facts and Figures 2001,* 2001. American Cancer Society, Inc. Reproduced by permission.

Figure 11.10. "Figure 7.2. Percentage of Adults Aged 18 and Older who Regularly Participated in Light or Moderate Leisure-Time Physical Activity, by Sex and Age Group: United States, 2000," in *National Health Interview Survey* [Online]. http://www.cdc.gov/nchs/data/nhis/measure07.pdf. [Accessed October 8, 2001].

CHAPTER 1

AMERICAN WOMEN—WHO ARE THEY?

POPULATION

Census 2000 reported the U.S. population as 143,368,343 females and 138,053,563 males. By 2010 the population of the United States is expected to reach almost 300 million, of which 153 million will be females.

Age and Race

According to the U.S. Census Bureau, as of 2000, 24.6 percent of the female population was under the age of 18, 61.1 percent was between 18 and 64 years of age, and 14.4 percent of the female population was 65 or older. (See Table 1.1.) The median age of American females in 2000 was 36.5 years, meaning that half of the females were younger than this and half were older.

Of the 98 percent of females identified in Census 2000 as belonging to a single race, 77 percent were white and 13 percent were African American. Asian women made up 4 percent of the female population, and Native American women, including Alaskan natives, comprised 0.9 percent. Native Hawaiians and other Pacific Islanders accounted for 0.1 percent of American women. Of the remainder, 5 percent were identified as belonging to some other race, and just over 2 percent of American women were multiracial. In addition, 12 percent of American women were Hispanics or Latinas of any racial designation. (See Table 1.1.)

Male-Female Ratios

According to Census 2000, females make up 50.9 percent of the population, compared to 51.3 percent in 1990. Over the decade the female population of the United States increased by 12.5 percent, whereas the male population increased by 13.9 percent. This difference is attributed to a decrease in male death rates and an increase in male immigration between 1990 and 2000.

There are 96.3 males for every 100 females in the United States. (See Table 1.2.) Among African Ameri-

FIGURE 1.1

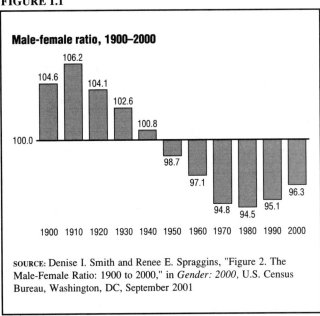

SOURCE: Denise I. Smith and Renee E. Spraggins, "Figure 2. The Male-Female Ratio: 1900 to 2000," in *Gender: 2000,* U.S. Census Bureau, Washington, DC, September 2001

cans, the ratio is 90.5 males for every 100 females. However, among Hispanics or Latinos of any race, there are 105.9 males for every 100 females.

Males outnumber females from birth until the age of five (104.8 males to 100 females). However, males experience a higher infant mortality rate and are subject to higher death rates at earlier ages than females. Nevertheless, males outnumber females until about age 30. From age 30 on, the proportion of females rises steadily. In the population older than 84 years, there are only 40.7 males per 100 females.

Figure 1.1 documents the change in the male-female ratio over the past century. Prior to the medical advances of the 20th century, it was common for women to die from complications of childbearing, and men often outlived several wives. The 1950 census was the first to record more women than men living in the United States.

TABLE 1.1

Female population by age, race and Hispanic origin, 2000

					Race						
					One race						
Age	Total population	Total	White	Black or African American	American Indian and Alaska Native	Asian	Native Hawaiian and Other Pacific Islander	Some other race	Two or more races	Hispanic or Latino (of any race)	White alone, not Hispanic or Latino
FIVE-YEAR AGE GROUPS											
Total population	143,368,343	139,962,733	107,687,432	18,193,005	1,241,974	5,294,257	196,206	7,349,859	3,405,610	17,144,023	99,395,043
Under 5 years	9,365,065	8,899,004	6,262,128	1,380,511	104,393	333,257	16,137	802,578	466,061	1,817,543	5,446,604
5 to 9 years	10,026,228	9,617,754	6,785,226	1,578,037	118,053	331,680	17,801	786,957	408,474	1,771,795	5,982,208
10 to 14 years	10,007,875	9,660,593	6,960,988	1,537,012	120,417	332,454	17,396	692,326	347,282	1,546,227	6,259,312
15 to 19 years	9,828,886	9,522,712	6,879,090	1,446,788	113,001	365,951	17,934	699,948	306,174	1,483,090	6,228,997
20 to 24 years	9,276,187	9,006,110	6,388,969	1,348,124	95,894	408,587	18,450	746,086	270,077	1,534,288	5,729,667
25 to 29 years	9,582,576	9,331,135	6,655,571	1,337,215	91,248	502,086	16,839	728,176	251,441	1,559,188	5,952,235
30 to 34 years	10,188,619	9,951,563	7,328,058	1,378,847	91,827	487,706	16,246	648,879	237,056	1,456,837	6,642,233
35 to 39 years	11,387,968	11,156,551	8,487,223	1,498,052	102,113	470,260	16,393	582,510	231,417	1,350,696	7,829,977
40 to 44 years	11,312,761	11,103,853	8,634,083	1,433,241	97,060	447,638	14,100	477,731	208,908	1,125,604	8,077,349
45 to 49 years	10,202,898	10,033,239	7,955,003	1,219,048	81,845	403,904	11,958	361,481	169,659	888,473	7,497,327
50 to 54 years	8,977,824	8,840,240	7,190,359	974,392	65,504	337,445	9,459	263,081	137,584	696,699	6,809,448
55 to 59 years	6,960,508	6,863,276	5,691,567	718,379	46,569	230,418	6,786	169,557	97,232	503,868	5,393,811
60 to 64 years	5,668,820	5,593,762	4,653,172	594,574	34,865	182,481	5,234	123,436	75,058	402,998	4,402,685
65 to 69 years	5,133,183	5,072,409	4,286,302	507,322	26,626	154,586	3,951	93,622	60,774	331,169	4,072,035
70 to 74 years	4,954,529	4,903,598	4,240,992	439,410	20,271	127,397	3,067	72,461	50,931	271,575	4,060,120
75 to 79 years	4,371,357	4,331,958	3,833,722	343,109	14,907	88,891	2,077	49,252	39,399	191,263	3,703,906
80 to 84 years	3,110,470	3,085,144	2,764,852	230,435	9,158	51,844	1,248	27,607	25,326	111,619	2,687,860
85 years and over	3,012,589	2,989,832	2,690,127	228,509	8,223	37,672	1,130	24,171	22,757	101,091	2,619,269
SELECTED AGE GROUPS											
Under 18 years	35,234,616	33,827,983	24,106,367	5,353,520	412,400	1,206,983	61,603	2,687,110	1,406,633	6,007,415	21,399,239
Under 1 year	1,856,631	1,756,329	1,234,112	270,275	20,606	63,290	3,124	164,922	100,302	376,442	1,065,448
1 to 4 years	7,508,434	7,142,675	5,028,016	1,110,236	83,787	269,967	13,013	637,656	365,759	1,441,101	4,381,156
5 to 13 years	18,061,432	17,370,463	12,360,187	2,820,144	215,095	597,182	31,775	1,346,080	690,969	3,025,311	10,986,886
14 to 17 years	7,808,119	7,558,516	5,484,052	1,152,865	92,912	276,544	13,691	538,452	249,603	1,164,561	4,965,749
18 to 64 years	87,551,599	85,751,809	65,765,070	11,090,700	750,389	3,626,884	123,130	4,395,636	1,799,790	10,129,891	60,852,614
18 to 24 years	13,269,625	12,878,190	9,170,034	1,936,952	139,358	564,946	26,115	1,040,785	391,435	2,145,528	8,247,549
25 to 44 years	42,471,924	41,543,102	31,104,935	5,647,355	382,248	1,907,690	63,578	2,437,296	928,822	5,492,325	28,501,794
45 to 64 years	31,810,050	31,330,517	25,490,101	3,506,393	228,783	1,154,248	33,437	917,555	479,533	2,492,038	24,103,271
65 years and over	20,582,128	20,382,941	17,815,995	1,748,785	79,185	460,390	11,473	267,113	199,187	1,006,717	17,143,190
16 years and over	112,014,898	109,894,023	86,303,651	13,409,517	875,695	4,228,859	141,461	4,934,840	2,120,875	11,719,571	80,460,102
18 years and over	108,133,727	106,134,750	83,581,065	12,839,485	829,574	4,087,274	134,603	4,662,749	1,998,977	11,136,608	77,995,804
21 years and over	102,162,061	100,343,307	79,430,369	11,956,696	765,372	3,850,798	123,039	4,217,033	1,818,754	10,214,809	74,241,120
50 years and over	42,189,280	41,680,219	35,351,093	4,036,130	226,123	1,210,734	32,952	823,187	509,061	2,610,282	33,749,134
55 years and over	33,211,456	32,839,979	28,160,734	3,061,738	160,619	873,289	23,493	560,106	371,477	1,913,583	26,939,686
60 years and over	26,250,948	25,976,703	22,469,167	2,343,359	114,050	642,871	16,707	390,549	274,245	1,409,715	21,545,875
62 years and over	23,883,016	23,641,077	20,531,824	2,093,220	98,891	565,869	14,422	336,851	241,939	1,238,640	19,713,648
67 years and over	18,506,704	18,333,357	16,099,929	1,534,060	67,605	395,638	9,757	226,368	173,347	866,363	15,516,680
72 years and over	13,428,535	13,311,980	11,813,197	1,056,840	43,747	250,604	6,218	141,374	116,555	556,560	11,433,430
75 years and over	10,494,416	10,406,934	9,288,701	802,053	32,288	178,407	4,455	101,030	87,482	403,973	9,011,035
Median age (years)	36.5	36.8	38.9	31.7	28.9	33.8	28.1	24.6	23.1	26.3	39.8
PERCENT DISTRIBUTION											
Total population	100.0	100.0	100.0	100.0	100.0	100.0	100.0	100.0	100.0	100.0	100.0
Under 18 years	24.6	24.2	22.4	29.4	33.2	22.8	31.4	36.6	41.3	35.0	21.5
Under 1 year	1.3	1.3	1.1	1.5	1.7	1.2	1.6	2.2	2.9	2.2	1.1
1 to 4 years	5.2	5.1	4.7	6.1	6.7	5.1	6.6	8.7	10.7	8.4	4.4
5 to 13 years	12.6	12.4	11.5	15.5	17.3	11.3	16.2	18.3	20.3	17.6	11.1
14 to 17 years	5.4	5.4	5.1	6.3	7.5	5.2	7.0	7.3	7.3	6.8	5.0
18 to 64 years	61.1	61.3	61.1	61.0	60.4	68.5	62.8	59.8	52.8	59.1	61.2
18 to 24 years	9.3	9.2	8.5	10.6	11.2	10.7	13.3	14.2	11.5	12.5	8.3
25 to 44 years	29.6	29.7	28.9	31.0	30.8	36.0	32.4	33.2	27.3	32.0	28.7
45 to 64 years	22.2	22.4	23.7	19.3	18.4	21.8	17.0	12.5	14.1	14.5	24.2
65 years and over	14.4	14.6	16.5	9.6	6.4	8.7	5.8	3.6	5.8	5.9	17.2

SOURCE: "Table 3. Female Population by Age, Race and Hispanic or Latino Origin for the United States: 2000," in *Census 2000 Summary File 1*, U.S. Census Bureau, Washington, DC, October 3, 2001 [Online] http://www.census.gov/population/cen2000/phc-t9/tab03.pdf [accessed October 6, 2001]

TABLE 1.2

Male-female ratio by race alone or in combination and Hispanic or Latino origin, 2000

Race and Hispanic or Latino origin	Total population	Male	Female	Male-female ratio[3]
Total population	281,421,906	138,053,563	143,368,343	96.3
White				
Alone	211,460,626	103,773,194	107,687,432	96.4
Alone or in combination[1]	216,930,975	106,521,196	110,409,779	96.5
Black				
Alone	34,658,190	16,465,185	18,193,005	90.5
Alone or in combination[1]	36,419,434	17,315,333	19,104,101	90.6
American Indian and Alaska Native				
Alone	2,475,956	1,233,982	1,241,974	99.4
Alone or in combination[1]	4,119,301	2,033,242	2,086,059	97.5
Asian				
Alone	10,242,998	4,948,741	5,294,257	93.5
Alone or in combination[1]	11,898,828	5,779,038	6,119,790	94.4
Native Hawaiian and other Pacific Islander				
Alone	398,835	202,629	196,206	103.3
Alone or in combination[1]	874,414	439,681	434,733	101.1
Some other race				
Alone	15,359,073	8,009,214	7,349,859	109.0
Alone or in combination[1]	18,521,486	9,635,774	8,885,712	108.4
Two or more races	6,826,228	3,420,618	3,405,610	100.4
Hispanic or Latino[2]	35,305,818	18,161,795	17,144,023	105.9
White alone, not Hispanic or Latino	194,552,774	95,157,731	99,395,043	95.7

[1] Alone or in combination with one or more of the other five races listed. Numbers for the six race groups add to more than the total population because individuals may report more than one race.
[2] May be of any race.
[3] Males per 100 females.

SOURCE: "Table 1. Male-Female Ratio by Race Alone or in Combination and Hispanic or Latino Origin in the United States: 2000," in *Census 2000 Summary File 1*, U.S. Census Bureau, Washington, DC, September 10, 2001 [Online] http://www.census.gov/population/www/cen2000/phc-t11.html [accessed September 18, 2001]

Life Expectancy

In 1999 the life expectancy at birth was 79.8 years for females and 74.1 years for males. (See Table 1.3.) Females had a longer life expectancy than males within each racial and ethnic group. Asian women had the longest life expectancy (86.5 years), and black women had the lowest (75.1 years). The U.S. Census Bureau projects that by the year 2100 female life expectancy at birth will be between 89.3 and 95.2 years.

Foreign-Born Women

The foreign-born population of the United States includes 14.2 million females, of which 39.1 percent were naturalized American citizens as of March 2000. (See Table 1.4.) Between 1990 and 1999, 5.5 million women immigrated to the United States. In recent years the majority of immigrants have been from Latin America.

The United States also is home to millions of undocumented foreign-born women, who may or may not have

TABLE 1.3

Projected life expectancy at birth by race and Hispanic origin, 1999–2100

(As of July 1. Resident population.)

Race and Hispanic origin	Middle series			
	1999	2025	2050	2100
Life expectancy at birth (years)				
Total population (male)	74.1	77.6	81.2	88.0
Total population (female)	79.8	83.6	86.7	92.3
White, non-Hispanic (male)	74.7	77.8	81.1	87.6
White, non-Hispanic (female)	80.1	83.6	86.4	91.8
Black, non-Hispanic (male)	68.4	73.6	78.5	86.9
Black, non-Hispanic (female)	75.1	80.5	84.6	91.5
American Indian, non-Hispanic (male)[1]	72.9	78.4	82.2	88.5
American Indian, non-Hispanic (female)[1]	82.0	86.5	89.2	93.6
Asian, non-Hispanic (male)[2]	80.9	82.4	84.8	89.4
Asian, non-Hispanic (female)[2]	86.5	87.7	89.7	93.4
Hispanic origin (male)[3]	77.2	80.0	83.0	88.6
Hispanic origin (female)[3]	83.7	86.1	88.4	92.9

[1] "American Indian" is used to describe the American Indian, Eskimo, and Aleut population.
[2] "Asian" is used to describe the Asian and Pacific Islander population.
[3] Hispanic origin may be of any race.

SOURCE: Adapted from Frederick W. Hollmann, Tammany J. Mulder, and Jeffrey E. Kallan, "Projected Life Expectancy at birth by Race and Hispanic Origin, 1999 to 2100," in *Methodology and Assumptions for the Population Projections of the United States: 1999 to 2100*, Population Division Working Paper No. 38, U.S. Census Bureau, Washington, DC, 2000

been counted in Census 2000. Sutapa Basu, director of the University of Washington Women's Center, told the *Seattle Times* (November 4, 2001) that approximately 50,000 women are illegally trafficked into the United States every year as mail-order brides, servants, factory workers, or forced laborers.

MARITAL STATUS

Married Women

The number of marriages has been declining since the early 1980s. In 1998, 2.32 million marriages were performed in the United States, according to the National Center for Health Statistics. The marriage rate in 1998, 8.4 per 1,000 people, was down from 9.4 per 1,000 in 1992.

In March 2000 about 56.5 million American women aged 15 and over were married and living with their spouses. (See Table 1.5.) Additionally, almost 1.4 million married women were not living with their spouses, and approximately 2.7 million women were legally separated from their spouses. In 2000 about 55 percent of all women over 14 were married, whereas in 1950 almost 66 percent of women over 13 were married.

Among individuals between the ages of 25 and 34, 57 percent of women and 50 percent of men were married

TABLE 1.4

Foreign-born population by citizenship status, year of entry, and sex, March 2000

(Numbers in thousands.)

	TOTAL		MALE		FEMALE	
Citizenship status and year of entry	Number	Percent	Number	Percent	Number	Percent
Total						
Total	28,379	100.0	14,200	100.0	14,179	100.0
1990–1999	11,206	39.5	5,692	40.1	5,514	38.9
1980–1989	8,022	28.3	4,186	29.5	3,836	27.1
1970–1979	4,605	16.2	2,243	15.8	2,362	16.7
Before 1970	4,547	16.0	2,079	14.6	2,468	17.4
Naturalized citizen						
Total	10,622	100.0	5,077	100.0	5,544	100.0
1990–1999	997	9.4	496	9.8	501	9.0
1980–1989	3,118	29.4	1,592	31.3	1,526	27.5
1970–1979	2,851	26.8	1,330	26.2	1,522	27.4
Before 1970	3,655	34.4	1,660	32.7	1,995	36.0
Not a citizen						
Total	17,758	100.0	9,123	100.0	8,635	100.0
1990–1999	10,209	57.5	5,196	57.0	5,013	58.1
1980–1989	4,904	27.6	2,594	28.4	2,310	26.7
1970–1979	1,754	9.9	913	10.0	840	9.7
Before 1970	892	5.0	419	4.6	472	5.5

SOURCE: "Table 8. Foreign-Born Population by Citizenship Status, Year of Entry, and Sex: March 2000," in *Current Population Survey, March 2000*. [Online] http://www.census.gov/population/socdemo/gender/ppl-121/tab08.txt [accessed October 11, 2001]

and living with their spouses in 2000. Among women between the ages of 35 and 64, almost 66 percent were married and living with their husbands. In contrast, only 41 percent of women over 64 were married and living with spouses, compared to 73 percent of men in that age group. (See Table 1.5.) Since men tend to die at younger ages than women, many women over 64 are widowed.

According to Census 2000, 57 percent of all white women aged 15 and over were married in 2000, compared to 63 percent in 1970. In 2000 only 36 percent of African American women over 14 were married, compared to 54 percent in 1970.

Single Women

The percentage of unmarried individuals continues to grow. In 2000, 45 percent of females age 15 and over were single, as were 42 percent of males. Although more men than women never marry, women are more likely to be single because they are less likely than men to remarry following divorce or the death of a spouse.

POSTPONING MARRIAGE. The age at which women marry continues to rise. In March 2000 the majority of single women under age 35 had yet to marry. (See Table 1.5.) As Table 1.6 shows, since 1890 women have consistently married at a younger median age than men, although the gap between men and women has narrowed over the years. The median age for a woman's first marriage rose from 22.0 years in 1890 and 20.1 years in 1956 to 25.1 years in 1999 and 2000. In March 2000, 72.8 per-

cent of women aged 20 to 24 had never been married, whereas in 1970 only 35.8 percent of women in that age group had not been married. (See Table 1.5.) Many women now postpone marriage to pursue their education and careers.

DIVORCED WOMEN. It is estimated that approximately half of all marriages end in divorce. According to the National Center for Health Statistics, there were 1.1 million divorces granted in 1998, for a divorce rate of 4.2 per 1,000 people. Although this figure is high compared to the divorce rate in 1980, it is down from the 1992 rate of 4.8 divorces per 1,000 people.

In March 2000 approximately 11.3 million American women aged 15 and over, or 10 percent of all women, were divorced and had not remarried. Women between the ages of 35 and 64 were most likely to be single because of divorce, and those aged 35 to 54 accounted for 57 percent of all divorced women. (See Table 1.5.) Overall, the percentage of women who were separated or divorced and not remarried increased from 5.7 percent in 1970 to 12.6 percent in 2000. (See Table 1.5.)

According to Census 2000, 10 percent of all white females 15 and over were divorced and had not remarried, compared to 8 percent of white males. Among African Americans 12 percent of women were divorced, compared to 9 percent of men. In 1970, 3 percent of white women and 4 percent of African American women were divorced.

TABLE 1.5

Marital status of people 15 years and over, March 1970 and March 2000

(In thousands)

Characteristic	March 2000 Number							Percent never married	March 1970 percent never married[1]
	Total	Married spouse present	Married spouse absent	Sepa-rated	Divorced	Widowed	Never married		
Both sexes									
Total 15 years old and over	213,773	113,002	2,730	4,479	19,881	13,665	60,016	28.1	24.9
15 to 19 years old	20,102	345	36	103	64	13	19,541	97.2	93.9
20 to 24 years old	18,440	3,362	134	234	269	11	14,430	78.3	44.5
25 to 29 years old	18,269	8,334	280	459	917	27	8,252	45.2	14.7
30 to 34 years old	19,519	11,930	278	546	1,616	78	5,071	26.0	7.8
35 to 44 years old	44,804	29,353	717	1,436	5,967	399	6,932	15.5	5.9
45 to 54 years old	36,633	25,460	492	899	5,597	882	3,303	9.0	6.1
55 to 64 years old	23,388	16,393	308	441	3,258	1,770	1,218	5.2	7.2
65 years old and over	32,620	17,827	485	361	2,193	10,484	1,270	3.9	7.6
Males									
Total 15 years old and over	103,113	56,501	1,365	1,818	8,572	2,604	32,253	31.3	28.1
15 to 19 years old	10,295	69	3	51	29	3	10,140	98.5	97.4
20 to 24 years old	9,208	1,252	75	70	101	—	7,710	83.7	54.7
25 to 29 years old	8,943	3,658	139	170	342	9	4,625	51.7	19.1
30 to 34 years old	9,622	5,640	151	205	712	15	2,899	30.1	9.4
35 to 44 years old	22,134	14,310	387	585	2,775	96	3,981	18.0	6.7
45 to 54 years old	17,891	13,027	255	378	2,377	157	1,697	9.5	7.5
55 to 64 years old	11,137	8,463	158	188	1,387	329	612	5.5	7.8
65 years old and over	13,885	10,084	197	171	849	1,994	590	4.2	7.5
Females									
Total 15 years old and over	110,660	56,501	1,365	2,661	11,309	11,061	27,763	25.1	22.1
15 to 19 years old	9,807	276	33	52	35	10	9,401	95.9	90.3
20 to 24 years old	9,232	2,110	59	164	168	11	6,720	72.8	35.8
25 to 29 years old	9,326	4,676	141	289	575	18	3,627	38.9	10.5
30 to 34 years old	9,897	6,290	127	341	904	63	2,172	21.9	6.2
35 to 44 years old	22,670	15,043	330	851	3,192	303	2,951	13.0	5.2
45 to 54 years old	18,742	12,433	237	521	3,220	725	1,606	8.6	4.9
55 to 64 years old	12,251	7,930	150	253	1,871	1,441	606	4.9	6.8
65 years old and over	18,735	7,743	288	190	1,344	8,490	680	3.6	7.7

— Represents zero or rounds to zero.

[1]The 1970 percentages include 14-year-olds, and thus are for 14+ and 14–19.

SOURCE: Jason Fields and Lynne M. Casper, "Table 5. Marital Status of People 15 Years and Over: March 1970 and March 2000," in *America's Families and Living Arrangements: March 2000,* Current Population Reports, P20-537, U.S. Census Bureau, Washington, DC, June 2001

WIDOWHOOD. The majority of single women over the age of 65 are widows. (See Table 1.5.) Of the nearly 11.1 million American widows in 2000, 77 percent were 65 or over. Widows made up 26 percent of the total population over age 64, and 45 percent of women in that age group were widowed. In contrast, only 2.6 million men were widowed, and only 14 percent of men over 64 were widowers. A total of 10 percent of all women 15 and over, as well as 10 percent of all white women, were widows in 2000, down from 12 percent in 1970.

Although the percentage of widows who remarry has increased since 1970, widowed women are much more likely than either widowed men or divorced women to remain single. In general, the older the woman, the less likely that she will remarry. White women are more likely to remarry than African American women, even though white women tend to become widows at an older age than African American women. The primary reason for the low rate of remarriage is the diminishing number of eligible older men, particularly among African Americans.

NEVER-MARRIED WOMEN. Being unmarried used to be considered a temporary or transitional state for most people. However, over the past 30 years there has been a large increase in the number of individuals who have never been married. Between 1970 and 2000 the percentage of never-married women increased significantly in every age group between 15 and 54. (See Table 1.5.) The percentages of never-married males likewise increased significantly in these age groups. In contrast, among women over age 64, only 3.6 percent had never married in 2000, compared to 7.7 percent in 1970. Although the Census Bureau estimates that 90 percent of women eventually marry, a few decades ago 95 percent of women married.

The total number of women ages 15 and over who had never been married increased from 22.1 percent in

TABLE 1.6

Estimated median age at first marriage, by sex, 1890–2000

Year	Men	Women
2000	26.8	25.1
1999	26.9	25.1
1998	26.7	25.0
1997	26.8	25.0
1996	27.1	24.8
1995	26.9	24.5
1994	26.7	24.5
1993	26.5	24.5
1992	26.5	24.4
1991	26.3	24.1
1990	26.1	23.9
1989	26.2	23.8
1988	25.9	23.6
1987	25.8	23.6
1986	25.7	23.1
1985	25.5	23.3
1984	25.4	23.0
1983	25.4	22.8
1982	25.2	22.5
1981	24.8	22.3
1980	24.7	22.0
1979	24.4	22.1
1978	24.2	21.8
1977	24.0	21.6
1976	23.8	21.3
1975	23.5	21.1
1974	23.1	21.1
1973	23.2	21.0
1972	23.3	20.9
1971	23.1	20.9
1970	23.2	20.8
1969	23.2	20.8
1968	23.1	20.8
1967	23.1	20.6
1966	22.8	20.5
1965	22.8	20.6
1964	23.1	20.5
1963	22.8	20.5
1962	22.7	20.3
1961	22.8	20.3
1960	22.8	20.3
1959	22.5	20.2
1958	22.6	20.2
1957	22.6	20.3
1956	22.5	20.1
1955	22.6	20.2
1954	23.0	20.3
1953	22.8	20.2
1952	23.0	20.2
1951	22.9	20.4
1950	22.8	20.3
1949	22.7	20.3
1948	23.3	20.4
1947	23.7	20.5
1940	24.3	21.5
1930	24.3	21.3
1920	24.6	21.2
1910	25.1	21.6
1900	25.9	21.9
1890	26.1	22.0

Notes: Figures for 1947 to 1999 are based on Current Population Survey data; figures for years prior to 1947 are based on decennial censuses. A standard error of 0.1 years is appropriate to measure sampling variability for any of the above estimated median ages at first marriage.

"Table MS-2. Estimated Median Age at First Marriage, by Sex: 1890 to the Present," in *Families and Living Arrangements,* U.S. Census Bureau, Washington, DC, June 29, 2001 [Online] http://www.census.gov/population/www/socdemo/hh-fam.html [accessed September 18, 2001]

1970 to 25.1 percent in 2000. (See Table 1.5.) Among white women, the total never-married increased from 21 to 22 percent over the 30-year period. However, among African American women 42 percent had never married in 2000, compared to only 28 percent in 1970. In 2000, 43 percent of single mothers had never been married.

Cohabitation

As attitudes change in America, marital status may no longer accurately reflect the personal relationships of individuals. Changes in attitudes toward cohabitation have contributed to the rise in the median age for first marriages, as well as to the increasing numbers of individuals who never marry or who do not remarry following divorce or death of a spouse. Among many Americans marriage is no longer viewed as a prerequisite for living together and raising children.

By the late 1990s more than 40 percent of women aged 15 to 44 and more than 50 percent of women between the ages of 25 and 29 had lived with men to whom they were not related. Seven percent of all women were living in an unmarried partnership, up from 6.4 percent in 1982. The March 2000 census counted 3.8 million unmarried male-female couples, compared to 56.5 million married couples.

Table 1.7 highlights several interesting differences between married and unmarried couples. Women in unmarried partnerships tend to be younger than married women. Those between the ages of 15 and 24 represent only 4.2 percent of married women, yet they comprise 24.5 percent of unmarried partners. In contrast, although 76.4 percent of married women are 35 and over, only 42.3 percent of women in unmarried couples are over 34. Furthermore, women in unmarried couples are more likely than those in married couples to be two or more years older than their male partners. A higher percentage of unmarried couples are black, interracial, or interethnic, as compared with married couples. Women in unmarried partnerships are more likely than married women to be in the labor force, to have more education than their male partners, and to earn significantly more money than their partners. (See Table 1.8.) Almost 41 percent of unmarried couples live with the children of one or both partners. This is only slightly less than the nearly 46 percent of married-partner families that include children under 18. (See Table 1.7.)

Despite these lifestyle trends, polls indicate that the majority of young Americans support more traditional family structures. A 1997–98 survey of college freshman conducted by Louis Harris and Associates for Northwestern Mutual Life found that 94 percent of the class of 2001 intended to be married by age 26, and 89 percent planned to have children. The majority of the students wanted to have three children. Although approximately 90 percent of the students agreed that "marriage is a cornerstone of

TABLE 1.7

Characteristics of unmarried partners and married spouses by sex, March 2000

	Number (In thousands)				Percent			
	Unmarried partners		Married spouses		Unmarried partners		Married spouses	
Characteristic	Men	Women	Men	Women	Men	Women	Men	Women
Total	3,822	3,822	56,497	56,497	100.0	100.0	100.0	100.0
Age								
15 to 24 years old	597	937	1,321	2,386	15.6	24.5	2.3	4.2
25 to 34 years old	1,413	1,269	9,296	10,964	37.0	33.2	16.5	19.4
35 years old and over	1,811	1,616	45,881	43,146	47.4	42.3	81.2	76.4
Race and Hispanic origin								
White	3,127	3,147	49,668	49,581	81.8	82.3	87.9	87.8
Non-Hispanic	2,710	2,742	44,350	44,142	70.9	71.7	78.5	78.1
Black	562	498	4,294	4,097	14.7	13.0	7.6	7.3
Asian and Pacific Islander	63	105	2,118	2,393	1.6	2.7	3.7	4.2
Hispanic (of any race)	453	433	5,550	5,671	11.9	11.3	9.8	10.0
Education								
Less than high school	683	599	8,314	7,160	17.9	15.7	14.7	12.7
High school graduate	1,441	1,357	17,506	19,950	37.7	35.5	31.0	35.3
Some college	996	1,223	14,002	14,968	26.1	32.0	24.8	26.5
College graduate	702	643	16,674	14,419	18.4	16.8	29.5	25.5
Labor force status								
Employed	3,179	2,894	42,854	34,067	83.2	75.7	75.9	60.3
Unemployed	187	178	992	961	4.9	4.7	1.8	1.7
Not in labor force	453	747	12,650	21,468	11.9	19.5	22.4	38.0
Personal earnings								
Without earnings	402	642	11,353	19,368	10.5	16.8	20.1	34.3
With earnings	3,419	3,178	45,144	37,132	89.5	83.2	79.9	65.7
Under $5,000 or loss	184	373	1,874	4,683	4.8	9.8	3.3	8.3
$5,000 to $9,999	286	395	1,665	4,183	7.5	10.3	2.9	7.4
$10,000 to $14,999	360	445	2,401	4,497	9.4	11.6	4.2	8.0
$15,000 to $19,999	410	441	3,101	4,427	10.7	11.5	5.5	7.8
$20,000 to $24,999	401	397	3,561	4,249	10.5	10.4	6.3	7.5
$25,000 to $29,999	336	315	3,595	3,429	8.8	8.2	6.4	6.1
$30,000 to $39,999	548	405	7,492	4,954	14.3	10.6	13.3	8.8
$40,000 to $49,999	337	201	6,096	2,976	8.8	5.3	10.8	5.3
$50,000 to $74,999	370	137	8,703	2,683	9.7	3.6	15.4	4.7
$75,000 and over	187	69	6,656	1,051	4.9	1.8	11.8	1.9
Presence of children								
With children[1]	1,563	1,563	25,771	25,771	40.9	40.9	45.6	45.6

[1]May be own children of either partner or both partners. Excludes ever married children under 18 years.
Note: Data are not shown separately for the American Indian and Alaska Native population because of the small sample size.

SOURCE: Jason Fields and Lynne M. Casper, "Table 7. Characteristics of Unmarried Partners and Married Spouses by Sex: March 2000," in *America's Families and Living Arrangements: March 2000*, U.S. Census Bureau, Washington, DC, June 2001

societal values," almost 70 percent felt that premarital sex was acceptable among individuals who loved each other. Furthermore, over 60 percent of the students believed that living together before marriage was a good idea. Surprisingly, only 2 out of 10 respondents believed that divorce was an acceptable resolution for an unhappy marriage.

Lesbian Partners

Lesbians are estimated to comprise somewhere between 1 and 6 percent of the adult female population. Many lesbian couples live together in long-term intimate relationships. In 1996 President Bill Clinton signed the "Defense of Marriage Act," which excluded same-gender couples from the definition of marriage and barred them from receiving the federal benefits and protections that are afforded to opposite-gender couples. As of June 2001,

35 states had passed laws prohibiting same-sex marriages. However, many lesbian couples consider themselves to be married and may have undergone a commitment or marriage ceremony. According to a 2001 report by The Urban Institute, a Washington, D.C.–based nonpartisan economic and social policy research organization, Census 2000 counted 297,061 lesbian families. Although this was a 314 percent increase over the 1990 census, the Human Rights Campaign suggests that the number of gay and lesbian families may have been undercounted by as much as 62 percent in 2000.

Many employers now offer the same benefits to same-sex and opposite-sex domestic partners of employees that they offer to the spouses of employees. As of October 2000 eight state governments offered same-sex domestic-partner benefits to their employees. On August 1, 2000,

TABLE 1.8

Characteristics of unmarried and married male-female couples, March 2000

Characteristic	Number (in thousands)		Percent	
	Unmarried couples	Married couples	Unmarried couples	Married couples
Number of couples				
Total	3,822	56,497	100.0	100.0
Age difference				
Male 6 or more years older than female	944	11,049	24.7	19.6
Male 2 to 5 years older than female	1,093	20,515	28.6	36.3
Within 1 year of each other	975	17,982	25.5	31.8
Female 2 to 5 years older than male	460	5,086	12.0	9.0
Female 6 or more years older than male	349	1,864	9.1	3.3
Race difference[1]				
Same race couples	3,614	55,029	94.6	97.4
Both White	3,040	48,917	79.5	86.6
Both Black	480	3,989	12.6	7.1
Both Asian and Pacific Islander	45	1,914	1.2	3.4
Interracial couples	165	1,047	4.3	1.9
Black/White	88	363	2.3	0.6
Black/Asian and Pacific Islander	9	25	—	—
White/Asian and Pacific Islander	67	655	1.8	1.2
Hispanic origin difference[2]				
Both Hispanic	332	4,739	8.7	8.4
Neither Hispanic	3,268	50,015	85.5	88.5
One Hispanic and one non-Hispanic	222	1,743	5.8	3.1
Education				
Male more education than female	885	13,843	23.2	24.5
Male and female same education	1,871	30,590	49.0	54.1
Female more education than male	1,065	12,064	27.9	21.4
Employment status				
Male only employed	695	12,642	18.2	22.4
Female only employed	410	3,855	10.7	6.8
Neither employed	230	9,787	6.0	17.3
Both employed	2,484	30,212	65.0	53.5
Earnings difference[3]				
Male $30,000 or more higher than female	546	16,679	14.3	29.5
Male $5,000 to $29,999 higher than female	1,553	16,549	40.6	29.3
Within $4,999 of each other	902	14,860	23.6	26.3
Female $5,000 to $29,999 higher than male	667	6,256	17.5	11.1
Female $30,000 or more higher than male	154	2,152	4.0	3.8

— Represents zero or rounds to zero.
[1]This race comparison is regardless of Hispanic origin.
[2]This difference does not consider race. People of Hispanic origin may be of any race.
[3]Includes people with no earnings or loss.
Note: Data are not shown separately for the American Indian and Alaska Native population because of the small sample size.

SOURCE: Jason Fields and Lynne M. Casper, "Table 8. Characteristics of Unmarried and Married Male-Female Couples: March 2000," in *America's Families and Living Arrangements: March 2000*, U.S. Census Bureau, Washington, DC, June 2001

the major auto manufacturers—Chrysler, Ford, and General Motors—began offering domestic-partner benefits to the same-sex partners of employees.

LIVING ARRANGEMENTS

More and more Americans are marrying later, choosing to remain single, divorcing, and cohabitating without marriage. Many people are choosing to raise children in homes other than a traditional married-couple household. As a result of these trends the living arrangements of America's households have changed in significant ways. The average household size has decreased dramatically since 1970, when almost 21 percent of households had five or more people. In 2000 only 10 percent of house-

holds were this large, and one-person households had increased from 17 percent of the total to more than 25 percent. The average household size decreased from 3.14 persons in 1970 to 2.62 in 2000. These trends, along with population growth, have resulted in a sharp increase in the number of households in the United States, from 63 million in 1970 to 105 million in 2000.

Types of Households

The Census Bureau defines a household as everyone who lives in a single housing unit. One of the people who owns, is buying, or rents the housing unit is designated the householder. Households are categorized by the Census Bureau as either family or nonfamily households. A family household comprises at least two persons who are related by birth, adoption, or marriage but may include other individuals who are not related. A nonfamily household consists of either a householder living alone or a householder who is not related to any of the other people that live in the same housing unit. These people may include roommates or unmarried partners. However, people other than the householder in a nonfamily household may be related to each other. The majority of households are family households, although the proportion of family households declined from 81 percent in 1970 to 69 percent in 2000. All types of nonfamily households, including women and men living alone, increased accordingly over the same period. (See Figure 1.2.)

Family Households

The proportion of households that included the householder's own children under 18 decreased from 45 percent in 1970 to 33 percent in 2000. In 1970, 40 percent of all households consisted of married couples with their own children. However, such family units made up only 24 percent of households in 2000. The percentage of households consisting of a married couple without their own children declined only slightly, from 30 percent in 1970 to 29 percent in 2000. This group includes couples who have not yet had children but intend to, couples who do not want or cannot have children, and older couples whose children have left home. Other types of family households, such as a householder living with his or her children or other relatives but without a spouse, increased from 11 percent to 16 percent of all households between 1970 and 2000. In approximately three-quarters of these families, the householder was female.

Whereas 56 percent of white householders, 55 percent of Hispanic householders of any race, and 60 percent of Asian and Pacific Islanders lived in married-couple households in 2000, only 32 percent of black householders lived in married-couple households. (See Table 1.9.) The average household size for married couples was 3.26 people. Related children under 18 lived in 48 percent of married-couple households, and 40 percent of these were families with two children. Only 6 percent of the families had four or more related children under 18. (See Table 1.9.) However, in 2000, 42.5 percent of women and 56.4 percent of men between the ages of 18 and 24 lived with at least one parent. (See Table 1.10.)

According to the Census Bureau, among families with children, the proportion of married-couple families declined from 87 percent to about 69 percent between 1970 and 2000, with most of the decline occurring prior to 1994. Families headed by single mothers increased from 3 million in 1970 to 10 million in 2000, and families headed by single fathers increased from 393,000 to 2 million.

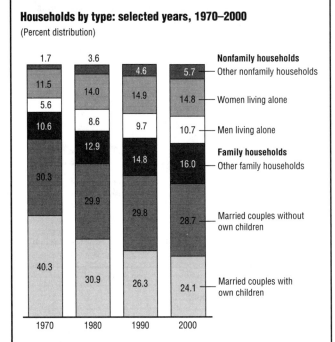

FIGURE 1.2

Households by type: selected years, 1970–2000
(Percent distribution)

SOURCE: Jason Fields and Lynne M. Casper, "Figure 1. Households by Type: Selected Years, 1970 to 2000," in *America's Families and Living Arrangements: March 2000,* Current Population Reports, P20-537, U.S. Census Bureau, Washington, DC, June 2001

Households headed by women with their own children under 18 and no husband present increased from 6.6 to 7.2 percent of all households between 1990 and 2000. Among whites and Asian and Pacific Islanders, 10 percent of all households were families headed by women, whereas 19 percent of Hispanic and 30 percent of black households were families with a female householder. (See Table 1.9.) Only 3 percent of non-Hispanic white households, 5 percent of black and Asian and Pacific Islander households, and 7 percent of Hispanic households were families headed by men with no spouse present. The majority of family households headed by men (52 percent) and by women (69 percent), with no spouse present, included related children under 18. The average size of a family household headed by a woman was 3.17 people.

According to the Census Bureau, in 1999 almost 6 percent of all children lived in their grandparents' homes, up from less than 4 percent in 1980. Almost 36 percent of these children had no parent living with them, and 46 percent had only their mother present. In 1980, 42 percent of these children had no parent present, and 40 percent had their mothers only. In 2000, 3.7 percent of all households were multigenerational, consisting of at least one grandparent, parent, and child. Black and Hispanic single mothers and their children were more likely to live with relatives than non-Hispanic white single mothers (18 and 22 percent versus 14 percent, respectively).

TABLE 1.9

Households by type and selected characteristics, March 2000

(In thousands, except average size)

Characteristic	All households	Family households				Nonfamily households		
		Total	Married couple	Other families		Total	Male householder	Female householder
				Male householder	Female householder			
All households	104,705	72,025	55,311	4,028	12,687	32,680	14,641	18,039
Age of householder								
15 to 24 years old	5,860	3,353	1,450	560	1,342	2,507	1,286	1,221
25 to 34 years old	18,627	13,007	9,390	886	2,732	5,620	3,448	2,172
35 to 44 years old	23,955	18,706	14,104	1,102	3,499	5,250	3,261	1,989
45 to 54 years old	20,927	15,803	12,792	713	2,299	5,123	2,583	2,541
55 to 64 years old	13,592	9,569	8,138	351	1,080	4,023	1,533	2,490
65 years old and over	21,744	11,587	9,437	416	1,735	10,157	2,530	7,626
Race and ethnicity of householder								
White	87,671	60,251	48,790	3,081	8,380	27,420	12,204	15,215
Non-Hispanic	78,819	53,066	43,865	2,468	6,732	25,753	11,278	14,475
Black	12,849	8,664	4,144	706	3,814	4,185	1,876	2,309
Asian and Pacific Islander	3,337	2,506	1,996	179	331	831	432	399
Hispanic (of any race)	9,319	7,561	5,133	658	1,769	1,758	974	783
Presence of related children under 18								
No related children	67,350	34,670	28,919	1,826	3,924	32,680	14,641	18,039
With related children	37,355	37,355	26,392	2,202	8,762	(X)	(X)	(X)
One related child under 18	15,493	15,493	9,897	1,321	4,275	(X)	(X)	(X)
Two related children under 18	14,020	14,020	10,567	644	2,809	(X)	(X)	(X)
Three related children under 18	5,510	5,510	4,238	185	1,087	(X)	(X)	(X)
Four or more related children under 18	2,332	2,332	1,690	52	591	(X)	(X)	(X)
Presence of own children under 18								
No own children	70,100	37,420	30,062	2,242	5,116	32,680	14,641	18,039
With own children	34,605	34,605	25,248	1,786	7,571	(X)	(X)	(X)
With own children under 1	2,939	2,939	2,264	174	501	(X)	(X)	(X)
With own children under 3	8,786	8,786	6,784	441	1,561	(X)	(X)	(X)
With own children under 6	14,986	14,986	11,393	706	2,887	(X)	(X)	(X)
With own children under 12	25,885	25,885	19,082	1,235	5,568	(X)	(X)	(X)
Size of households								
1 person	26,724	(X)	(X)	(X)	(X)	26,724	11,181	15,543
2 people	34,666	29,834	22,899	1,730	5,206	4,832	2,607	2,225
3 people	17,152	16,405	11,213	1,106	4,086	746	570	177
4 people	15,309	15,064	12,455	682	1,927	245	179	66
5 people	6,981	6,894	5,723	307	864	87	70	17
6 people	2,445	2,413	1,916	130	366	32	26	6
7 or more	1,428	1,415	1,105	73	237	13	8	5
Average size	2.62	3.24	3.26	3.16	3.17	1.25	1.34	1.17

X Not applicable.

Note: Data are not shown separately for the American Indian and Alaska Native population because of the small sample size.

SOURCE: Jason Fields and Lynne M. Casper, "Table 1. Households by Type and Selected Characteristics: March 2000," in *America's Families and Living Arrangements: March 2000*, Current Population Reports, P20-537, U.S. Census Bureau, Washington, DC, June 2001

Unmarried Partners

The percentage of households consisting of individuals who are not related by birth, adoption, or marriage increased from 1.7 percent in 1970 to 5.7 percent in 2000 (see Figure 1.2). Census 2000 identified 5.5 million unmarried-partner households, up from 1.6 million in 1980. Unmarried partners accounted for 5.2 percent of all households, up from 3.5 percent in 1990. These may be identified as either family or nonfamily households, depending on whether other individuals in the household are related to the householder. Sixty-one percent of unmarried-couple families included their own children under 18, as compared with only 46 percent of married-couple families.

The actual numbers of unmarried-partner households may be higher, since individuals are sometimes reluctant to identify themselves as partners and may instead say they are roommates, housemates, or friends. Furthermore, since only householders and their partners are counted as unmarried couples, any additional couples in the household are identified as unmarried partners.

In 1998 the Census Bureau estimated that there were almost 1.7 million households of same-sex partners. The majority of same-sex partners were under age 35 and had never been married. Only about 10 percent of such households included children under 15.

Women Living Alone

The majority of nonfamily households consist of women or men living alone. Women made up 58 percent of all one-person households in 2000. (See Table 1.9.) However, only 6.6 percent of women between the ages of 18 and 34 lived alone. Older adults were most likely to be living alone in 2000. Almost 39.6 percent of all women 65 and over lived alone, compared to 17 percent of men in that age group. Over 49.4 percent of all women over 74 lived alone. (See Table 1.10.) In 1970 only 37 percent of women over 74 lived alone. Men over 64 were much more likely to be living with their spouse, a reflection of women's longer life expectancy. The Census Bureau predicts that the number of single-occupant residences will grow another 26 percent by 2010.

Women and Housing

HOMEOWNERS VERSUS RENTERS. In 1999 almost 81.8 percent of all married-couple households owned or were buying their homes, up from 78.2 percent in 1985. (See Table 1.11.) In contrast, only 48.2 percent of female heads of family households with no spouse present were homeowners, although this was up from 45.8 percent in 1985. Male heads of family households with no spouse present were more likely to own their homes (56.1 percent). Interestingly, 57.6 percent of women living alone owned their homes, compared to only 46.3 percent of men living alone. In addition, 41.5 percent of women heads of other types of nonfamily households owned their homes, compared to 37.2 percent of men in that category.

HOMELESS WOMEN. The U. S. Conference of Mayors' 25-city annual survey, *A Status Report on Hunger and Homelessness in America's Cities* (Washington, D.C., December 2000) found that families with children accounted for 36 percent of the homeless population, up from 27 percent in 1985. Single parents, most often mothers, headed 63 percent of these families. Requests for shelter from families with children increased by about 17 percent over the previous year, and 27 percent of the requests went unmet. Two-parent families were often forced to separate to obtain shelter, because fathers could not be accommodated with their families. As a result, many families stayed together on the streets rather than in shelters.

In the Conference of Mayors' survey, single women accounted for 13 percent of the homeless population, compared to just 3 percent in 1963. Other surveys of homelessness have found higher proportions of single women, although the proportion has remained fairly constant since 1984. However, the actual number of homeless single women has increased by 180 percent since 1984. Homeless single women may find it difficult to obtain shelter and other services because most programs that serve women are designed for families.

TABLE 1.10

Living arrangements of younger and older adults, March 2000
(In thousands)

Characteristic	Number		Percent	
	Men	Women	Men	Women
YOUNGER ADULTS				
18 to 34 years old				
Total	31,854	32,464	100.0	100.0
Living alone	2,830	2,156	8.9	6.6
Married spouse present	10,603	13,298	33.3	41.0
Not married spouse present - child of householder	9,737	6,661	30.6	20.5
None of the above	8,684	10,349	27.3	31.9
18 to 24 years old				
Total	13,291	13,242	100.0	100.0
Living alone	551	588	4.1	4.4
Married spouse present	1,305	2,332	9.8	17.6
Not married spouse present - child of householder	7,497	5,629	56.4	42.5
None of the above	3,938	4,693	29.6	35.4
25 to 34 years old				
Total	18,563	19,222	100.0	100.0
Living alone	2,279	1,568	12.3	8.2
Married spouse present	9,298	10,966	50.1	57.0
Not married spouse present - child of householder	2,240	1,032	12.1	5.4
None of the above	4,746	5,656	25.6	29.4
OLDER ADULTS				
65 years old and over				
Total	13,886	18,735	100.0	100.0
Living alone	2,355	7,427	17.0	39.6
Married spouse present	10,084	7,743	72.6	41.3
None of the above	1,447	3,565	10.4	19.0
65 to 74 years old				
Total	8,049	9,747	100.0	100.0
Living alone	1,108	2,983	13.8	30.6
Married spouse present	6,170	5,156	76.7	52.9
None of the above	771	1,608	9.6	16.5
75 years old and over				
Total	5,837	8,988	100.0	100.0
Living alone	1,247	4,444	21.4	49.4
Married spouse present	3,914	2,587	67.1	28.8
None of the above	676	1,957	11.6	21.8

SOURCE: Jason Fields and Lynne M. Casper, "Table 6. Living Arrangements of Younger and Older Adults: March 2000," in *America's Families and Living Arrangements: March 2000,* Current Population Reports, P20-537, U.S. Census Bureau, Washington, DC, June 2001

The majority of America's homeless are African American (50 percent in the Conference of Mayors' survey) and 26 percent are employed. Although lack of affordable housing has been identified as the single most important cause of homelessness, many women are homeless because they are escaping domestic violence.

Women's Mobility

Mobility can be a factor in women's living arrangements and may determine where they reside. Fewer women than men are licensed to drive. The difference is small between young males and females, but it increases dramatically above age 40. According to the Federal Highway Administration, in 1996, 2 percent fewer women than men between the ages of 40 and 44 had driver's

TABLE 1.11

Homeownership rates, by family status, selected years, 1985–99

[In percent. Represents the proportion of owner households to the total number of occupied households.]

	1985	1990	1992	1993[1]	1994	1995	1996	1997	1998	1999
United States	63.9	63.9	64.1	64.5	64.0	64.7	65.4	65.7	66.3	66.8
FAMILY STATUS										
Family households:										
Married-couple families	78.2	78.1	78.7	79.1	78.8	79.6	80.2	80.8	81.5	81.8
Male householder, no spouse present	57.8	55.2	53.6	54.6	52.8	55.3	55.5	54.0	55.7	56.1
Female householder, no spouse present	45.8	44.0	43.6	44.5	44.2	45.1	46.1	46.1	47.0	48.2
Nonfamily households:										
One-person	45.8	49.0	49.8	50.0	49.8	50.5	51.4	51.8	52.1	52.7
Male householder	38.8	42.4	43.5	43.2	43.1	43.8	44.9	45.2	45.7	46.3
Female householder	51.3	53.6	54.1	54.8	54.5	55.4	56.0	56.7	56.9	57.6
Other:										
Male householder	30.1	31.7	32.4	33.2	33.6	34.2	35.5	35.9	36.7	37.2
Female householder	30.6	32.5	34.0	35.6	34.3	33.0	35.9	39.5	40.3	41.5

[1] Based on 1990 census controls.

SOURCE: Adapted from "No. 1213. Homeownership Rates by Age of Householder and Family Status: 1985 to 1999," in *Statistical Abstract of the United States: 2000*, U.S. Census Bureau, Washington, DC, 2001

licenses. Between the ages of 70 and 74, almost 19 percent fewer women than men had driver's licenses. Although 72 percent of men 85 and over were licensed drivers, only 29 percent of women in that age group were able to drive. Furthermore, women drove only about half as many miles as men annually. Thus, women are more dependent than men on public transportation and transportation provided by friends, relatives, and social service agencies. This dependence increases with a woman's age and may limit where she is able to reside.

CHAPTER 2
WOMEN'S EDUCATION

Prior to the 19th century, few American girls attended school. By the early part of the 19th century, female seminaries were being established, primarily to teach domestic chores and social graces. Mount Holyoke, founded in 1837, was one of the first female seminaries to stress academics, and in 1888 it became a women's college. Most of the graduates of the early female seminaries and normal schools became teachers. In the 1830s Oberlin College in Ohio became the first coeducational institute of higher learning. In the second half of the 19th century, American and European women undertook a major campaign to gain admission to medical schools, laying the groundwork for subsequent struggles for women's equity in education. Although by the 20th century most public universities admitted at least a few women, it wasn't until the 1960s and 1970s that elite universities such as Harvard, Yale, and Princeton began to accept women students. Many of the women's colleges also became coeducational during this period.

However, a century ago few young women even completed high school. Those who did go beyond high school usually trained to be teachers, nurses, or social workers. Business schools prepared young women for clerical duties, never for management. Now at the turn of the 21st century, increasing numbers of American women are undertaking higher levels of education and preparing for essentially all occupations.

EDUCATIONAL ATTAINMENT

According to the Department of Education's National Center for Education Statistics (NCES), in 1940, 12 percent of females and 15 percent of males over age 24 had attended less than five years of elementary school, and 26 percent of American females and 23 percent of males had completed high school. Only 4 percent of women and 6 percent of men had completed four years of college. Most African Americans had only an elementary school education in 1940.

Table 2.1 shows that by 1999, 83.4 percent of all adult Americans had graduated high school. More white women than black women or Asian and Pacific Islanders had finished high school, and only about 56 percent of Hispanic males and females had graduated. According to the NCES, however, in 2000, 95 percent of white women between the ages of 25 and 29 had completed high school, as had 86 percent of black women and 66 percent of Hispanic females. More female than male high school graduates in this age group had some college education by 2000, and 38 percent of white females, 20 percent of African Americans, and 17 percent of Hispanic females had earned bachelor's degrees. Furthermore, in 1999, 23.1 percent of all adult women had at least a bachelor's degree, compared to 27.5 percent of men. (See Table 2.1.) Although only 11 percent of Hispanic women had four-year college degrees, 39 percent of all Asian and Pacific Islander women had degrees. Only 16.4 percent of black women had college degrees, but this was up from 3.3 percent in 1960. According to the NCES, in 1998 far more American women had secondary and higher educations than did women in other developed countries (G-7 member countries).

SCHOOL ATTENDANCE AND ACHIEVEMENT

The Educational Attainment Level of Women Surpasses That of Men

In 1999, 55.5 percent of all females between the ages of 3 and 34 were enrolled in school. (See Table 2.2.) This was up from 51.5 percent in 1975. Between the ages of 7 and 15, over 98 percent of girls were attending school in 1999. Similar numbers of males and females were enrolled in preschool through high school. Of children entering kindergarten in 1999, 59 percent had attended preschool, up from about 5 percent in 1964. In 1999 in the 18- to 24-year-old population, there were fewer female dropouts (12 percent) than male (14 percent), more

TABLE 2.1

Educational attainment by race, Hispanic origin, and sex, 1960–99

[In percent.]

Year	All races [1]		White		Black		Asian and Pacific Islander		Hispanic [2]	
	Male	Female	Male	Female	Male	Female	Male	Female	Male	Female
COMPLETED 4 YEARS OF HIGH SCHOOL OR MORE										
1960	39.5	42.5	41.6	44.7	18.2	21.8	(NA)	(NA)	(NA)	(NA)
1965	48.0	49.9	50.2	52.2	25.8	28.4	(NA)	(NA)	(NA)	(NA)
1970	51.9	52.8	54.0	55.0	30.1	32.5	(NA)	(NA)	37.9	34.2
1975	63.1	62.1	65.0	64.1	41.6	43.3	(NA)	(NA)	39.5	36.7
1980	67.3	65.8	69.6	68.1	50.8	51.5	(NA)	(NA)	67.3	65.8
1985	74.4	73.5	76.0	75.1	58.4	60.8	(NA)	(NA)	48.5	47.4
1990	77.7	77.5	79.1	79.0	65.8	66.5	84.0	77.2	50.3	51.3
1995[3]	81.7	81.6	83.0	83.0	73.4	74.1	(NA)	(NA)	52.9	53.8
1997[3]	82.0	82.2	82.9	83.2	73.5	76.0	(NA)	(NA)	54.9	54.6
1998[3]	82.8	82.9	83.6	83.8	75.2	76.7	(NA)	(NA)	55.7	55.3
1999[3]	83.4	83.4	84.2	84.3	76.7	77.2	86.9	82.8	56.0	56.3
COMPLETED 4 YEARS OF COLLEGE OR MORE										
1960	9.7	5.8	10.3	6.0	2.8	3.3	(NA)	(NA)	(NA)	(NA)
1965	12.0	7.1	12.7	7.3	4.9	4.5	(NA)	(NA)	(NA)	(NA)
1970	13.5	8.1	14.4	8.4	4.2	4.6	(NA)	(NA)	7.8	4.3
1975	17.6	10.6	18.4	11.0	6.7	6.2	(NA)	(NA)	8.3	4.6
1980	20.1	12.8	21.3	13.3	8.4	8.3	(NA)	(NA)	9.4	6.0
1985	23.1	16.0	24.0	16.3	11.2	11.0	(NA)	(NA)	9.7	7.3
1990	24.4	18.4	25.3	19.0	11.9	10.8	44.9	35.4	9.8	8.7
1995[3]	26.0	20.2	27.2	21.0	13.6	12.9	(NA)	(NA)	10.1	8.4
1997[3]	26.2	21.7	27.0	22.3	12.5	13.9	(NA)	(NA)	10.6	10.1
1998[3]	26.5	22.4	27.3	22.8	13.9	15.4	(NA)	(NA)	11.1	10.9
1999[3]	27.5	23.1	28.5	23.5	14.2	16.4	46.2	39.0	10.7	11.0

NA Not available.
[1] Includes other races, not shown separately.
[2] Persons of Hispanic origin may be of any race.
[3] Beginning 1995, persons high school graduates and those with a BA degee or higher.

SOURCE: "No. 250. Educational Attainment by Race, Hispanic Origin, and Sex: 1960 to 1999," in *Statistical Abstract of the United States: 2000* [Online] http://www.census.gov/prod/2001pubs/statab/sec04.pdf [accessed October 11, 2001]

---

female high school graduates (83 versus 79 percent), and more female college students (37 versus 31 percent.)

In 1999 more males between the ages of 15 and 17 (36 percent) than females (25 percent) were at a grade level lower than expected for their age. According to the Census Bureau, although the annual dropout rate for grades 10 through 12 remained stable for males, at just over 5 percent between 1967 and 2000, the dropout rate for females decreased from 5.2 percent to 3.9 percent. The 2000 dropout rate was 3.6 percent for white non-Hispanic females, 3.8 percent for African American females, 0.5 percent for Asian and Pacific Islander females, and 6.5 percent for Hispanic females. According to the Federal Interagency Forum on Child and Family Statistics, girls between the ages of 16 and 19 were more likely than boys to be neither enrolled in school nor employed, although the percentage of such girls declined from 14 percent in 1984 to 9 percent in 2000. In this same age group 32 percent of females were both working and attending school (up from 25 percent in 1984), compared to 29 percent of males.

According to the NCES, among high school seniors in 1998, 61 percent of girls and 50 percent of boys planned to graduate from a four-year college. This was up from 37 percent of girls and 35 percent of boys in 1983. Among girls, 19 percent planned to graduate from a two-year college program, as did 17 percent of boys, up from 15 percent of girls and 11 percent of boys in 1983. Only 7 percent of females and 9 percent of males planned to attend a technical or vocational school after graduation. This was down from 9 and 10 percent, respectively, in 1983. Among girls, 24 percent planned to attend graduate or professional schools, up from 11 percent in 1983. Only 17 percent of senior boys planned to go on to graduate or professional school.

Test Scores

Girls score higher than boys in reading exams at every age level. (See Table 2.3.) Although boys score better than girls in mathematics, by 1999 the difference among 17-year-olds was only three points, compared to an eight-point spread in 1973. (See Table 2.4.) In 1973 younger girls scored higher than boys in math. By 1990 girls' math

TABLE 2.2

Percent of the population 3 to 34 years old enrolled in school, by race/ethnicity, sex, and age, October 1999

Year and age	Total				Male				Female			
	All races	White, non-Hispanic	Black, non-Hispanic	Hispanic origin	All races	White, non-Hispanic	Black, non-Hispanic	Hispanic origin	All races	White, non-Hispanic	Black, non-Hispanic	Hispanic origin
1	2	3	4	5	6	7	8	9	10	11	12	13
1999												
Total, 3 to 34 years	56.0	56.2	58.6	51.1	56.4	56.7	60.3	50.3	55.5	55.7	56.9	52.1
3 and 4 years	54.2	58.6	56.7	36.9	53.3	59.2	52.8	33.5	55.2	57.9	60.5	40.5
5 and 6 years	96.0	96.0	97.7	93.9	95.9	96.1	98.2	92.8	96.1	95.9	97.1	95.0
7 to 9 years	98.5	98.4	98.1	99.0	98.3	98.4	97.6	98.7	98.7	98.5	98.6	99.2
10 to 13 years	98.8	98.9	98.7	98.3	98.7	98.7	98.9	98.5	98.9	99.1	98.5	98.0
14 and 15 years	98.2	98.4	98.1	97.6	98.0	98.2	97.8	98.1	98.3	98.6	98.4	96.9
16 and 17 years	93.6	94.5	93.9	88.1	93.7	94.3	94.5	87.9	93.5	94.8	93.2	88.2
18 and 19 years	60.6	64.1	57.2	44.5	60.3	63.7	59.3	45.3	60.9	64.6	55.3	43.6
20 and 21 years	45.3	50.0	40.4	22.6	44.7	48.9	43.2	21.5	45.8	51.1	37.9	23.6
22 to 24 years	24.5	26.3	21.9	15.0	23.6	26.8	16.4	11.2	25.4	25.7	26.0	19.2
25 to 29 years	11.1	10.9	10.7	9.1	10.7	10.7	9.4	8.6	11.4	11.0	11.8	9.5
30 to 34 years	6.2	5.9	7.8	5.6	5.8	5.8	6.6	3.9	6.6	6.1	8.8	7.3

NOTE: Includes enrollment in any type of graded public, parochial, or other private schools. Includes nursery schools, kindergartens, elementary schools, high schools, colleges, universities, and professional schools. Attendance may be on either a full-time or part-time basis and during the day or night. Enrollments in "special" schools, such as trade schools, business colleges, or correspondence schools, are not included. Beginning in 1995, preprimary enrollment was collected using new procedures. May not be comparable to figures for earlier years. Data are based upon sample surveys of the civilian noninstitutional population.

SOURCE: Adapted from "Table 7. Percent of the Population 3 to 34 Years Old Enrolled in School, by Race/Ethnicity, Sex, and Age: October 1975 to October 1999," in *Digest of Educational Statistics 2000*, National Center for Education Statistics, Washington, DC, January 2001

scores were dropping relative to boys' scores. Girls score below boys in science at every age level. (See Table 2.5.)

SATS. Female college-bound high school seniors score below males on both the verbal and mathematics sections of the Scholastic Assessment Test (SAT), although this gender gap has been narrowing slowly since 1991. According to the College Entrance Examination Board, women averaged 7 points lower than men on the verbal exam (502 versus 509) and 35 points lower on math (498 versus 533). However, since the early 1970s more women than men have taken the SAT. In 2001 females comprised 54 percent of SAT-takers. This contributes to girls' lower scores, since lower average scores are to be expected when more people from a self-selected population take the exam.

In 1966–67, females averaged 545 in verbal and 495 in math and males averaged 540 in verbal and 535 in math. At that time it was still a common belief that girls were more verbal and boys more mathematical. This is no longer an acceptable explanation for the gender gap in scores. Some observers believe that girls' lower scores stem from a bias in the examination. The College Board, however, claims that every effort has been made to eliminate gender and racial/ethnic bias in the tests. They suggest that gender differences reflect differences in the ways that boys and girls are raised and educated.

According to the Census Bureau, in 1999 more females than males took advanced placement exams. However, far more boys than girls took advanced place-

ment exams in calculus, chemistry, computer science, economics, and physics. Far more girls than boys took advanced placement exams in art, biology, English, French, Spanish, psychology, and history.

The Congressional Commission on the Advancement of Women and Minorities in Science, Engineering and Technology Development (CAWMSET) reported in 2000 that high school girls were taking advanced mathematics and science courses at the same rate as boys. However, of the SAT-takers who were planning to major in engineering and computer science, three-quarters were male. By the eighth grade, twice as many boys as girls were interested in science and engineering careers. Although eighth-grade girls did as well as boys in math, their interest and self-confidence in math had diminished compared to younger girls. Fewer girls than boys enrolled in computer science classes or felt confident using computers. Biology was the only scientific field that attracted more high school girls than boys. These differences are attributed to the attitudes of parents, teachers, and peers who—consciously or not—steer girls away from math and science. Furthermore, female role models in science and technology remain rare, and women scientists and engineers are underrepresented in the media.

HIGHER EDUCATION

College Enrollment

During the 1930s approximately equal numbers of men and women attended college, but the overall numbers were quite small. Between 1940 and 1970 the number of

TABLE 2.3

Average reading scale scores, by sex and age, 1971–99

Year	Male			Female		
	Age 9	Age 13	Age 17	Age 9	Age 13	Age 17
1971	*201	*250	279	214	*261	291
1975	*204	*250	280	216	262	291
1980	210	254	282	*220	263	*289
1984	207	253	284	214	*262	294
1988	207	252	*286	216	263	294
1990	204	251	284	215	263	296
1992	206	254	284	215	265	296
1994	207	251	282	215	266	295
1996	207	251	281	218	264	295
1999	209	254	281	215	265	295

* Significantly different from 1999.

SOURCE: "Table 10-3. Average Reading Scale Scores, by Sex and Age: 1971–99," in *The Condition of Education 2001*, National Center for Education Statistics, Washington, DC, July 2001

TABLE 2.5

Average science scores, by sex and age, 1970–99

Year	Male			Female		
	Age 9	Age 13	Age 17	Age 9	Age 13	Age 17
1970	228	257	*314	*223	253	*297
1973	*223	*252	304	*218	*247	288
1977	*222	*251	297	*218	*244	*282
1982	*221	256	*292	*221	*245	*275
1986	227	256	*295	*221	*247	*282
1990	230	259	*296	227	252	*285
1992	*235	260	299	227	*256	289
1994	232	259	300	230	254	289
1996	231	260	300	228	252	292
1999	231	259	300	228	253	291

*Significantly different from 1999.

SOURCE: "Table 13-3. Average Science Scale Scores, by Sex and Age: 1970–99," in *The Condition of Education 2001*, National Center for Education Statistics, Washington, DC, July 2001

TABLE 2.4

Average mathematics scale scores, by sex and age, 1973–99

Year	Male			Female		
	Age 9	Age 13	Age 17	Age 9	Age 13	Age 17
1973	*218	*265	309	*220	*267	*301
1978	*217	*264	*304	*220	*265	*297
1982	*217	*269	*301	*221	*268	*296
1986	*222	*270	*305	*222	*268	*299
1990	*229	*271	*306	230	*270	*303
1992	231	*274	309	*228	272	305
1994	232	276	309	230	273	304
1996	233	276	310	229	272	305
1999	233	277	310	231	274	307

* Significantly different from 1999.

SOURCE: "Table 12-3. Average Mathematics Scale Scores, by Sex and Age: 1973–99," in *The Condition of Education 2001*, National Center for Education Statistics, Washington, DC, July 2001

men who attended college increased dramatically as a result of the G.I. bill, which offered tuition assistance to servicemen returning from World War II, the Korean conflict, and the Vietnam War. However, the past two decades have seen a tremendous growth in the number of women attending colleges and universities.

In 2000 one out of every four American women was a college graduate. In 1960 only 37.9 percent of females entered college, compared to 54 percent of males. (See Table 2.6.) In every year since 1978, more women than men were enrolled in college. Women accounted for about 96 percent of the increase in college and university enrollment from 1976 to 1984 and 70 percent of the increase from 1984 to 1992. In 1999, 64 percent of female high school graduates entered college, compared to 61 percent of males. The National Center for Education Statistics, *The Condition of Education 2001*, projects that college enroll-

ment by women will continue to increase at a faster rate than male enrollment, reaching an all-time high by 2010.

According to the Census Bureau, in 1998, 22 percent of female college students were between the ages of 25 and 34 and 20 percent were 35 or over. Women made up 57 percent of college students over 24 and 65 percent of those over 34. Older students are more likely to attend college part-time, and 36 percent of women students were part-time in 1998, compared to 30 percent of male students. The Census Bureau projects that in 2003, 45 percent of women students and 40 percent of male students will be enrolled in higher education part-time.

Associate and Bachelor's Degrees

Women earned 15 percent of the bachelor's degrees awarded in 1969–70. (See Table 2.7.) Since 1977 they have earned more associate degrees then men, and since 1981 they have earned more bachelor's degrees than men. In 2001–02 women are expected to earn 62 percent of associate degrees and 57 percent of bachelor's degrees. In 2009–10 women are projected to earn 63 percent of all associate degrees and 59 percent of all bachelor's degrees. About half of associate degrees awarded to women are academic and the other half are occupational.

Of bachelor's degrees earned by women in 1997–98, 76 percent went to white women, 10 percent to black women, 6 percent each to Hispanic and Asian and Pacific Islander women, and 0.7 percent to Native American women. (See Table 2.8.) An additional 3 percent of women's bachelor's degrees went to foreign students.

FIELDS OF STUDY. The proportion of degrees earned by women in most major fields has steadily increased since 1971 at all degree levels. Women earned high percentages of the bachelor's degrees granted in such traditional female

TABLE 2.6

College enrollment rates of high school graduates, by sex, 1960–99

[Numbers in thousands]

Year	Total high school graduates [1]			Enrolled in college [2]					
	Total	Males	Females	Total		Males		Females	
				Number	Percent	Number	Percent	Number	Percent
1	2	3	4	5	6	7	8	9	10
1960	1,679	756	923	758	45.1	408	54.0	350	37.9
1961	1,763	790	973	847	48.0	445	56.3	402	41.3
1962	1,838	872	966	900	49.0	480	55.0	420	43.5
1963	1,741	794	947	784	45.0	415	52.3	369	39.0
1964	2,145	997	1,148	1,037	48.3	570	57.2	467	40.7
1965	2,659	1,254	1,405	1,354	50.9	718	57.3	636	45.3
1966	2,612	1,207	1,405	1,309	50.1	709	58.7	600	42.7
1967	2,525	1,142	1,383	1,311	51.9	658	57.6	653	47.2
1968	2,606	1,184	1,422	1,444	55.4	748	63.2	696	48.9
1969	2,842	1,352	1,490	1,516	53.3	812	60.1	704	47.2
1970	2,757	1,343	1,414	1,427	51.8	741	55.2	686	48.5
1971	2,872	1,369	1,503	1,535	53.4	788	57.6	747	49.7
1972	2,961	1,420	1,541	1,457	49.2	749	52.7	708	45.9
1973	3,059	1,458	1,601	1,425	46.6	730	50.1	695	43.4
1974	3,101	1,491	1,610	1,474	47.5	736	49.4	738	45.8
1975	3,186	1,513	1,673	1,615	50.7	796	52.6	819	49.0
1976	2,987	1,450	1,537	1,458	48.8	685	47.2	773	50.3
1977	3,140	1,482	1,658	1,590	50.6	773	52.2	817	49.3
1978	3,161	1,485	1,676	1,584	50.1	758	51.0	826	49.3
1979	3,160	1,474	1,686	1,559	49.3	743	50.4	816	48.4
1980	3,089	1,500	1,589	1,524	49.3	701	46.7	823	51.8
1981	3,053	1,490	1,563	1,646	53.9	816	54.8	830	53.1
1982	3,100	1,508	1,592	1,568	50.6	739	49.0	829	52.1
1983	2,964	1,390	1,574	1,562	52.7	721	51.9	841	53.4
1984	3,012	1,429	1,583	1,662	55.2	800	56.0	862	54.5
1985	2,666	1,286	1,380	1,539	57.7	754	58.6	785	56.9
1986	2,786	1,331	1,455	1,499	53.8	744	55.9	755	51.9
1987	2,647	1,278	1,369	1,503	56.8	746	58.4	757	55.3
1988	2,673	1,334	1,339	1,575	58.9	761	57.0	814	60.8
1989	2,454	1,208	1,245	1,463	59.6	696	57.6	767	61.6
1990	2,355	1,169	1,185	1,410	59.9	676	57.8	735	62.0
1991	2,276	1,139	1,137	1,420	62.4	656	57.6	763	67.1
1992	2,398	1,216	1,182	1,479	61.7	725	59.6	754	63.8
1993	2,338	1,118	1,219	1,464	62.6	668	59.7	797	65.4
1994	2,517	1,244	1,273	1,559	61.9	754	60.6	805	63.2
1995	2,599	1,238	1,361	1,610	61.9	775	62.6	835	61.4
1996	2,660	1,297	1,363	1,729	65.0	779	60.1	950	69.7
1997	2,769	1,354	1,415	1,856	67.0	860	63.5	995	70.3
1998	2,810	1,452	1,358	1,844	65.6	906	62.4	938	69.1
1999	2,897	1,474	1,423	1,822	62.9	905	61.4	917	64.4

[1] Individuals age 16 to 24 who graduated from high school during the preceding 12 months.
[2] Enrollment in college as of October of each year for individuals age 16 to 24 who graduated from high school during the preceding 12 months.

NOTE: Data are based upon sample surveys of the civilian population. High school graduate data in this table differ from figures appearing in other tables because of varying survey procedures and coverage. High school graduates include GED recipients. Detail may not sum to totals due to rounding.

SOURCE: "Table 185. College Enrollment Rates of High School Graduates, by Sex: 1960 to 1999," in *Digest of Education Statistics 2000,* National Center for Education Statistics, Washington, DC, January 2001

---

subjects as home economics (89 percent), health professions (82 percent), library science (77 percent), education (75 percent), psychology (74 percent), and English (69 percent). They earned much lower proportions of the degrees in traditionally male fields such as mechanics (2 percent), construction trades (7 percent), engineering and related technologies (18 and 10 percent, respectively), and physical sciences (38 percent). (See Table 2.8.)

Business is by far the most common field of study for both men and women, although the growth of business degrees has slowed in recent years. One-fifth of all bache-

lor's degrees in 1997–98 were in business, and women earned more than 48 percent of them. (See Table 2.8.) In 1971 women earned only 9 percent of business degrees.

Although the number of women earning bachelor's degrees in life sciences, physical sciences, and computer science has increased significantly since 1971, women continue to earn fewer degrees in science, engineering, and technology than men at all degree levels. CAWMSET reports that the percentage of women earning computer and information science degrees declined from 37 percent in 1984 to 27 percent in 1997–98. The percentage of

TABLE 2.7

Earned degrees conferred by degree-granting institutions, by level of degree and sex of student, 1869–70 to 2009–10

Year	Associate degrees			Bachelor's degrees			Master's degrees			First-professional degrees			Doctor's degrees [1]		
	Total	Men	Women	Total	Men	Women	Total	Men	Women	Total	Men	Women	Total	Men	Women
1	2	3	4	5	6	7	8	9	10	11	12	13	14	15	16
1869–70	—	—	—	[2] 9,371	[2] 7,993	[2] 1,378	0	0	0	[3]	[3]	[3]	1	1	0
1879–80	—	—	—	[2] 12,896	[2] 10,411	[2] 2,485	879	868	11	[3]	[3]	[3]	54	51	3
1889–90	—	—	—	[2] 15,539	[2] 12,857	[2] 2,682	1,015	821	194	[3]	[3]	[3]	149	147	2
1899–1900	—	—	—	[2] 27,410	[2] 22,173	[2] 5,237	1,583	1,280	303	[3]	[3]	[3]	382	359	23
1909–10	—	—	—	[2] 37,199	[2] 28,762	[2] 8,437	2,113	1,555	558	[3]	[3]	[3]	443	399	44
1919–20	—	—	—	[2] 48,622	[2] 31,980	[2] 16,642	4,279	2,985	1,294	[3]	[3]	[3]	615	522	93
1929–30	—	—	—	[2] 122,484	[2] 73,615	[2] 48,869	14,969	8,925	6,044	[3]	[3]	[3]	2,299	1,946	353
1939–40	—	—	—	[2] 186,500	[2] 109,546	[2] 76,954	26,731	16,508	10,223	[3]	[3]	[3]	3,290	2,861	429
1949–50	—	—	—	[2] 432,058	[2] 328,841	[2] 103,217	58,183	41,220	16,963	[3]	[3]	[3]	6,420	5,804	616
1959–60	—	—	—	[2] 392,440	[2] 254,063	[2] 138,377	74,435	50,898	23,537	[3]	[3]	[3]	9,829	8,801	1,028
1960–61	—	—	—	365,174	224,538	140,636	84,609	57,830	26,779	25,253	24,577	676	10,575	9,463	1,112
1961–62	—	—	—	383,961	230,456	153,505	91,418	62,603	28,815	25,607	24,836	771	11,622	10,377	1,245
1962–63	—	—	—	411,420	241,309	170,111	98,684	67,302	31,382	26,590	25,753	837	12,822	11,448	1,374
1963–64	—	—	—	461,266	265,349	195,917	109,183	73,850	35,333	27,209	26,357	852	14,490	12,955	1,535
1964–65	—	—	—	493,757	282,173	211,584	121,167	81,319	39,848	28,290	27,283	1,007	16,467	14,692	1,775
1965–66	111,607	63,779	47,828	520,115	299,287	220,828	140,602	93,081	47,521	30,124	28,982	1,142	18,237	16,121	2,116
1966–67	139,183	78,356	60,827	558,534	322,711	235,823	157,726	103,109	54,617	31,695	30,401	1,294	20,617	18,163	2,454
1967–68	159,441	90,317	69,124	632,289	357,682	274,607	176,749	113,552	63,197	33,939	32,402	1,537	23,089	20,183	2,906
1968–69	183,279	105,661	77,618	728,845	410,595	318,250	193,756	121,531	72,225	35,114	33,595	1,519	26,158	22,722	3,436
1969–70	206,023	117,432	88,591	792,316	451,097	341,219	208,291	125,624	82,667	34,918	33,077	1,841	29,866	25,890	3,976
1970–71	252,311	144,144	108,167	839,730	475,594	364,136	230,509	138,146	92,363	37,946	35,544	2,402	32,107	27,530	4,577
1971–72	292,014	166,227	125,787	887,273	500,590	386,683	251,633	149,550	102,083	43,411	40,723	2,688	33,363	28,090	5,273
1972–73	316,174	175,413	140,761	922,362	518,191	404,171	263,371	154,468	108,903	50,018	46,489	3,529	34,777	28,571	6,206
1973–74	343,924	188,591	155,333	945,776	527,313	418,463	277,033	157,842	119,191	53,816	48,530	5,286	33,816	27,365	6,451
1974–75	360,171	191,017	169,154	922,933	504,841	418,092	292,450	161,570	130,880	55,916	48,956	6,960	34,083	26,817	7,266
1975–76	391,454	209,996	181,458	925,746	504,925	420,821	311,771	167,248	144,523	62,649	52,892	9,757	34,064	26,267	7,797
1976–77	406,377	210,842	195,535	919,549	495,545	424,004	317,164	167,783	149,381	64,359	52,374	11,985	33,232	25,142	8,090
1977–78	412,246	204,718	207,528	921,204	487,347	433,857	311,620	161,212	150,408	66,581	52,270	14,311	32,131	23,658	8,473
1978–79	402,702	192,091	210,611	921,390	477,344	444,046	301,079	153,370	147,709	68,848	52,652	16,196	32,730	23,541	9,189
1979–80	400,910	183,737	217,173	929,417	473,611	455,806	298,081	150,749	147,332	70,131	52,716	17,415	32,615	22,943	9,672
1980–81	416,377	188,638	227,739	935,140	469,883	465,257	295,739	147,043	148,696	71,956	52,792	19,164	32,958	22,711	10,247
1981–82	434,526	196,944	237,582	952,998	473,364	479,634	295,546	145,532	150,014	72,032	52,223	19,809	32,707	22,224	10,483
1982–83	449,620	203,991	245,629	969,510	479,140	490,370	289,921	144,697	145,224	73,054	51,250	21,804	32,775	21,902	10,873
1983–84	452,240	202,704	249,536	974,309	482,319	491,990	284,263	143,595	140,668	74,468	51,378	23,090	33,209	22,064	11,145
1984–85	454,712	202,932	251,780	979,477	482,528	496,949	286,251	143,390	142,861	75,063	50,455	24,608	32,943	21,700	11,243

women earning degrees in engineering and physics has not grown since the 1980s, despite programs such as Purdue University's highly successful Women in Engineering Program, launched in 1969. In 2000, 22 percent of the engineering students at Purdue were women. Smith College, one of the nation's top private women's colleges, established an engineering department in 1999.

Master's Degrees

In 1879–80 women earned only 1 percent of the 879 master's degrees awarded in the United States. (See Table 2.7.) Since 1985–86, women have earned more master's degrees every year than have men, and women's share of these degrees continues to increase. In 2001–02 women are expected to earn 58 percent of all master's degrees, and in 2009–10 they are projected to earn 60 percent. The percentages of master's degrees awarded to women in various racial groups in 1997–98 were similar to the percentages of bachelor's degrees for each group, except that 8 percent of women's master's degrees in the United States were awarded to foreign students. (See Table 2.9.)

Fields of study for master's degrees were similar to those for bachelor's degrees in 1997–98. Women earned most of the master's degrees in home economics (83 percent), library science (79 percent), health professions and sciences (78 percent), education (76 percent), and psychology (73 percent). They earned 59 percent of the master's degrees in visual and performing arts and 52 percent of the degrees in biological sciences but only 29 percent of the degrees in computer science and 20 percent of the engineering degrees. However, in 1970–71 women earned only 10 percent of the master's degrees in computer and information science and 1 percent of the engineering degrees. In 1997–98 women earned 43 percent of the master's degrees in agriculture and natural resources, up from only 6 percent in 1970–71. They earned 36 percent of the physical science degrees in 1997–98, up from 13 percent in 1970–71. (See Table 2.9.)

In 1997–98 women were awarded 39 percent of master's of business administration (MBA) degrees, up from 4 percent in 1970–71. (See Table 2.9.) An MBA degree is often a prerequisite for a successful business career. However, the enrollment of women in MBA programs has not

TABLE 2.7

Earned degrees conferred by degree-granting institutions, by level of degree and sex of student, 1869–70 to 2009–10 [CONTINUED]

Year	Associate degrees			Bachelor's degrees			Master's degrees			First-professional degrees			Doctor's degrees [1]		
	Total	Men	Women	Total	Men	Women	Total	Men	Women	Total	Men	Women	Total	Men	Women
1	2	3	4	5	6	7	8	9	10	11	12	13	14	15	16
1985–86	446,047	196,166	249,881	987,823	485,923	501,900	288,567	143,508	145,059	73,910	49,261	24,649	33,653	21,819	11,834
1986–87	436,304	190,839	245,465	991,264	480,782	510,482	289,349	141,269	148,080	71,617	46,523	25,094	34,041	22,061	11,980
1987–88	435,085	190,047	245,038	994,829	477,203	517,626	299,317	145,163	154,154	70,735	45,484	25,251	34,870	22,615	12,255
1988–89	436,764	186,316	250,448	1,018,755	483,346	535,409	310,621	149,354	161,267	70,856	45,046	25,810	35,720	22,648	13,072
1989–90	455,102	191,195	263,907	1,051,344	491,696	559,648	324,301	153,653	170,648	70,988	43,961	27,027	38,371	24,401	13,970
1990–91	481,720	198,634	283,086	1,094,538	504,045	590,493	337,168	156,482	180,686	71,948	43,846	28,102	39,294	24,756	14,538
1991–92	504,231	207,481	296,750	1,136,553	520,811	615,742	352,838	161,842	190,996	74,146	45,071	29,075	40,659	25,557	15,102
1992–93	514,756	211,964	302,792	1,165,178	532,881	632,297	369,585	169,258	200,327	75,387	45,153	30,234	42,132	26,073	16,059
1993–94	530,632	215,261	315,371	1,169,275	532,422	636,853	387,070	176,085	210,985	75,418	44,707	30,711	43,185	26,552	16,633
1994–95	539,691	218,352	321,339	1,160,134	526,131	634,003	397,629	178,598	219,031	75,800	44,853	30,947	44,446	26,916	17,530
1995–96	555,216	219,514	335,702	1,164,792	522,454	642,338	406,301	179,081	227,220	76,734	44,748	31,986	44,652	26,841	17,811
1996–97	571,226	223,948	347,278	1,172,879	520,515	652,364	419,401	180,947	238,454	78,730	45,564	33,166	45,876	27,146	18,730
1997–98	558,555	217,613	340,942	1,184,406	519,956	664,450	430,164	184,375	245,789	78,598	44,911	33,687	46,010	26,664	19,346
1998–99[4]	561,000	218,000	343,000	1,178,000	517,000	661,000	405,000	172,000	233,000	80,300	45,600	34,700	45,900	27,300	18,600
1999–2000[4]	559,000	216,000	342,000	1,185,000	517,000	668,000	398,000	168,000	230,000	78,400	44,700	33,600	45,200	26,700	18,500
2000–01[4]	569,000	215,000	354,000	1,194,000	515,000	678,000	396,000	166,000	230,000	76,500	43,200	33,300	45,000	26,500	18,500
2001–02[4]	571,000	216,000	355,000	1,210,000	516,000	694,000	396,000	165,000	231,000	75,400	42,100	33,300	44,900	26,400	18,500
2002–03[4]	577,000	217,000	359,000	1,220,000	522,000	697,000	399,000	165,000	233,000	75,200	41,600	33,600	45,000	26,400	18,600
2003–04[4]	581,000	218,000	363,000	1,240,000	527,000	712,000	402,000	166,000	236,000	75,400	41,500	33,900	45,100	26,400	18,700
2004–05[4]	583,000	218,000	364,000	1,253,000	529,000	725,000	406,000	167,000	239,000	75,900	41,500	34,400	45,300	26,500	18,800
2005–06[4]	587,000	219,000	367,000	1,264,000	533,000	731,000	411,000	168,000	243,000	76,700	41,800	35,000	45,600	26,600	19,000
2006–07[4]	591,000	220,000	371,000	1,277,000	536,000	741,000	417,000	169,000	248,000	77,700	42,100	35,600	46,000	26,700	19,300
2007–08[4]	596,000	221,000	374,000	1,290,000	538,000	751,000	425,000	171,000	254,000	78,700	42,300	36,400	46,400	26,800	19,600
2008–09[4]	603,000	223,000	380,000	1,304,000	542,000	761,000	432,000	173,000	260,000	80,100	42,700	37,400	46,800	27,000	19,800
2009–10[4]	611,000	224,000	387,000	1,324,000	547,000	776,000	439,000	175,000	264,000	81,600	43,200	38,400	47,100	27,100	20,000

—Not available.

[1] Includes Ph.D., Ed.D., and comparable degrees at the doctoral level. Excludes first-professional degrees, such as M.D., D.D.S., and law degrees.

[2] Includes first-professional degrees.

[3] First-professional degrees are included with bachelor's degrees.

[4] Projected data for higher education institutions.

NOTE: Data for 1869–70 to 1994–95 and 1998–99 to 2009–10 are for institutions of higher education. Institutions of higher education were accredited by an agency or association that was recognized by the U.S. Department of Education, or recognized directly by the Secretary of Education. The new degree-granting classification is very similar to the earlier higher education classification, except that it includes some additional institutions, primarily 2-year colleges, and excludes a few higher education institutions that did not award associate or higher degrees. Some data have been revised from previously published figures. Detail may not sum to totals due to rounding.

SOURCE: "Table 248. Earned Degrees Conferred by Degree-Granting Institutions, by Level of Degree and Sex of Student: 1869–70 to 2009–10," in *Digest of Education Statistics 2000*, National Center for Education Statistics, Washington, DC, January 2001

kept pace with their enrollment increases in other graduate programs. The admissions offices at several business schools uncovered some reasons for this. Women were less willing than men to meet the common requirement of working for several years before beginning their MBA studies. They worried that by postponing their education, they would be starting careers just when they hoped to start families. Women also worried that after spending as much as $130,000 to earn an MBA, they could not command salaries comparable to those of their male counterparts. In addition, women were worried about sexual harassment in the workplace and hitting the "glass ceiling" that prevents women from advancing in their careers beyond a certain level. Finally, they feared that if they chose to have children, they would be forced into the slower-moving career path called the "mommy track."

Doctoral Degrees

Just 3 of the 54 doctoral degrees awarded in 1879–80 went to women. (See Table 2.7.) Both the number of female doctorates and the percent of doctoral degrees going to women have increased steadily over the years. In 1960–61, women earned 1,112 doctoral degrees, 11 percent of the total. From 1976 until the late 1980s, the number of men earning doctorates declined slightly, whereas the number of women earning doctorates doubled. In 2001–02, an estimated 18,500 women will earn doctorates, or 41 percent of the total doctoral degrees granted. Women are projected to earn 42 percent of doctorates in 2009–10.

Non-Hispanic white women earned 69 percent of the doctoral degrees awarded to females in 1997–98. African American women earned 6 percent and Hispanic women earned 3 percent. Five percent of the degrees went to Asian and Pacific Islander women, whereas Native American women earned only 0.5 percent. Foreign students accounted for 16 percent of female doctorates.

In 1999 women earned the majority of doctoral degrees in social sciences and education. (See Figure 2.1.) According to the NCES, women also earned the majority

TABLE 2.8

Bachelor's degrees conferred by degree-granting institutions, by racial/ethnic group, major field of study, and sex of student, 1997–98

	Men							Women						
Major field of study	Total	White non-His-panic	Black, non-His-panic	His-panic	Asian/ Pacific Is-lander	Amer-ican Indian/ Alas-kan Native	Non-resi-dent alien	Total	White, non-His-panic	Black non-His-panic	His-panic	Asian/ Pacific Is-lander	Amer-ican Indian/ Alas-kan Native	Non-resi-dent alien
1	2	3	4	5	6	7	8	9	10	11	12	13	14	15
All fields, total	519,360	399,105	34,469	27,648	33,405	3,148	21,585	663,673	501,212	63,663	38,289	38,187	4,746	17,576
Agriculture and natural resources	13,809	12,547	301	343	283	106	229	9,475	8,250	339	308	349	85	144
Architecture and related programs	4,966	3,694	204	347	386	30	305	2,686	1,857	88	187	309	10	235
Area, ethnic, and cultural studies	2,045	1,198	236	257	235	31	88	4,108	2,428	503	473	515	49	140
Biological sciences/life sciences	29,589	21,466	1,483	1,476	4,290	196	678	36,279	25,604	3,181	1,731	4,808	214	741
Business	120,069	90,868	7,983	6,153	6,855	551	7,659	113,050	79,271	12,643	6,334	8,055	739	6,008
Communications	19,631	16,033	1,477	879	557	111	574	29,754	23,059	2,950	1,561	1,106	154	924
Communications technologies	383	304	40	13	13	2	11	346	231	62	12	13	4	24
Computer and information sciences	19,686	13,543	1,378	815	2,368	74	1,508	7,166	3,871	1,323	396	919	35	622
Construction trades	169	152	9	1	3	1	3	13	11	2	0	0	0	0
Education	26,302	22,178	2,081	1,029	495	267	252	79,666	68,211	5,578	3,340	1,260	685	592
Engineering	48,852	34,480	2,028	2,544	5,573	211	4,016	11,058	7,041	1,060	685	1,596	48	628
Engineering-related technologies	12,330	9,800	1,078	435	418	86	513	1,397	997	246	55	42	15	42
English language and literature/letters	16,477	13,950	925	797	569	90	146	33,231	26,939	2,697	1,660	1,383	199	353
Foreign languages and literatures	4,342	3,145	144	707	187	26	133	10,109	7,115	405	1,658	520	55	356
Health professions and related sciences	15,082	11,653	1,080	758	1,198	145	248	69,297	55,849	6,157	2,566	3,612	456	657
Home economics and vocational home economics	1,980	1,557	171	87	101	11	53	15,316	12,807	1,127	498	575	87	222
Law and legal studies	569	418	61	47	32	9	2	1,448	1,114	178	76	56	17	7
Liberal arts and sciences, general studies, and humanities	11,866	9,052	1,148	801	470	116	279	21,336	15,295	2,664	1,963	843	218	353
Library science	17	15	1	1	0	0	0	56	48	4	0	1	2	1
Mathematics	6,596	4,961	498	334	471	40	292	5,732	4,286	554	302	400	28	162
Mechanics and repairers	89	62	4	7	1	0	15	2	2	0	0	0	0	0
Multi/interdisciplinary studies	8,866	6,566	677	644	720	61	198	17,297	12,342	1,614	1,894	1,106	129	212
Parks, recreation, leisure and fitness studies	8,350	6,967	603	451	165	37	127	8,431	7,237	506	337	173	60	118
Philosophy and religion	5,178	4,285	227	290	261	25	90	3,029	2,454	178	140	172	23	62
Physical sciences and science tech-nologies	11,955	9,615	540	363	940	67	430	7,461	5,476	629	259	807	43	247
Precision production trades	296	240	30	7	9	4	6	111	87	11	3	6	0	4
Protective services	14,934	11,453	1,744	1,197	354	111	75	10,142	6,634	2,164	985	173	121	65
Psychology	18,959	14,339	1,590	1,325	1,259	151	295	55,013	41,352	5,437	3,867	3,109	377	871
Public administration and services	3,881	2,568	739	321	154	44	55	16,527	11,401	3,140	1,178	416	214	178
R.O.T.C. and military sciences	3	3	0	0	0	0	0	0	0	0	0	0	0	0
Social sciences and history	63,537	49,010	4,578	3,810	3,708	390	2,041	61,503	43,941	6,886	4,357	4,102	494	1,723
Theological studies and religious vocations	4,260	3,826	138	121	69	10	96	1,643	1,414	82	46	41	6	54
Transportation and material moving workers	2,809	2,300	137	144	64	25	139	397	342	27	11	7	1	9
Visual and performing arts	21,483	16,857	1,136	1,144	1,197	120	1,029	30,594	24,246	1,228	1,407	1,713	178	1,822

NOTE: Reported racial/ethnic distributions of students by level of degree, field of degree, and sex were used to estimate race/ethnicity for students whose race/ethnicity was not reported. Excludes 596 men and 777 women whose racial/ethnic group and field of study were not available. To facilitate trend comparisons, certain aggregations have been made of the degree fields: "Agriculture and natural resources" includes Agricultural business and production, Agricultural sciences, and Conservation and renewable natural resources; and "Business" includes Business management and administrative services, Marketing operations/marketing and distribution, and Consumer and personal services.

SOURCE: Adapted from "Table 266. Bachelor's Degrees Conferred by Degree-Granting Institutions, by Racial/Ethnic Group, Major Field of Study, and Sex of Student: 1997–98," in *Digest of Education Statistics 2000*, National Center for Education Statistics, Washington, DC, January 2001

of doctoral degrees in English and foreign languages, home economics, and library science in 1997–98, but only about 31.4 percent of business doctorates.

According to the National Science Foundation, in 1999, 35 percent of all science and engineering doctorates went to women, compared to 28 percent in 1990. Of doctorates in biological sciences, 43 percent went to women in 1999, compared to 37 percent in 1990. Women earned 67 percent of doctorates in psychology and 63 percent of those in health professions and sciences in 1997–98. Although women's share of the degrees in physical sciences and engineering has increased consistently, the number of women is still quite small. They earned only 16 percent of the doctorates in computer science. Among 1999 science and engineering graduates, most women

TABLE 2.9

Master's degrees conferred by degree-granting institutions, by racial/ethnic group, major field of study, and sex of student, 1997–98

Major field of study		Men							Women						
	Total	White non-His-panic	Black, non-His-panic	His-panic	Asian/ Pacific Is-lander	Amer-ican Indian/ Alas-kan Native	Non-resi-dent alien	Total	White, non-His-panic	Black non-His-panic	His-panic	Asian/ Pacific Is-lander	Amer-ican Indian/ Alas-kan Native	Non-resi-dent alien
1	2	3	4	5	6	7	8	9	10	11	12	13	14	15
All fields, total	183,982	125,343	9,631	6,499	10,239	780	31,490	245,314	182,244	20,466	9,716	10,849	1,269	20,770
Agriculture and natural resources	2,552	1,880	59	54	50	17	492	1,923	1,423	85	48	46	9	312
Architecture and related programs	2,537	1,676	78	103	140	7	533	1,810	1,147	79	77	148	9	350
Area, ethnic, and cultural studies	709	477	44	49	31	6	102	908	598	69	57	58	9	117
Biological sciences/life sciences	2,981	2,116	72	87	304	10	392	3,280	2,255	128	87	298	13	499
Business	62,713	43,509	2,939	1,908	3,846	205	10,306	39,458	25,518	3,644	1,339	2,825	144	5,988
Communications	2,110	1,451	150	72	65	9	363	3,501	2,223	338	123	169	8	640
Communications technologies	282	179	17	12	17	0	57	282	137	35	10	17	0	83
Computer and information sciences	7,987	3,253	246	126	975	12	3,375	3,259	994	158	68	661	3	1,375
Construction trades	9	2	3	0	2	0	2	7	3	1	0	0	0	3
Education	27,070	21,828	2,314	1,318	476	174	960	87,621	71,288	7,927	3,911	1,676	477	2,342
Engineering	20,813	10,330	496	583	1,924	48	7,432	5,123	2,322	256	155	658	9	1,723
Engineering-related technologies	876	647	81	20	25	4	99	260	192	23	8	6	2	29
English language and literature/letters	2,643	2,250	96	98	74	18	107	5,152	4,239	243	159	188	32	291
Foreign languages and literatures	932	602	23	107	28	1	171	1,995	1,206	52	237	97	6	397
Health professions and related sciences	8,751	6,442	454	350	854	53	598	30,509	24,776	2,036	914	1,641	149	993
Home economics and vocational home economics	494	374	31	27	21	0	41	2,420	1,860	181	93	75	18	193
Law and legal studies	2,070	911	50	60	66	8	975	1,158	463	65	36	46	7	541
Liberal arts and sciences, general studies, and humanities	1,023	827	53	37	26	5	75	1,778	1,447	119	48	38	7	119
Library science	1,015	885	38	22	23	7	40	3,856	3,346	183	68	115	20	124
Mathematics	2,151	1,240	76	48	119	4	664	1,492	884	84	42	110	8	364
Multi/interdisciplinary studies	1,076	838	44	28	35	12	119	1,601	1,256	106	66	52	16	105
Parks, recreation, leisure and fitness studies	1,053	871	52	39	23	2	66	971	824	63	16	13	6	49
Philosophy and religion	848	655	34	24	45	4	86	459	366	22	15	17	2	37
Physical sciences and science tech-nologies	3,435	2,123	84	73	158	14	983	1,926	1,147	68	44	135	11	521
Precision production trades	10	3	1	2	0	0	4	5	3	0	0	2	0	0
Protective services	1,172	936	143	37	20	10	26	828	598	171	30	12	4	13
Psychology	3,699	2,983	273	193	97	37	116	10,048	7,911	851	537	316	80	353
Public administration and services	7,025	4,828	894	430	232	41	600	18,119	13,208	2,580	1,015	602	141	573
R.O.T.C. and military technologies	0	0	0	0	0	0	0	0	0	0	0	0	0	0
Social sciences and history	7,960	5,311	413	294	275	38	1,629	6,978	4,622	543	296	329	41	1,147
Theological studies and religious vocations	2,726	2,002	156	80	123	6	359	1,966	1,533	115	35	93	10	180
Transportation and material moving workers	664	598	26	15	10	5	10	72	60	11	0	0	0	1
Visual and performing arts	4,596	3,316	191	203	155	23	708	6,549	4,395	230	182	406	28	1,308

NOTE: Reported racial/ethnic distributions of students by level of degree, field of degree, and sex were used to estimate race/ethnicity for students whose race/ethnicity was not reported. Excludes 393 men and 475 women whose racial/ethnic group and field of study were not available. To facilitate trend comparisons, certain aggregations have been made of the degree fields: "Agriculture and natural resources" includes Agricultural business and production, Agricultural sciences, and Conservation and renewable natural resources; and "Business" includes Business management and administrative services, Marketing operations/marketing and distribution, and Consumer and personal services.

SOURCE: Adapted from "Table 269. Master's Degrees Conferred by Degree-Granting Institutions, by Racial/Ethnic Group, Major Field of Study, and Sex of Student: 1997–98," in *Digest of Education Statistics 2000,* National Center for Education Statistics, Washington, DC, January 2001

planned to pursue postdoctoral studies (43 percent) or seek academic employment (25 percent). More male graduates than female graduates planned to seek employment in industry (26 versus 15 percent).

First Professional Degrees

In 2001–02 women are expected to earn 33,300 first professional degrees in fields including medicine, den-tistry, pharmacy, veterinary medicine, theology, and law. This is 44 percent of the total number of first professional degrees. (See Table 2.7.) In 2009–10 women are expected to earn 47 percent of these degrees. In 1960–61, women earned only 676 such degrees, or 3 percent of the total.

Non-Hispanic white women earned 72 percent of women's first professional degrees, and Asian and Pacific Islander women earned 11 percent. (See Table 2.10.)

FIGURE 2.1

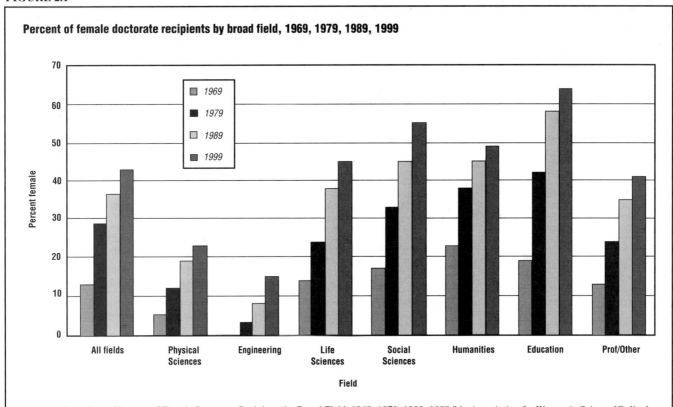

Percent of female doctorate recipients by broad field, 1969, 1979, 1989, 1999

SOURCE: Megan Pratt, "Percent of Female Doctorate Recipients by Broad Field, 1969, 1979, 1989, 1999," in *Association for Women in Science* [Online] http://www.awis.org/statistics/science_human.JPG [accessed October 11, 2001]

TABLE 2.10

First professional degrees conferred by degree-granting institutions, by racial/ethnic group, major field of study, and sex of student, 1997–98

Major field of study		Men						Women						
	Total	White non-His-panic	Black, non-His-panic	His-panic	Asian/ Pacific Is-lander	Amer-ican Indian/ Alas-kan Native	Non-resi-dent alien	Total	White, non-His-panic	Black non-His-panic	His-panic	Asian/ Pacific Is-lander	Amer-ican Indian/ Alas-kan Native	Non-resi-dent alien
1	2	3	4	5	6	7	8	9	10	11	12	13	14	15
All fields	44,769	35,069	2,303	1,971	3,993	291	1,142	33,584	24,204	3,180	1,576	3,719	270	635
Dentistry (D.D.S. or D.M.D.)	2,490	1,773	71	76	416	18	136	1,542	866	110	67	383	4	112
Medicine (M.D.)	9,006	6,391	484	458	1,503	60	110	6,418	4,167	696	315	1,109	59	72
Optometry (O.D.)	594	446	10	25	74	1	38	680	425	22	32	163	4	34
Osteopathic medicine (D.O.)	1,337	1,102	31	53	122	13	16	773	595	29	29	104	9	7
Pharmacy (Pharm.D.)	1,197	853	80	22	205	3	34	2,463	1,587	211	53	533	3	76
Podiatry (Pod.D. or D.P.) or podiatric medicine (D.P.M.)	418	324	5	17	53	1	18	176	110	13	13	30	0	10
Veterinary medicine (D.V.M.)	754	677	24	30	11	7	5	1,439	1,330	29	34	31	9	6
Chiropractic medicine (D.C. or D.C.M.)	2,712	2,143	38	78	178	12	263	1,023	800	28	36	60	6	93
Law (LL.B. or J.D.)	21,876	17,941	1,233	1,111	1,191	165	235	17,455	13,071	1,816	974	1,262	170	162
Theology (M.Div., M.H.L., B.D., or Ord.)	4,343	3,382	326	100	238	10	287	1,530	1,174	222	22	44	5	63
Other	42	37	1	1	2	1	0	85	79	4	1	0	1	0

NOTE: Reported racial/ethnic distributions of students by level of degree, field of degree, and sex were used to estimate race/ethnicity for students whose race/ethnicity was not reported. Excludes 142 men and 103 women whose racial/ethnic group and field of study were not available.

SOURCE: Adapted from "Table 275. First-Professional Degrees Conferred by Degree-Granting Institutions, by Racial/Ethnic Group, Major Field of Study, and Sex of Student: 1997–98," in *Digest of Education Statistics 2000*, National Center for Education Statistics, Washington, DC, January 2001

Non-Hispanic black women earned 9 percent, Hispanic women earned 5 percent, and American Indian/Alaskan Native women earned less than 1 percent. Foreign students earned 2 percent of the first professional degrees awarded to women.

The majority (52 percent) of women's professional degrees were in law. (See Table 2.10.) Women earned 44 percent of all law degrees in 1997–98, as compared to 7 percent in 1970–71. According to Catalyst Fact Sheet, "Women in Law: Making the Case" (2001), it is expected that in 2001–02 more women than men will be enrolled in law school. Medical doctor (MD) degrees accounted for 19 percent of the degrees to women, and 42 percent of all MD degrees went to women, up from 9 percent in 1970–71. Women earned 67 percent of the degrees in pharmacy, 66 percent of those in veterinary medicine, and 38 percent of dentistry degrees, but only 26 percent of theology degrees.

Continuing Education

According to the Census Bureau, almost 49 million women, or 48 percent of the adult female population, were enrolled in adult education courses in 1998–99. This compares with 43 percent of the adult male population. Half of these women were taking courses for personal or social reasons, compared to only 34 percent of the men, and 50 percent of the women were taking courses for job advancement. Training for a new job was the reason given by 12 percent of the women, and 9 percent were completing a degree or diploma.

ACHIEVING EDUCATIONAL EQUITY

Single-Sex or Coeducational Schools?

Prior to the late 1960s many private high schools and colleges were single-sex schools. By the end of the 20th century, most schools were coeducational. However, there is renewed interest in single-sex education, particularly for girls, and the number of single-sex schools increased in the 1990s.

In 1992 the American Association of University Women (AAUW) published a study, *How Schools Short-change Girls*. The study reported that teachers paid more attention to boys and that girls received less encouragement in math and science. A second AAUW study, *Gaining a Foothold: Women's Transitions Through Work and College* (1999), found that high school boys were more likely than girls to take all three core science courses (biology, chemistry, and physics) and that far fewer girls than boys took physics. Girls made up only a small percentage of students in computer science and computer design classes.

However, another AAUW study, *Separated by Sex: A Critical Look at Single-Sex Education for Girls* (1998),

found that girls could succeed in coed classrooms if they were treated fairly and that all children achieved in small classes with a strong curriculum. AAUW Educational Foundation president Maggie Ford concluded that "separating by sex is not the answer to inequities in the schools."

In January 2000 the Goodman Research Group conducted a survey for the National Coalition of Girls' Schools (NCGS). They surveyed 4,274 alumnae from the graduating classes of 1983, 1987, 1991, and 1995, from 64 NCGS schools. The report, *Achievement, Leadership & Success: A Report on Educational, Professional, and Life Outcomes at Girls' Schools in the United States*, found that a large majority of the alumnae believed that girls' schools were more relevant to the academic, personal, and social development of females, as compared to coeducational schools. A large majority of the alumnae (91 percent), rated their schools as very good or excellent at challenging students academically and preparing them for college. Most respondents believed that they were better prepared for college, both academically and socially, than were their peers from coeducational high schools. In particular, they felt that their schools had provided them with more leadership opportunities and had encouraged them in math, science, and technology. The NCGS alumnae had higher-than-average SAT scores, and almost all attended college, where 13 percent of them majored in math and science, as compared to 2 percent of females nationwide. Most alumnae (78 percent) rated their schools as very good or excellent at instilling self-confidence in students. Most (88 percent) said they would choose a girls' school again, and 84 percent said they would encourage their daughters to attend a girls' school.

Educators have found that girls in single-sex classrooms participate much more than they do in coeducational classes. At the Bronx High School of Science, girls in a single-sex physics class worked together cooperatively, learned concepts better, and asked more questions. The coed physics class was dominated by boys and was very competitive, with little interaction among the students.

Increasingly, public school systems are experimenting with single-sex education. In 1996, The Young Women's Leadership School opened in East Harlem with 56 seventh-grade girls. In 1999–2000 it served 275 middle and high school girls. In 1999, their reading and math scores far exceeded the New York City–wide average. As of 2001, 16 states were offering single-sex classes for girls in public schools.

The NCGS reported a 6 percent increase in enrollment at girls' schools from kindergarten through high school during the 1990s. Between 1995 and 2000, 32 new girls' schools opened in the United States. Although only 2.5 percent of college women attend a single-sex college, enrollment is increasing there as well. The Women's

TABLE 2.11

High school students engaged in organized physical activity, 1999

[In percent. For students in grades 9 to 12.]

Characteristic	Enrolled in physical education class			Played on a sports team
	Total	Attended daily	Exercised 20 minutes or more per class	
All students	56.1	29.1	76.3	55.1
Male	60.7	31.9	82.1	61.7
Grade 9	82.3	44.0	84.4	63.9
Grade 10	65.3	32.8	79.4	62.3
Grade 11	44.6	23.5	82.0	58.8
Grade 12	43.8	23.6	82.3	60.7
Female	51.5	26.3	69.6	48.5
Grade 9	75.6	40.3	72.5	53.4
Grade 10	56.6	27.9	70.2	50.9
Grade 11	36.8	16.6	68.0	45.8
Grade 12	29.4	16.6	60.1	42.3
White, non-Hispanic	56.1	28.3	78.7	56.9
Male	60.2	30.8	83.8	63.0
Female	51.7	25.8	72.4	50.5
Black, non-Hispanic	52.9	29.2	67.8	48.7
Male	59.2	33.1	78.4	62.0
Female	47.1	25.5	55.8	36.3
Hispanic	59.3	40.4	75.5	50.8
Male	65.1	44.6	79.6	57.2
Female	53.6	36.2	70.8	44.5

SOURCE: "No. 431. High School Students Engaged in Organized Physical Activity: 1999," in *Statistical Abstract of the United States: 2000,* U.S. Census Bureau, Washington, DC, 2001

TABLE 2.12

Change in number of women participants for NAIA and NCAA schools. 1981–82 to 1998–99

Sport	1981–82	1998–99	Change in number of participants	Percentage change
Soccer	1,855	19,987	18,132	977%
Indoor track	6,026	15,927	9,901	164
Outdoor track	11,933	19,611	7,678	64
Cross-country	5,560	13,048	7,488	135
Softball	10,816	17,320	6,504	60
Rowing	1,187	5,628	4,441	374
Basketball	12,699	17,118	4,419	35
Volleyball	11,762	15,603	3,841	33
Swimming	6,570	10,086	3,516	54
Golf	1,060	3,140	2,080	196
Lacrosse	2,648	4,749	2,101	79
Tennis	7,849	9,319	1,470	19
Water polo	19	746	727	3,826
Ice hockey	336	900	564	168
Equestrian	101	633	532	527
Skiing	359	535	176	49
Squash	238	365	127	53
Rifle	90	184	94	104
Synchronized swimming	49	108	59	120
Archery	75	106	31	41
Badminton	141	94	-47	-33
Bowling	88	20	-68	-77
Fencing	765	594	-171	-22
Field hockey	5,701	5,472	-229	-4
Gymnastics	2,173	1,490	-683	-31
Total	**90,100**	**162,783**	**72,683**	**81%**

Note: Athletes who participate in more than one intercollegiate sport are counted as participants in each sport. Information for schools that were members of both NAIA and NCAA was counted only once to avoid overstating the number of participants at these schools. This table excludes sports that were neither championship nor emerging NCAA sports in 1998–99. In 1981–82, this represented 222 participants in six sports—cricket, judo, pistol, polo, rugby, and sailing.

SOURCE: "Table 1. Change in Number of Women Participants for NAIA and NCAA Schools," in *Intercollegiate Athletics: Four-Year Colleges' Experiences Adding and Discontinuing Teams,* U.S. General Accounting Office, Washington, DC, March 2001

College Coalition reports that graduates of women's colleges are more than twice as likely to earn doctoral degrees as women graduates of coeducational institutions.

Military Schools

As increasing numbers of women sought out all-female institutions, other women were trying to break into all-male schools. Following the ruling of a federal district court judge that a publicly financed school could not bar women, The Citadel, a college that trains future military officers, was forced to admit women. In 1994 Shannon Faulkner became the first full-time female student at The Citadel, although she withdrew before completing introductory training.

Hoping to retain their male-only status, both The Citadel and the Virginia Military Institute (VMI) set up separate "leadership programs" for women. In 1996 the U.S. Supreme Court, in *United States v. Virginia* (508 U.S. 946), ruled that the all-male admissions policies violated the Constitution and that the alternative leadership programs were inadequate. The Court further ruled that women could not be kept out of state-supported military colleges.

In the fall of 1997, 30 women enrolled at VMI. Two women graduated from VMI in 1999, and The Citadel graduated its first woman in that same year. Women made up 15 percent of the 1999 graduating class of the Naval Academy in Annapolis, Maryland. Five of their top 10 graduates were women.

HIGH SCHOOL AND COLLEGE ATHLETICS

Title IX of the Education Amendments of 1972 prohibits sex discrimination in any education program or activity that receives federal funding, including athletics. In 1999, 51.5 percent of high school girls and 60.7 percent of boys were enrolled in physical education classes, although the majority of students did not attend on a daily basis. (See Table 2.11.) The number of females participating in high school athletic programs increased from 294,105 in 1971 to 2.7 million in 1998–99. Over the same period the number of males participating in high school sports remained fairly constant. Among high school students, 62 percent of boys and 49 percent of girls played on a sports team. Basketball was the most popular sport among girls and the second-most popular among boys. Track and field, soccer, tennis, cross country, and swimming and diving were among the top 10 sports for both genders.

Title IX has increased the opportunities for college scholarships for female athletes. As Table 2.12 shows, there has been an 81 percent increase in the participation of women athletes at National Collegiate Athletic Association (NCAA) and National Association of Intercollegiate Athletics (NAIA) schools since 1981–82. In 1981–82, 3.9 percent of female undergraduates participated in sports, compared to 5.5 percent in 1998–99. The number of women's teams increased from 5,695 to 9,479, resulting in more women's teams than men's teams. Almost 20,000 women played college soccer in 1998–99, an increase of 977 percent since 1981–82. The number of women's soccer teams increased by 1,058 percent. Women's rowing increased by 374 percent over the same period. Participation in women's gymnastics decreased by 31 percent. Although there continue to be far more male than female college athletes, the percentage of male athletes remained stable between 1981–82 and 1998–99.

CHAPTER 3

WOMEN IN THE LABOR FORCE

A LEGACY OF WORK

Women have always labored hard. Early American women worked long hours, primarily in their own homes and on their farms and ranches. In 1800 only 5 percent of white women worked outside the home. Over the next 50 years that percentage doubled as more white women became domestic servants, seamstresses, tavern keepers, and storeowners. African American women slaves labored in the fields and homes of their owners and tended their own small gardens. By the end of the American Civil War 14 percent of both African American and white women were in the paid labor force.

By the turn of the 20th century, one woman in five was working for pay outside of the home. For the most part, these were young, single women or widows; many of them were nonwhite. Most women had low-paying, low-skilled jobs that were considered to be temporary arrangements prior to marriage. Although most women were denied educations that would prepare them for prestigious professions, increasing numbers of women did move into newer fields, such as nursing, teaching, and social work. Other women worked for volunteer causes and became political activists. As a result, by the early 20th century there existed a large population of women with impressive organizational and administrative skills.

With the onset of the Great Depression in 1929, many women lost their jobs. Some state and local governments limited or banned the employment of married women. Even employed women who were the sole support of their families were seen as taking jobs away from men.

By 1940, 28 percent of American women worked outside the home, and nearly half of all single women and those aged 20 to 24 were in the labor force. With the United States' entry into World War II, the need for additional workers became so great that even married women were encouraged to enter the labor force. In some cases, child care was made available to working mothers. An estimated 6 million women who had never worked outside the home took jobs during the war years. By 1944, 36 percent of American women were in the labor force, 5.2 million more than in 1940.

With the end of World War II women were expected to return to their homes, making jobs available for discharged servicemen. However the postwar economy was strong enough to support working women, and more educated, middle-class, married women began entering the labor force. In 1946, 31 percent of American women were still in the labor force.

LABOR FORCE PARTICIPATION AND EMPLOYMENT

1950 to the Present

The U.S. Department of Labor's Bureau of Labor Statistics carefully tracks labor force participation and employment and unemployment. Since the labor force includes the unemployed who are actively looking for work, a distinction is made between labor force participation and employment.

In 1950, 33.9 percent of women 16 and over were in the civilian labor force; however, the labor force participation rates of men and women differed by 52.5 percent. (See Table 3.1.) More women began joining the labor force in the 1960s, and their participation has continued to grow steadily, although growth slowed during the 1990s. In 2000, 60.2 percent of women over 15, or 65.6 million women, were in the labor force, compared to 42.7 percent in 1969. (See Table 3.2.)

In 2000 about 75 percent of men over 15 were in the labor force. The percentage of men in the labor force has dropped in every age group since 1950, with an overall drop of 11.5 percent. (See Table 3.1.) This decline usually is attributed to the increased availability of pensions and

TABLE 3.1

Civilian labor force participation rates by sex and age, 1950–1998 and projected, 2015–2025

[In percent]

Group	1950	1960	1970	1980	1990	1998	2015	2025
Total, 16 and older	59.2	59.4	60.4	63.8	66.4	67.1	66.9	63.2
16 to 24	59.9	56.4	59.8	68.1	67.3	65.9	67.1	66.1
25 to 34	63.5	65.4	69.7	79.9	83.6	84.6	86.6	86.4
35 to 44	67.5	69.4	73.1	80.0	85.2	84.7	87.0	86.9
45 to 54	66.4	72.2	73.5	74.9	80.7	82.5	85.2	85.0
55 to 64	56.7	60.9	61.8	55.7	55.9	59.3	64.8	63.1
65 and older	26.7	20.8	17.0	12.5	11.8	11.9	14.5	14.0
Men, 16 years and older	86.4	83.3	79.7	77.4	76.1	74.9	72.2	68.8
16 to 24	77.3	71.7	69.4	74.4	71.5	68.4	68.9	68.1
25 to 34	96.0	97.5	96.4	95.2	94.2	93.2	93.1	93.0
35 to 44	97.6	97.7	96.8	95.5	94.4	92.6	92.2	92.1
45 to 54	95.8	95.7	94.3	91.2	90.7	89.2	88.4	88.3
55 to 64	86.9	87.3	83.0	72.1	67.7	68.1	69.1	67.7
65 and older	45.8	33.1	26.8	19.0	16.4	16.5	19.8	19.1
Women, 16 years and older	33.9	37.7	43.3	51.5	57.5	59.8	61.9	58.1
16 to 24	43.9	42.8	51.3	61.9	63.1	63.3	65.3	64.1
25 to 34	34.0	36.0	45.0	65.5	73.6	76.3	80.5	80.0
35 to 44	39.1	43.4	51.1	65.5	76.5	77.1	82.0	81.9
45 to 54	37.9	49.9	54.4	59.9	71.2	76.2	82.0	81.8
55 to 64	27.0	37.2	43.0	41.3	45.3	51.2	60.8	58.8
65 and older	9.7	10.8	9.7	8.1	8.7	8.6	10.3	9.9
White, 16 years and older	—	—	—	64.1	66.8	67.3	67.4	63.9
Black, 16 years and older	—	—	—	61.0	63.3	65.6	62.5	60.1
Asian and other, 16 years and older[1]	—	—	—	64.6	64.9	67.0	63.8	61.9
Hispanic origin, 16 years and older	—	—	—	64.0	67.0	67.9	65.1	63.1
Other than Hispanic origin, 16 years and older	—	—	—	63.7	66.3	67.0	67.1	63.5
White non-Hispanic	—	—	—	64.0	66.8	67.2	67.9	64.1

	Change						
Group	1950–60	1960–70	1970–80	1980–90	1990–98	1998–2015	2015–25
Total, 16 and older	.2	1.0	3.4	2.6	.7	–.2	–3.6
16 to 24	–3.5	3.4	8.2	–.8	–1.4	1.2	–1.0
25 to 34	1.9	4.3	10.2	3.7	1.0	2.0	–.2
35 to 44	1.9	3.7	6.9	5.2	–.5	2.2	–.1
45 to 54	5.8	1.3	1.4	5.8	1.8	2.6	–.2
55 to 64	4.2	.9	–6.1	.2	3.4	5.5	–1.8
65 and older	–5.9	–3.8	–4.4	–.7	.1	2.5	–.4
Men, 16 years and older	–3.1	–3.6	–2.3	–1.3	–1.2	–2.7	–3.4
16 to 24	–5.6	–2.2	5.0	–2.9	–3.2	.6	–.9
25 to 34	1.5	–1.1	–1.2	–1.0	–1.0	–.1	–.1
35 to 44	.1	–.9	–1.4	–1.0	–1.8	–.4	–.1
45 to 54	–.1	–1.4	–3.1	–.5	–1.5	–.8	–.2
55 to 64	.4	–4.3	–10.8	–4.4	.4	1.0	–1.4
65 and older	–12.7	–6.3	–7.8	–2.6	.0	3.3	–.7
Women, 16 years and older	3.8	5.6	8.1	6.0	2.4	2.1	–3.8
16 to 24	–1.1	8.5	10.6	1.2	.2	1.9	–1.1
25 to 34	2.0	9.0	20.5	8.2	2.7	4.2	–.5
35 to 44	4.3	7.7	14.4	11.0	.6	4.9	–.1
45 to 54	12.0	4.5	5.5	11.3	5.0	5.8	–.2
55 to 64	10.2	5.8	–1.7	4.0	5.9	9.7	–2.1
65 and over	1.1	–1.1	–1.6	.6	.0	1.6	–.4
White, 16 years and older	—	—	—	2.8	.5	.1	–3.6
Black, 16 years and older	—	—	—	2.4	2.2	–3.0	–2.4
Asian and other, 16 years and older 1	—	—	—	.4	2.1	–3.2	–1.9
Other than Hispanic origin, 16 years and older	—	—	—	2.6	.7	.1	–3.6
White non-Hispanic	—	—	—	2.8	.4	.6	–3.8

	Difference between men and women's labor force participation rates						
Group	1950	1960	1970	1980	1990	1998	2015	2025
Total, 16 and older	52.5	45.6	36.3	25.9	18.6	15.0	10.3	10.6
16 to 24	33.4	28.8	18.1	12.5	8.4	5.0	3.6	3.9
25 to 34	62.0	61.5	51.4	29.7	20.5	16.9	12.6	13.0
35 to 44	58.5	54.3	45.7	30.0	18.0	15.6	10.2	10.2
45 to 54	57.9	45.8	39.9	31.3	19.5	13.0	6.4	6.5
55 to 64	59.9	50.1	39.9	30.8	22.4	16.9	8.2	8.9
65 and older	36.1	22.3	17.1	10.9	7.7	7.8	9.5	9.3

[1] The "Asian and other" group includes (1) Asians and Pacific Islanders and (2) American Indians and Alaska Natives. The historical data are derived by subtracting "black" from the "black and other" group; projections are made directly, not by subtraction.

NOTE: Dash indicates data not available.

SOURCE: Howard N. Fullerton, Jr., "Table 1. Civilian Labor Force Participation Rates by Sex and Age, 1950 to 1998 and Projected, 2015 to 2025," in "Labor Force Participation: 75 Years of Change, 1950–98 and 1998–2025," *Monthly Labor Review*, vol. 122, no. 12, December 1999

TABLE 3.2

Employment status of the civilian noninstitutional population 16 years and over by sex, 1969 to date

(Numbers in thousands)

Year	Civilian noninsti-tutional population	Civilian labor force									Not in labor force
		Total	Percent of population	Employed				Unemployed			
				Total	Percent of population	Agri-culture	Nonagricultural industries	Number	Percent of labor force		

Men

Year	Civ. pop.	Total	Pct pop	Total	Pct pop	Agri	Nonag	Number	Pct LF	Not in LF
1969	62,898	50,221	79.8	48,818	77.6	2,963	45,855	1,403	2.8	12,677
1970	64,304	51,228	79.7	48,990	76.2	2,862	46,128	2,238	4.4	13,076
1971	65,942	52,180	79.1	49,390	74.9	2,795	46,595	2,789	5.3	13,762
1972[1]	67,835	53,555	78.9	50,896	75.0	2,849	48,047	2,659	5.0	14,280
1973[1]	69,292	54,624	78.8	52,349	75.5	2,847	49,502	2,275	4.2	14,667
1974	70,808	55,739	78.7	53,024	74.9	2,919	50,105	2,714	4.9	15,069
1975	72,291	56,299	77.9	51,857	71.7	2,824	49,032	4,442	7.9	15,993
1976	73,759	57,174	77.5	53,138	72.0	2,744	50,394	4,036	7.1	16,585
1977	75,193	58,396	77.7	54,728	72.8	2,671	52,057	3,667	6.3	16,797
1978[1]	76,576	59,620	77.9	56,479	73.8	2,718	53,761	3,142	5.3	16,956
1979	78,020	60,726	77.8	57,607	73.8	2,686	54,921	3,120	5.1	17,293
1980	79,398	61,453	77.4	57,186	72.0	2,709	54,477	4,267	6.9	17,945
1981	80,511	61,974	77.0	57,397	71.3	2,700	54,697	4,577	7.4	18,537
1982	81,523	62,450	76.6	56,271	69.0	2,736	53,534	6,179	9.9	19,073
1983	82,531	63,047	76.4	56,787	68.8	2,704	54,083	6,260	9.9	19,484
1984	83,605	63,835	76.4	59,091	70.7	2,668	56,423	4,744	7.4	19,771
1985	84,469	64,411	76.3	59,891	70.9	2,535	57,356	4,521	7.0	20,058
1986[1]	85,798	65,422	76.3	60,892	71.0	2,511	58,381	4,530	6.9	20,376
1987	86,899	66,207	76.2	62,107	71.5	2,543	59,564	4,101	6.2	20,692
1988	87,857	66,927	76.2	63,273	72.0	2,493	60,780	3,655	5.5	20,930
1989	88,762	67,840	76.4	64,315	72.5	2,513	61,802	3,525	5.2	20,923
1990[1]	90,377	69,011	76.4	65,104	72.0	2,546	62,559	3,906	5.7	21,367
1991	91,278	69,168	75.8	64,223	70.4	2,589	61,634	4,946	7.2	22,110
1992	92,270	69,964	75.8	64,440	69.8	2,575	61,866	5,523	7.9	22,306
1993	93,332	70,404	75.4	65,349	70.0	2,478	62,871	5,055	7.2	22,927
1994[1]	94,355	70,817	75.1	66,450	70.4	2,554	63,896	4,367	6.2	23,538
1995	95,178	71,360	75.0	67,377	70.8	2,559	64,818	3,983	5.6	23,818
1996	96,206	72,087	74.9	68,207	70.9	2,573	65,634	3,880	5.4	24,119
1997[1]	97,715	73,261	75.0	69,685	71.3	2,552	67,133	3,577	4.9	24,454
1998[1]	98,758	73,959	74.9	70,693	71.6	2,553	68,140	3,266	4.4	24,799
1999[1]	99,722	74,512	74.7	71,446	71.6	2,432	69,014	3,066	4.1	25,210
2000[2]	100,731	75,247	74.7	72,293	71.8	2,434	69,859	2,954	3.9	25,484

Women

Year	Civ. pop.	Total	Pct pop	Total	Pct pop	Agri	Nonag	Number	Pct LF	Not in LF
1969	71,436	30,513	42.7	29,084	40.7	643	28,441	1,429	4.7	40,924
1970	72,782	31,543	43.3	29,688	40.8	601	29,087	1,855	5.9	41,239
1971	74,274	32,202	43.4	29,976	40.4	599	29,377	2,227	6.9	42,072
1972[1]	76,290	33,479	43.9	31,257	41.0	635	30,622	2,222	6.6	42,811
1973[1]	77,804	34,804	44.7	32,715	42.0	622	32,093	2,089	6.0	43,000
1974	79,312	36,211	45.7	33,769	42.6	596	33,173	2,441	6.7	43,101
1975	80,860	37,475	46.3	33,989	42.0	584	33,404	3,486	9.3	43,386
1976	82,390	38,983	47.3	35,615	43.2	588	35,027	3,369	8.6	43,406
1977	83,840	40,613	48.4	37,289	44.5	612	36,677	3,324	8.2	43,227
1978[1]	85,334	42,631	50.0	39,569	46.4	669	38,900	3,061	7.2	42,703
1979	86,843	44,235	50.9	41,217	47.5	661	40,556	3,018	6.8	42,608
1980	88,348	45,487	51.5	42,117	47.7	656	41,461	3,370	7.4	42,861
1981	89,618	46,696	52.1	43,000	48.0	667	42,333	3,696	7.9	42,922
1982	90,748	47,755	52.6	43,256	47.7	665	42,591	4,499	9.4	42,993
1983	91,684	48,503	52.9	44,047	48.0	680	43,367	4,457	9.2	43,181
1984	92,778	49,709	53.6	45,915	49.5	653	45,262	3,794	7.6	43,068
1985	93,736	51,050	54.5	47,259	50.4	644	46,615	3,791	7.4	42,686
1986[1]	94,789	52,413	55.3	48,706	51.4	652	48,054	3,707	7.1	42,376
1987	95,853	53,658	56.0	50,334	52.5	666	49,668	3,324	6.2	42,195
1988	96,756	54,742	56.6	51,696	53.4	676	51,020	3,046	5.6	42,014
1989	97,630	56,030	57.4	53,027	54.3	687	52,341	3,003	5.4	41,601
1990[1]	98,787	56,829	57.5	53,689	54.3	678	53,011	3,140	5.5	41,957
1991	99,646	57,178	57.4	53,496	53.7	680	52,815	3,683	6.4	42,468
1992	100,535	58,141	57.8	54,052	53.8	672	53,380	4,090	7.0	42,394
1993	101,506	58,795	57.9	54,910	54.1	637	54,273	3,885	6.6	42,711
1994[1]	102,460	60,239	58.8	56,610	55.3	855	55,755	3,629	6.0	42,221
1995	103,406	60,944	58.9	57,523	55.6	881	56,642	3,421	5.6	42,462
1996	104,385	61,857	59.3	58,501	56.0	871	57,630	3,356	5.4	42,528
1997[1]	105,418	63,036	59.8	59,873	56.8	847	59,026	3,162	5.0	42,382
1998[1]	106,462	63,714	59.8	60,771	57.1	825	59,945	2,944	4.6	42,748
1999[1]	108,031	64,855	60.0	62,042	57.4	849	61,193	2,814	4.3	43,175
2000[2]	108,968	65,616	60.2	62,915	57.7	871	62,044	2,701	4.1	43,352

[1] Not strictly comparable with data for prior years.
[2] Beginning in January 2000, data are not strictly comparable with data for 1999 and earlier years because of revisions in the population controls used in the household survey.

SOURCE: "2. Employment Status of the Civilian Noninstitutional Population 16 Years and Over, by Sex, 1969 to Date," in "Average Annual Tables," *Employment and Earnings,* vol. 48, no. 1, January 2001

disability payments. By 2000 the primary reason for the higher labor force participation rates of men was that many more women than men were over age 65.

NEW JOBS FOR WOMEN. According to the Department of Labor Women's Bureau, of the more than 70 million new jobs created in the United States between 1964 and 1999, 43 million went to women. Service industries accounted for 43 percent of all new jobs, retail trade for 20 percent, and government for 15 percent. Each of these sectors provided more new jobs for women than for men. The number of women's jobs doubled in every industry except manufacturing. Within the service sector, 6.6 million new jobs for women were created in health services alone. Within the government sector, 4 million new jobs for women were created in state and local education.

AGE. Since 1950 the biggest increase in labor force participation has been among women between the ages of 25 and 54. In the early post–World War II era, the highest rates of labor force participation were among women under age 25, the age by which women had left the labor force to raise their children. As more women enroll in higher education and marry and have children at later ages, the pattern of women's labor force participation has come to resemble that of men. (See Table 3.1.) As women complete their education, their presence in the labor force increases steadily, peaking between the ages of 35 and 44. After age 45 labor force participation begins a slow decline, as workers start to retire or are downsized. Among women over age 64, only 9 percent were in the labor force in 2000, compared to 10 percent in 1950. The labor force participation of men over 64 dropped from 46 percent to 18 percent during the same period. Most of the labor force participants in this group are between the ages of 65 and 69.

RACE. African Americans have the highest labor force participation rates among women, and Hispanics have the lowest. In contrast, Hispanics have the highest labor force participation rates among men and African Americans have the lowest.

In 1890 nearly two out of five nonwhite women between the ages of 20 and 64 were in the labor force. Often these women were supplementing their husbands' meager earnings. By the turn of the century many African Americans were leaving rural areas and seeking employment in northern cities. Most African American women found work in private households or laundries. In 1947 only 31 percent of white women were in the labor force, compared to 44 percent of women of other races. During the 1960s and 1970s many white and black women entered the labor force, but the increase was higher for white women. In August 2001, 65.6 percent of black women 20 and over were in the labor force, as were 60.1 percent of white women. (See Table 3.3.)

Among Hispanic women 59 percent of those over 19 were in the labor force in 2000, up from about 50 percent in 1986. More women of Mexican and Puerto Rican heritage than Cuban women have entered the labor force.

Among Asian women and those of other races, 60 percent over age 15 were in the labor force in 2000. However, the percentages of younger Asian women in the labor force were lower than for other racial groups, presumably because of the large proportion of Asian women who were enrolled in higher education.

MARITAL STATUS. As in the past, single women are more likely to be in the labor force than married women. Furthermore, the population of single women has increased, as more people postpone marriage, divorce, or choose not to marry. Among women who maintained families, 66 percent were employed in 2000. (See Table 3.4.)

As more families require two incomes and as more women choose to pursue careers after marriage, the proportion of married women in the labor force has increased, from 44 percent in the mid-1970s to 59 percent in 2000. In 53.2 percent of married-couple families, both partners were employed. Only the husband was employed in 19.2 percent of such families. (See Table 3.4.)

CHILDREN. According to the Women's Research and Education Institute, a Washington, D.C. –based organization that focuses on women's issues, the labor force participation of women with children under 18 increased from 60 percent in 1978 to 78 percent in 1998. For women with children under six, the rate increased from 44 percent to 65 percent. For women with children under three, the rate increased from 39 percent to 62 percent.

In married-couple families with children under 18, in which the parents were unlikely to be retired, 68.3 percent of the mothers were employed in 2000. (See Table 3.5.) In 64.2 percent of married-couple families with children under 18, both parents worked. Only the father was employed in 29.2 percent of such families. In married-couple families with children under age six, 59.9 percent of mothers were employed. The labor force participation rate for married mothers with children under one year began declining in 1994, to 53 percent in 2000. More married African American mothers were employed than white mothers.

The labor force participation rate for unmarried mothers was 79 percent in 2000, up almost 12 percent from 1994. The labor force participation rate was 59 percent for unmarried mothers with children under one year, up 13 percent since 1994. Among families maintained by a woman with no spouse present and with children under 18, 76 percent of the mothers were employed in 2000. Among such families with children under age six, 69 percent of the mothers were employed. (See Table 3.5.)

TABLE 3.3

Employment status of the civilian population by race, sex, age, and Hispanic origin
(Numbers in thousands)

Employment status, race, sex, age, and Hispanic origin	Seasonally adjusted Aug. 2001
WHITE	
Civilian noninstitutional population	176,069
Civilian labor force	117,726
Participation rate	66.9
Employed	112,703
Employment-population ratio	64.0
Unemployed	5,024
Unemployment rate	4.3
Men, 20 years and over	
Civilian labor force	60,575
Participation rate	76.7
Employed	58,297
Employment-population ratio	73.8
Unemployed	2,278
Unemployment rate	3.8
Women, 20 years and over	
Civilian labor force	50,656
Participation rate	60.1
Employed	48,839
Employment-population ratio	57.9
Unemployed	1,817
Unemployment rate	3.6
Both sexes, 16 to 19 years	
Civilian labor force	6,495
Participation rate	50.7
Employed	5,567
Employment-population ratio	43.4
Unemployed	928
Unemployment rate	14.3
Men	15.8
Women	12.7
BLACK	
Civilian noninstitutional population	25,604
Civilian labor force	16,712
Participation rate	65.3
Employed	15,195
Employment-population ratio	59.3
Unemployed	1,517
Unemployment rate	9.1
Men, 20 years and over	
Civilian labor force	7,424
Participation rate	72.3
Employed	6,752
Employment-population ratio	65.8
Unemployed	672
Unemployment rate	9.0
Women, 20 years and over	
Civilian labor force	8,424
Participation rate	65.6
Employed	7,842
Employment-population ratio	61.0
Unemployed	582
Unemployment rate	6.9
Both sexes, 16 to 19 years	
Civilian labor force	864
Participation rate	34.8
Employed	601
Employment-population ratio	24.2
Unemployed	263
Unemployment rate	30.4
Men	32.5
Women	28.1
HISPANIC ORIGIN	
Civilian noninstitutional population	23,222
Civilian labor force	15,772
Participation rate	67.9
Employed	14,778
Employment-population ratio	63.6
Unemployed	994
Unemployment rate	6.3

NOTE: Detail for the above race and Hispanic-origin groups will not sum to totals because data for the "other races" group are not presented and Hispanics are included in both the white and black population groups.

SOURCE: Adapted from "Table A-2. Employment Status of the Civilian Population by Race, Sex, Age, and Hispanic Origin," in "The Employment Situation: August 2001," *BLS News,* Bureau of Labor Statistics, Washington, DC, September 7, 2001

TABLE 3.4

Families by presence and relationship of employed members, annual averages 1999–2000
(Numbers in thousands)

Characteristic	Number 1999	Number 2000	Percent distribution 1999	Percent distribution 2000
MARRIED-COUPLE FAMILIES				
Total	54,468	54,704	100.0	100.0
Member(s) employed, total	45,800	45,967	84.1	84.0
Husband only	10,533	10,500	19.3	19.2
Wife only	2,980	2,946	5.5	5.4
Husband and wife	28,882	29,128	53.0	53.2
Other employment combinations	3,404	3,394	6.3	6.2
No member(s) employed	8,668	8,737	15.9	16.0
FAMILIES MAINTAINED BY WOMEN[1]				
Total	12,625	12,775	100.0	100.0
Members(s) employed, total	9,797	10,026	77.6	78.5
Householder only	5,566	5,581	44.1	43.7
Householder and other member(s)	2,663	2,806	21.1	22.0
Other member(s), not householder	1,568	1,639	12.4	12.8
No member(s) employed	2,827	2,749	22.4	21.5
FAMILIES MAINTAINED BY MEN[1]				
Total	4,158	4,200	100.0	100.0
Members(s) employed, total	3,588	3,632	86.3	86.5
Householder only	1,718	1,761	41.3	41.9
Householder and other member(s)	1,353	1,358	32.5	32.3
Other member(s), not householder	517	514	12.4	12.2
No member(s) employed	569	567	13.7	13.5

[1]No spouse present.
NOTE: Data for 2000 are not strictly comparable with data for 1999 and earlier years because of the introduction of revised population controls in the household survey in January 2000. Detail may not sum to totals due to rounding.

SOURCE: "Table 2. Families by Presence and Relationship of Employed Members and Family Type, 1999-2000," in *Employment Characteristics of Families in 2000,* Bureau of Labor Statistics, Washington, DC, April 19, 2001 [Online] ftp://146.142.4.23/pub/news.release/famee.txt [accessed September 23, 2001]

Employment Sectors

As seen in Table 3.6, fewer than 1 million women aged 16 and over were employed in agriculture in 2000, compared to over 1.5 million men. Of the more than 58.6 million female wage and salary workers, 81 percent were employed in private industry, of which almost 2 percent worked in private households. The remaining wage and salary workers were government employees. Men were more likely than women to be employed by private industry, but only a very small fraction of men were employed in private households. Of the 8.7 million self-employed Americans in 2000, 39 percent were women, 57 percent of whom were between the ages of 35 and 54. Finally, women were much more likely than men to work within the family without pay.

Far more women than men in all age groups work in service industries. According to the Census Bureau, in 1999 women accounted for 62 percent of all service jobs. Women accounted for 79 percent of professional and related services such as health care, social and legal services, and education. They accounted for 92 percent of

TABLE 3.5

Employment status of parents by age of youngest child and family type, annual averages 1999–2000

(Numbers in thousands)

Characteristic	Number		Percent distribution	
	1999	2000	1999	2000
WITH OWN CHILDREN UNDER 18 YEARS				
Total	34,340	34,340	100.0	100.0
Parent(s) employed	31,493	31,601	91.7	92.0
No parent employed	2,847	2,739	8.3	8.0
Married-couple families	24,904	24,915	100.0	100.0
Parent(s) employed	24,243	24,282	97.3	97.5
Mother employed	16,995	17,012	68.2	68.3
Both parents employed	15,958	15,996	64.1	64.2
Mother employed, not father	1,037	1,016	4.2	4.1
Father employed, not mother	7,249	7,270	29.1	29.2
Neither parent employed	661	633	2.7	2.5
Families maintained by women[1]	7,653	7,613	100.0	100.0
Mother employed	5,713	5,751	74.6	75.5
Mother not employed	1,940	1,862	25.4	24.5
Families maintained by men[1]	1,782	1,812	100.0	100.0
Father employed	1,537	1,568	86.3	86.5
Father not employed	245	244	13.7	13.5
WITH OWN CHILDREN 6 TO 17 YEARS, NONE YOUNGER				
Total	19,364	19,382	100.0	100.0
Parent(s) employed	17,824	17,892	92.0	92.3
No parent employed	1,540	1,490	8.0	7.7
Married-couple families	13,565	13,628	100.0	100.0
Parent(s) employed	13,174	13,248	97.1	97.2
Mother employed	10,113	10,247	74.6	75.2
Both parents employed	9,446	9,575	69.6	70.3
Mother employed, not father	667	672	4.9	4.9
Father employed, not mother	3,061	3,001	22.6	22.0
Neither parent employed	391	380	2.9	2.8
Families maintained by women[1]	4,722	4,668	100.0	100.0
Mother employed	3,737	3,715	79.1	79.6
Mother not employed	985	954	20.9	20.4
Families maintained by men[1]	1,077	1,086	100.0	100.0
Father employed	913	929	84.8	85.6
Father not employed	164	157	15.2	14.4
WITH OWN CHILDREN UNDER 6 YEARS				
Total	14,976	14,958	100.0	100.0
Parent(s) employed	13,669	13,708	91.3	91.6
No parent employed	1,307	1,249	8.7	8.4
Married-couple families	11,340	11,287	100.0	100.0
Parent(s) employed	11,069	11,034	97.6	97.8
Mother employed	6,882	6,765	60.7	59.9
Both parents employed	6,512	6,421	57.4	56.9
Mother employed, not father	370	344	3.3	3.0
Father employed, not mother	4,187	4,269	36.9	37.8
Neither parent employed	270	254	2.4	2.2
Families maintained by women[1]	2,931	2,945	100.0	100.0
Mother employed	1,976	2,036	67.4	69.1
Mother not employed	956	909	32.6	30.9
Families maintained by men[1]	705	726	100.0	100.0
Father employed	624	639	88.5	88.0
Father not employed	81	87	11.5	12.0

[1]No spouse present.
NOTE: Children include sons, daughters, step-children and adopted children. Not included are nieces, nephews, grandchildren, and other related and unrelated children. Data for 2000 are not strictly comparable with data for 1999 and earlier years because of the introduction of revised population controls in the household survey in January 2000. Detail may not sum to totals due to rounding.

SOURCE: "Table 4. Families With Own Children: Employment Status of Parents by Age of Youngest Child and Family Type, 1999-2000 Annual Averages," in *Employment Characteristics of Families in 2000*, Bureau of Labor Statistics, Washington, DC, April 19, 2001 [Online] ftp:// 146.142.4.23/pub/news.release/famee.txt [accessed September 23, 2001]

personal household employees and 56 percent of the jobs in hotels and lodgings. Women accounted for 58 percent of the jobs in the finance, insurance, and real estate industries, 48 percent of jobs in wholesale and retail trade, and 45 percent of jobs in government and public administration. Women accounted for 32 percent of manufacturing jobs and were more likely to work in the manufacture of nondurable goods, whereas far more men were employed in the manufacture of durable goods. Many more men than women were employed in the transportation, public utilities, construction, and mining industries.

In 1999, 13 percent of employed female wage and salary workers were represented by unions and 11 percent were union members, compared to 17 percent of males who were represented by unions and 16 percent who were union members. Only 12 percent of white and Hispanic women were represented by unions, as compared to 17 percent of African American women. The median usual weekly earnings of women not represented by unions were only 74 percent of the earnings of women with union representation.

Job Tenure

In general, men have worked at their current jobs for longer than women. According to the Census Bureau, in 1998, 27 percent of men and 29 percent of women had worked at their current jobs for less than 12 months. Only 7 percent of women, compared to 11 percent of men, had been at their current jobs for 20 years or more.

WELFARE REFORM

One of the major objectives of the 1996 Personal Responsibility and Work Opportunity Reconciliation Act (PRWORA: PL 104-193) was to move single mothers off welfare and into the labor force. A program called Temporary Assistance for Needy Families (TANF) provided federal aid for a lifetime maximum of five years to families transitioning from welfare to work. Recipients had to be in work-related activities within two years, and states could be penalized for having too few welfare recipients transitioning to work. In some states work or schooling to prepare for work were conditions for receiving TANF benefits, and mothers with children under age six had to work at least 20 hours per week to receive TANF benefits. Beginning in 2000 mothers of children over six were required to work 30 hours per week.

However, most American women with children work less than 30 hours a week year-round. It has been estimated that only 32 percent of women with children under the age of three work at least 30 hours per week. Women with less education work fewer hours than more educated women.

A December 2000 report from The Urban Institute, a Washington, D.C.–based nonpartisan economic and social

TABLE 3.6

Employed persons in agriculture and nonagricultural industries by age, sex, and class of worker
(In thousands)

	Agriculture			2000 Nonagricultural industries						
					Wage and salary workers					
						Private industries				
Age and sex	Wage and salary workers	Self-employed workers	Unpaid family workers	Total	Total	Private household workers	Other private industries	Government	Self-employed workers	Unpaid family workers
Total, 16 years and over	2,034	1,233	38	123,128	104,076	890	103,186	19,053	8,674	101
16 to 19 years	198	24	14	6,972	6,636	91	6,545	336	58	11
16 to 17 years	83	15	9	2,651	2,551	45	2,506	100	16	4
18 to 19 years	115	9	4	4,321	4,085	46	4,039	236	42	7
20 to 24 years	272	32	7	12,772	11,690	96	11,594	1,082	230	8
25 to 34 years	500	140	1	28,450	24,705	136	24,569	3,745	1,395	14
35 to 44 years	511	267	7	33,320	28,116	198	27,918	5,203	2,566	27
45 to 54 years	304	286	4	26,676	20,905	182	20,723	5,771	2,425	22
55 to 64 years	171	256	3	11,816	9,422	126	9,297	2,394	1,369	12
65 years and over	78	229	2	3,122	2,601	61	2,541	520	630	8
Men, 16 years and over	1,512	898	24	64,574	56,359	67	56,292	8,215	5,256	29
16 to 19 years	150	20	11	3,493	3,353	11	3,343	139	33	7
16 to 17 years	59	13	7	1,315	1,269	7	1,262	46	8	3
18 to 19 years	90	7	4	2,178	2,084	4	2,080	93	25	4
20 to 24 years	211	25	4	6,625	6,195	8	6,187	430	138	6
25 to 34 years	373	108	–	15,224	13,610	15	13,595	1,614	786	3
35 to 44 years	369	196	4	17,656	15,446	11	15,434	2,210	1,543	2
45 to 54 years	224	195	1	13,649	11,182	9	11,173	2,467	1,489	3
55 to 64 years	121	180	1	6,229	5,140	8	5,132	1,090	852	6
65 years and over	65	173	2	1,698	1,434	5	1,428	265	415	3
Women, 16 years and over	521	336	14	58,554	47,717	823	46,894	10,838	3,417	72
16 to 19 years	48	3	2	3,480	3,283	80	3,202	197	25	4
16 to 17 years	24	1	2	1,336	1,282	39	1,243	54	8	1
18 to 19 years	24	2	–	2,143	2,001	42	1,959	142	17	3
20 to 24 years	61	7	3	6,147	5,495	88	5,407	653	92	2
25 to 34 years	127	32	1	13,227	11,095	122	10,974	2,132	609	11
35 to 44 years	142	71	3	15,663	12,670	187	12,484	2,993	1,023	25
45 to 54 years	81	91	3	13,027	9,723	173	9,550	3,304	936	19
55 to 64 years	50	76	2	5,587	4,283	118	4,164	1,304	517	6
65 years and over	13	56	1	1,423	1,168	55	1,113	256	215	5

NOTE: Beginning in January 2000, data reflect revised population controls used in the household survey.

SOURCE: "15. Employed Persons in Agriculture and Nonagricultural Industries by Age, Sex, and Class of Worker," in "Average Annual Tables," *Employment and Earnings*, vol. 48, no. 1, January 2001

policy research organization, indicated that as a result of PRWORA, large numbers of single mothers were transitioning from welfare to the labor force and that wages and employment levels were rising for these women. However, most women transitioning off welfare are poorly educated and enter at the bottom level of the labor force, with low pay, few or no benefits, and little job security. The lack of adequate child-care facilities and arrangements in some areas has proved to be a major obstacle for many women, particularly since low-level jobs frequently have nonstandard or irregular hours. Lack of transportation also has been a major obstacle for mothers attempting to juggle work and child care. Whereas most welfare families live in the central cities, most of the job growth in recent years has been on the outskirts of urban areas.

According to a December 2000 report by the Institute for Women's Policy Research, a research organization that studies public policy issues of importance to women and their families, prior to PRWORA many welfare mothers cycled between welfare and work because of a lack of jobs and the instability of jobs for women with few skills. Former welfare recipients are unlikely to find jobs that pay health benefits or paid sick or vacation leave. Thus, they are more likely to lose their jobs when forced to take time off for family issues such as a sick child. In most states low-wage women may not qualify for unemployment insurance if they lose their jobs, and part-time workers are not usually eligible for unemployment insurance.

ALTERNATIVE WORK ARRANGEMENTS

Part-Time Work

According to the Census Bureau in 2000, 59 percent of working women worked full-time year-round,

TABLE 3.7

Persons at work in nonagricultural industries by age, sex, race, marital status, and usual full- or part-time status

(Numbers in thousands)

Age, sex, race, and marital status	Total at work	Worked 1 to 34 hours		For noneconomic reasons		Worked 35 hours or more	Average hours	
		Total	For economic reasons	Usually work full time	Usually work part time		Total at work	Persons who usually work full time
TOTAL								
Total, 16 years and over	126,433	28,732	3,045	7,521	18,165	97,701	39.7	43.3
16 to 19 years	6,795	4,662	324	242	4,097	2,132	25.7	39.3
16 to 17 years	2,561	2,236	69	43	2,125	324	19.6	37.9
18 to 19 years	4,234	2,426	255	199	1,972	1,808	29.4	39.6
20 years and over	119,639	24,070	2,721	7,280	14,069	95,569	40.4	43.4
20 to 24 years	12,621	3,849	529	699	2,621	8,772	36.6	41.5
25 years and over	107,018	20,221	2,192	6,581	11,448	86,797	40.9	43.6
25 to 54 years	91,023	15,460	1,883	5,600	7,977	75,563	41.5	43.7
55 years and over	15,995	4,761	310	981	3,471	11,234	37.5	43.0
Men, 16 years and over	67,531	10,637	1,458	3,592	5,587	56,894	42.5	44.8
16 to 19 years	3,418	2,178	164	125	1,890	1,240	27.1	39.8
16 to 17 years	1,271	1,077	38	21	1,018	194	20.7	38.7
18 to 19 years	2,146	1,101	126	104	871	1,046	31.0	40.0
20 years and over	64,113	8,458	1,294	3,467	3,697	55,655	43.3	44.9
20 to 24 years	6,602	1,647	283	325	1,039	4,955	38.4	42.3
25 years and over	57,512	6,811	1,011	3,142	2,658	50,700	43.8	45.2
25 to 54 years	48,772	4,765	863	2,633	1,269	44,007	44.5	45.3
55 years and over	8,739	2,046	148	509	1,389	6,693	40.0	44.3
Women, 16 years and over	58,902	18,095	1,587	3,929	12,579	40,807	36.4	41.4
16 to 19 years	3,377	2,484	160	117	2,207	893	24.2	38.7
16 to 17 years	1,289	1,159	31	21	1,106	130	18.6	36.8
18 to 19 years	2,088	1,325	129	95	1,101	762	27.7	39.0
20 years and over	55,525	15,611	1,427	3,813	10,372	39,914	37.2	41.4
20 to 24 years	6,019	2,202	246	374	1,582	3,817	34.6	40.4
25 years and over	49,506	13,409	1,181	3,439	8,790	36,097	37.5	41.5
25 to 54 years	42,250	10,694	1,019	2,967	6,708	31,556	38.0	41.6
55 years and over	7,256	2,715	162	472	2,082	4,540	34.5	41.2
Race								
White, 16 years and over	105,736	24,604	2,404	6,287	15,913	81,132	39.7	43.6
Men	57,439	9,040	1,174	3,078	4,788	48,399	42.7	45.0
Women	48,297	15,564	1,230	3,209	11,125	32,733	36.1	41.4
Black, 16 years and over	14,590	2,897	488	923	1,487	11,692	39.3	41.9
Men	6,822	1,085	210	361	514	5,737	41.0	43.1
Women	7,767	1,812	277	561	973	5,955	37.9	40.8
Marital status								
Men, 16 years and over:								
Married, spouse present	40,473	4,491	546	2,210	1,735	35,981	44.3	45.5
Widowed, divorced, or separated	8,165	1,118	225	472	420	7,047	43.0	44.6
Single (never married)	18,893	5,027	686	909	3,431	13,866	38.2	43.0
Women, 16 years and over:								
Married, spouse present	31,122	9,482	624	2,085	6,773	21,640	36.4	41.2
Widowed, divorced, or separated	11,901	2,872	386	886	1,600	9,029	38.6	41.8
Single (never married)	15,879	5,742	577	959	4,206	10,138	34.9	41.4

NOTE: Beginning in January 2000, data reflect revised population controls used in the household survey.

SOURCE: "22. Persons at Work in Nonagricultural Industries by Age, Sex, Race, Marital Status, and Usual Full- or Part-time Status," in "Average Annual Tables," *Employment and Earnings*, vol. 48, no. 1, January 2001

compared to 57 percent in 1999. In 2000, 31 percent of employed women worked less than 35 hours per week, as compared to 16 percent of men. (See Table 3.7.) Women made up 63 percent of all part-time workers. Among white employed women, 32 percent worked part-time, compared to 23 percent of black women. Never-married women were more likely to work part-time (36 percent),

compared to married women (30 percent) and widowed, divorced, or separated women (24 percent).

Most people worked part-time for noneconomic reasons, such as caring for a child or other family member. Many of these people, including 21 percent of white women and 31 percent of black women, usually worked

FIGURE 3.1

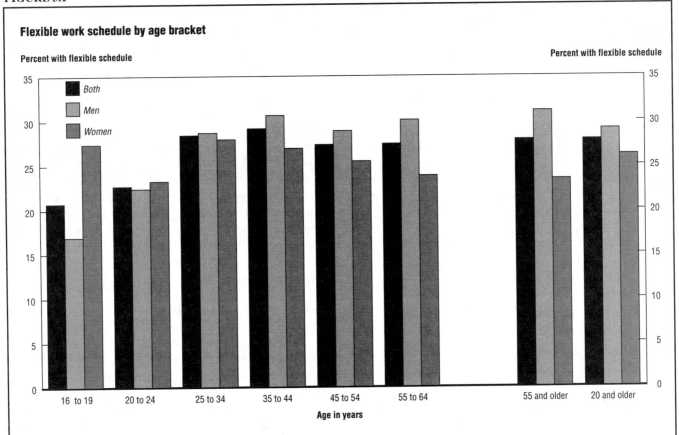

Flexible work schedule by age bracket

Percent with flexible schedule

Percent with flexible schedule

SOURCE: Lonnie Golden, "Chart 1. Flexible work schedule, by age bracket," in "Flexible Work Schedules: What Are We Trading Off to Get Them?" *Monthly Labor Review*, Bureau of Labor Statistics, Washington, DC, vol. 124, no. 3, March 2001

full-time. Men (14 percent) were more likely than women (9 percent) to be working part-time because of economic reasons such as job cutbacks or the inability to find full-time work. However, 15 percent of black women work part-time for such economic reasons. (See Table 3.7.)

Nearly 9 out of 10 companies offer some benefits to part-time workers, most of whom are in clerical and sales positions. The federal government is the largest employer of part-time workers as a result of the Federal Employees Part-Time Career Employment Act of 1978 (PL 95-437). This act gave part-time federal employees benefits and permanent status. The federal Office of Personnel Management reported that the number of part-time managers and executives has risen more than 150 percent since the enactment of the legislation. Both companies and the federal government now use part-time status as a way to recruit talented women who do not want to work full-time or are unable to do so because of other commitments.

Some women manage to work part-time by sharing what would be otherwise be full-time jobs. In particular, some teachers, librarians, receptionists, and health-care professionals have been able to job-share successfully.

Flextime

Changes in the structure of the American family have led businesses to offer alternatives to the traditional 40-hour workweek. Flextime enables employees to vary their work hours to accommodate family needs, education, or other situations. In its 2001 annual survey of the 100 best companies for working mothers, *Working Mother* magazine focused on flextime, advancement, and equitable distribution of benefits. The magazine viewed flextime as essential for working moms. However, Figure 3.1 shows that men are somewhat more likely than women to have flexible work schedules. Only women under age 24 have more access to flextime than men, although an increasing number of women have flexible schedules during their peak childbearing years.

Flextime is most available to professionals, such as scientists, lawyers, and teachers, and those in sales occupations. Others, such as computer equipment operators, farm and forestry workers, and transportation and construction workers, as well as many part-time workers, often work variable hours out of choice or at the convenience of their employer. Women and nonwhites are more likely to have unpredictable work schedules, in part because of the types of jobs they hold.

TABLE 3.8

Employed workers with alternative and traditional work arrangements by selected characteristics, February 2001
(Percent distribution)

	Workers with alternative arrangements				Workers with traditional arrangements
Characteristic	Independent contractors	On-call workers	Temporary help agency workers	Workers provided by contract firms	
Age and sex					
Total, 16 years and over	100.0	100.0	100.0	100.0	100.0
16 to 19 years	1.2	9.7	3.5	1.1	5.1
20 to 24 years	2.7	14.8	18.8	10.9	10.1
25 to 34 years	15.3	17.0	26.5	23.3	22.9
35 to 44 years	29.0	25.7	24.9	28.9	27.2
45 to 54 years	28.1	17.9	14.1	23.9	22.0
55 to 64 years	15.8	9.1	10.6	7.6	10.0
65 years and over	7.9	5.7	1.5	4.4	2.6
Men, 16 years and over	64.5	53.1	41.1	70.6	52.2
16 to 19 years	.7	3.9	1.3	1.1	2.6
20 to 24 years	1.4	8.5	7.0	8.9	5.2
25 to 34 years	9.0	11.7	11.1	18.2	12.2
35 to 44 years	19.0	12.0	13.2	21.8	14.3
45 to 54 years	18.0	8.6	4.4	12.0	11.2
55 to 64 years	10.6	4.7	3.6	6.1	5.2
65 years and over	5.7	3.6	.6	2.4	1.5
Women, 16 years and over	35.5	46.9	58.9	29.4	47.8
16 to 19 years	.5	5.8	2.2	-	2.5
20 to 24 years	1.3	6.3	11.8	1.9	5.0
25 to 34 years	6.3	5.3	15.4	5.1	10.6
35 to 44 years	9.9	13.7	11.8	7.1	12.9
45 to 54 years	10.1	9.3	9.7	11.9	10.8
55 to 64 years	5.2	4.5	7.0	1.4	4.8
65 years and over	2.2	2.1	.9	2.0	1.2
Race and Hispanic origin					
White	88.3	83.6	68.4	76.8	83.8
Black	7.0	13.3	25.4	14.9	11.4
Hispanic origin	7.2	11.1	17.6	10.4	11.0
Full- or part-time status					
Full-time workers	75.2	52.6	79.2	89.7	83.2
Part-time workers	24.8	47.4	20.8	10.3	16.8

NOTE: Workers with traditional arrangements are those who do not fall into any of the "alternative arrangements" categories. Detail for the above race and Hispanic-origin groups will not sum to totals because data for the "other races" group are not presented and Hispanics are included in both the white and black population groups. Detail for other characteristics may not sum to totals due to rounding.

SOURCE: "Table 6. Employed Workers with Alternative and Traditional Work Arrangements by Selected Characteristics, February 2001," in *Contingent and Alternative Employment Arrangements* Bureau of Labor Statistics, Washington, DC, [Online] http://www.bls.gov/news.release/conemp.t06.htm [accessed September 25, 2001]

Nontraditional Work Arrangements

Table 3.8 shows that more women than men had nontraditional or alternative work arrangements in February 2001. However, women made up 46.9 percent of on-call workers and 58.9 percent of those who worked through temporary help agencies, whereas 64.5 percent of independent contractors and 70.6 percent of those who work through contract firms were men. Thus, women with nontraditional arrangements tended to work in lower-skilled, lower-paying jobs. Although there are numerous types of contract workers, many women contract workers are poorly paid immigrants performing tasks such as garment work at home. In recent years there has been a resurgence in this type of arrangement, which was very common in the 19th century, when it was called "outworking."

Telecommuting

Personal and laptop computers, cellular phones, and other new technologies are enabling a growing number of Americans to work from home. Telework America's 2000 annual research survey, sponsored by AT&T, found that there were 16.5 million telecommuters in America. These are defined as people who are regularly employed and work from home at least one day per month. This was an increase of almost 21 percent over the previous year. More than 9 million American telecommuters worked from home at least one full day per week. The study projects that there may be as many as 30 million regular telecommuters by the end of 2004.

Although some telecommuters worked at telework centers, 89 percent performed most of their telework from home. The majority (54 percent) of these home-based teleworkers were employees; the remainder of home-based teleworkers were contract workers, self-employed, or operators of home-based businesses. The majority (65 percent) of home-based teleworkers were male, although females make up the majority of workers who began telecommuting in 1999 to 2000. Most teleworkers were experienced professionals over age 40.

Telecommuting allows workers to be available for children and other family members while generating income. It eliminates commuting time and costs. Telecommuting also saves money for businesses. Telework America estimates that teleworking increases worker productivity by 15 to 30 percent. In 1998, 16,000 AT&T employees worked from home. According to Mark Trierweiler, a vice-president in Denver for AT&T, the company's remote work program saves it about $6,000 annually per telecommuting employee. An increasing number of American businesses of all sizes are turning to telecommuting as a means of saving money and increasing worker productivity and job satisfaction.

Multiple Jobholders

In August 2001, 5.2 percent of employed women held more than one job. In 2000, 5.7 percent of employed women, or almost 3.6 million women, held more than one job, as did 5.5 percent of employed men. (See Table 3.9.) In 1999, 6 percent of women held multiple jobs. Women between the ages of 20 and 24 were most likely to hold more than one job (almost 7 percent). White women were more likely than blacks or Hispanics to hold multiple jobs. Single women were more likely to be multiple jobholders, as compared to married women living with their spouses. Most women with multiple jobs (49 percent) had

TABLE 3.9

Multiple jobholders by selected demographic and economic characteristics

(Numbers in thousands)

Characteristic	Both sexes Number 1999	Both sexes Number 2000	Both sexes Rate[1] 1999	Both sexes Rate[1] 2000	Men Number 1999	Men Number 2000	Men Rate[1] 1999	Men Rate[1] 2000	Women Number 1999	Women Number 2000	Women Rate[1] 1999	Women Rate[1] 2000
AGE												
Total, 16 years and over[2]	7,802	7,556	5.8	5.6	4,104	3,968	5.7	5.5	3,698	3,588	6.0	5.7
16 to 19 years	343	346	4.8	4.8	153	145	4.1	3.9	190	201	5.5	5.6
20 years and over	7,460	7,210	5.9	5.6	3,952	3,822	5.8	5.6	3,508	3,388	6.0	5.7
20 to 24 years	751	752	5.8	5.6	341	337	5.1	4.8	410	415	6.7	6.6
25 years and over	6,708	6,458	5.9	5.6	3,610	3,485	5.9	5.7	3,098	2,972	5.9	5.6
25 to 54 years	5,886	5,614	6.1	5.8	3,146	3,011	6.1	5.8	2,740	2,604	6.1	5.8
55 years and over	822	843	4.8	4.8	464	474	4.9	4.9	358	369	4.7	4.6
55 to 64 years	701	695	5.3	5.1	387	379	5.3	5.1	314	317	5.2	5.1
65 years and over	122	148	3.1	3.6	77	95	3.4	4.1	45	52	2.7	3.1
RACE AND HISPANIC ORIGIN												
White	6,674	6,462	5.9	5.7	3,514	3,433	5.7	5.6	3,159	3,029	6.2	5.8
Black	831	818	5.5	5.3	442	396	6.3	5.5	389	422	4.8	5.2
Hispanic origin	490	490	3.6	3.4	280	298	3.5	3.5	210	192	3.7	3.2
MARITAL STATUS												
Married, spouse present	4,309	4,156	5.6	5.4	2,566	2,499	5.9	5.8	1,744	1,656	5.2	4.9
Widowed, divorced, or separated	1,356	1,299	6.5	6.1	490	469	5.8	5.3	866	830	7.0	6.6
Single (never married)	2,137	2,101	5.9	5.7	1,048	1,000	5.3	5.0	1,089	1,102	6.7	6.6
FULL- OR PART-TIME STATUS												
Primary job full time, secondary job part time	4,293	4,173	–	–	2,497	2,409	–	–	1,796	1,764	–	–
Primary and secondary job both part time	1,657	1,595	–	–	519	518	–	–	1,138	1,077	–	–
Primary and secondary jobs both full time	298	317	–	–	204	210	–	–	94	106	–	–
Hours vary on primary or secondary job	1,513	1,429	–	–	861	811	–	–	652	618	–	–

[1] Multiple jobholders as a percent of all employed persons in specified group.
[2] Includes a small number of persons who work part time on their primary job and full time on their secondary jobs(s), not shown separately.
NOTE: Detail for the above race and Hispanic-origin groups will not sum to totals because data for the "other races" group are not presented and Hispanics are included in both the white and black population groups. Beginning in January 2000, data reflect revised population controls used in the household survey.

SOURCE: "36. Multiple Jobholders by Selected Demographic and Economic Characteristics," in "Average Annual Tables," *Employment and Earnings*, vol. 48, no. 1, January 2001

---

one full-time and one part-time job. Another 30 percent had two part-time jobs.

According to the Census Bureau, most women hold multiple jobs to meet household expenses. About 1 in 10 women has a second job in order to pay off debts, and another 10 percent are working because they enjoy their second job. Smaller numbers of women are working multiple jobs to save for the future or to save up to buy something special. Other reasons include obtaining additional experience, building up a business, or helping out a friend or relative.

UNEMPLOYMENT

The labor force includes both those who are employed and those who are looking for work. In 2000, 96 percent of women in the labor force were employed.

Unemployment Rates

In August 2001 the seasonally adjusted unemployment rate for women 20 and over was 4.2 percent. It was 15.5 percent for young women aged 16 and 17, but only 2.7 percent for women 55 and over. The rate for women 20 and over was 3.6 percent for white women and 6.9 percent for black women. (See Table 3.3.) The unemployment rate was 3.0 percent for married women living with their spouses but 6.7 percent for women maintaining families.

In 2000, 4.1 percent of women workers 16 and over were unemployed and 3.2 percent of those over 24 were unemployed. (See Table 3.10.) This was down slightly from the 1999 rates but higher than the unemployment rates for men in 2000. The unemployment rate for women in 2000 was the lowest since before 1969. (See Table 3.2.) The unemployment rate for men in 1969 was 2.8 percent, but it was 4.7 percent for women in that year. In 1982, the unemployment rate was 9.4 percent for women and 9.9 percent for men.

Race and Age

The unemployment rate was highest for never-married blacks ages 16 and over: 10.7 percent for women and 13.7 percent for men in 2000. The unemployment rates for never-married blacks over 24 were 7.0 percent for women and 8.5 percent for men. In general, unemployment rates were lower for whites than for blacks and for

TABLE 3.10

Unemployed persons by marital status, race, age, and sex

Marital status, race, and age	Men				Women			
	Thousands of persons		Unemployment rates		Thousands of persons		Unemployment rates	
	1999	2000	1999	2000	1999	2000	1999	2000
Total, 16 years and over	3,066	2,954	4.1	3.9	2,814	2,701	4.3	4.1
Married, spouse present	990	891	2.2	2.0	921	923	2.7	2.7
Widowed, divorced, or separated	411	400	4.6	4.4	585	553	4.5	4.2
Single (never married)	1,665	1,663	7.8	7.6	1,308	1,224	7.4	6.9
White, 16 years and over	2,274	2,165	3.6	3.4	1,999	1,934	3.8	3.6
Married, spouse present	797	706	2.1	1.8	749	755	2.5	2.5
Widowed, divorced, or separated	320	304	4.3	4.0	427	412	4.2	4.0
Single (never married)	1,157	1,154	6.7	6.6	823	767	6.3	5.8
Black, 16 years and over	626	636	8.2	8.1	684	633	7.8	7.2
Married, spouse present	130	127	3.8	3.7	119	114	4.2	4.0
Widowed, divorced, or separated	77	82	6.3	6.7	134	123	6.1	5.5
Single (never married)	419	426	14.0	13.7	430	395	11.7	10.7
Total, 25 years and over	1,870	1,800	3.0	2.8	1,805	1,736	3.3	3.2
Married, spouse present	925	841	2.1	2.0	828	817	2.5	2.5
Widowed, divorced, or separated	393	383	4.5	4.3	544	518	4.3	4.1
Single (never married)	553	576	4.9	5.0	433	401	4.9	4.5
White, 25 years and over	1,415	1,343	2.6	2.5	1,294	1,266	2.9	2.8
Married, spouse present	744	669	2.0	1.8	671	667	2.4	2.3
Widowed, divorced, or separated	305	289	4.3	3.9	396	383	4.0	3.8
Single (never married)	366	386	4.2	4.3	227	217	3.8	3.6
Black, 25 years and over	345	360	5.4	5.6	423	380	5.9	5.2
Married, spouse present	120	119	3.6	3.5	107	101	4.0	3.7
Widowed, divorced, or separated	74	81	6.2	6.7	127	118	5.9	5.3
Single (never married)	152	160	8.4	8.5	188	161	8.1	7.0

NOTE: Beginning in January 2000, data reflect revised population controls used in the household survey.

SOURCE: "24. Unemployed Persons by Marital Status, Race, Age, and Sex," in "Average Annual Tables," *Employment and Earnings,* vol. 48, no. 1, January 2001

married women living with their spouses than for single women. (See Table 3.10.) The unemployment rate for Hispanic women aged 16 and over was 6.7 percent in 2000, down from 7.6 percent in 1999. The rate was 5.9 percent for Hispanic women 20 and over in 2000.

Young workers are most likely to be unemployed. In 2000 the unemployment rate for white women aged 16 or 17 was 12.5 percent. It was 15.2 percent for white men of that age. The rate was 25.7 percent for 16- and 17-year-old African American women and 28.6 percent for African American men of that age.

Unemployed Mothers

The unemployment rate for single mothers with children under 18 was 7.5 percent in 2000, compared to 2.5 percent for married mothers. Many unmarried mothers have a lower socioeconomic status, lack job skills, and have limited access to child care. More financially well-off mothers often choose to remain at home until their children reach school age, either because of inadequate child care or from a desire to spend more time with their children during the formative years. Many of these women return to work when their children are older.

Duration of Unemployment

In 2000 the majority of unemployed persons, including 43.8 percent of unemployed women aged 20 and over, had been out of work for less than five weeks. (See Table 3.11.) Among unemployed women over 19, 31.6 percent had been out of work between 5 and 14 weeks and 24.6 percent had been unemployed for at least 15 weeks. On average, women in every age group remained unemployed for a shorter period than men in the same age group.

African Americans and Hispanics remain unemployed longer than whites, although both white and African American women remain unemployed, on average, a shorter period than men of the same race. However, Hispanic women remain unemployed longer than Hispanic men.

Never-married men and women remain unemployed for a shorter average period than married individuals living with their spouses. Widowed, divorced, or separated individuals remain unemployed for longer periods.

Reasons for Unemployment

Among unemployed women aged 20 and over in 2000, 42 percent had lost their jobs or had completed temporary jobs. One-third of these women were on temporary

TABLE 3.11

Unemployed persons by reason for unemployment, sex, age, and duration

(Percent distribution)

	2000						
	Total unemployed		Duration of unemployment				
					15 weeks and over		
Reason, sex, and age	Thousands of persons	Percent	Less than 5 weeks	5 to 14 weeks	Total	15 to 26 weeks	27 weeks and over
Total, 16 years and over	5,655	100.0	45.0	31.9	23.1	11.8	11.4
Job losers and persons who completed temporary jobs	2,492	100.0	45.4	31.7	22.9	12.7	10.2
On temporary layoff	842	100.0	58.1	30.6	11.3	7.8	3.6
Not on temporary layoff	1,650	100.0	39.0	32.3	28.8	15.2	13.6
Permanent job losers	1,108	100.0	35.7	33.0	31.2	16.6	14.7
Persons who completed temporary jobs	542	100.0	45.5	30.7	23.7	12.4	11.3
Job leavers	775	100.0	50.4	30.7	18.9	9.5	9.4
Reentrants	1,957	100.0	42.6	31.8	25.6	12.1	13.5
New entrants	431	100.0	43.4	35.4	21.2	9.1	12.1
Men, 20 years and over	2,350	100.0	42.0	31.7	26.3	12.5	13.8
Job losers and persons who completed temporary jobs	1,398	100.0	43.7	32.3	24.0	12.9	11.1
On temporary layoff	484	100.0	56.4	31.8	11.7	8.0	3.7
Not on temporary layoff	914	100.0	37.0	32.5	30.5	15.5	15.0
Permanent job losers	609	100.0	33.9	33.4	32.7	16.6	16.1
Persons who completed temporary jobs	306	100.0	43.1	30.7	26.1	13.2	12.9
Job leavers	324	100.0	48.3	31.0	20.7	9.5	11.2
Reentrants	574	100.0	35.4	30.8	33.8	13.1	20.7
New entrants	54	100.0	29.7	29.2	41.2	15.8	25.3
Women, 20 years and over	2,212	100.0	43.8	31.6	24.6	12.8	11.8
Job losers and persons who completed temporary jobs	934	100.0	43.9	32.2	23.9	13.9	10.0
On temporary layoff	302	100.0	56.0	31.7	12.3	8.7	3.6
Not on temporary layoff	632	100.0	38.1	32.5	29.4	16.4	13.1
Permanent job losers	441	100.0	34.9	33.3	31.8	17.8	14.1
Persons who completed temporary jobs	191	100.0	45.6	30.5	23.9	13.1	10.8
Job leavers	340	100.0	49.6	30.5	19.9	9.8	10.1
Reentrants	860	100.0	41.9	31.2	26.9	13.1	13.8
New entrants	78	100.0	37.8	33.6	28.6	8.6	20.0
Both sexes, 16 to 19 years	1,093	100.0	53.8	32.9	13.3	8.0	5.3
Job losers and persons who completed temporary jobs	160	100.0	68.9	23.9	7.2	4.1	3.1
On temporary layoff	57	100.0	82.9	14.0	3.1	1.0	2.1
Not on temporary layoff	103	100.0	61.2	29.3	9.5	5.8	3.6
Permanent job losers	58	100.0	60.9	27.6	11.5	7.0	4.5
Persons who completed temporary jobs	45	100.0	61.6	31.5	6.9	4.3	2.6
Job leavers	111	100.0	59.0	30.3	10.7	8.3	2.4
Reentrants	522	100.0	51.8	33.8	14.4	9.2	5.2
New entrants	300	100.0	47.4	37.0	15.7	8.0	7.7

NOTE: Beginning in January 2000, data reflect revised population controls used in the household survey.

SOURCE: "29. Unemployed Persons By Reason for Unemployment, Sex, Age, and Duration of Unemployment," in "Average Annual Tables," *Employment and Earnings*, vol. 48, no. 1, January 2001

layoff. Another 39 percent of unemployed women over 19 were trying to reenter the labor force after having left for a time. Women who had left their jobs accounted for 15 percent of unemployed women. The remaining 4 percent of unemployed women were trying to enter the labor force for the first time.

Of unemployed women aged 20 and over in 2000, 81 percent were looking for full-time work. Young white women between 16 and 19 were somewhat more likely to be looking for part-time work, whereas young African American women were more likely to be looking for full-time work.

Displaced workers are people aged 20 years and older who have lost jobs because their plants or companies have closed or moved, because there is insufficient work for them to do, or because their positions or shifts have been abolished. According to the Census Bureau, women are more likely than men to be unemployed or out of the labor force after being displaced.

Out of the Labor Force

Underemployed workers are part-time workers who would prefer full-time employment. Discouraged workers are job seekers who have stopped looking and those who are unable to work because they lack child care or transportation. Discouraged workers are not considered to be part of the labor force.

According to the Bureau of Labor Statistics, of the more than 44 million women who were not in the labor

TABLE 3.12

Employment status of the civilian noninstitutional population 25 years and over by educational attainment, sex, race, and Hispanic origin

(Numbers in thousands)

Educational attainment	Total 1999	Total 2000	Men 1999	Men 2000	Women 1999	Women 2000	White 1999	White 2000	Black 1999	Black 2000	Hispanic origin 1999	Hispanic origin 2000
TOTAL												
Civilian noninstitutional population	173,746	175,247	82,657	83,426	91,089	91,821	145,992	147,000	19,761	20,060	16,644	17,277
Civilian labor force	117,101	118,148	62,903	63,372	54,198	54,777	98,025	98,737	13,540	13,704	11,563	12,129
Percent of population	67.4	67.4	76.1	76.0	59.5	59.7	67.1	67.2	68.5	68.3	69.5	70.2
Employed	113,425	114,612	61,032	61,571	52,392	53,041	95,316	96,127	12,771	12,964	10,985	11,596
Employment-population ratio	65.3	65.4	73.8	73.8	57.5	57.8	65.3	65.4	64.6	64.6	66.0	67.1
Unemployed	3,676	3,537	1,870	1,800	1,805	1,736	2,709	2,610	768	740	578	533
Unemployment rate	3.1	3.0	3.0	2.8	3.3	3.2	2.8	2.6	5.7	5.4	5.0	4.4
Less than a high school diploma												
Civilian noninstitutional population	28,337	27,942	13,388	13,219	14,948	14,722	22,765	22,357	4,247	4,271	7,189	7,419
Civilian labor force	12,110	12,054	7,347	7,287	4,763	4,767	9,815	9,783	1,684	1,669	4,226	4,471
Percent of population	42.7	43.1	54.9	55.1	31.9	32.4	43.1	43.8	39.6	39.1	58.8	60.3
Employed	11,294	11,283	6,921	6,889	4,372	4,394	9,235	9,232	1,488	1,490	3,926	4,190
Employment-population ratio	39.9	40.4	51.7	52.1	29.2	29.8	40.6	41.3	35.0	34.9	54.6	56.5
Unemployed	817	771	426	398	391	373	580	550	196	179	300	282
Unemployment rate	6.7	6.4	5.8	5.5	8.2	7.8	5.9	5.6	11.6	10.7	7.1	6.3
High school graduates, no college												
Civilian noninstitutional population	57,559	57,559	26,158	26,337	31,402	31,222	48,629	48,510	7,008	7,046	4,566	4,794
Civilian labor force	37,327	37,170	19,785	19,762	17,542	17,409	31,145	30,927	4,944	4,929	3,370	3,549
Percent of population	64.8	64.6	75.6	75.0	55.9	55.8	64.0	63.8	70.5	69.9	73.8	74.0
Employed	36,017	35,886	19,125	19,086	16,893	16,799	30,211	30,015	4,631	4,609	3,213	3,410
Employment-population ratio	62.6	62.3	73.1	72.5	53.8	53.8	62.1	61.9	66.1	65.4	70.4	71.1
Unemployed	1,310	1,285	661	675	649	609	934	913	313	320	158	139
Unemployment rate	3.5	3.5	3.3	3.4	3.7	3.5	3.0	3.0	6.3	6.5	4.7	3.9
Less than a bachelor's degree[1]												
Civilian noninstitutional population	43,358	44,364	19,997	20,412	23,360	23,951	36,349	37,260	5,318	5,414	3,049	3,109
Civilian labor force	32,115	32,844	16,212	16,515	15,903	16,329	26,621	27,271	4,219	4,295	2,437	2,489
Percent of population	74.1	74.0	81.1	80.9	68.1	68.2	73.2	73.2	79.3	79.3	79.9	80.1
Employed	31,209	31,965	15,778	16,093	15,430	15,871	25,944	26,610	4,032	4,124	2,356	2,412
Employment-population ratio	72.0	72.1	78.9	78.8	66.1	66.3	71.4	71.4	75.8	76.2	77.3	77.6
Unemployed	906	879	434	422	473	458	677	661	187	171	81	78
Unemployment rate	2.8	2.7	2.7	2.6	3.0	2.8	2.5	2.4	4.4	4.0	3.3	3.1
Some college, no degree												
Civilian noninstitutional population	30,111	30,481	14,192	14,412	15,919	16,069	25,077	25,453	3,895	3,923	2,205	2,219
Civilian labor force	21,778	22,001	11,251	11,439	10,527	10,562	17,863	18,086	3,067	3,076	1,755	1,763
Percent of population	72.3	72.2	79.3	79.4	66.1	65.7	71.2	71.1	78.7	78.4	79.6	79.4
Employed	21,129	21,374	10,941	11,133	10,189	10,240	17,388	17,615	2,924	2,949	1,696	1,706
Employment-population ratio	70.2	70.1	77.1	77.3	64.0	63.7	69.3	69.2	75.1	75.2	76.9	76.9
Unemployed	648	628	310	306	338	322	475	471	143	128	60	57
Unemployment rate	3.0	2.9	2.8	2.7	3.2	3.0	2.7	2.6	4.7	4.2	3.4	3.2
Associate degree												
Civilian noninstitutional population	13,247	13,883	5,806	6,000	7,441	7,883	11,272	11,807	1,423	1,491	844	890
Civilian labor force	10,337	10,843	4,961	5,075	5,376	5,767	8,758	9,186	1,152	1,219	682	727
Percent of population	78.0	78.1	85.4	84.6	72.2	73.2	77.7	77.8	81.0	81.8	80.8	81.6
Employed	10,079	10,591	4,838	4,960	5,242	5,631	8,556	8,995	1,108	1,176	660	706
Employment-population ratio	76.1	76.3	83.3	82.7	70.4	71.4	75.9	76.2	77.9	78.9	78.3	79.3
Unemployed	258	252	123	116	134	136	202	190	44	43	21	21
Unemployment rate	2.5	2.3	2.5	2.3	2.5	2.4	2.3	2.1	3.8	3.5	3.1	2.8
College graduates												
Civilian noninstitutional population	44,492	45,382	23,113	23,457	21,379	21,925	38,249	38,873	3,188	3,328	1,840	1,955
Civilian labor force	35,548	36,080	19,558	19,808	15,990	16,272	30,444	30,756	2,693	2,810	1,530	1,620
Percent of population	79.9	79.5	84.6	84.4	74.8	74.2	79.6	79.1	84.5	84.4	83.2	82.9
Employed	34,905	35,478	19,208	19,503	15,697	15,975	29,925	30,270	2,621	2,741	1,491	1,585
Employment-population ratio	78.5	78.2	83.1	83.1	73.4	72.9	78.2	77.9	82.2	82.3	81.0	81.1
Unemployed	643	602	350	305	293	296	519	486	73	70	39	35
Unemployment rate	1.8	1.7	1.8	1.5	1.8	1.8	1.7	1.6	2.7	2.5	2.6	2.2

[1] Includes the categories, some college, no degree, and associate degree.

NOTE: Detail for the above race and Hispanic-origin groups will not sum to totals because data for the "other races" group are not presented and Hispanics are included in both the white and black population groups. Beginning in January 2000, data reflect revised population controls used in the household survey.

SOURCE: "7. Employment Status of the Civilian Noninstitutional Population 25 Years and Over by Educational Attainment, Sex, Race, and Hispanic Origin," in "Average Annual Tables," *Employment and Earnings*, vol. 48, no. 1, January 2001

TABLE 3.13

Employment and total job openings by education and training category, 1998–2008

[Numbers in thousands of jobs]

Education and training category	Employment				Change, 1998-2008		Total job openings due to growth and net replacements, 1998-2008[1]	
	Number		Percent distribution					Percent distribution
	1998	2008	1998	2008	Number	Percent	Number	
Total, all occupations	140,514	160,795	100.0	100.0	20,281	14.4	55,008	100.0
First professional degree	1,908	2,215	1.4	1.4	308	16.1	617	1.1
Doctoral degree	996	1,228	.7	.8	232	23.3	502	.9
Master's degree	940	1,115	.7	.7	174	18.6	374	.7
Work experience plus bachelor's or higher degree	9,595	11,276	6.8	7.0	1,680	17.5	3,372	6.1
Bachelor's degree	17,379	21,596	12.4	13.4	4,217	24.3	7,822	14.2
Associate degree	4,930	6,467	3.5	4.0	1,537	31.2	2,422	4.4
Postsecondary vocational training	4,508	5,151	3.2	3.2	643	14.3	1,680	3.1
Work experience in a related occupation	11,174	12,490	8.0	7.8	1,316	11.8	3,699	6.7
Long-term on-the-job training	13,436	14,604	9.6	9.1	1,168	8.7	4,411	8.0
Moderate-term on-the-job training	20,521	21,952	14.6	13.7	1,430	7.0	6,218	11.3
Short-term on-the-job training	55,125	62,701	39.2	39.0	7,576	13.7	23,890	43.4

[1]Total job openings represent the sum of employment increases and net replacements. If employment change is negative, job openings due to growth are zero and total job openings equal net replacements.

Note: Detail may not equal total or 100 percent due to rounding.

SOURCE: "Table 4. Employment and Total Job Openings, 1998-2008, by Education and Training Category," in *BLS Releases New 1998-2008 Employment Projections*, Bureau of Labor Statistics, Washington, DC, November 30, 1999 [Online] ftp://146.142.4.23/pub/news.release/ecopro.txt [accessed September 23, 2001]

force as of August 2000, 7 percent wanted to be working. Of this 7 percent, 22 percent were available to work and had looked for work in the past 12 months, but they were not currently looking for work and were therefore not considered to be part of the labor force. Of the 646,000 women in this category, 25 percent had become discouraged with their job prospects. They may have been unable to find a job or they may lack training or education. This also includes women who may have been discriminated against, perhaps for being a single mother or of the wrong age or race. The remaining 75 percent of the women in this category had been unable to look for work in the past four weeks for other reasons, such as lack of child care or transportation.

In 1999 the Census Bureau found that 6 percent of women who were not in the labor force wanted to be. Of these women, 62 percent had not looked for a job in the previous year. Of those who had looked for a job and were available for work, 18 percent were not currently looking because they were discouraged, 16 percent because of family responsibilities, and 16 percent because they were in school or training. Another 9 percent were not currently looking because of poor health or disability. However, 40 percent of the women were not looking for a job because of other reasons such as lack of child care or transportation.

EDUCATION AND THE LABOR FORCE

There is a strong correlation between a woman's education and her labor force status. (See Table 3.12.) Over-all, 59.7 percent of the civilian female population aged 25 and over was in the labor force in 2000. However, of those with less than a high school diploma, only 32.4 percent were in the labor force. Of female high school graduates with no college, 55.8 percent were in the labor force, as were 65.7 percent of those with some college but without a bachelor's degree. Over 70 percent of women with associate or four-year college degrees were in the labor force.

Likewise, although 57.8 percent of the female population 25 and over was employed in 2000, only 29.8 percent of women with less than a high school diploma were employed, and the unemployment rate for these women was 7.8 percent, compared to 3.2 percent for all women over 25. The percent employed increased with education to 72.9 percent for college graduates, and the unemployment rate decreased to 1.8 percent. The correlation between education and employment also held for men and for white, black, and Hispanic individuals. (See Table 3.12.)

These trends are expected to continue. As Table 3.13 shows, the Bureau of Labor Statistics projects a total employment growth of 14.4 percent between 1998 and 2008. Of these new jobs, 31.2 percent will require associate degrees, 24.3 percent bachelor's degrees, and 23.3 percent doctoral degrees. Only 13.7 percent will require nothing but short-term on-the-job training. Over the same period, there are projected to be 55 million job openings because of replacements and new jobs. Of these, 55 percent will require only short- or medium-term on-the-job training. However, 14.2 percent are expected to require a bachelor's degree.

LABOR FORCE PROJECTIONS

As the baby boom generation ages, the labor force will become older. As this generation retires, the labor force will become younger and more diverse.

Although the Bureau of Labor Statistics projects slightly more population growth between 1998 and 2008 than occurred in the previous 10 years, labor force growth is expected to be slower than it was from 1988 to 1998. Between 1998 and 2008, it is projected that 21 million women will enter the labor force, as will a similar number of men. Although 11 million women will leave the labor force, 52 million will stay, for a net increase of almost 10 million women. Since women in the current labor force tend to be younger than men in the labor force, more men than women will leave. Thus, the number of women in the labor force will continue to grow at a faster rate than the number of men. However, the rate of growth will slow. In 2008 it is projected that women will make up 48 percent of the labor force. Of these women, 33 percent will be white, 6 percent African American, 6 percent of Hispanic origin, and 3 percent Asian and other races.

The participation of women in the labor force is projected to continue its growth through 2015, when women's labor force participation rate will be 61.9 percent, compared to 72.2 percent for men. It is projected that 82 percent of women between the ages of 35 and 54 will be in the labor force. (See Table 3.1.) African American women will continue to have the highest labor force participation rates among women, at 65 percent. The participation rate of white women will be 62 percent, whereas 59 percent of Asian and other women and 58 percent of Hispanic women will be in the labor force. The participation rate of men is expected to continue its decline in all age groups except for men 16 to 24 and 55 and older.

By 2025 the percentage of women in the labor force is expected to drop to 58.1 percent. (See Table 3.1.) This drop will occur across all age groups. Men's participation in the labor force is also expected to decline in all age groups. In 2025 the difference between the labor force participation rates of men and women is expected to be only about 11 percent. Since Hispanics and Asians are younger populations, their labor force participation rates will decline less than those of non-Hispanic whites.

CHAPTER 4
WOMEN'S OCCUPATIONS

Until recent times women's occupations outside of the home were restricted primarily to a very few selected fields in which women would be unlikely to compete with men. Thus, women were household servants and nannies, farmworkers, shop girls, seamstresses, barmaids, and waitresses. Early businesswomen were shopkeepers and innkeepers. With the Industrial Revolution, lower-class women went to work in factories, particularly in the garment industry. As women's educational opportunities improved, women became teachers of young children, nurses, and social workers. Other women began replacing men as clerical workers and secretaries.

LEGAL RESTRICTIONS

Tradition was codified into law in the latter part of the 19th century when the appalling conditions of factory sweatshops brought together diverse groups, including labor leaders and feminists, in support of labor laws for the protection of women and children. *U.S. v. Martin,* (18 Stat 737, 1868) and other court rulings and laws that followed limited the hours that women could work and banned them from certain occupations that required exertion or that might be "morally corrupting." In some states women were banned from bartending and setting pins in bowling alleys as well as from freight handling and mining.

For the most part, barring women from secondary or higher education was enough to keep them out of professions in which they could compete with men. If that failed, the law was called upon. In *Bradwell v. Illinois* (83 US, 16 Wall, 1872), the U.S. Supreme Court upheld an Illinois law prohibiting women from practicing law. The high court held that:

> The natural proper timidity and delicacy which belongs to the female sex unfits it for many occupations of civil life. The constitution of the family organization, which, if founded in the divine ordinance, as well as in the nature of things, indicates the domestic sphere as that

which properly belongs to the domain and functions of womanhood.

Well into the 20th century employers were able to use labor laws and court rulings to justify not hiring women for certain jobs or for restricting their hours and paying them less than men. When the Civil Rights Act of 1964 (PL 88-352) and the case law built on it freed women to enter nearly any occupation, some employers resorted to old arguments about the reproductive functions of women in order to bar them from jobs.

Johnson Controls adopted a policy barring all women, regardless of age, from jobs involving contact with lead in its car battery manufacturing plant, unless the women had medical proof of sterility. As a result women were kept out of some of the highest-paying jobs at the plant. In 1991 in *United Automobile Workers v. Johnson Controls* (499 U.S. 187), the Supreme Court ruled that the Civil Rights Act of 1964 prohibited companies from barring women from jobs that might jeopardize a developing fetus. The court noted that "decisions about the welfare of future children must be left to the parents who conceive, bear, support and raise them rather than to the employers who hire those parents."

TRADITIONAL FEMALE OCCUPATIONS

Most women in the American labor force still work in what may be considered traditionally female occupations. Among the 20 leading occupations of employed women in 2000, women comprised 97.8 percent of registered nurses, 90 percent of nursing aides, orderlies, and attendants, and 91.2 percent of hairdressers and cosmetologists. (See Table 4.1.) There were more women working in sales than in any other occupation, and women made up 63.5 percent of all retail and personal services sales workers. In addition, women comprised 77.5 percent of all cashiers. However, they comprised only 40.3 percent of sales supervisors and proprietors. There were 2.6 million

TABLE 4.1

Twenty leading occupations of employed women, annual averages, 2000
(In thousands)

Occupations	Total employed women	Total employed (men and women)	Percent women	Women's median usual weekly earnings[1]	Ratio women's earnings to men's earnings
Total, 16 years and over	62,915	135,208	46.5	$491	76.0
Sales workers, retail and personal services	4,306	6,782	63.5	301	55.8
Secretaries	2,594	2,623	98.9	450	N.A.
Managers and administrators, n.e.c.[2]	2,418	7,797	31.0	733	66.3
Cashiers	2,277	2,939	77.5	276	88.2
Sales supervisors and proprietors	1,989	4,937	40.3	485	69.8
Registered nurses	1,959	2,111	97.8	782	87.9
Elementary school teachers	1,814	2,177	83.3	701	81.5
Nursing aides, orderlies, and attendants	1,784	1,983	90.0	333	88.1
Bookkeepers, accounting, & auditing clerks	1,584	1,719	92.1	478	88.7
Receptionists	984	1,017	96.8	388	N.A.
Sales workers, other commodities[3,4]	949	1,428	66.5	319	69.3
Accountants and auditors	903	1,592	56.7	690	72.4
Cooks	899	2,076	43.3	290	89.5
Investigators and adjusters, exclud. insurance	833	1,097	75.9	459	82.6
Janitors and cleaners	811	2,233	36.3	309	83.1
Secondary school teachers	764	1,319	57.9	741	88.6
Hairdressers and cosmetologists	748	820	91.2	339	N.A.
General office clerks	722	864	83.6	430	91.3
Mgrs, food serving and lodging establishments	677	1,446	46.8	475	73.0
Teachers' aides	646	710	91.0	338	N.A.

[1]Wage and salary for full-time workers.
[2]Not elsewhere classified.
[3]Included in sales workers, personal and retail workers.
[4]Includes foods, drugs, heath, and other commodities.
N.A.: Median not available where base is less than 50,000 male workers.

SOURCE: "20 Leading Occupations of Employed Women 2000 Annual Averages," in *Statistics and Data* U.S. Department of Labor, Washington, DC [Online] http://www.dol.gov/dol/wb/public/wb_pubs/20lead2000.htm [accessed September 21, 2001]

female secretaries in 2000, and 98.9 percent of all secretaries were women. In addition, 96.8 percent of all receptionists, 92.1 percent of all bookkeepers and accounting clerks, and 83.6 percent of all general office clerks were women. Yet only 31 percent of managers and administrators were women. Women made up 83.3 percent of elementary school teachers and 91 percent of teachers' aides, but only 57.9 percent of secondary school teachers.

As is evident from Table 4.1, in every leading female occupation women earned substantially less than men with the same occupation. In retail and personal service sales, women earned only 55.8 percent of what salesmen earned.

Over 25 million American women were in technical, sales, and administrative support occupations in 2000, compared to some 14 million men. (See Table 4.2.) About 23 percent of employed women were in administrative support, including clerical occupations, accounting for 79 percent of all such positions.

Approximately equal numbers of men and women (about 20 million) were managers and professionals. Of all employed white women, 33.4 percent were in this occupational category, compared to 24.8 percent of employed black women. (See Table 4.3.) More women than men were professionals and more men than women were managers, executives, and administrators. Women accounted for 78 percent of medicine and health managers but only 10 percent of construction inspectors. Among professionals, far more men than women were engineers and computer scientists in 2000. Women accounted for 86 percent of all persons employed in health care below the level of physician, including 91 percent of occupational therapists. Women accounted for about three-quarters of teachers below the college level, including 99 percent of kindergarten and prekindergarten teachers.

More than 11 million American women over the age of 15 were in service occupations in 2000, compared to about 7 million men. Of employed white women, 16.4 percent were in service occupations, compared to 25.2 percent of employed black women. (See Table 4.3.) Far more men than women were in protective service occupations, and almost all private household workers were women. Far more women than men were in health and personal service occupations. (See Table 4.2.) Women accounted for 96 percent of dental assistants and 98 percent of all child-care workers.

TABLE 4.2

Employed persons by occupation, sex, and age

(Numbers in thousands)

Occupation	Total 16 years and over 1999	Total 16 years and over 2000	Men 16 years and over 1999	Men 16 years and over 2000	Men 20 years and over 1999	Men 20 years and over 2000	Women 16 years and over 1999	Women 16 years and over 2000	Women 20 years and over 1999	Women 20 years and over 2000
Total	133,488	135,208	71,446	72,293	67,761	68,580	62,042	62,915	58,555	59,352
Managerial and professional specialty	40,467	40,887	20,446	20,543	20,285	20,401	20,021	20,345	19,846	20,140
Executive, administrative, and managerial	19,584	19,774	10,744	10,814	10,682	10,754	8,840	8,960	8,784	8,900
Officials and administrators, public administration	745	753	381	380	381	379	364	373	363	372
Other executive, administrative, and managerial	13,960	14,089	8,303	8,291	8,245	8,243	5,657	5,797	5,616	5,747
Management-related occupations	4,879	4,932	2,060	2,143	2,056	2,132	2,819	2,789	2,805	2,780
Professional specialty	20,883	21,113	9,702	9,728	9,603	9,648	11,181	11,385	11,062	11,241
Engineers	2,081	2,093	1,860	1,886	1,857	1,882	221	207	221	206
Mathematical and computer scientists	1,847	2,074	1,272	1,422	1,267	1,409	575	652	575	651
Natural scientists	578	566	404	376	404	376	174	190	173	190
Health diagnosing occupations	1,071	1,038	813	757	813	757	258	281	257	281
Health assessment and treating occupations	3,019	2,966	431	425	430	424	2,588	2,541	2,582	2,539
Teachers, college and university	978	961	563	541	558	539	414	420	407	414
Teachers, except college and university	5,277	5,353	1,325	1,317	1,301	1,294	3,952	4,036	3,898	3,962
Lawyers and judges	964	926	685	651	685	650	279	275	278	275
Other professional specialty occupations	5,068	5,134	2,348	2,352	2,289	2,316	2,721	2,782	2,670	2,723
Technical, sales, and administrative support	38,921	39,442	14,079	14,288	13,155	13,383	24,842	25,154	23,049	23,328
Technicians and related support	4,355	4,385	2,094	2,118	2,047	2,071	2,261	2,267	2,216	2,222
Health technologists and technicians	1,701	1,724	320	336	313	331	1,380	1,388	1,352	1,367
Engineering and science technicians	1,266	1,272	961	955	935	932	305	316	295	301
Technicians, except health, engineering, and science	1,388	1,389	813	827	798	808	576	562	570	554
Sales occupations	16,118	16,340	8,049	8,231	7,439	7,618	8,069	8,110	6,946	6,986
Supervisors and proprietors	4,896	4,937	2,891	2,948	2,868	2,918	2,005	1,989	1,975	1,960
Sales representatives, finance and business services	2,735	2,934	1,534	1,628	1,511	1,596	1,201	1,306	1,169	1,268
Sales representatives, commodities, except retail	1,526	1,581	1,118	1,146	1,112	1,139	408	435	397	429
Sales workers, retail and personal services	6,866	6,782	2,476	2,476	1,918	1,935	4,391	4,306	3,344	3,257
Sales-related occupations	95	107	31	33	30	31	64	74	61	72
Administrative support, including clerical	18,448	18,717	3,936	3,939	3,669	3,694	14,512	14,778	13,887	14,120
Supervisors	675	710	287	282	285	280	388	428	386	427
Computer equipment operators	356	323	153	166	143	157	203	157	200	151
Secretaries, stenographers, and typists	3,457	3,328	73	67	68	60	3,383	3,262	3,294	3,181
Financial records processing	2,181	2,269	200	186	190	182	1,982	2,083	1,952	2,051
Mail and message distributing	990	978	572	575	551	561	417	403	405	394
Other administrative support, including clerical	10,789	11,108	2,650	2,663	2,432	2,454	8,138	8,445	7,650	7,916
Service occupations	17,915	18,278	7,093	7,245	6,093	6,197	10,822	11,034	9,599	9,808
Private household	831	792	40	35	33	31	791	757	701	679
Protective service	2,440	2,399	1,980	1,944	1,921	1,896	460	455	415	414
Service, except private household and protective	14,644	15,087	5,074	5,265	4,138	4,270	9,570	9,822	8,482	8,715
Food service	6,091	6,327	2,576	2,675	1,860	1,924	3,516	3,651	2,772	2,888
Health service	2,521	2,557	273	269	259	251	2,249	2,288	2,149	2,190
Cleaning and building service	3,021	3,127	1,647	1,719	1,530	1,598	1,373	1,407	1,308	1,339
Personal service	3,011	3,077	578	601	489	497	2,433	2,476	2,254	2,299
Precision production, craft, and repair	14,593	14,882	13,286	13,532	12,974	13,202	1,307	1,351	1,270	1,316
Mechanics and repairers	4,868	4,875	4,633	4,625	4,532	4,531	235	250	227	247
Construction trades	5,801	6,120	5,654	5,960	5,486	5,776	148	160	140	151
Other precision production, craft, and repair	3,923	3,887	2,999	2,946	2,956	2,895	924	941	903	918
Operators, fabricators, and laborers	18,167	18,319	13,793	13,988	12,748	12,925	4,374	4,331	4,161	4,115
Machine operators, assemblers, and inspectors	7,386	7,319	4,637	4,622	4,459	4,453	2,749	2,697	2,672	2,616
Transportation and material moving occupations	5,516	5,557	4,968	5,003	4,845	4,870	548	554	535	536
Motor vehicle operators	4,202	4,222	3,718	3,736	3,619	3,634	484	486	472	470
Other transportation and material moving occupations	1,314	1,335	1,250	1,267	1,226	1,236	64	68	63	66
Handlers, equipment cleaners, helpers, and laborers	5,265	5,443	4,188	4,363	3,444	3,603	1,077	1,080	954	963
Construction laborers	920	1,015	882	977	797	883	38	38	35	38
Other handlers, equipment cleaners, helpers, and laborers	4,346	4,428	3,306	3,386	2,647	2,720	1,039	1,042	918	925
Farming, forestry, and fishing	3,426	3,399	2,749	2,698	2,506	2,472	676	701	631	645
Farm operators and managers	1,134	1,125	855	839	848	832	280	286	278	284
Other farming, forestry, and fishing occupations	2,292	2,274	1,895	1,859	1,658	1,641	397	415	352	361

NOTE: Beginning in January 2000, data reflect revised population controls used in the household survey.

SOURCE: "9. Employed Persons by Occupation, Sex, and Age," in "Average Annual Tables," *Employment and Earnings*, vol. 48, no. 1, January 2001

TABLE 4.3

Employed persons by occupation, race, and sex

(Percent distribution)

Occupation and race	Total 1999	Total 2000	Men 1999	Men 2000	Women 1999	Women 2000
TOTAL						
Total, 16 years and over (thousands)	133,488	135,208	71,446	72,293	62,042	62,915
Percent	100.0	100.0	100.0	100.0	100.0	100.0
Managerial and professional specialty	30.3	30.2	28.6	28.4	32.3	32.3
Executive, administrative, and managerial	14.7	14.6	15.0	15.0	14.2	14.2
Professional specialty	15.6	15.6	13.6	13.5	18.0	18.1
Technical, sales, and administrative support	29.2	29.2	19.7	19.8	40.0	40.0
Technicians and related support	3.3	3.2	2.9	2.9	3.6	3.6
Sales occupations	12.1	12.1	11.3	11.4	13.0	12.9
Administrative support, including clerical	13.8	13.8	5.5	5.4	23.4	23.5
Service occupations	13.4	13.5	9.9	10.0	17.4	17.5
Private household	.6	.6	.1	(1)	1.3	1.2
Protective service	1.8	1.8	2.8	2.7	.7	.7
Service, except private household and protective	11.0	11.2	7.1	7.3	15.4	15.6
Precision production, craft, and repair	10.9	11.0	18.6	18.7	2.1	2.1
Operators, fabricators, and laborers	13.6	13.5	19.3	19.3	7.0	6.9
Machine operators, assemblers, and inspectors	5.5	5.4	6.5	6.4	4.4	4.3
Transportation and material moving occupations	4.1	4.1	7.0	6.9	.9	.9
Handlers, equipment cleaners, helpers, and laborers	3.9	4.0	5.9	6.0	1.7	1.7
Farming, forestry, and fishing	2.6	2.5	3.8	3.7	1.1	1.1
White						
Total, 16 years and over (thousands)	112,235	113,475	61,139	61,696	51,096	51,780
Percent	100.0	100.0	100.0	100.0	100.0	100.0
Managerial and professional specialty	31.3	31.1	29.5	29.2	33.4	33.4
Executive, administrative, and managerial	15.4	15.3	15.9	15.8	14.7	14.8
Professional specialty	15.9	15.8	13.6	13.4	18.7	18.6
Technical, sales, and administrative support	29.2	29.2	19.7	19.7	40.6	40.5
Technicians and related support	3.2	3.2	2.9	2.9	3.6	3.5
Sales occupations	12.4	12.5	11.7	11.9	13.3	13.2
Administrative support, including clerical	13.5	13.5	5.1	5.0	23.6	23.7
Service occupations	12.2	12.4	8.9	9.1	16.2	16.4
Private household	.6	.6	(1)	(1)	1.3	1.2
Protective service	1.7	1.6	2.6	2.5	.6	.6
Service, except private household and protective	10.0	10.2	6.3	6.5	14.3	14.6
Precision production, craft, and repair	11.5	11.6	19.4	19.5	2.1	2.1
Operators, fabricators, and laborers	13.0	12.9	18.3	18.4	6.5	6.4
Machine operators, assemblers, and inspectors	5.2	5.1	6.2	6.1	4.0	3.9
Transportation and material moving occupations	4.0	3.9	6.6	6.6	.8	.8
Handlers, equipment cleaners, helpers, and laborers	3.8	3.9	5.5	5.8	1.7	1.6
Farming, forestry, and fishing	2.8	2.8	4.1	4.0	1.2	1.3
Black						
Total, 16 years and over (thousands)	15,056	15,334	7,027	7,180	8,029	8,154
Percent	100.0	100.0	100.0	100.0	100.0	100.0
Managerial and professional specialty	21.5	21.8	18.0	18.5	24.5	24.8
Executive, administrative, and managerial	9.9	9.9	8.5	8.9	11.1	10.7
Professional specialty	11.6	12.0	9.5	9.6	13.5	14.1
Technical, sales, and administrative support	28.9	29.3	18.4	18.8	38.2	38.6
Technicians and related support	3.1	3.2	2.7	2.6	3.5	3.7
Sales occupations	9.3	9.4	7.6	7.6	10.8	10.9
Administrative support, including clerical	16.5	16.8	8.1	8.5	23.9	24.0
Service occupations	21.8	21.5	17.4	17.4	25.6	25.2
Private household	.8	.8	.1	(1)	1.5	1.4
Protective service	3.2	3.1	4.9	4.7	1.8	1.6
Service, except private household and protective	17.7	17.7	12.4	12.6	22.4	22.1
Precision production, craft, and repair	7.8	7.8	14.3	14.2	2.1	2.1
Operators, fabricators, and laborers	18.9	18.5	29.8	29.0	9.4	9.1
Machine operators, assemblers, and inspectors	7.6	7.0	9.3	8.8	6.1	5.5
Transportation and material moving occupations	5.8	6.0	11.0	11.1	1.3	1.4
Handlers, equipment cleaners, helpers, and laborers	5.5	5.4	9.5	9.1	2.0	2.2
Farming, forestry, and fishing	1.1	1.1	2.2	2.1	.2	.2

[1] Less than 0.05 percent.

NOTE: Beginning in January 2000, data reflect revised population controls used in the household survey.

SOURCE: "10. Employed Persons by Occupation, Race, and Sex," in "Average Annual Tables," *Employment and Earnings,* vol. 48, no. 1, January 2001

In contrast, women accounted for only about 9 percent of those in precision production, craft, and repair occupations. Furthermore, within this broad category, women were concentrated in traditionally female occupations, comprising 93 percent of all dressmakers and 80 percent of all food batchmakers. Women accounted for about 24 percent of operators, fabricators, and laborers, but less than 1 percent of these women were construction laborers. More black women (9.1 percent of those employed) than white women (6.4 percent) pursued these types of occupations. Farming, forestry, and fishing occupations were about 21 percent female but accounted for only 1.3 percent of employed white women and 0.2 percent of employed black women. (See Table 4.3.)

Most occupations with a disproportionate number of women pay less than equivalent occupations that are male-dominated. Major male-female salary differences exist even when occupational classifications are almost identical. For example, female waitresses predominate in coffeeshops and inexpensive restaurants, whereas luxury restaurants may hire male waiters who earn considerably higher wages and tips. Likewise in sales, women tend to be concentrated in lower-paying retail positions, whereas most men work in better-paying wholesale positions.

NEW OCCUPATIONS FOR WOMEN

Although the majority of women continue to work in traditionally female occupations, the proportions of women in some traditional fields, such as waiting tables and cashiering, have fallen in the past quarter century. Over the same period, women have made impressive inroads into other occupations, even if the numbers remain small. According to the Bureau of Labor Statistics, women comprised 1 percent of engineers in 1975 but 10 percent in 2000. In 1975, 3 percent of police and detectives were women, compared to 14 percent in 2000. The proportion of female physicians increased from 13 percent to 28 percent over the same period. It is often easier for women to enter new or rapidly growing occupations. For example, the proportion of female financial managers has increased from 24 percent to 50 percent in the past 25 years. As the numbers of women enrolling in higher education increases, the proportions of women in skilled and professional occupations will continue to rise.

Construction

The construction industry boomed during the 1990s, resulting in a serious labor shortage. Department of Labor projections indicate that the industry must recruit and train 240,000 workers annually for the foreseeable future.

According to the National Association of Women in Construction, although women account for only 10 percent of construction jobs, the number of women in these occupations has increased 33 percent from 617,000 in 1993 to 913,000 in 2000. Although 46 percent of these women are in technical, sales, and administrative support, 32 percent are in managerial occupations and professional specialties. Another 14 percent are in precision production and crafts, and 6 percent are operators, fabricators, and laborers. The labor shortage is particularly severe in skilled construction trades. In 2000 women filled only 2.6 percent of these positions.

Law

According to the Bureau of Labor Statistics, only 7 percent of lawyers were women in 1975, compared to 30 percent in 2000. This increase in women lawyers has had a profound effect on American society. Women lawyers have championed the legal rights of women, and record numbers of women have entered government and politics at every level.

A large number of women entered law school in the 1970s. As they advance in their careers, record numbers of women are being appointed and elected judges. According to GenderGap.com, a Web site that tracks women in politics and government, the judicial branch of the U.S. government included 332 female federal judges in 2001, 21 percent of the total. This is up from 10 percent in 1997. Most of these female judges are white, although the number of women judges of other races is increasing. In 1981 Sandra Day O'Connor became the first woman ever appointed as one of the nine justices of the U.S. Supreme Court. She was joined on the court in 1993 by Justice Ruth Bader Ginsberg.

In contrast, women make up only 16 percent of law partners and only 14 percent of general counsels for *Fortune* 500 companies (the 500 largest U.S.-based corporations), according to *Women in Law: Making the Case*, a 2001 study by Catalyst, a New York–based nonprofit research and advocacy organization that works to advance women in business.

Wall Street

Just as large numbers of young women went into law in the 1970s, the 1980s saw a huge increase in the number of young people studying business and finance and earning MBAs. The proportion of female financial managers doubled after 1975. With the booming economy of the 1990s, record numbers of women became stockbrokers, stock analysts, and administrators, and many women now manage major stock portfolios. However, these gains have not come without legal battles.

MERRILL LYNCH. In 1997 eight female financial consultants filed a sexual discrimination lawsuit against their employer, the Merrill Lynch investment firm. Merrill Lynch settled in January 1998, agreeing to permit employees to bring future discrimination complaints to mediation, and then to federal court, rather than to binding arbitration panels, which were controlled by older, white male industry leaders. Under the terms of the settlement, financial consultants who worked at the firm between January 1994 and June 1998 could file discrimination claims. Most of the complaints filed were based on unfair economic practices: male employees were given most of the accounts, and female employees' earnings were below those of less-qualified male employees.

SMITH BARNEY. In November 1997 Smith Barney, Inc. (now Salomon Smith Barney), a large Wall Street securities firm, faced a class-action suit brought by 25 former and current female brokers. The firm agreed to a multimillion-dollar settlement after the women demonstrated that they had been routinely subjected to discrimination and sexual harassment by male co-workers. The settlement included an uncapped (no maximum amount) compensation fund to cover approximately 20,000 female brokers who had worked for the firm since May 1993. As part of the settlement, Smith Barney set up a diversity office to investigate discrimination complaints. The company also established hiring and promotion quotas for women and minorities and will pay a $100,000 penalty to anyone who is improperly denied a promotion.

As part of the settlement, Smith Barney funded Catalyst to undertake an independent survey of 838 men and women employed at seven leading securities firms (*Women in Financial Services: The Word on the Street*, 2001). More than half (65 percent) of the women reported that they had to work harder than men for the same rewards. Only 13 percent of the male respondents believed that women had to work harder. A majority of the women (51 percent), but only 8 percent of the men, believed that women were paid less for the same work at their firms. Overall, the survey results indicate that many more men than women believe that women are treated fairly and have ample opportunities for advancement.

Women in the Corporate World

In 1978 women made up only 26 percent of executives, managers, and administrators. In 2000 women made up 45 percent (8.9 million) of those employed in these occupations. (See Table 4.2.) They made up 50 percent of managers and professional specialists in 2000. Women are more likely to be managers and executives in industries with more female employees at lower levels, such as insurance, banking, and retail trade. Women also appear to advance more rapidly in fast-growing industries such as business services and direct marketing, and in industries such as telecommunications that are undergoing changes such as deregulation and restructuring. Women managers and executives are much less common in the communications, transportation, and utilities industries. According to Catalyst, 86 percent of women in management and administrative positions in the private sector are white.

Working Mother's 100 Best Companies

Each year, *Working Mother* magazine publishes a list of the 100 best companies for working mothers. In addition to rating companies on issues such as the percentage of women employees, distribution of benefits, flexible hours, child care, parental leave, and other work/life issues, the companies are rated on their records for advancing women up the corporate ladder. In October 2001 the magazine named Booz Allen & Hamilton, a Washington, D.C.–area strategy and technology consulting firm, as number one for advancing women. At Merck & Company, a New Jersey pharmaceutical firm that was in the top 100, 40 percent of the senior executives and managers were women, including 2 women in the top 14 executive posts. *Working Mother's* top 10 companies of 2001 included:

- Bristol-Myers Squibb, a New York–based pharmaceutical company

- Citigroup, a New York financial services company

- Fannie Mae, a Washington, D.C., mortgage company

- IBM Corporation, a New York–based technology conglomerate

- Marriot International, a Washington, D.C.–based hotel chain

- Morgan Stanley, a New York investment firm

- PricewaterhouseCoopers, a New York–based global consulting firm

- Procter & Gamble, an Ohio-based food, drug, and home products company

- Prudential, a New Jersey insurance, real estate, and investment firm

- Texas Instruments, a Texas-based semiconductor company

This annual survey by *Working Mother* has stimulated important changes in the work/life status and advancement of corporate women.

THE FORTUNE 500. The *2000 Catalyst Census of Women Corporate Officers and Top Earners of the Fortune 500* found that although women comprised about half of the managerial and professional positions in *Fortune* 500 companies, they made up only 12.5 percent of corporate officers (1,622 out of 12,945). However, this was up from 11.9 percent in 1999 and 8.7 percent in 1995. Corporate line officers were up only 2 percent from 1997, to 7.3 percent. These are individuals with profit-or-loss or direct client responsibilities. Ninety of the *Fortune* 500 companies had no women corporate officers. However, Catalyst projects that by the year 2020, 27.4 percent of the corporate officers in the *Fortune* 500 will be female.

Women represented 4.1 percent (93 out of 2,255) of the top earners in *Fortune* 500 companies in 2000, up from 3.3 percent in 1999. Only 29 companies had female top earners in 1995, compared to 83 companies in 2000. Ten companies had two top women earners in 2000, up from three companies in 1995.

Women comprised 11.7 percent of *Fortune* 500 board directors in 2000, up only 2.2 percent from 1995. Out of 2,488 such positions, 154 women (6.2 percent) held top titles such as chairman, CEO (chief executive officer), vice chairman, or president. This was up 5.1 percent over 1999. Catalyst reports that in 2001 there were five women CEOs of *Fortune* 500 companies.

THE "GLASS CEILING". Although more women and minorities have professional occupations than ever before, they are usually confined to the lower levels of management. Over a decade ago *The Wall Street Journal*'s "Corporate Woman" column dubbed this invisible barrier the "glass ceiling." The Department of Labor, in *A Report on the Glass Ceiling Initiative* (Washington, D.C., 1991), defined the glass ceiling as "artificial barriers based on attitudinal or organizational bias that prevent qualified individuals from advancing upward in their organization into management level positions."

As a result of the report, the Civil Rights Act of 1991 established the Glass Ceiling Commission. In *Good for Business: Making Full Use of the Nation's Human Capital* (Washington, D.C., 1995), the commission found three types of artificial barriers to the advancement of women and minorities in the private sector:

- Societal barriers that may be outside the direct control of business. These include what the commission calls the supply barrier, related to educational opportunity and attainment, and the difference barrier, characterized by conscious and unconscious stereotyping, prejudice, and bias related to gender, race, and/or ethnicity.

- Internal structure barriers that are within the direct control of business. Some of these include corporate climates that alienate and isolate women and minorities; lack of mentoring, management training, and opportunities for career development; and biased rating and testing systems.

- Government barriers. These include a lack of adequate, consistent monitoring and law enforcement and inadequate reporting and dissemination of information about the glass ceiling.

The commission found that corporate executives and women have very different perceptions of the glass ceiling and how much progress has been made. The majority of CEOs in the survey believed that the glass ceiling was no longer a problem for women, regardless of race. Without exception they expressed strong support for women's advancement to senior management. Most believed that white and minority women had reached pay equity, although they recognized that the disparity between men's and women's earnings had not been resolved.

The report cited a number of studies suggesting "that the glass ceiling exists because of the perception of many White males that as a group they are losing—losing the corporate game, losing control, and losing opportunity." In essence the report found that many white males at the middle- and upper-middle levels of management saw the rise of minorities and women as a direct threat to their own chances for advancement.

A survey of senior women executives found that a number of stereotypes and preconceptions were applied to women regardless of race or ethnicity. Men tended to view women as not wanting to work, not being as committed as men, not tough enough, unwilling or unable to work long or unusual hours, unwilling to relocate, unwilling or unable to make decisions, too emotional, not sufficiently aggressive, too aggressive, too passive, and lacking quantitative skills. On the other hand, women also were perceived by male managers to be good with people, warm and nurturing, creative, hardworking, loyal, and good team players.

In *A Solid Investment: Making Full Use of the Nation's Human Capital* (Washington, D.C., 1995), the Glass Ceiling Commission offered several recommendations for business:

- Demonstrate commitment to change from the highest level (CEOs)

- Include diversity in strategic business plans

- Use affirmative action as a tool

- Select, promote, and train qualified workers

- Prepare minorities and women for senior positions in the corporate ranks

- Initiate family-friendly policies

The report stated that the government should lead by example and make equal opportunity a reality, strengthen enforcement of antidiscrimination laws, improve data collection, and increase disclosure of diversity data.

THE GLASS CEILING TODAY. In the Catalyst 2001 Wall Street survey, 70 percent of the women believed that lack of mentoring opportunities was an obstacle to women's advancement. Almost as many women believed that their exclusion from informal networks and lack of female role models were obstacles. In other words, the "old boy network" was as strong as ever. Family and personal responsibilities were seen as obstacles by 69 percent of the women respondents. The majority of women also believed that they suffered from sexual stereotyping and

TABLE 4.4

Scientists and engineers in the labor force, by occupation, race/ethnicity, and sex, 1997

Occupation	Total		White		Asian/Pacific Islander		Black		Hispanic		American Indian/ Alaskan Native	
	Women	Men	Women	Men	Women	Men	Women	Men	Women	Men	Women	Men
Total scientists and engineers	780,300	2,641,900	624,000	2,208,200	83,800	273,100	41,700	73,600	27,600	78,600	2,800	7,300
Computer/mathematical scientists	287,500	766,600	222,800	627,700	37,800	90,700	17,800	27,600	8,200	18,700	600	1,200
Computer scientists	250,500	695,900	192,600	569,600	35,000	83,000	15,500	25,100	6,900	17,200	500	1,000
Mathematical scientists	12,100	23,200	10,000	19,100	1,000	2,100	500	1,200	300	300	—	100
Postsecondary computer/ mathematics teachers	24,900	47,400	20,100	39,000	1,900	5,600	1,800	1,300	1,000	1,300	100	100
Life and related scientists	119,200	209,900	97,400	180,200	14,500	19,100	3,400	4,800	3,600	4,800	400	1,000
Agricultural/food scientists	11,000	32,800	10,000	29,000	500	2,100	100	1,000	300	600	—	—
Biological scientists	78,500	108,600	61,300	88,800	12,400	13,500	2,300	2,800	2,200	2,800	300	700
Environmental scientists	3,200	17,000	3,100	16,400	—	100	—	100	100	300	—	200
Postsecondary life science teachers	26,500	51,600	23,000	46,000	1,600	3,500	900	900	900	1,100	—	100
Physical and related scientists	63,400	226,000	48,500	195,000	8,900	19,500	3,300	5,200	2,400	5,500	200	800
Chemists	32,600	89,200	22,700	73,200	6,600	10,000	2,000	3,600	1,100	2,300	—	100
Earth/geology/oceanographers	11,200	58,600	9,700	53,300	400	3,200	600	400	400	1,500	100	200
Physicists and astronomers	3,100	28,700	2,500	24,500	400	3,300	100	300	—	600	—	100
Other physical scientists	5,600	11,700	5,100	10,800	100	500	200	—	200	200	—	200
Postsecondary physical science teachers	10,800	37,800	8,500	33,100	1,300	2,600	300	800	600	900	100	200
Social and related scientists	183,500	169,000	158,100	147,500	6,100	7,200	9,400	7,500	8,600	5,900	1,200	800
Economists	15,600	30,100	12,800	25,900	1,600	2,400	400	1,100	1,000	700	—	—
Political scientists	115,500	67,800	102,100	59,900	2,100	800	5,400	3,900	5,200	2,700	700	400
Psychologists	8,800	7,300	7,500	6,300	300	200	600	500	300	400	100	—
Sociologists/anthropologists	3,800	5,500	3,300	5,100	200	200	100	—	300	200	—	—
Other social scientists	7,400	4,700	6,100	4,400	400	100	500	100	200	—	100	100
Postsecondary social science teachers	32,300	53,600	26,400	45,900	1,700	3,600	2,400	1,900	1,600	1,900	200	300
Engineers	126,800	1,270,300	97,200	1,057,800	16,400	136,500	7,800	28,500	4,900	43,600	400	3,500
Aerospace engineers	5,700	68,000	4,300	58,100	700	5,700	400	1,900	200	1,700	—	500
Chemical engineers	10,600	66,800	7,800	54,800	1,800	8,000	700	1,100	300	2,800	—	100
Civil engineers	19,600	190,400	15,100	155,800	2,800	22,700	600	3,300	900	8,100	100	400
Electrical engineers	24,600	346,400	16,600	276,300	5,300	46,900	1,900	9,000	700	13,300	100	900
Industrial engineers	8,900	72,400	7,300	60,500	400	5,500	500	3,300	700	2,800	—	400
Mechanical engineers	16,600	257,900	13,300	220,700	1,700	24,500	1,100	5,000	400	6,700	—	900
Other engineers	37,600	237,300	30,200	208,200	3,300	17,700	2,400	3,900	1,600	7,000	100	400
Postsecondary engineering teachers	3,200	31,100	2,600	23,400	400	5,400	100	1,000	100	1,100	—	—

KEY: — = Fewer than 50 estimated.
NOTE: Figures are rounded to nearest hundred. Details may not add to total because of rounding. Total includes "other" race/ethnicity not shown separately. The term "scientists and engineers" includes all persons who have ever received a bachelor's degree or higher in a science or engineering field, plus persons holding a non-science and -engineering bachelor's or higher degree who were employed in a science or engineering occupation.

SOURCE: "Appendix table 5-3. Scientists and Engineers in the U. S. Labor Force, by Occupation, Race/Ethnicity, and Sex: 1997," in *Women, Minorities, and Persons With Disabilities in Science and Engineering: 2000,* National Science Foundation, Arlington, VA, 2000

were excluded from choice assignments. In the Catalyst 2001 report *Women in Law*, the majority of female lawyers cited the same obstacles to advancement. In a 1999 study Catalyst reported that for women of color, the glass ceiling has become a concrete ceiling.

Science, Engineering, and Technology

Although the glass ceiling concept was originally applied to women in the corporate world, in recent years the metaphor has been used to describe the situation of women in science and engineering professions and in academia in general. The proportion of women earning degrees in science and engineering has increased significantly in recent years. However, women accounted for only 23 percent of the science and engineering labor force in 1997, approximately the same percentage as in 1993.

THE NATIONAL SCIENCE FOUNDATION REPORT. Every two years, the National Science Foundation (NSF) publishes a congressionally mandated report on the status of women and minorities in science and engineering. The latest report, *Women, Minorities, and Persons with Disabilities in Science and Engineering: 2000*, found that 80 percent of women in the science and engineering labor force were white and 11 percent were Asian/Pacific Islander, but only 5 percent were black, 4 percent Hispanic, and 0.4 percent American Indian/Alaskan Native. (See Table 4.4.) Although 32 percent of these women were computer scientists, women accounted for only 26 percent of all computer scientists, and the percentage of women who were computer/mathematical scientists decreased from 31 to 27 percent between 1993 and 1997. Women accounted for 52 percent of the workforce in social and related sciences in 1997, and 63 percent of these women

FIGURE 4.1

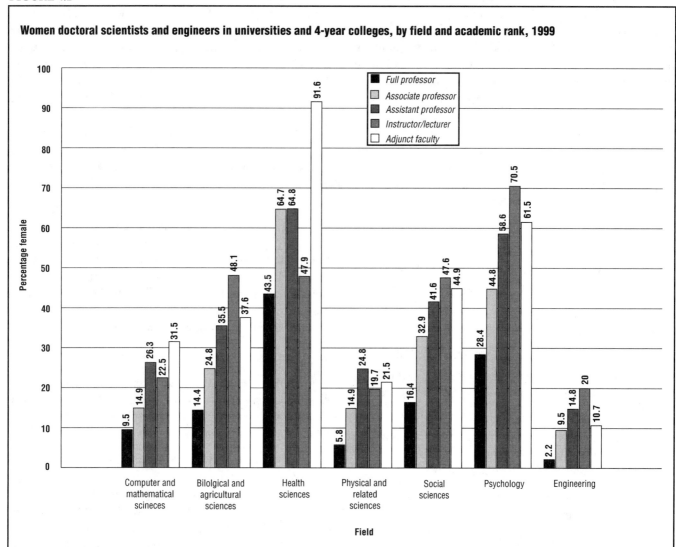

Women doctoral scientists and engineers in universities and 4-year colleges, by field and academic rank, 1999

SOURCE: Megan Pratt, "Women as a percentage of employed doctoral scientists and engineers in universities and 4-year colleges, by broad field of doctorate and academic rank: 1999," in *Women in Science Statistics*, Association for Women in Science, Washington, DC, n.d. [Online] http://www.awis.org/statistics/statistics.html [accessed October, 2001]

were political scientists. Women accounted for 36 percent of life scientists, up from 34 percent in 1993. Only 9 percent of women were engineers in 1997.

About 13 percent of both men and women in the science and engineering labor force hold doctorates. Figure 4.1 illustrates the positions of female doctoral scientists and engineers employed by universities and four-year colleges in 1999. In every field a high proportion of women were adjunct faculty, the lowest faculty position. In the health sciences women made up 91.6 percent of adjunct faculty; however, they also accounted for 43.5 percent of full professors, the highest academic rank. In engineering women accounted for only 2.2 percent of the full professors. Women scientists and engineers were less likely to be tenured than their male counterparts (35 versus 60 percent in four-year colleges and universities). Minority women were less likely than white women to be full pro-

fessors or tenured. Furthermore, many women scientists were employed by smaller four-year and two-year colleges, where pay scales and opportunities for professional advancement are lower than at large research universities.

REPORT OF THE CONGRESSIONAL COMMISSION ON THE ADVANCEMENT OF WOMEN AND MINORITIES IN SCIENCE, ENGINEERING AND TECHNOLOGY DEVELOPMENT. According to the Report of the Congressional Commission on the Advancement of Women and Minorities in Science, Engineering and Technology Development (CAWMSET), *Land of Plenty: Diversity as America's Competitive Edge in Science, Engineering and Technology* (September 2000), women made up only 19 percent of the science, engineering, and technology (SET) workforce employed in industry in 1997. However, industry employed 62 percent of the female SET workforce. About one-quarter (23 percent) of women worked in an educational institution, and women made up 30 percent of the total SET workforce in academia. The remaining women in the SET workforce were employed by local, state, and federal governments. The positions held by minority women in the SET workforce were similar to those held by white women, although Asian women were more likely to be involved in research and development than in management and administration. Unemployment rates were far higher for women than for men in SET occupations. Many more women than men who were not working (38 percent versus 2 percent) cited family responsibilities as the reason. Men who were not working were much more likely to be retired.

The commission made a number of recommendations for the advancement of women in the SET workforce:

- Implement high standards in math and science curricula, teacher qualifications, and technology in schools

- Intervene to promote SET careers among women, underrepresented minorities, and disabled students in high schools, community colleges, and universities

- Significantly increase federal and state expenditures to support underrepresented groups in SET higher education

- Make public and private SET employers accountable for the career development and advancement of women and underrepresented minorities

- Establish a representative body to transform the image of SET professionals into one that is positive and inclusive of women, minorities, and those with disabilities

- Establish a collaborative body to continue the work of the commission

AAAS SURVEY OF LIFE SCIENTISTS. In the summer of 2001 the American Association for the Advancement of Science (AAAS) surveyed 19,000 members who worked in the life sciences. Of the respondents, 93 percent had Ph.D.'s, MDs, or both. Women made up 27 percent of the respondents and, on average, were younger than the male respondents. Only 72 percent of the female scientists were married, compared to 88 percent of the male scientists, and many of the women were married to scientists. The survey found that although industry paid better than academia, men made one-third more money than women across the board. According to the report, "women are paid less for similar work even when type of employer is held constant." The women in the survey felt that they had less job security than the men and that they got less recognition than men as exemplified by prestige, promotion, and salaries. Most of the married women scientists said that their careers had been constrained by the career needs of their husbands. In contrast, only 7 percent of the men said that their careers had been affected by their wives' career decisions.

OBSTACLES TO ADVANCEMENT. According to the NSF, some but not all of the disparities between men and women scientists and engineers are the result of age differences. The science and engineering labor force is made up of individuals who have earned their degrees since the 1940s, long before large numbers of women began enrolling in higher education. Thus, women scientists and engineers tend to be younger than their male counterparts. For example, in 1997, 35 percent of women scientists and engineers were younger than 35, compared to 27 percent of the men. Therefore, women should be moving up the SET pipeline.

However, SET careers, both in industry and academia, are known to be very fast-paced and may involve long, stressful hours. For women who bear the brunt of family and household responsibilities, the pace can be overwhelming. Both companies and universities are looking for new ways to improve the work/life situation for women and to enable them to advance in their careers without sacrificing promotions or academic tenure.

Women in Academia

Women account for 44 percent of college and university teachers. (See Table 4.2.) Many of the issues confronting women scientists and engineers apply to women in academia in general.

In 1994 Nancy H. Hopkins, a professor of biology at the Massachusetts Institute of Technology (MIT), had her request for more laboratory space turned down. She took out her tape measure and discovered that, on average, the male faculty in her department had 50 percent more lab space than the women. That summer Hopkins joined with two other tenured women in the MIT School of Science to conduct an informal poll of female faculty. This led in the following year to the establishment of a committee to analyze the status of women in the School of Science. The committee report, which was printed in 1999 and distributed over the World Wide Web, engendered a great deal of publicity, including front-page stories in major newspapers, as well as controversy. The report found that although junior women faculty worried that work-family conflicts would negatively affect their careers, it was the older, tenured women faculty who were extremely dissatisfied. They felt marginalized in their departments and discriminated against in salaries, laboratory space, resources, and awards, despite career accomplishments that were equal to those of the men. In an almost unprecedented step, MIT admitted discrimination against women and developed a five-year plan for improving the situation. More women faculty were hired and promoted, and the number of tenured women faculty in the School of Science increased by 40 percent.

Following the MIT report, a number of other universities began analyzing the status of their female faculty, with

TABLE 4.5

Active duty servicewomen by branch of service, rank, race, and Hispanic origin, May 31, 1999

Service and Rank[1]	Number of Women	Women as a Percentage of Total Personnel	Percent Distribution of Women[2]			
			White	Black	Hispanic	Other
Total DOD forces[3]						
Enlisted	160,383	14.1	50.8	34.9	7.9	6.4
Officers	30,425	13.9	75.1	14.7	3.5	6.7
Army						
Enlisted	58,119	15.0	38.7	47.0	7.2	7.1
Officers	10,219	13.2	67.3	21.8	4.1	6.8
Navy						
Enlisted	39,572	12.8	52.0	30.9	10.2	6.9
Officers	7,711	14.3	78.9	10.3	4.7	6.1
Marine Corps						
Enlisted	9,060	5.9	55.8	23.5	14.4	6.2
Officers	866	4.8	77.1	12.5	5.0	5.4
Air Force						
Enlisted	53,632	18.7	62.3	26.6	5.7	5.3
Officers	11,629	16.7	79.3	11.6	2.0	7.1
Coast Guard						
Enlisted	2,726	10.0	73.4	12.8	7.5	6.3
Officers	685	9.8	81.3	7.3	4.5	6.9

[1]Officers include warrant officers.
[2]Percentages may not total 100.0 due to rounding.
[3]"Defense Department (DOD) forces do not include Coast Guard.

SOURCE: Lory Manning and Vanessa R. Wright, "Table 7-1: Active Duty Servicewomen by Branch of Service, Rank, Race, and Hispanic origin, May 31, 1999," in *Women in the Military: Where They Stand,* 3rd edition, Women's Research and Education Institute, Washington, DC, 2000

FIGURE 4.2

Active duty servicewomen in the department of defense services by officer/enlisted status, 1972–99

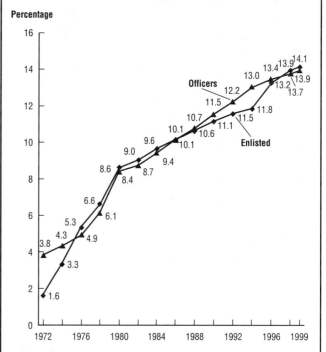

Note: Does not include the Coast Guard, which is part of the Department of Transportation.

SOURCE: Lory Manning and Vanessa R. Wright, "Figure 7-1: Active Duty Servicewomen in the Department of Defense Services by Officer/Enlisted Status, 1972–1999 (in percentages)," in *Women in the Military: Where They Stand,* 3rd Edition, Women's Research and Education Institute, Washington, DC, 2000

findings similar to those at MIT. Early in 2001 a class-action suit representing as many as 2,000 women was filed against the University of Washington in Seattle. The suit charged broad gender inequalities in pay, promotion, teaching loads, and access to grants and research funds.

Women in the Military

In 1973, when the male military draft was replaced by an all-volunteer force, the number of women joining the military began increasing. As of May 1999, 194,219 women were serving in the armed services, about 14 percent of the total military. Although the largest number of women was serving in the army, the air force had the highest percentage of women, at 18.7 percent of enlisted personnel and 16.7 percent of officers. The Marine Corps had the lowest percentage of women at 5.9 percent of enlistees and 4.8 percent of officers. (See Table 4.5.) Between 1972 and 1999 the percentage of enlisted women in the Department of Defense (DOD) services increased eightfold, and the percentage of female officers nearly tripled. (See Figure 4.2.) The Coast Guard is under the jurisdiction of the Department of Transportation rather than the DOD.

About 55 percent of military women in 1999 were white, accounting for 50.8 percent of female enlisted personnel and 75.1 percent of female officers. (See Table 4.5.) Black women made up almost half of the women enlisted in the army, Hispanic women accounted for one in seven of enlisted women in the Marine Corps, and white women accounted for almost three-quarters of the women in the Coast Guard.

MILITARY OCCUPATIONS. Among enlisted women in 1999, 33 percent were in support and administration and 17 percent were in health-care positions. Technical specialties accounted for 3 percent of women, and 10 percent were in communications and intelligence, compared to 9 percent of enlisted men. Only 4 percent of enlisted women were in infantry, gun crew, and seamanship. Although major changes to combat restriction laws in the 1990s opened up new occupations and positions to women, most of the women on active duty in 1999 had enlisted prior to these changes.

Although about 16 percent of both women and men in the DOD services were officers in 1999, there were significant occupational differences between the genders. (See Figure 4.3.) Whereas 43.6 percent of the women officers were in the health-care field, compared to 13.1 percent of male officers, 41.9 percent of men were in tactical

FIGURE 4.3

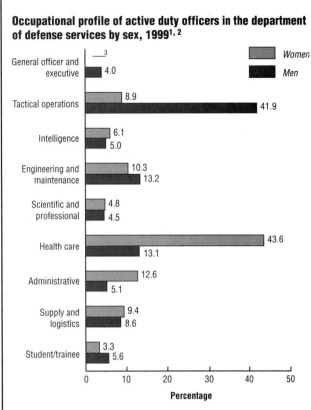

Occupational profile of active duty officers in the department of defense services by sex, 1999[1, 2]

Note: Chart showing Women (light gray) and Men (dark/black) percentages by occupation:

- General officer and executive: Women [3], Men 4.0
- Tactical operations: Women 8.9, Men 41.9
- Intelligence: Women 6.1, Men 5.0
- Engineering and maintenance: Women 10.3, Men 13.2
- Scientific and professional: Women 4.8, Men 4.5
- Health care: Women 43.6, Men 13.1
- Administrative: Women 12.6, Men 5.1
- Supply and logistics: Women 9.4, Men 8.6
- Student/trainee: Women 3.3, Men 5.6

X-axis: Percentage (0, 10, 20, 30, 40, 50)

[1]Does not include the Coast Guard, which is part of the Department of Transportation.
[2]Percentages may not total 100.0 due to rounding.
[3]Less than one-tenth of one percent.

Note: The changes on the combat restriction laws in the early-to-mid 90's opened air and sea combat positions to women officers. However, infantry, armor, most field artillery and special forces positions remain closed to them. Thus women in the Navy and Air Force can now enter most of their services' key warfighting occupations whereas women in the Army and Marine Corps can enter only into aviation combat positions.

SOURCE: "Figure 7-5. Occupational Profile of Active Duty Officers in the Department of Defense Services by Sex, 1999 (percent distributions)," in *The American Woman 2001–2002: Getting to the Top*, 3rd Edition, Women's Research and Education Institute, Washington, DC, 2000

---

operations, compared to 8.9 percent of women officers. The changes in combat restriction laws in the 1990s opened up air and sea combat positions to women officers. Women are still barred from infantry, armor, and most field artillery and Special Forces positions.

In 1972 less than 1 percent of enlisted women were in senior pay grades. By 1999 more than 10 percent of enlisted women in the army and the air force were in senior pay grades. Only about 5 percent of enlisted Marine Corps women were in senior pay grades. Likewise in 1972, 1 percent or less of female officers were in a colonel/navy captain pay grade. By 1999 about 9 percent of female navy officers were at a captain's pay grade; however, only about 2 percent of Marine Corps officers had reached that pay grade.

The number of female army colonels, navy captains, and air force colonels is rising as women who joined the military in the last 20 years gain seniority. In addition, growing proportions of junior women officers are entering mainstream combat occupations. These include pilots, navigators, and aircrews in all of the services, and surface warfare in the navy. Successful careers in these positions can lead to top leadership positions in the armed forces.

WOMEN-OWNED BUSINESSES

Women entrepreneurs are significantly affecting the American economy. Between 1987 and 1999 the number of companies owned by women more than doubled. (See Table 4.6.) Women owned 9.1 million U.S. businesses in 1999, 38 percent of the total. More than 27.5 million people were employed by these businesses, over four times the number in 1987. Sales from women-owned businesses amounted to almost $3.7 trillion in 1999, more than a fivefold increase since 1987.

One-half of all women-owned businesses were in service industries in 1999. Another 18 percent were in retail trade, and 10 percent were in finance, insurance, and real estate. However, the largest increases in the number of women-owned businesses between 1992 and 1999 were in nontraditional fields. The number of agriculture, construction, manufacturing, wholesale trade, and transportation, communications, and public utilities businesses all increased by 50 percent or more.

According to the National Foundation for Women Business Owners (NFWBO), the most important reason that women start businesses is to improve the situation for themselves and their families. Other important reasons include working for oneself rather than an employer and fulfilling a long-standing dream.

Businesses Owned by Women of Color

According to a 1998 report, *Women Business Owners of Color: Challenges and Accomplishments*, prepared by the NFWBO, underwritten by AT&T, and sponsored by IBM, women of color own one out of eight women-owned businesses in the United States. The top 10 metropolitan areas for minority women-owned firms, based on the number of firms, employment, and sales, were Los Angeles, Orange County, San Francisco, and Oakland in California, and Miami, New York, Chicago, Houston, Washington, D.C., and Honolulu.

Financing

Female business owners are applying for more bank credit and using more credit for business expansion than ever before. A 1998 study, *Capital, Credit, and Financing: An Update Comparing Women and Men Business Owners' Sources and Uses of Capital*, was prepared by the NFWBO, underwritten by Wells Fargo Bank, and

TABLE 4.6

Firms owned by women, 1987–99

	1987[1]	1992[2]	1996[3]	1999[4]	% Change, 1992–99
Total U.S.					
Number of firms	4,476,616	6,406,715	7,951,000	9,108,900	42.2
Employment	6,559,213	13,217,066	18,543,000	27,523,200	108.2
Sales ($000)	$681,440,025	$1,574,090,448	$2,288,211,000	$3,655,283,600	132.2
Industry					
Agriculture					
Number of firms	51,471	88,532	118,000	140,400	58.6
Employment	37,871	106,671	162,000	287,100	169.1
Sales ($000)	$3,142,675	$8,109,567	$12,083,000	$20,477,400	152.5
Mining					
Number of firms	29,002	40,841	50,000	57,400	40.6
Employment	26,293	67,012	100,000	167,700	150.2
Sales ($000)	$3,427,939	$12,240,629	$19,291,000	$38,809,300	217.1
Construction					
Number of firms	119,687	233,128	324,000	391,900	68.1
Employment	362,138	746,591	1,054,000	1,584,100	112.2
Sales ($000)	$39,805,405	$90,147,198	$130,421,000	$206,142,300	128.7
Manufacturing					
Number of firms	118,332	191,863	251,000	294,800	53.7
Employment	1,044,755	2,306,397	3,316,000	5,169,500	162.9
Sales ($000)	$124,554,898	$365,173,381	$557,668,000	$1,011,287,500	176.9
TCPU[5]					
Number of firms	94,020	166,926	225,000	269,000	61.1
Employment	345,948	943,274	1,421,000	2,480,000	162.9
Sales ($000)	$42,484,415	$100,312,077	$146,574,000	$236,907,200	136.2
Wholesale Trade					
Number of firms	113,756	213,059	293,000	352,100	65.3
Employment	513,635	1,055,021	1,488,000	2,231,800	111.5
Sales ($000)	$104,298,424	$304,204,870	$464,130,000	$839,361,000	175.9
Retail Trade					
Number of firms	882,425	1,207,966	1,468,000	1,663,700	37.7
Employment	1,756,319	2,979,122	3,957,000	5,347,900	79.5
Sales ($000)	$149,651,297	$273,053,643	$371,776,000	$522,860,800	91.5
FIRE[6]					
Number of firms	484,615	667,932	815,000	924,600	38.4
Employment	355,474	962,150	1,447,000	2,516,l00	161.5
Sales ($000)	$71,298,670	$206,891,735	$315,366,000	$568,782,900	174.9
Services					
Number of firms	2,377,162	3,308,965	4,054,000	4,613,500	39.4
Employment	1,881,266	3,972,773	5,646,000	8,594,900	116.3
Sales ($000)	$95,362,262	$203,983,463	$290,880,000	$445,878,200	118.6

[1]Estimate of 1987 totals including C corporations using 1992 ratios.
[2]Bureau of the Census figure.
[3]NFWBO estimate using 1987–1992 Census growth rates.
[4]NFWBO estimate using modeling of 1987–1996 data.
[5]Transportation, communications, public utilities.
[6]Finance, insurance, real estate.

SOURCE: "Women-Owned Firms in the United States: 1987-1999," Bureau of the Census and the Center for Women's Business Research, Washington, DC, 1999

supported by AT&T Credit Corporation. The survey found that the share of women-owned companies that applied for financing increased from 27 percent in 1996 to 33 percent in 1998. The share of women-owned businesses with bank credit increased from 46 percent in 1996 to 52 percent in 1998.

However, female entrepreneurs generally have lower credit available to them than male business owners. Only 34 percent of women-owned businesses with bank credit have $50,000 or more available to them, compared to 58 percent of male-owned businesses. Approximately 10 percent of women business owners have $100,000 to $499,999 in bank credit, compared to 20 percent of male entrepreneurs. Only 7 percent of women business owners have $500,000 or more in bank credit, compared to 16 percent of men.

Home-Based Businesses

Of the 3.5 million home-based women-owned businesses in the United States, 63 percent have employees other than the owner. These provide full- or part-time employment for approximately 14 million people, about 60 percent of whom are employed part-time or are contract employees. Home-based businesses are generally newer

FIGURE 4.4

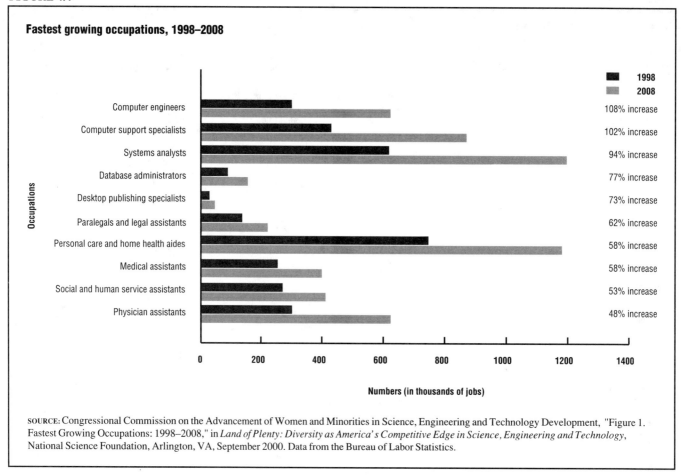

Fastest growing occupations, 1998–2008

SOURCE: Congressional Commission on the Advancement of Women and Minorities in Science, Engineering and Technology Development, "Figure 1. Fastest Growing Occupations: 1998–2008," in *Land of Plenty: Diversity as America's Competitive Edge in Science, Engineering and Technology*, National Science Foundation, Arlington, VA, September 2000. Data from the Bureau of Labor Statistics.

and smaller than other women-owned businesses. Women-owned home-based businesses are more likely to finance growth using private sources and personal credit rather than business earnings. They also take out fewer business loans, lease less equipment, and use less vendor credit.

WOMEN'S OCCUPATIONS IN THE FUTURE

Until the 1970s most women had occupations that were very different from those of most men. A number of factors have been responsible for the movement of women into previously male-dominated occupations:

- The influence of the feminist movement beginning in the 1960s

- Civil rights laws prohibiting discrimination based on sex

- Increased female enrollment in higher education

- Increased women's labor force participation

- Decreased gender stereotyping in education and employment

Since the 1970s, women have been moving out of blue-collar, service, and administrative support jobs and into professional and managerial positions. However, traditional ideas of "women's work" and "men's work" are still preva-

lent in American society: For example, men are truck drivers and women are child caregivers. Although the stereotypes of women's occupations are beginning to disappear, men in traditional female roles, such as kindergarten teachers, secretaries, or manicurists, are still considered unusual.

Obstacles Remain

Despite equal opportunity laws and regulations and affirmative action policies, various personnel practices, including the wording of job descriptions and the structure of the corporate ladder, can keep women from entering male-dominated occupations. Women starting out in new fields in recent years lack the seniority necessary for advancing in their careers. Women entering male-dominated occupations may face suspicion, distrust, or outright hostility. Off-color comments or jokes, gossip, outright sexual harassment, or the refusal of help by co-workers may make the workplace intolerable for women.

Women consistently identify mentoring as a crucial factor for success. Since the majority of senior positions are occupied by men, it may be difficult for a female to find a mentor. As more women achieve higher-echelon jobs, more mentors will be available for younger women. Isolation and exclusion from an old-boy network also are cited as important obstacles for women moving into new occupations. As more women make their way up the pipeline to more influential positions, this too may begin to change.

Other obstacles may be more difficult to eradicate. Many careers, particularly in science, technology, and the corporate world, may require relocating numerous times. This can be very difficult for married women, particularly if they have children and if their husbands are also pursuing careers.

Growing Occupations

As can be seen in Figure 4.4, the five fastest-growing occupations between 1998 and 2008 are in the computer science and information technology fields. A critical labor shortage in these fields might be avoided if more women enter these occupations. It remains to be seen whether more women will move into these male-dominated fields, since the next five fastest-growing occupations are more traditionally female service jobs.

CHAPTER 5
MONEY, INCOME, AND POVERTY

Women earn less money than men, have fewer assets, and are far more likely to live in poverty. According the Center on Budget and Policy Priorities (CBPP), a Washington, D.C.–based nonpartisan research organization and policy institute, income disparities between high-, middle-, and low-income families are the highest they have been since before World War II. In 2000 the median money income for women 45 to 54 years of age (the highest-income age group) was $24,196, up 3.6 percent from 1999. (See Table 5.1.) Median income means that one-half of the women had more income than this and one-half had less. In addition to earnings from employment, money income may include such sources as child support payments, alimony, interest, dividends, capital gains, and other investment income. For men in this age group, the median income in 2000 was $41,072, down 2.9 percent from 1999 in inflation-adjusted dollars.

Although they have far less money than men, women are responsible for spending $0.80 of every U.S. dollar, according to Catalyst, a New York–based nonprofit research and advocacy organization. Furthermore, 40 percent of all American investors are women investing their own resources.

MONEY INCOME

In the past three decades women's income has risen substantially, while the real income of most men has increased very little. In 2000 the median money income for all females 15 and over was $16,190. For all men the median income in 2000 was $28,272. Among women who worked full-time year-round in 2000 the median income was $28,823, compared to $39,020 for men who worked all year. (See Table 5.1.) In 1999 the mean (average) income for women was $21,311 and for men was $38,352. Women's median income in 1967 was $8,266 (in 1999 dollars), and their mean income was $11,396. Men's median money income in 1967 was $25,486, and their mean income was $27,785.

In general, black women have less money income than non-Hispanic white women, and Hispanic women have even less. The median income for all black women in 2000 was $16,081. In 1967 African American women had a median income of $6,701. Non-Hispanic white women had a median income in 2000 of $16,805. (See Table 5.1.) In 1972 non-Hispanic white women had a median income of $9,906. For Hispanic women the median in 2000 was $12,255. In 1972 Hispanic women had a median income of $9,933. In 1999 Asian and Pacific Islander women had a median income of $16,840 and a mean income of $23,951.

As Table 5.1 shows, money income rises with educational attainment. Women with doctoral degrees had the highest median money income in 2000 ($48,894). In contrast, men with professional degrees had the highest median income at $81,602. The median income of women aged 25 and over with less than a ninth-grade education was $8,404.

Families and Households

Over 5.4 million families, or 7 percent of all families, had annual incomes under $10,000 in 2000. (See Table 5.2.) Of these families, 65 percent were headed by women. Only 28 percent were married-couple families. More than one-quarter (27 percent) of American families had incomes above $75,000. Married-couple families made up 93 percent of this group. Many of these were "dual-earner" families with both partners working. Among high-income households, 79 percent had two or more earners.

According to the Census Bureau, the median income of American households in 2000 was $42,148, the same as in 1999. For married-couple families, the median income was $55,346. For female-headed families with no husband present, the median income in 2000 was only $28,116; however, this was up 4 percent from 1999 and 29 percent from 1993, compared to a 17 percent increase for married-couple families over that period. Asian and

TABLE 5.1

Median income of people by selected characteristics, 1999 and 2000

[People 15 years old and over as of March of the following year. An asterisk (*) preceding percent change indicates statistically significant change at the 90-percent confidence level.]

Characteristic	Male				Female			
	Number with income (1,000)	2000 Median income Value (dollars)	Standard error (dollars)	Percent change in real median income (1999-2000)	Number with income (1,000)	2000 Median income Value (dollars)	Standard error (dollars)	Percent change in real median income (1999-2000)
TOTAL								
All males / All females	96,976	28,272	230	0.3	99,966	16,190	103	*2.3
Region								
Northeast	18,283	30,457	274	2.4	19,747	16,386	222	0.5
Midwest	22,867	29,952	374	-1.0	23,280	16,432	222	2.5
South	33,831	26,701	215	-0.4	35,352	15,716	164	*3.2
West	21,994	28,012	484	-0.3	21,586	16,653	253	*3.6
Race and Hispanic Origin								
White	82,213	29,696	253	0.6	82,894	16,218	114	*2.1
Non-Hispanic White	72,400	31,213	141	*-1.3	74,290	16,805	125	*2.1
Black	10,123	21,662	338	1.8	12,525	16,081	280	*5.3
Hispanic origin[1]	10,249	19,833	322	*5.2	9,079	12,255	222	*4.8
Relationship to Family Householder								
In families	75,909	29,757	262	*2.1	76,839	15,359	119	*3.0
Householder	42,369	35,730	216	-1.3	27,357	17,655	233	1.7
Spouse of householder	16,524	36,618	310	0.3	35,321	16,961	190	1.5
Other relative of householder	17,016	11,016	173	*9.1	14,161	8,410	188	*8.2
In unrelated subfamilies	224	14,938	1,355	4.7	627	16,129	856	7.8
Unrelated individuals	20,843	25,550	236	*-2.3	22,501	19,321	272	*4.4
Age								
Under 65 years	83,038	30,675	122	-0.3	81,647	18,332	158	*4.7
15 to 24 years	14,476	9,557	221	*11.4	14,018	7,746	197	*12.0
25 to 34 years	17,822	30,634	195	-0.8	17,140	20,937	213	*4.4
35 to 44 years	21,684	37,087	247	-0.9	20,971	21,861	213	*2.3
45 to 54 years	18,156	41,072	271	*-2.9	18,117	24,196	373	*3.6
55 to 64 years	10,900	34,412	702	-1.1	11,400	16,465	317	0.1
65 years and over	13,938	19,168	233	*-2.8	18,319	10,899	115	*-3.6
65 to 74 years	8,060	21,361	396	-3.0	9,378	10,793	190	*-4.8
75 years and over	5,879	17,023	296	-1.8	8,941	10,982	143	*-2.8

TABLE 5.1

Median income of people by selected characteristics, 1999 and 2000 [CONTINUED]

[People 15 years old and over as of March of the following year. An asterisk (*) preceding percent change indicates statistically significant change at the 90-percent confidence level.]

Male [CONT'D]

	Number with income (1,000)	2000 Median income		Percent change in real median income (1999-2000)
Occupation Group of Longest Job[2] (Earnings)		Value (dollars)	Standard error (dollars)	
Total with earnings[3]	79,095	31,040	111	-0.2
Executive, administrators, and managerial	11,409	52,282	567	-1.3
Professional specialty	10,290	51,276	397	*-1.5
Technical and related support	2,218	41,012	622	4.4
Sales	8,804	31,824	388	-1.8
Administrative support, including clerical	4,430	25,895	501	1.9
Precision production, craft, and repair	14,480	31,264	184	*-1.6
Machine operators, assemblers, and inspectors	4,874	26,172	371	-1.2
Transportation and material moving	5,476	27,456	500	1.9
Handlers, equipment cleaners, helpers, and laborers	5,190	15,021	440	0.6
Service workers	8,137	16,703	305	*6.5
Private household	49	—	—	—
Service workers, except private household	8,088	16,754	304	*6.3
Farming, forestry, and fishing	3,157	13,659	541	*9.0
Educational attainment				
Total, 25 years and over	82,500	32,092	118	*-1.8
Less than 9th grade	5,498	14,149	285	1.9
9th to 12 grade (no diploma)	6,982	18,953	331	3.6
High school graduate (includes equivalency)	26,091	27,666	305	-1.7
Some college, no degree	14,331	33,039	566	-2.3
Associate degree	6,139	37,953	616	0.2

Female [CONT'D]

	Number with income (1,000)	2000 Median income		Percent change in real median income (1999-2000)
Occupation Group of Longest Job[2] (Earnings)		Value (dollars)	Standard error (dollars)	
Total with earnings[3]	70,709	20,311	108	*6.9
Executive, administrators, and managerial	10,061	33,527	674	1.6
Professional specialty	12,152	32,429	319	0.1
Technical and related support	2,651	27,426	604	*5.0
Sales	9,265	12,303	205	*4.2
Administrative support, including clerical	16,308	20,268	155	1.4
Precision production, craft, and repair	1,373	21,243	453	0.8
Machine operators, assemblers, and inspectors	3,053	16,723	317	*7.4
Transportation and material moving	689	14,103	1,117	-1.6
Handlers, equipment cleaners, helpers, and laborers	1,248	11,687	543	-4.6
Service workers	13,063	10,441	140	2.6
Private household	924	6,261	567	20.3
Service workers, except private household	12,139	10,728	147	1.0
Farming, forestry, and fishing	773	9,014	768	*38.9
Educational attainment				
Total, 25 years and over	85,948	18,025	145	*2.1
Less than 9th grade	5,113	8,404	149	-1.3
9th to 12 grade (no diploma)	7,337	9,996	172	0.5
High school graduate (includes equivalency)	28,662	15,119	152	-0.5
Some college, no degree	15,384	20,181	218	-0.7
Associate degree	7,856	23,269	411	2.5

TABLE 5.1

Median income of people by selected characteristics, 1999 and 2000 [CONTINUED]

[People 15 years old and over as of March of the following year. An asterisk (*) preceding percent change indicates statistically significant change at the 90-percent confidence level.]

Male [CONT'D]

	Number with income (1,000)	2000 Median income Value (dollars)	Standard error (dollars)	Percent change in real median income (1999-2000)
Bachelor's degree				
or more	23,457	53,457	709	-1.0
Bachelor's degree	15,151	49,178	729	0.5
Master degree	5,164	59,376	1,274	-2.5
Professional degree	1,695	81,602	2,529	-3.6
Doctorate degree	1,448	71,738	2,621	-1.5
FULL-TIME, YEAR-ROUND WORKERS				
Male				
All males	58,738	39,020	293	0.5
Region				
Northeast	10,948	41,889	304	*-1.7
Midwest	13,780	40,330	308	*-2.6
South	20,751	36,324	235	-0.4
West	13,259	39,632	631	0.5
Race and Hispanic Origin				
White	49,950	40,350	165	-0.7
Non-Hispanic White	43,490	42,223	172	*-1.3
Black	5,804	30,893	350	-1.3
Hispanic origin[1]	6,766	25,041	430	3.8
Relationship to Family Householder				
In families	46,351	40,748	168	-0.8
Householder	28,221	43,914	540	0.7
Spouse of householder	11,933	44,205	882	2.4
Other relative of householder	6,197	22,123	191	-0.5
In unrelated subfamilies	93	21,834	2,808	13.6
Unrelated individuals	12,294	33,685	593	-1.8
Age				
Under 65 years	57,391	38,793	298	0.3
15 to 24 years	4,676	20,825	226	*3.2
25 to 34 years	14,095	34,218	558	1.6
35 to 44 years	17,896	41,560	258	*-1.7
45 to 54 years	14,360	46,674	410	*-2.3
55 to 64 years	6,365	46,752	610	2.2
65 years and over	1,347	47,985	1,651	1.4
65 to 74 years	1,097	48,185	1,582	-0.7
75 years and over	249	45,578	6,308	8.6

Female [CONT'D]

	Number with income (1,000)	2000 Median income Value (dollars)	Standard error (dollars)	Percent change in real median income (1999-2000)
Bachelor's degree				
or more	21,598	33,365	392	*2.0
Bachelor's degree	14,858	30,487	294	*3.2
Master degree	5,323	40,249	598	-2.0
Professional degree	840	45,999	3,434	-2.2
Doctorate degree	576	48,894	3,137	1.7
FULL-TIME, YEAR-ROUND WORKERS				
Female				
All females	41,583	28,823	203	*1.9
Region				
Northeast	7,633	31,364	280	—
Midwest	9,470	28,908	366	2.3
South	15,689	26,653	196	-1.0
West	8,791	30,599	309	*4.0
Race and Hispanic Origin				
White	33,147	29,659	220	*2.4
Non-Hispanic White	29,281	30,776	160	*1.4
Black	6,390	25,745	248	50.9
Hispanic origin[1]	4,080	21,026	310	1.4
Relationship to Family Householder				
In families	32,232	27,805	230	0.1
Householder	12,720	28,374	361	-0.2
Spouse of householder	15,401	30,028	265	*2.7
Other relative of householder	4,110	21,160	319	-2.5
In unrelated subfamilies	282	25,499	1,112	*16.7
Unrelated individuals	9,070	31,735	290	0.8
Age				
Under 65 years	40,927	28,739	205	*1.7
15 to 24 years	3,822	18,960	346	2.8
25 to 34 years	9,775	27,953	353	1.4
35 to 44 years	12,053	30,471	262	1.1
45 to 54 years	10,790	31,981	283	0.3
55 to 64 years	4,487	30,282	423	1.9
65 years and over	656	34,159	1,485	*10.1
65 to 74 years	548	33,276	1,906	6.3
75 years and over	109	36,846	3,020	26.5

TABLE 5.1

Median income of people by selected characteristics, 1999 and 2000 [CONTINUED]

[People 15 years old and over as of March of the following year. An asterisk (*) preceding percent change indicates statistically significant change at the 90-percent confidence level.]

FULL-TIME, YEAR-ROUND WORKERS [CONT'D]
Male
Educational attainment

	Number with income (1,000)	2000 Median income Value (dollars)	Standard error (dollars)	Percent change in real median income (1999-2000)
Associate degree	4,729	41,948	460	*-2.5
Bachelor's degree or more	17,387	61,868	303	-0.6
Bachelor's degree	11,395	56,334	573	*2.9
Master degree	3,681	68,309	1,502	-0.2
Professional degree	1,274	99,435	5,165	-3.8
Doctorate degree	1,038	80,256	2,439	-4.9

FULL-TIME, YEAR-ROUND WORKERS [CONT'D]
Female
Educational attainment

	Number with income (1,000)	2000 Median income Value (dollars)	Standard error (dollars)	Percent change in real median income (1999-2000)
Associate degree	4,118	31,069	307	*-2.8
Bachelor's degree or more	11,585	42,701	438	-1.0
Bachelor's degree	7,899	40,413	284	*2.9
Master degree	2,824	50,139	734	0.9
Professional degree	509	58,978	3,553	-4.7
Doctorate degree	354	57,078	2,993	-8.1

1 People of Hispanic origin may be of any race.
2 Amounts shown are median earnings.
3 Includes people whose longest job was in the Armed Forces.

SOURCE: "Table 7. Median Income of People by Selected Characteristics: 2000, 1999, and 1998," in *Income 2000* [Online] http://www.census.gov/hhes/income/income00/inctab7.html [accessed November 7, 2001]

Pacific Islander households had the highest median income at $55,521; Hispanics had the lowest at $33,447.

Wealthy Women

Clearly men control the lion's share of wealth in America. Nevertheless, at least 23 American women were among the 538 billionaires in the world in 2001, according to *Forbes* magazine. Some of these women are becoming increasingly wealthy. All but one of them inherited their wealth from husbands, fathers, grandfathers, or other relatives. However, several of the women are actively involved in managing their corporate interests, as board members or corporate officers. Several of the women own sports teams, and others devote themselves to philanthropy.

The richest women in America are members of the Walton family. Helen R. Walton, the widow of the founder of Wal-Mart, the world's largest retailer, and her daughter Alice L. Walton, are each worth $18.5 billion. Two nieces of Wal-Mart's founder also are billionaires. Barbara Cox Anthony and Anne Cox Chambers, the daughters of the founder of Cox Communications, are each worth $11.7 billion. The only self-made female American billionaire is Doris Feigenbaum who, with her husband, founded The Gap chain of retailers.

THE EARNINGS GAP

A wage survey taken in 1833 in Philadelphia found that the majority of women workers in local textile factories received less for working 78 hours per week than men were getting for one 10-hour day (W. Chafe, *The American Woman: Her Changing Social, Economic and Political Roles, 1920–1970*, London, 1972). Women entered the labor market by filling the lowest-paying jobs and mirroring the work they customarily did at home—cleaning, cooking, sewing, and child care. Despite women's increased education and participation in the workforce, women's generally lower status and salaries continue in the 21st century. The AFL-CIO labor organization has noted that as more women enter a new occupation, the wages for that occupation begin to fall.

Men continue to earn substantially more money than women. Figure 5.1 illustrates the median annual earnings of men and women from 1967 to 2000. The median earnings of women who worked full-time year-round were $27,355 in 2000, unchanged from 1999, but up 7 percent from 1993. Men's median earnings dropped 1 percent between 1999 and 2000 to $37,339. Some of the rise in women's earnings is the result of the large increase in the number of women working full-time year-round.

The "earnings gap" is quantified as women's earnings as a percentage of men's earnings (100 percent). (See Table 5.3.) The gap between women's and men's earnings has narrowed significantly as women's earnings have increased and men's have declined in real terms. In 1973 women earned only 56.6 percent as much as men. The earnings gap was smallest in 1996–97 and again in 2000 when women's earnings were about 74 percent of men's. The earnings gap is widest between non-Hispanic white women and men and the gap is smallest between Hispanic women and men.

According to the AFL-CIO, working families lose $200 billion annually due to the earnings gap. The average 25-year-old working woman will lose $523,000 to the earnings gap during her working lifetime. Furthermore, women in low-wage jobs typically have few or no employee benefits, lower Social Security earnings, less job security and less access to unemployment insurance, and less access to credit.

Women's median pay is so much lower than men's for several reasons. Many women leave the workforce to stay at home while their children are young. Women are more likely to be in low-paying, entry-level jobs, and they often work fewer hours and have fewer job skills than men. In part the earnings gap is closing because women are accumulating job experience. Women's educational attainment has increased dramatically in recent years, and fewer women are leaving their jobs. Women with degrees tend to work for more years than women without degrees.

Annual Earnings

Men earned more than women at all levels of educational attainment. According to the Census Bureau, in 2000 the median earnings for women high school graduates or equivalent, aged 25 and over, were $15,119, compared to $27,666 for male graduates. The median earnings for women with bachelor's degrees were $30,487, compared to $49,178 for men. Women with professional degrees earned $45,999, compared to professional men's median earnings of $81,602.

Executives, administrators, and managers had the highest median earnings among women in 2000, according to the Census Bureau. Although private household workers and women working in farming, forestry, and fishing had the lowest median earnings ($6,621 and $9,014, respectively), these represented increases of 20 percent and 39 percent, respectively, over 1999.

Weekly Earnings

Weekly earnings may be a more accurate measure of the earnings gap than annual earnings, since many women do not work year-round. About half of all women leave the workforce at some point to care for children, and many women do not work when their children are out of school during the summer months. According to the Bureau of Labor Statistics, in the second quarter of 2001 women's median weekly earnings for full-time wage and salary workers were $514, or 77 percent of men's median earnings. In 2000 the average median weekly earnings for

TABLE 5.2

Family groups by type and selected characteristics, March 2000
(In thousands)

Characteristic	Total	Married couple	Other family groups Total	Male	Female
All family groups	75,579	56,497	19,083	4,286	14,797
Family type					
Family household	72,025	55,311	16,715	4,028	12,687
Related subfamily	2,983	1,149	1,834	201	1,633
Unrelated subfamily	571	37	534	57	477
Size of family group					
1 person	(X)	(X)	(X)	(X)	(X)
2 people	33,749	23,794	9,955	2,529	7,426
3 people	16,909	11,497	5,412	1,016	4,396
4 people	14,800	12,640	2,160	446	1,714
5 people	6,622	5,668	954	168	786
6 or more	3,498	2,897	601	126	475
Number of own children under 18					
No own children	38,084	30,726	7,358	2,242	5,116
1 child	16,221	9,682	6,539	1,300	5,239
2 children	13,949	10,452	3,497	543	2,954
3 children	5,235	4,076	1,159	146	1,013
4 or more children	2,091	1,561	530	55	475
Presence of own children under 18					
No own children	38,084	30,726	7,358	2,242	5,116
With own children	37,496	25,771	11,725	2,044	9,681
With own children under 1	3,370	2,350	1,020	196	824
With own children under 3	9,832	7,002	2,830	511	2,319
With own children under 6	16,645	11,711	4,934	819	4,115
With own children under 12	28,297	19,519	8,778	1,441	7,337
Family income					
Under $10,000	5,426	1,505	3,921	393	3,528
$10,000-$14,999	3,919	1,817	2,102	320	1,782
$15,000-$19,999	4,706	2,675	2,031	341	1,690
$20,000-$24,999	4,694	3,008	1,686	304	1,382
$25,000-$29,999	4,606	3,060	1,546	365	1,181
$30,000-$39,999	8,702	6,323	2,379	638	1,741
$40,000-$49,999	7,835	6,147	1,688	476	1,212
$50,000-$74,999	15,495	13,238	2,257	788	1,469
$75,000 and over	20,198	18,723	1,475	663	812
Metropolitan residence					
Metropolitan	60,461	44,580	15,881	3,564	12,317
In central cities	20,803	13,532	7,271	1,501	5,770
Outside central cities	39,658	31,048	8,610	2,063	6,547
Nonmetropolitan	15,119	11,917	3,202	722	2,480
Tenure					
Owns/buying	56,029	46,280	9,749	2,505	7,244
Rents	18,562	9,561	9,001	1,707	7,294
Occupies without payment	987	655	332	74	258

X Not applicable.

SOURCE: Jason Fields and Lynne M. Casper, "Table 2. Family Groups by Type and Selected Characteristics of the Family: March 2000," in *America's Families and Living Arrangements: March 2000*, U.S. Census Bureau, Washington, DC, June 2001

all female full-time wage and salary workers ages 16 and over were 76 percent of men's earnings. (See Table 5.4.) In 1979 the median usual weekly earnings of full-time working women were 63 percent of men's earnings. The median usual weekly earnings of women 25 and over, as a percent of men's, increased from 62 percent in 1979 to 74 percent in 2000. Some of this narrowing of the earnings gap was the result of declines in men's real earnings.

Women working part-time had median weekly earnings that were 36 percent of the median for women work-

ing full-time. Males working part-time earned even less; however, part-time male workers, unlike female part-time workers, tend to be very young.

AGE AND RACIAL DIFFERENCES. As Figure 5.2 shows, the earnings gap varies with age. For young women, the female-male earnings ratio is 91 percent, whereas for women 55 to 64 the ratio is 68.5 percent. Women between 35 and 44 and women 65 and over earned only about 71 percent as much as the men in those age groups. (See Table 5.4.)

FIGURE 5.1

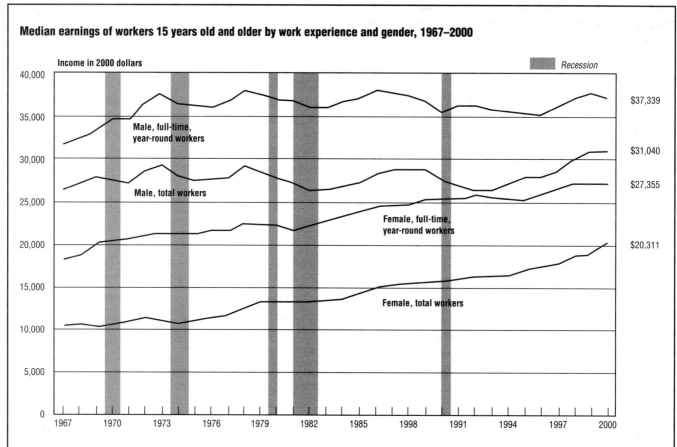

Median earnings of workers 15 years old and older by work experience and gender, 1967–2000

Income in 2000 dollars

Recession

Male, full-time, year-round workers $37,339

Male, total workers $31,040

Female, full-time, year-round workers $27,355

Female, total workers $20,311

SOURCE: Carmen DeNavas-Walt, Robert W. Cleveland, and Marc I. Roemer, "Figure 3. Median Earnings of Workers 15 Years Old and Over by Work Experience and Sex: 1967 to 2000," in *Money Income in the United States: 2000,* Current Population Reports, P60-213, U.S. Census Bureau, Washington, DC, September 2001

In the second quarter of 2001 the median earnings of white women were $522, compared to $460 for African American women and $537 for African American men. Hispanic women's median earnings were $383. The female-male earnings ratios were highest for Hispanics and African Americans at 86 percent, compared to 76 percent for whites.

Hispanic women made 88 percent of Hispanic men's weekly earnings in 2000, and black women made 85 percent of what black men made. However, white women made only 75 percent of what white men made. This is because of the relatively low earnings of Hispanic and black men compared to white men. The median weekly earnings of white women were nearly identical to those of black men and substantially higher than those of Hispanic men. The median for white women was $500 per week, compared to $429 for black women and $364 for Hispanic women. The median for white men was $669 per week, compared to $503 for black men and $414 for Hispanic men. (See Table 5.4.)

The inflation-adjusted earnings of white women rose 23 percent between 1979 and 2000, whereas African American women's earnings rose only 15 per-

cent and Hispanic women's rose only 5 percent. However, white and African American men's real earnings changed very little between 1979 and 2000, and Hispanic men's earnings fell. Thus, the median usual weekly earnings of full-time working African American women, as a percent of African American men's earnings, increased from 74 percent to 85 percent, and Hispanic women's earnings, as a percent of Hispanic men's, increased from 72 to 88 percent.

MARITAL STATUS AND CHILDREN. Married women living with their spouses and working full-time had higher median usual weekly earnings ($517) than did women with other marital statuses ($461). (See Table 5.5.) Women without children had higher earnings than those with children under 18, and those with children under 6 had the lowest earnings. On average, men with children had higher weekly median earnings than men without children. Thus, the earnings gap was largest for parents, with mothers earning only two-thirds as much as fathers.

The median usual weekly earnings for unmarried women in 2000 were closer to those of unmarried men than they were for married women compared to married

TABLE 5.3

Women's earnings as a percentage of men's earnings by race and Hispanic origin, 1960–99

Year	All races	White	Black[1]	Asian Pacific Islander	Hispanic origin[2]	Non-Hispanic White
1999	72.2	71.6	80.7	77.9	84.6	68.0
1998	73.2	72.6	83.7	77.7	86.3	71.2
1997	74.2	72.0	83.4	80.1	87.8	70.8
1996	73.8	73.3	81.3	74.2	88.6	70.2
1995[20]	71.4	71.2	84.6	78.8	84.3	68.8
1994[19]	72.0	71.6	83.9	76.3	86.5	71.1
1993[18]	71.5	70.8	86.1	78.8	83.2	70.0
1992[17]	70.8	70.0	88.2	74.7	87.4	69.0
1991	69.9	68.7	84.8	70.2	82.2	67.9
1990	71.6	69.4	85.4	79.7	81.9	67.6
1989	68.7	66.3	85.1	75.9	85.3	64.2
1988	66.0	65.4	81.2	71.3	83.2	64.1
1987[16]	65.2	64.4	82.4	(NA)	83.3	63.5
1986	64.3	63.3	80.3	(NA)	82.3	(NA)
1985[15]	64.6	63.0	81.9	(NA)	76.6	(NA)
1984[14]	63.7	62.2	82.5	(NA)	74.1	(NA)
1983	63.6	62.7	78.6	(NA)	72.1	(NA)
1982	61.7	60.9	78.3	(NA)	72.2	(NA)
1981	59.2	58.5	76.0	(NA)	72.9	(NA)
1980	60.2	58.9	78.8	(NA)	71.4	(NA)
1979[13]	59.7	58.8	74.6	(NA)	68.2	(NA)
1978	59.4	58.9	71.5	(NA)	68.8	(NA)
1977	58.9	57.6	77.5	(NA)	69.7	(NA)
1976[12]	60.2	59.0	75.7	(NA)	68.0	(NA)
1975[11]	58.8	57.6	74.6	(NA)	68.3	(NA)
1974[11/10]	58.8	57.9	75.3	(NA)	66.7	(NA)
1973	56.6	55.9	69.6	(NA)	(NA)	(NA)
1972[9]	57.9	56.6	70.5	(NA)	(NA)	(NA)
1971[8]	59.5	58.5	75.2	(NA)	(NA)	(NA)
1970	59.4	58.7	69.8	(NA)	(NA)	(NA)
1969	58.9	58.1	68.2	(NA)	(NA)	(NA)
1968	58.2	58.2	65.6	(NA)	(NA)	(NA)
1967[7]	57.8	57.9	66.9	(NA)	(NA)	(NA)
1966[6]	57.6	(NA)	(NA)	(NA)	(NA)	(NA)
1965[5]	59.9	(NA)	(NA)	(NA)	(NA)	(NA)
1964	59.1	(NA)	(NA)	(NA)	(NA)	(NA)
1963	58.9	(NA)	(NA)	(NA)	(NA)	(NA)
1962[4]	59.3	(NA)	(NA)	(NA)	(NA)	(NA)
1961[3]	59.2	(NA)	(NA)	(NA)	(NA)	(NA)
1960	60.7	(NA)	(NA)	(NA)	(NA)	(NA)

NA Not available.

[1] Before 1967, data are for "Black and other races" combined.

[2] People of Hispanic origin may be of any race.

[3] Data reflect implementation of first hotdeck procedure to impute missing income entries (all income data imputed if any missing). Data also reflect introduction of 1960 census-based sample design.

[4] Data reflect full implementation of 1960 census-based sample design and population controls.

[5] Data reflect implementation of new procedures to impute missing data only.

[6] Questionnaire expanded to ask eight income questions.

[7] Data reflect implementation of a new March CPS processing system.

[8] Data reflect introduction of 1970 census-based sample design and population controls.

[9] Data reflect full implementation of 1970 census-based sample design.

[10] Data reflect implementation of a new March CPS processing system. Questionnaire expanded to ask 11 income questions.

[11] Some of these estimates were derived using Pareto interpolation and may differ from published data which were derived using linear interpolation.

[12] First year medians were derived using both Pareto and linear interpolation. Before this year, all medians were derived using linear interpolation.

[13] Data reflect implementation of 1980 census population controls. Questionnaire expanded to show 27 possible values from 51 possible sources of income.

[14] Data reflect implementation of Hispanic population weighting controls and introduction of 1980 census-based sample design.

[15] Recording of amounts for earnings from longest job were increased to $299,999. Data reflect full implementation of 1980 census-based sample design.

[16] Data reflect implementation of a new March CPS processing system.

[17] Data reflect implementation of 1990 census population controls.

[18] Data collection method changed from paper and pencil to computer-assisted interviewing. In addition, the March 1994 income supplement was revised to allow for the coding of different income amounts on selected questionnaire items. Child support and alimony limits decreased to $49,999. Limits increased in the following categories: earnings to $999,999; social security to $49,999; supplemental security income and public assistance income to $24,999; and veterans' benefits to $99,999.

[19] Data reflect introduction of 1990 census-based sample design.

[20] Data reflect full implementation of the 1990 census-based sample design and metropolitan definitions, 7,000 household sample reduction, and revised race edits.

Note: Based on median earnings of full-time, year-round workers 15 years old and over as of March of the following year. Before 1989, based on median earnings for full-time, year-round civilian workers only.

SOURCE: "Table p-40. Women's Earnings as a Percentage of Men's Earnings by Race and Hispanic Origin: 1960 to 1999," in *Historical Income Tables – People* U.S. Census Bureau, Washington, DC [Online] http://www.census.gov/hhes/income/histinc/p40.html [accessed September 23, 2001]

TABLE 5.4

Median usual weekly earnings of full-time wage and salary workers by selected characteristics, 2000 annual averages

Characteristic	Both sexes			Women			Men			Women's earnings as percent of men's[1]
	Number of workers (in thousands)	Median weekly earnings	Standard error of median	Number of workers (in thousands)	Median weekly earnings	Standard error of median	Number of workers (in thousands)	Median weekly earnings	Standard error of median	
AGE										
Total, 16 years and over	99,917	$576	$1	43,644	$491	$1	56,273	$646	$2	76.0
16 to 24 years	11,934	361	2	5,147	342	2	6,786	376	2	91.0
16 to 19 years	2,303	294	2	926	279	3	1,377	304	3	91.9
20 to 24 years	9,631	383	2	4,221	364	2	5,409	396	2	91.9
25 years and over	87,984	611	1	38,497	515	1	49,487	700	2	73.6
25 to 34 years	25,272	550	3	10,826	493	2	14,445	603	3	81.9
35 to 44 years	28,926	631	3	12,407	520	3	16,519	731	4	71.1
45 to 54 years	23,044	671	3	10,578	565	4	12,466	777	5	72.7
55 to 64 years	9,383	617	4	4,129	505	4	5,254	738	6	68.5
65 years and over	1,359	442	12	557	378	10	802	537	36	70.5
RACE AND HISPANIC ORIGIN										
White	82,475	591	1	34,897	500	1	47,578	669	2	74.7
Black	12,556	468	3	6,568	429	3	5,989	503	3	85.2
Hispanic origin	11,738	396	3	4,477	364	4	7,261	414	3	87.7
MARITAL STATUS										
Never married	25,676	459	2	11,000	436	3	14,676	478	3	91.3
Married, spouse present	57,423	638	2	22,856	517	2	34,566	735	2	70.3
Other marital status	16,819	528	3	9,788	486	2	7,031	616	4	78.9
Divorced	11,456	571	4	6,637	509	3	4,819	650	7	78.4
Separated	3,812	466	6	1,957	421	5	1,855	517	7	81.4
Widowed	1,551	478	8	1,194	443	9	357	624	23	70.9
UNION AFFILIATION[2]										
Members of unions[3]	14,822	696	3	5,649	616	4	9,173	739	4	83.4
Represented by unions[4]	16,306	691	3	6,418	613	3	9,888	737	4	83.2
Not represented by a union	83,611	542	2	37,226	472	1	46,385	620	2	76.2
EDUCATIONAL ATTAINMENT										
Total, 25 years and over	87,984	611	1	38,497	515	1	49,487	700	2	73.6
Less than a high school diploma	8,523	360	2	3,034	303	2	5,490	409	3	74.1
High school graduates, no college	27,637	506	1	12,088	421	2	15,549	594	2	70.9
Some college or associate degree	24,452	598	2	11,442	504	2	13,010	699	3	72.2
College graduates, total	27,372	896	4	11,934	760	3	15,438	1022	6	74.4

[1] These figures are computed using unrounded medians and may differ slightly from percents computed using the rounded medians displayed in this table.
[2] Differences in earnings levels between workers with and without union affiliation reflect a variety of factors in addition to coverage by a collective bargaining agreement, including the distribution of male and female employees by occupation, industry, firm size, or geographic region.
[3] Data refer to members of a labor union or an employee association similar to a union.
[4] Data refer to members of a labor union or an employee association similar to a union as well as workers who report no union affiliation but whose jobs are covered by a union or an employee association contract.

NOTE: Detail for the above race and Hispanic-origin groups will not sum to totals because data for the "other races" group are not presented and Hispanics are included in both the white and black population groups.

SOURCE: "Table 1. Median Usual Weekly Earnings of Full-Time Wage and Salary Workers by Selected Characteristics, 2000 Annual Averages," in *Highlights of Women's Earnings in 2000,* Report 952, Bureau of Labor Statistics, Washington, DC, August 2001

men. Never-married women made, on average, 91 percent of what never-married men earned, whereas married women living with their spouses made only 70 percent as much as married men. (See Table 5.4.)

OCCUPATIONAL DIFFERENCES. Professionals, particularly engineers, computer scientists, pharmacists, and lawyers, had the highest median weekly earnings among women in 2001 ($745), although according to the AFL-CIO, the median weekly earnings of female lawyers is $300 less than that of male lawyers and women physicians earn $500 less per week than male doctors. To some extent this difference is the result of

women choosing lower-paying specialties than men. For example, women physicians are more likely to choose family practice over surgery. Furthermore, most women professionals are employed in lower-paying traditionally female occupations such as nursing and teaching. Female nurses (95 percent of all nurses) make $30 less per week than the 5 percent of nurses who are male. Female professors make $170 less per week than male professors, and women elementary school teachers make $70 less per week than the 11 percent of elementary school teachers who are male. Female food service supervisors make $60 less per week than men with the same job, and waitresses make $50 less per week than

FIGURE 5.2

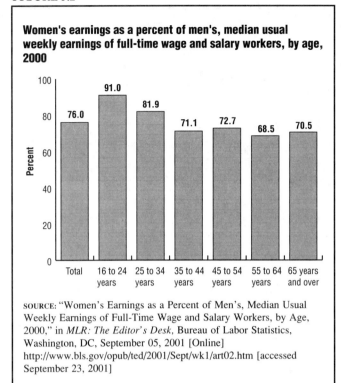

Women's earnings as a percent of men's, median usual weekly earnings of full-time wage and salary workers, by age, 2000

SOURCE: "Women's Earnings as a Percent of Men's, Median Usual Weekly Earnings of Full-Time Wage and Salary Workers, by Age, 2000," in *MLR: The Editor's Desk,* Bureau of Labor Statistics, Washington, DC, September 05, 2001 [Online] http://www.bls.gov/opub/ted/2001/Sept/wk1/art02.htm [accessed September 23, 2001]

TABLE 5.5

Median usual weekly earnings of full-time wage and salary workers by gender, marital status, and presence and age of own children under 18, 2000

Characteristic	Number of workers (in thousands)	Median weekly earnings	Standard error of median
WOMEN			
Total, all marital statuses	43,644	$491	$1
With children under 18 years old	17,104	479	2
With children 6 to 17, none younger	10,585	492	2
With children under 6 years old	6,519	456	4
With no children under 18 years old	26,540	499	2
Total, married, spouse present	22,856	517	2
With children under 18 years old	11,476	507	2
With children 6 to 17, none younger	7,056	512	3
With children under 6 years old	4,421	501	3
With no children under 18 years old	11,380	527	3
Total, other marital statuses[1]	20,788	461	2
With children under 18 years old	5,628	418	3
With children 6 to 17, none younger	3,529	453	5
With children under 6 years old	2,099	374	4
With no children under 18 years old	15,160	479	2
MEN			
Total, all marital statuses	56,273	646	2
With children under 18 years old	22,008	721	3
With children 6 to 17, none younger	11,706	756	4
With children under 6 years old	10,303	681	4
With no children under 18 years old	34,265	601	2
Total, married, spouse present	34,566	735	2
With children under 18 years old	20,484	733	3
With children 6 to 17, none younger	10,808	765	4
With children under 6 years old	9,676	696	4
With no children under 18 years old	14,083	738	3
Total, other marital statuses[1]	21,707	512	2
With children under 18 years old	1,524	570	13
With children 6 to 17, none younger	898	643	18
With children under 6 years old	626	476	11
With no children under 18 years old	20,182	510	2

[1] Includes never-married, divorced, separated, and widowed persons.
NOTE: Children refer to "own" children and include sons, daughters, stepchildren, and adopted children. Excluded are other related children such as grandchildren, nieces, nephews, and cousins, and unrelated children.

SOURCE: "Table 9. Median Usual Weekly Earnings of Full-Time Wage and Salary Workers by Sex, Marital Status, and Presence and Age of Own Children Under 18 Years Old, 2000 Annual Averages," in *Highlights of Women's Earnings in 2000,* Report 952, Bureau of Labor Statistics, Washington, DC, August 2001

waiters. According to the Bureau of Labor Statistics, female private household workers had the lowest median weekly earnings in 2001 ($246).

As is evident from Table 5.6, the gap in median weekly earnings narrowed from 66.6 percent in 1983 to 76 percent in 2000. However, the ratios varied substantially among occupations. Among the leading occupations for women in 2000, the ratio of women's usual median weekly earnings to men's earnings was 55.8 percent for sales workers and 91.3 percent for general office clerks. (See Table 4.1.) The narrowest earnings gap was for private police and guards (99 percent) and the widest gap was among physicians (58 percent) and securities and financial services salespeople (57 percent). Between 1983 and 2000 the earnings gap narrowed for most occupations. However, for some occupations, such as transportation and material movers, handlers, equipment cleaners, helpers, and laborers, the gap increased. For managerial and professional women, the gap narrowed only slightly, from 69.2 to 71.3 percent. However, these are among the highest-paying careers for both women and men, and the proportion of women in these occupations has increased significantly since 1983. (See Table 5.6.)

The earnings gap also varies by state, in part because major occupations and the age of the labor force vary by state. Washington, D.C., had the highest female-to-male earnings ratio (over 89 percent in 2000), and Wyoming had the lowest at 69 percent.

EDUCATION AND EARNINGS. In 2000 the median weekly earnings for women aged 25 and over without a high school diploma were $303, compared to $409 for men. Female college graduates had median earnings of $760 compared to $1,022 for men. (See Table 5.4.)

However, between 1979 and 2000 women's earnings grew more than men's at all educational levels. (See Figure 5.3.) Men without a high school diploma lost more than 27 percent in constant (inflation-adjusted) dollar earnings over the period, whereas women lost only about 9 percent. The earnings of men with only a high school diploma declined more than 10 percent, whereas the earnings of women high school graduates increased about 3 percent. Women with some college or an associate degree

TABLE 5.6

Median usual weekly earnings of full-time wage and salary workers by occupation and gender, 1983 and 2000

	1983					2000				
	Number of workers (in thousands)	Percent women	Median weekly earnings		Women's earnings as percent of men's[1]	Number of workers (in thousands)	Percent women	Median weekly earnings		Women's earnings as percent of men's[1]
Occupation			Women	Men				Women	Men	
Total, 16 years and over	70,976	40.4	$252	$379	66.6	99,917	43.7	$491	$646	76.0
Managerial and professional specialty	17,451	40.9	358	516	69.2	31,455	49.5	709	994	71.3
Executive, administrative, and managerial	8,117	34.2	340	530	64.0	15,368	47.0	686	1,014	67.7
Professional specialty	9,334	46.8	368	506	72.6	16,087	51.9	725	977	74.2
Technical, sales, and administrative support	21,641	62.5	247	386	64.0	28,252	61.7	452	655	69.0
Technicians and related support	2,574	44.5	299	424	70.6	3,652	48.4	541	761	71.1
Sales occupations	6,313	39.0	205	389	52.7	10,133	44.9	407	684	59.6
Administrative support, including clerical	12,755	77.7	249	362	68.7	14,468	76.8	449	563	79.8
Service occupations	7,321	49.2	173	256	67.8	11,020	52.1	316	414	76.2
Private household	278	96.0	116	(2)	(3)	368	94.7	261	(2)	(3)
Protective service	1,453	9.5	251	356	70.4	2,112	16.1	500	659	75.9
Service, except private household and protective	5,590	57.1	176	218	81.0	8,540	59.1	314	357	88.2
Precision production, craft, and repair	9,963	7.9	256	387	66.1	12,163	8.9	445	628	70.9
Operators, fabricators, and laborers	13,319	26.2	205	308	66.5	15,411	23.2	351	487	72.2
Machine operators, assemblers, and inspectors	6,990	40.8	202	320	63.3	6,636	36.1	355	495	71.6
Transportation and material moving occupations	3,358	4.7	253	335	75.5	4,587	8.0	407	558	72.9
Handlers, equipment cleaners, helpers, and laborers	2,970	16.0	211	252	83.9	4,189	19.4	320	394	81.2
Farming, forestry, and fishing	1,280	11.2	169	201	84.2	1,616	15.0	294	347	84.9

[1]These figures are computed using unrounded medians and may differ slightly from percents computed using the rounded medians displayed in this table.
[2]Data not shown where base is less than 50,000.
[3]Data not shown where base for either the numerator or denominator is less than 50,000.

SOURCE: "Table 2. Median Usual Weekly Earnings of Full-Time Wage and Salary Workers by Occupation and Sex, 1983 and 2000 Annual Averages," in *Highlights of Women's Earnings in 2000,* Report 952, Bureau of Labor Statistics, Washington, DC, August 2001

saw their earnings rise over 8 percent, whereas men with a comparable amount of education lost about 4 percent in real earnings. Women college graduates saw their earnings rise about 30 percent, whereas the men's earnings rose only 17 percent.

Hourly Wages

Gender comparisons of hourly earnings also are useful, since many more women than men work part-time, and since minimum wage laws are based on hourly wages. In 2000 similar numbers of men and women worked for hourly wages (over 36 million of each sex.) (See Table 5.7.) About 63 percent of women in the labor force are paid by the hour. Overall women's median wage was $9.03 per hour, 83 percent of men's median of $10.85 per hour. In the low-paying jobs held by 16- to 19-year-olds, women made 95 percent as much as men. Women represented by unions earned 77 percent of men's hourly wages, $11.87 per hour, compared to a median of $8.79 per hour for nonunionized women. Women with college degrees earned 89 percent as much as male graduates, whereas women high school graduates made only 74 percent as much as male high school graduates.

In 2000, 4.8 percent of women 16 and over who were paid hourly wages earned at or below the prevailing federal minimum wage of $5.15 per hour, compared to 2.6 per-

cent of men. (See Table 5.8.) Of women between ages 16 and 24, 11 percent made at or below minimum wage, compared to 6.3 percent of men. A higher percentage of white women made at or below minimum wage, compared to black or Hispanic women. Part-time workers of either sex were much more likely to be paid at or below minimum wage. In 2000, 6.8 percent of women age 65 and over earned at or below the federal minimum wage.

Employee Health Coverage

According to the CBPP, more than one-third of low-income working families do not have access to heath insurance. Almost half of all workers earning under $20,000 per year are not offered health insurance by their employer, and many of those who are eligible cannot afford the premiums. Retail and service industries, which employ large numbers of women, often do not provide health insurance to their employees. Furthermore, part-time employees and those who have not worked for an employer for very long, including large numbers of women, often do not qualify for employee health coverage. Most low-income working women do not qualify for government-subsidized health insurance.

Unions

In 2000 women who were union members or were represented by unions made about 83 percent as much as unionized men, whereas nonunionized women made only 76.2 percent as much as nonunionized men. (See Table 5.4.) According to the AFL-CIO, the average female union member earns 38 percent more per week than nonunion women. Unionized women of color make 39 percent more than nonunionized women of color.

Equal Pay Laws

The Equal Pay Act of 1963 (PL 88-38) made it illegal to pay women less than men working at the same job. However, equal pay for equal work laws have little effect when the workplace is gender-segregated and it is nearly impossible to define equal work. Furthermore, the laws may be poorly enforced. A 1999 study, *Equal Pay for Working Families: National and State Data on the Pay Gap and Its Costs* (Washington, D.C.), conducted by the AFL-CIO and the Institute for Women's Policy Research (IWPR), asserts that if equal pay were enforced by the states, the poverty rate for all working women would be cut by as much as 12 percent. In the AFL-CIO's 2000 "Ask a Working Woman" survey, equal pay was the number one policy issue among the respondents, with 87 percent saying that stronger equal pay laws were important. There is a growing movement toward replacing equal pay laws with laws providing for pay equity or comparable worth for men and women. Such laws would provide for equal pay if men's and women's jobs are merely comparable rather than identical.

POVERTY IN AMERICA

The federal government defines poverty as having an income below the poverty threshold as shown in Table 5.9. However, calculations of poverty levels are controversial, and the Census Bureau is experimenting with new types of poverty calculations. For example, the poverty threshold is usually calculated using food costs, without taking into consideration skyrocketing housing costs in many regions of the country.

The poverty threshold depends on family size and the age of the householder. In 1999 over 32.3 million Americans were living in poverty, of which 57 percent were female, 13.2 percent of all American females. Among females 18 and over, 11.8 percent lived in poverty, compared to 8.2 percent of males under 65 and 6.9 percent of males 65 and over. (See Table 5.10.) In 2000 over 31 million Americans (11 percent) had a family income below the poverty level, and 4.4 percent of Americans were living with a family income of less than half of the poverty threshold. Only 5 percent of married-couple families lived in poverty in 2000, compared to 25 percent of families headed by a woman with no spouse present.

Although poverty rates dropped in 2000, far more women than men continue to be poor. Gender-based wage disparities and the segregation of women into low-paying jobs account for much of this difference, which has

FIGURE 5.3

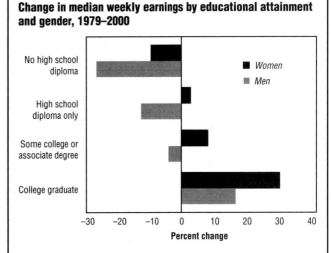

Change in median weekly earnings by educational attainment and gender, 1979–2000

NOTE: Data relate to full-time wage and salary workers 25 years and over. Changes are calculated from constant-dollar annual averages.

SOURCE: "Chart 3. Percent Change Between 1979 and 2000 Median Usual Weekly Earnings by Educational Attainment and Sex," in *Highlights of Women's Earnings in 2000,* Report 952, Bureau of Labor Statistics, Washington, DC, August 2001

become a global phenomenon, often called the "feminization of poverty."

Single Mothers

Over two-thirds of all families headed by females with no one working lived in poverty in 2000, compared to 28.7 percent of all families and 14.6 percent of married-couple families. (See Figure 5.4.) However, the poverty rate for families headed by women was at an all-time low of 25 percent, down from 28 percent in 1999. That was the first year that the rate had fallen below 30 percent since 1959, when data was first gathered. In 1959, 43 percent of all such families lived in poverty. The poverty rate for families headed by women fell even though the numbers of such families steadily increased, from 10 percent of all families in 1959 to 17 percent in 2000. The poverty rate for families headed by non-Hispanic white women reached a record low of 17 percent in 2000. The poverty rate for families headed by African American and Hispanic women was 35 percent. Until 1989 more than half of all families headed by African American women lived in poverty. The poverty rate for families headed by Hispanic women did not fall below 50 percent until 1998. Between 1993 and 2000 the percentage of married-couple families living below the poverty level decreased by almost 2 percent.

Table 5.11 shows that in 2000 families and individuals living below the poverty line had a per capita deficit, meaning that they spent more than their income. Families headed by females with no spouse present had an average per person deficit of over $2,000. Men and women living

TABLE 5.7

Median hourly earnings of wage and salary workers paid hourly rates, 2000

Characteristic	Both sexes			Women			Men			Women's earnings as percent of men's[1]
	Number of workers (in thousands)	Median hourly earnings	Standard error of median	Number of workers (in thousands)	Median hourly earnings	Standard error of median	Number of workers (in thousands)	Median hourly earnings	Standard error of median	
AGE										
Total, 16 years and over	72,744	$9.91	$0.01	36,516	$9.03	$0.02	36,228	$10.85	$0.03	83.2
16 to 24 years	16,938	7.21	.02	8,194	6.97	.02	8,743	7.59	.04	91.8
16 to 19 years	6,698	6.37	.02	3,336	6.22	.02	3,362	6.57	.04	94.7
20 to 24 years	10,240	8.06	.02	4,859	7.78	.03	5,381	8.40	.07	92.6
25 years and over	55,806	10.93	.02	28,321	9.89	.02	27,485	12.41	.06	79.7
25 to 34 years	16,497	10.18	.02	7,861	9.69	.06	8,636	10.98	.05	88.2
35 to 44 years	17,982	11.56	.08	9,135	10.05	.03	8,847	13.24	.09	76.0
45 to 54 years	13,326	11.85	.04	7,102	10.19	.04	6,224	13.94	.07	73.1
55 to 64 years	6,236	10.81	.08	3,289	9.75	.07	2,947	12.82	.15	76.1
65 years and over	1,764	8.00	.06	934	7.76	.08	830	8.29	.19	93.7
RACE AND HISPANIC ORIGIN										
White	59,374	9.98	.01	29,404	9.06	.02	29,970	11.04	.03	82.1
Black	10,105	9.27	.05	5,457	8.82	.04	4,648	9.91	.04	89.0
Hispanic origin	9,847	8.50	.09	4,060	7.89	.04	5,787	9.01	.05	87.5
MARITAL STATUS										
Never married	25,198	8.05	.02	11,539	7.72	.03	13,659	8.45	.06	91.3
Married, spouse present	35,463	11.18	.04	17,489	9.89	.02	17,975	13.01	.04	76.1
Other marital status	12,083	10.14	.03	7,488	9.60	.07	4,595	11.86	.06	80.9
Divorced	7,733	10.86	.06	4,650	9.97	.04	3,084	12.62	.20	79.0
Separated	2,894	9.42	.15	1,642	8.78	.10	1,252	10.04	.07	87.5
Widowed	1,455	9.09	.12	1,196	8.83	.12	259	10.90	.46	81.0
UNION AFFILIATION[2]										
Members of unions[3]	10,691	14.22	.09	3,711	11.91	.07	6,980	15.68	.15	75.9
Represented by unions[4]	11,624	14.08	.05	4,182	11.87	.07	7,442	15.34	.14	77.4
Not represented by a union	61,120	9.29	.03	32,333	8.79	.02	28,786	10.01	.02	87.8
EDUCATIONAL ATTAINMENT										
Total, 25 years and over	55,806	10.93	.02	28,321	9.89	.02	27,485	12.41	.06	79.7
Less than a high school diploma	7,949	8.21	.04	3,299	7.23	.03	4,649	9.33	.12	77.5
High school graduates, no college	22,630	10.53	.05	11,184	9.21	.03	11,446	12.44	.09	74.0
Some college or associate degree	17,259	11.90	.03	9,367	10.65	.06	7,892	13.83	.07	77.0
College graduates, total	7,968	15.02	.05	4,471	14.20	.15	3,497	15.96	.14	89.0

[1] These figures are computed using unrounded medians and may differ slightly from percents computed using the rounded medians displayed in this table.

[2] Differences in earnings levels between workers with and without union affiliation reflect a variety of factors in addition to coverage by a collective bargaining agreement, including the distribution of male and female employees by occupation, industry, firm size, or geographic region.

[3] Data refer to members of a labor union or an employee association similar to a union.

[4] Data refer to members of a labor union or an employee association similar to a union as well as workers who report no union affiliation but whose jobs are covered by a union or an employee association contract.

NOTE: Hourly-paid workers account for approximately three-fifths of all wage and salary workers. Detail for the above race and Hispanic-origin groups will not sum to totals because data for the "other races" group are not presented and Hispanics are included in both the white and black population groups.

SOURCE: "Table 10. Median Hourly Earnings of Wage and Salary Workers Paid Hourly Rates by Selected Characteristics, 2000 Annual Averages," in *Highlights of Women's Earnings in 2000,* Report 952, Bureau of Labor Statistics, Washington, DC, August 2001

alone or with unrelated individuals had the highest deficits. In contrast, those living above poverty had average per capita surpluses, although families headed by females had the lowest surplus of any group.

The Working Poor

According to the CBPP, the vast majority of poor and near-poor (within 200 percent of the poverty level) families include at least one adult working most of the year. According to the Census Bureau in 2000, 45 percent of all families in poverty had someone in the family working full-time. Although 69.8 percent of families headed by women and with no working members were below the poverty threshold in 2000, 21.4 percent of all female-head-

ed households with at least one working member remained in poverty. (See Figure 5.4.) Only 7.6 percent of all families and 4.8 percent of married-couple families with at least one working member were below the poverty line.

According to the CBPP, unemployment in 2000 reached its lowest level in more than three decades, and poverty rates dropped to the lowest level since 1979. However, unemployment soared in 2001 and poverty rates are expected to rise accordingly.

Welfare Reform and Government Benefits

The Personal Responsibility and Work Opportunity Reconciliation Act (PRWORA) was designed to move people, primarily single mothers, off welfare and into the workforce. However, a 2001 study by the CBPP found that although earnings by single working mothers increased in the late 1990s because of a strong economy, the earned income tax credit, and improved child care options, these gains were completely offset by declines in government benefits. As a group, single working mothers were no better off than before, and those who were already poor became poorer. The proportion of single mothers who worked increased from 68 percent in 1993 to 82 percent in 1999. However, the study found that the poverty rate for working single mothers in 1999 was just as high as in 1995, before PRWORA, even after government benefits were figured in. The poverty gap also increased for working single-mother families between 1995 and 1999. (The poverty gap is the total amount of money needed to lift all families that are below the poverty line up to the poverty line. The poverty gap, therefore, is a measure of not only the numbers in poverty but the depth of their poverty.) In contrast, both the poverty status and the poverty gap of other types of working families with children improved. The report concluded that since 1995 government safety-net programs for the poor have been less effective in improving the poverty status of working single-mother families. With the slowing of the economy and the rise in unemployment in 2001, the number of women in poverty was expected to increase.

After taking into consideration government benefits and taxes, the poverty rate for all single-mother families was 27.7 percent in 1999, down from 41 percent in 1993. (See Table 5.12.) This compares to an after-benefit poverty rate for all families with children of 6.8 percent in 1999. The poverty rate for families headed by single working mothers, taking into account benefits and taxes, remained at 19.4 percent in 1999, up from 19.2 percent in 1995. The poverty rate for single mothers without earnings, after government benefits, was 64 percent in 1999, down from 72 percent in 1993.

Table 5.13 shows that 42.2 percent of working single-mother families in 1999 were above the poverty threshold only because of government benefits. Among these benefits, the earned- income tax credit was the most important. The impact of other benefits declined by half between 1993 and 1999. These benefits included Social Security, unemployment insurance, housing subsidies, and the school lunch program. Between 1995 and 1999 the number of single-mother families receiving cash assistance in the form of Aid to Families with Dependent Children (AFDC) or Temporary Assistance for Needy Families (TANF) decreased dramatically. The TANF program provided federal aid for a lifetime maximum of five years to families transitioning from welfare to work. Recipients had to be in work-related activities within two years, and states could be penalized for having too few welfare

TABLE 5.8

Wage and salary workers paid hourly rates with earnings at or below the prevailing federal minimum wage by selected characteristics

(Numbers in thousands)

	2000				
	Workers paid hourly rates				
				Total at or below prevailing Federal minimum wage	
Characteristic	Total	Below prevailing Federal minimum wage	At prevailing Federal minimum wage	Number	Percent of hourly-paid workers
Sex and age					
Total, 16 years and over	72,744	1,844	866	2,710	3.7
16 to 24 years	16,938	938	510	1,447	8.5
25 years and over	55,806	906	357	1,263	2.3
Men, 16 years and over	36,228	632	322	954	2.6
16 to 24 years	8,743	346	202	548	6.3
25 years and over	27,485	286	120	406	1.5
Women, 16 years and over	36,516	1,212	544	1,757	4.8
16 to 24 years	8,194	592	308	899	11.0
25 years and over	28,321	621	237	857	3.0
Race, Hispanic origin, and sex					
White, 16 years and over	59,374	1,555	687	2,242	3.8
Men	29,970	506	246	752	2.5
Women	29,404	1,049	441	1,490	5.1
Black, 16 years and over	10,105	213	148	361	3.6
Men	4,648	94	63	157	3.4
Women	5,457	119	85	204	3.7
Hispanic origin, 16 years and over	9,847	189	129	318	3.2
Men	5,787	91	50	141	2.4
Women	4,060	99	78	177	4.4
Full- and part-time status and sex[1]					
Full-time workers	55,701	736	289	1,025	1.8
Men	30,856	286	113	400	1.3
Women	24,845	450	176	626	2.5
Part-time workers	16,909	1,096	577	1,673	9.9
Men	5,308	342	208	550	10.4
Women	11,601	754	369	1,123	9.7

[1] The distinction between full- and part-time workers is based on hours usually worked. These data will not sum to totals because full- or part-time status on the principal job is not identifiable for a small number of multiple jobholders.

NOTE: The prevailing Federal minimum wage was $5.15 per hour in 2000. Data are for wage and salary workers, excluding the incorporated self-employed. They refer to a person's earnings on their sole or principal job, and pertain only to workers who are paid hourly rates. Salaried workers and other nonhourly workers are not included. The presence of workers with hourly earnings below the minimum wage does not necessarily indicate violations of the Fair Labor Standards Act, as there are exceptions to the minimum wage provisions of the law. In addition, some survey respondents might have rounded hourly earnings to the nearest dollar, and, as a result, reported hourly earnings below the minimum wage even though they earned the minimum wage or higher. Detail for the above race and Hispanic-origin groups will not sum to totals because data for the "other races" group are not presented and Hispanics are included in both the white and black population groups.

SOURCE: "Table 44. Wage and Salary Workers Paid Hourly Rates with Earnings At or Below the Prevailing Federal Minimum Wage by Selected Characteristics," in "Average Annual Tables," *Employment and Earnings*, vol. 48, no. 1, January 2001

recipients transitioning to work. In some states work or schooling to prepare for work were conditions for receiving the benefits, and mothers with children under age six had to work at least 20 hours per week to qualify. Beginning in 2000 mothers of children over age six were required to work 30 hours per week.

TABLE 5.9

Poverty thresholds by size of family and number of related children under 18 years, 2000

(Dollars)

Size of family unit	Related children under 18 years								
	None	One	Two	Three	Four	Five	Six	Seven	Eight or more
One person (unrelated individual):									
Under 65 years	8,959								
65 years and over	8,259								
Two people:									
Householder under 65 years	11,531	11,869							
Householder 65 years and over	10,409	11,824							
Three people	13,470	13,861	13,874						
Four people	17,761	18,052	17,463	17,524					
Five people	21,419	21,731	21,065	20,550	20,236				
Six people	24,636	24,734	24,224	23,736	23,009	22,579			
Seven people	28,347	28,524	27,914	27,489	26,696	25,772	24,758		
Eight people	31,704	31,984	31,408	30,904	30,188	29,279	28,334	28,093	
Nine people or more	38,138	38,322	37,813	37,385	36,682	35,716	34,841	34,625	33,291

SOURCE: Joseph Dalaker, "Poverty Thresholds in 2000 by Size of Family and Number of Related Children under 18 Years," in *Poverty in the United States: 2000,* Current Population Reports, P60-214, U. S. Census Bureau, Washington, DC, September 2001

TABLE 5.10

Poverty status of the population in 1999 by age and sex, 2000

(Numbers in thousands.)

Poverty status and age	Total		Sex			
			Male		Female	
	Number	Percent	Number	Percent	Number	Percent
Total [1]						
Total	273,493	100.0	133,647	100.0	139,846	100.0
Below poverty level	32,258	11.8	13,813	10.3	18,445	13.2
Above poverty level	241,235	88.2	119,834	89.7	121,401	86.8
Under 18 years						
Total	71,731	100.0	36,746	100.0	34,985	100.0
Below poverty level	12,109	16.9	6,058	16.5	6,051	17.3
Above poverty level	59,622	83.1	30,688	83.5	28,934	82.7
18 to 64 years						
Total	169,141	100.0	83,015	100.0	86,126	100.0
Below poverty level	16,982	10.0	6,795	8.2	10,187	11.8
Above poverty level	152,159	90.0	76,220	91.8	75,939	88.2
65 years and over						
Total	32,621	100.0	13,886	100.0	18,735	100.0
Below poverty level	3,167	9.7	960	6.9	2,207	11.8
Above poverty level	29,454	90.3	12,926	93.1	16,528	88.2

[1] Poverty statistics excludes unrelated individuals under 15 years.

SOURCE: "Table 16. Poverty Status of the Population in 1999 by Age and Sex: March 2000," in *Women in the United States: March 2000,* Current Population Survey Supplement, PPL-121, U. S. Census Bureau, Washington, DC, March 15, 2001

FIGURE 5.4

Poverty rates of people in families by family type and presence of workers, 2000

(Percent)

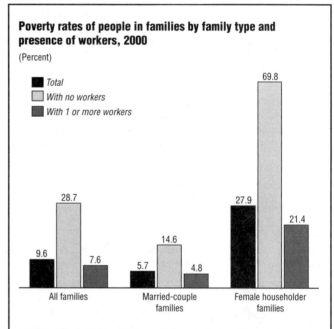

SOURCE: Joseph Dalaker, "Figure 6. Poverty Rates of People in Families by Family Type and Presence of Workers: 2000," in *Poverty in the United States: 2000,* Current Population Reports, P60-214, U.S. Census Bureau, Washington, DC, September 2001

In 1998 writer and researcher Barbara Ehrenreich set out to experience the life of a woman entering the workforce at the bottom rung, as was happening to many welfare mothers. In her account, *Nickel and Dimed: On (Not) Getting By in America* (Metropolitan Books, New York, 2001), she describes her experiences as a waitress, a cleaning woman, a nursing home aide, and a Wal-Mart sales clerk in three different regions of the country.

Ehrenreich had several advantages as compared to many low-income women in the workforce: She was white and healthy with a car and no young children. Although she sometimes had to work two jobs simultaneously, she managed to feed herself. Finding affordable housing and saving up enough for the move-in costs (deposits and first and last months' rent) were much more difficult, if not impossible.

TABLE 5.11

Income deficit or surplus of families and unrelated individuals by poverty status, 2000

(Numbers in thousands)

Characteristic	Total	Under $500	$500 to $999	$1,000 to $1,999	$2,000 to $2,999	$3,000 to $3,999	$4,000 to $4,999	$5,000 to $5,999	$6,000 to $6,999	$7,000 to $7,999	$8,000 or more	Average deficit	Deficit per capita
						Size of deficit or surplus							
Deficit for Those Below Poverty													
All families	6,226	261	302	623	561	471	472	481	393	402	2,259	6,820	1,922
Married-couple families	2,638	139	145	289	237	223	222	191	136	139	916	6,612	1,712
Families with female householders, no husband present	3,099	98	137	290	275	229	205	246	230	206	1,183	7,018	2,084
Unrelated individual	8,530	557	779	1,427	1,206	707	493	454	449	454	2,004	4,388	4,388
Male	3,458	186	308	515	481	237	217	173	204	197	939	4,724	4,724
Female	5,073	371	471	912	725	470	276	281	245	257	1,065	4,159	4,159
Surplus for Those Above Poverty													
All families	66,158	386	318	768	808	820	774	829	865	816	59,773	56,427	18,001
Married-couple families	52,968	205	171	404	440	453	477	492	511	539	49,276	62,599	19,490
Families with female householders, no husband present	9,427	146	124	293	317	290	257	280	266	234	7,219	27,778	9,701
Unrelated individual	36,590	540	629	1,549	1,237	1,361	1,166	1,038	1,257	967	26,846	26,622	26,622
Male	18,171	223	172	618	428	539	479	401	594	399	14,318	31,067	31,067
Female	18,419	317	457	931	809	822	687	637	663	569	12,529	22,237	22,237

SOURCE: Joseph Dalaker, "Table F. Income Deficit or Surplus of Families and Unrelated Individuals by Poverty Status: 2000," in *Poverty in the United States: 2000,* Current Population Reports, P60-214, U.S. Census Bureau, Washington, DC, September 2001

TABLE 5.12

Poverty rates for people in families with children, 1993–99

	1993	1994	1995	1996	1997	1998	1999
Single-mother families							
Before counting government benefits	55.1%	53.8%	50.8%	49.8%	50.6%	45.9%	42.8%
After counting government benefits	41.0%	37.2%	33.5%	33.3%	33.7%	30.0%	27.7%
Other families with children							
Before counting government benefits	14.7%	13.8%	12.8%	12.6%	11.9%	11.4%	10.6%
After counting government benefits	10.7%	9.3%	8.2%	8.1%	7.6%	7.3%	6.8%

SOURCE: Kathryn H. Porter and Allen Dupree, "Table 2: Poverty Rates for People in Families with Children," in *Poverty Trends for Families Headed by Working Single Mothers: 1993 to 1999,* Center on Budget and Policy Priorities, Washington, DC, August 2001

TABLE 5.13

People in working single-mother families lifted out of poverty by government benefits, 1993–99

Type of assistance	1993	1994	1995	1996	1997	1998	1999
Cash assistance and food stamps	11.0%	13.9%	15.5%	12.0%	9.8%	11.1%	10.4%
Cash assistance	6.1%	6.8%	6.9%	5.3%	4.6%	5.0%	5.0%
Food stamps	4.9%	7.1%	8.6%	6.7%	5.3%	6.2%	5.4%
Earned Income Tax Credit	11.2%	16.4%	20.0%	20.8%	24.9%	25.4%	26.7%
Other benefits	10.8%	11.0%	10.5%	10.6%	9.6%	7.8%	5.2%
Total government benefits and taxes	32.9%	41.2%	46.0%	43.4%	44.3%	44.3%	42.2%

SOURCE: Kathryn H. Porter and Allen Dupree, "Table 6. People in Working Single-Mother Families Lifted out of Poverty by Government Benefits," in *Poverty Trends for Families Headed by Working Single Mothers: 1993 to 1999,* Center on Budget and Policy Priorities, Washington, DC, August 2001

FOOD PROGRAMS. Although government expenditures for food programs such as school breakfasts and lunches, child and adult care, and the Special Supplemen-tal Nutrition Program for Women, Infants, and Children (WIC) increased between 1993 and 1999, expenditures for the food stamp program, by far the largest government

TABLE 5.14

Expenditures for federal government nutrition assistance programs, 1990 and 1999

Nutrition assistance program	Nominal expenditures		Real expenditures[1]		Change, FY 1990-99
	FY 1990	FY 1999[2]	FY 1990	FY 1999[2]	
	Million dollars		Million dollars		Percent
All programs	24,874.0	32,862.3	31,986.4	32,862.3	2.7
Food Stamp	15,491.1	17,665.2	19,920.6	17,665.2	-11.3
National School Lunch	3,833.7	5,985.6	4,929.9	5,985.6	21.4
WIC	2,122.2	3,922.3	2,729.0	3,922.3	43.7
Child and Adult Care	812.9	1,613.5	1,045.3	1,613.5	54.3
School Breakfast	596.2	1,333.6	766.7	1,333.6	73.9

[1]Real expenditures were calculated using the Consumer Price Index for All Urban Consumers (CPI-U) and are reported in fiscal 1999 dollars.
[2]1999 data subject to change with later reporting.

SOURCE: Victor Oliveira, "Table 1. Real Expenditures for the Food Stamp Program Were Lower in Fiscal 1999 Than in Fiscal 1990, While Other Nutrition Assistance Programs Grew," in "Food Assistance Expanded, Then Contracted in the 1990's," *FoodReview*, vol. 23, no. 3, September-December, 2000

nutrition assistance program, decreased by 11.3 percent. (See Table 5.14.) Participation in WIC increased from less than 2 million in 1980 to more than 7 million in 1999. (See Figure 5.5.) The *FoodReview* January–April 2001 issue states that almost half of all American infants participated in WIC. In contrast, the number of food stamp participants decreased by almost 34 percent from the participation peak in 1994. Much of this decrease resulted from the strong economy of the late 1990s and to restrictions placed on food stamp participation by PRWORA. Table 5.15 shows that food insecurity increased between 1995 and 1999 for many low-income households, including women living alone, but did not increase significantly for single mothers with children. Nevertheless 41.4 percent of single-mother households not receiving food stamps experienced food insecurity in 1999, although hunger dropped by almost 4 percent for this group between 1995 and 1999.

CHILD SUPPORT. When President Bill Clinton signed PRWORA in 1996, he stated, "If every parent paid the child support that he or she owes legally today, we could move 800,000 women and children off welfare immediately." The IWPR, in *How Much Can Child Support Provide? Welfare, Family Income, and Child Support* (1999), examined the role of child support in helping welfare recipients and other low-income single-mother families to become self-sufficient. The study found that child support generally provided only a small portion of the income of single-mother families.

According to the Census Bureau, the majority of custodial mothers have child support awards, and most of them receive at least some of their child support. However, the IWPR study found that very few custodial parents received support without an agreement. Most of those without a child support agreement were young, minority women with little education and few job skills. Even if

these women had support agreements, the award was likely to be small and difficult to collect. These are the same women who had difficulty finding a stable, well-paying job. The report concluded that child support does not constitute a safety net or a substitute for government assistance to single mothers.

In March 2000 The Urban Institute reported that child support kept 500,000 children out of poverty. However, in an April 2001 report they found that two-thirds of the nearly 11 million fathers who did not live with their children also did not pay formal child support. Approximately 2.5 million of these fathers lived in poverty themselves and more than 40 percent of them had less than a high school education. Furthermore, 29 percent of these fathers were institutionalized, primarily in prisons. The remainder had little access to government benefits for the poor, such as job training.

Elderly Women

Poverty among older women and men has declined over the past decades with the establishment of Medicare and increases in Social Security benefits. In addition Supplemental Security Income (SSI) has become available to more people. During the rapid economic expansion following World War II, Americans accumulated pensions and built equity in their homes.

Nevertheless, although the poverty rate among the elderly decreased from 29 percent in 1966 to 10.5 percent in 1998, many older women remain poor or may sink into poverty when medical expenses deplete their savings. According to the Census Bureau, almost 11 percent of women aged 55 to 64 were poor in 1998, compared to 7 to 8 percent of men. Among those 65 and older, 15 percent of women and 8 percent of men were below the poverty level. Among those over 75, 10 percent of men and 20 percent of

TABLE 5.15

Food insecurity among low-income households not receiving food stamps, 1995–99

| Type of household | Food insecurity (with or without hunger) | | | Hunger | | |
| | 1995 | 1999 | Change | 1995 | 1999 | Change |
	Percent		Percentage points	Percent		Percentage points
All households	11.8	10.1	-1.7	4.2	3.0	-1.2
Households with incomes above 130 percent of poverty line	6.2	5.6	-.6	1.9	1.3	-.6
Low-income households (income below 130 percent of poverty line)	31.5	32.4	—	11.9	10.7	-1.2
Low-income households not receiving food stamps during the previous month	23.2	28.2	5.0	8.8	8.9	—
Noncitizens	33.3	34.2	—	12.1	9.3	—
Citizens	22.1	27.4	5.3	8.4	8.8	—
Two-parent with children	26.6	32.0	5.5	6.4	6.1	—
Single mother with children	36.3	41.4	—	14.9	11.1	-3.8
Multi-adult with no children	16.8	20.9	4.2	6.3	8.3	—
Men living alone	23.9	29.7	5.8	12.8	12.1	—
Women living alone	16.9	19.9	3.0	6.7	8.0	—
Low-income households receiving food stamps during the previous month	48.9	48.8	—	18.6	17.9	—
Noncitizens	51.5	52.7	—	17.3	17.7	—
Citizens	48.6	48.5	—	18.8	17.9	—
Two-parent with children	49.5	52.4	—	17.4	10.9	—
Single mother with children	51.3	47.5	—	19.0	15.3	—
Multi-adult with no children	46.8	43.6	—	16.7	23.6	—
Men living alone	54.8	55.6	—	33.8	24.7	—
Women living alone	38.6	50.2	11.6	15.3	24.6	9.3

— = Change was not significant at 90-percent confidence level.

SOURCE: Mark Nord, "Table 2. Food Insecurity Among Low-Income Households Not Receiving Food Stamps Rose Between 1995 and 1999," in "Food Stamp Participation and Food Security," *FoodReview*, vol. 24, no. 1, January-April 2001

women lived in poverty. The highest poverty rates were among divorced and widowed women aged 80 and above.

Nine percent of women 65 and over continue to work to supplement limited incomes. In 1998, 2.2 percent of older women and 2.7 percent of older men who worked full-time year-round remained below the poverty level.

According to a May 2001 study by the IWPR, *The Gender Gap in Pension Coverage: What Does the Future Hold?*, there is a substantial gender gap in all forms of retirement income, including Social Security, pensions, savings, and earnings from postretirement employment. Despite the growing participation of women in the labor force, they continue to receive fewer traditional pension and Social Security benefits than men. Furthermore, women live longer than men and therefore require more retirement income.

SOCIAL SECURITY. According to the CBPP, Social Security has been more effective in lifting people out of poverty than all other government programs combined. More women than men depend on Social Security as their only income, and many of these women live at or just above the poverty level. Without Social Security, almost 53 percent of women age 65 and older would be poor, as

FIGURE 5.5

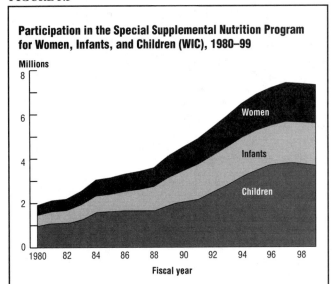

Participation in the Special Supplemental Nutrition Program for Women, Infants, and Children (WIC), 1980–99

SOURCE: Victor Oliveira and Craig Gundersen, "Figure 1. Participation in WIC Increased During Most of the 1990's," in "WIC Increases the Nutrient Intake of Children," *FoodReview*, vol. 24, no. 1, January-April 2001

would 41 percent of men. Although women pay only 38 percent of all Social Security payroll taxes, they receive 53 percent of the benefits because they live longer than men and Social Security benefits increase annually to keep up with inflation. In addition, more women than men receive spousal Social Security benefits, regardless of their labor force participation.

Even with Social Security benefits, 20 percent of widows, 24 percent of divorced women, 28 percent of never-married women, and 47 percent of separated elderly women lived in poverty in 1998. Divorced and never-married women form an increasing proportion of the elderly. The proportion of elderly African American and Hispanic women living in poverty was almost three times the proportion of white elderly women, and the proportion of divorced and never-married elderly African American women is growing rapidly.

THE PENSION GAP. According to the IWRP study, women are about half as likely as men to receive a pension, either their own or that of their spouse. Low-wage workers, including a large proportion of women, are less likely to have an employer-sponsored pension plan. Women who do have pensions receive only about half as much as men. Women who are dependent on their husbands' pension may lose it through divorce or have it reduced if their husbands die. According to the Department of Labor, only 39 percent of female workers are covered by private pension plans, compared to 46 percent of men. Furthermore, only 32 percent of female retirees over age 55 receive pension benefits, compared to 55 percent of male retirees.

Because of the earnings gap, women's pensions are smaller than men's. According to the AFL-CIO, in 1998 one-half of all older women with private pensions received less than $3,486 per year, compared to a median

pension income of $7,020 for men. The average annual pension payment in 1998 was $3,700 for women and $6,400 for men, according to The Urban Institute.

According to the IWPR study, more women than ever before are participating in employee-sponsored pension plans, and for women who work full-time the plans are nearly equal to those of men. Among older employees, however, 44 percent of women lack pension plans, compared to only 36 percent of male employees. Less than one-third of part-time workers, primarily women, have pension plans. Of women aged 35 to 64, 35 percent work too few hours to participate in their employers' pension plans, compared to only 20 percent of men. Approximately half of all women leave the workforce at some point to care for children. During these absences, women workers cannot contribute to their pensions and retirement savings plans.

Women do not stay at the same jobs as long as men. According to the Bureau of Labor Statistics, women averaged only 3.8 years at their current jobs. Many employers do not offer pension benefits until an employee has worked for five years. The IWPR study found that for women whose employers offered pension plans, the most common reason for not participating was that the women had not worked long enough for that employer. The second most common reason for nonparticipation was that they worked part-time and so did not qualify.

When employees leave a job, they often receive a lump-sum distribution of their pension fund assets. The IWPR study found that women are much less likely than men to roll over their distribution into another retirement fund. Rather, they use the distribution to pay off bills or loans or for their children's education. In part this is because women average only about one-half of the lump-sum distributions that men receive.

CHAPTER 6
WOMEN AND THEIR CHILDREN

Although more and more women are joining the workforce and pursuing educational opportunities and new careers, raising children remains a focal point of life for most of them. Surveys of college women find that 90 percent intend to have children. The development of effective methods of contraception, particularly birth control pills, the legalization of abortion, the "morning-after" pill, and increased condom use to combat the spread of the human immunodeficiency virus (HIV) and other sexually transmitted diseases have contributed to falling fertility and birth rates and have enabled women to time their childbearing. The advent of fertility pills and other reproductive technologies have allowed many women to delay childbearing. Increases in maternal age, in single motherhood, and in labor force participation by women have affected many aspects of women's relationships with their children.

FERTILITY AND BIRTH RATES

American women are having fewer children than in the past. The fertility rate is defined as the total number of live births per 1,000 women aged 15 to 44 within population categories other than age. The fertility rate increased dramatically during the post-World War II baby boom of the 1940s and 1950s. (See Figure 6.1.) In the early 1960s, when far fewer women were active in the labor force and larger families were more common, the fertility rate was 118 live births per 1,000 women. However, the fertility rate declined in the 1960s and early 1970s to a level below that of the 1930s. By 1972 the fertility rate had dropped to 73.1 per 1,000. Between 1990 and 1997 the fertility rate declined by another 8 percent. Since 1997 the fertility rate has increased slightly. The estimated fertility rate for 2000 was 67.6 per 1,000 women aged 15 to 44, up 3 percent from 1999. (See Table 6.1.) Preliminary data indicates that the number of births rose 3 percent between 1999 and 2000, to just over 4 million annually.

FIGURE 6.1

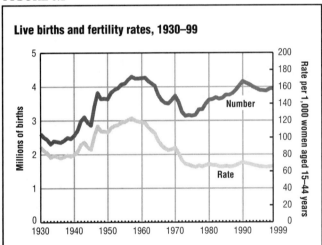

Live births and fertility rates, 1930–99

NOTE: Beginning with 1959, trend lines are based on registered live births; trend lines for 1930–59 are based on live births adjusted for underregistration.

SOURCE: Stephanie J. Ventura, Joyce A. Martin, Sally C. Curtin, Fay Menacker, and Brady E. Hamilton, "Live Births and Fertility Rates: United States, 1930–99," in "Births: Final Data for 1999," *National Vital Statistics Reports,* vol. 49, no. 1, April 17, 2001

Birth rates are defined as the number of live births per 1,000 people in a specified group. The Census Bureau estimates that 4.2 to 4.3 million women between the ages of 15 and 50 gave birth in 2000, for a birth rate of 59 per 1,000 women. The highest birth rate in 2000, 121.7, was among women aged 25 to 29. The birth rate increased steadily with age up to 25 and declined steadily with age after 29. (See Table 6.1.)

Increasing Maternal Age

The rising birth rate among older mothers was a remarkable feature of the late 20th century. (See Figure 6.2.) As the teenage birth rate declined and the rates for women in their 20s remained fairly stable, the birth rates

TABLE 6.1

Birth rates by age of mother, live-birth order, and race and Hispanic origin of mother, preliminary 2000

[Data are based on a continuous file of records received from the States. Rates per 1,000 women in specified age and racial group]

Live-birth order and race/Hispanic origin of mother	15-44 years[1]	Age of mother							
		10-14 years	15-19 years	20-24 years	25-29 years	30-34 years	35-39 years	40-44 years	45-49 years[2]
All races	67.6	0.9	48.7	112.5	121.7	94.2	40.3	7.9	0.5
1st child	27.1	0.9	38.2	51.7	44.2	27.2	9.0	1.7	0.1
2d child	22.0	0.0	8.8	38.8	42.0	34.0	13.1	2.2	0.1
3d child	11.3	*	1.5	15.9	22.5	19.6	9.5	1.6	0.1
4th child and over	7.2	*	0.2	6.0	13.0	13.3	8.7	2.4	0.2
White, total[3]	66.7	0.6	43.9	108.3	124.9	97.6	40.7	7.7	0.4
1st child	26.9	0.6	35.2	51.8	46.4	28.4	9.2	1.7	0.1
2d child	22.0	0.0	7.5	37.8	44.0	35.6	13.2	2.1	0.1
3d child	11.2	*	1.1	14.3	22.9	20.6	9.8	1.6	0.1
4th child and over	6.6	*	0.1	4.5	11.6	12.9	8.5	2.3	0.1
White, non-Hispanic	58.7	0.3	32.8	90.1	113.4	94.2	39.0	7.2	0.4
1st child	24.3	0.3	27.0	44.9	46.1	29.5	9.4	1.7	0.1
2d child	19.9	*	5.0	31.1	40.3	35.8	13.3	2.1	0.1
3d child	9.5	*	0.6	11.0	18.5	18.7	9.2	1.5	0.1
4th child and over	5.1	*	0.1	3.1	8.5	10.1	7.1	1.9	0.1
Black, total[3]	71.4	2.5	79.2	143.7	104.8	67.0	32.0	7.1	0.4
1st child	26.7	2.4	58.7	53.7	25.5	14.2	5.8	1.2	0.1
2d child	21.2	0.1	16.4	48.7	33.5	20.9	9.1	1.7	0.1
3d child	12.8	*	3.5	26.6	24.0	15.6	7.5	1.6	0.1
4th child and over	10.7	*	0.6	14.7	21.8	16.4	9.6	2.7	0.2
American Indian, total[3,4]	71.3	1.3	67.9	135.4	106.7	68.0	32.7	7.4	0.3
1st child	25.0	1.3	51.8	49.8	21.0	9.8	3.9	0.9	*
2d child	20.0	*	13.6	50.0	31.0	16.1	6.4	1.1	*
3d child	12.6	*	2.2	24.9	26.8	15.5	6.6	1.1	*
4th child and over	13.6	*	0.2	10.8	28.0	26.5	15.7	4.2	*
Asian or Pacific Islander, total[3]	70.7	0.3	21.8	72.2	125.7	120.6	60.2	12.7	0.9
1st child	33.0	0.3	17.5	43.6	68.5	47.5	16.6	3.1	0.2
2d child	24.1	*	3.5	19.8	38.2	48.2	24.7	4.3	0.2
3d child	8.7	*	0.7	6.0	12.3	16.3	11.9	2.7	0.1
4th child and over	4.9	*	0.1	2.8	6.6	8.5	7.1	2.6	0.3
Hispanic[5]	105.9	1.9	94.4	184.6	170.8	109.0	48.6	11.6	0.6
1st child	39.5	1.8	72.1	80.2	45.2	20.5	7.2	1.5	0.1
2d child	32.3	0.0	18.7	65.8	58.7	32.3	11.8	2.3	0.1
3d child	19.9	*	3.1	28.1	41.7	29.6	12.7	2.5	0.1
4th child and over	14.2	*	0.4	10.4	25.1	26.6	17.0	5.3	0.3

0.0 Quantity more than zero but less than 0.05.

*Figure does not meet standards of reliability or precision; based on fewer than 20 births in the numerator.

[1] The rate shown is the fertility rate, which is defined as the total number of births, regardless of age of mother, per 1,000 women aged 15-44 years.

[2] The birth rate for ages 45-49 years is computed by relating births to women aged 45-54 years to women aged 45-49 years, because most of the births in this group are to women aged 45-49.

[3] Race and Hispanic origin are reported separately on the birth certificate. Data for persons of Hispanic origin are included in the data for each race group according to the mother's reported race.

[4] Includes births to Aleuts and Eskimos.

[5] Includes all persons of Hispanic origin of any race.

NOTE: Data are subject to sampling and/or random variation.

SOURCE: Joyce A. Martin, Brady E. Hamilton, and Stephanie J. Ventura, "Birth Rates by Age of Mother, Live-Birth Order, and Race and Hispanic Origin of Mother: United States, Preliminary 2000," in "Births: Preliminary Data for 2000," *National Vital Statistics Reports,* vol. 49, no. 5, July 24, 2001

for women in their 30s increased steadily. According to the National Center for Health Statistics (NCHS), between 1975 and 1990 the birth rate for women aged 30 to 34 increased 3 percent per year. During the 1990s the increase slowed to about 1 percent annually. The birth rate for women in their later 30s more than doubled between 1978 and 1999, increasing 4 percent per year from 1978 to 1990. The increase slowed in the 1990s to about 2 percent annually. The 1999 birth rate for women aged 35 to 39 equaled the previous high in 1967, and the number of births to women in this age group increased by more than

one-third during the 1990s. The birth rate for women in their early 40s increased by one-third in the 1990s, and the number of births to women aged 40 to 44 increased 71 percent. Between 1982 and 1995 fertility drug treatment increased significantly among childless women aged 35 to 44 who had been unable to conceive.

Among women aged 45 to 49 the birth rate increased in 2000 to 0.5, up from 0.4 in 1998 and 1999. The number of births to women in their late 40s was the highest since 1966, in part because of the increased numbers of women

FIGURE 6.2

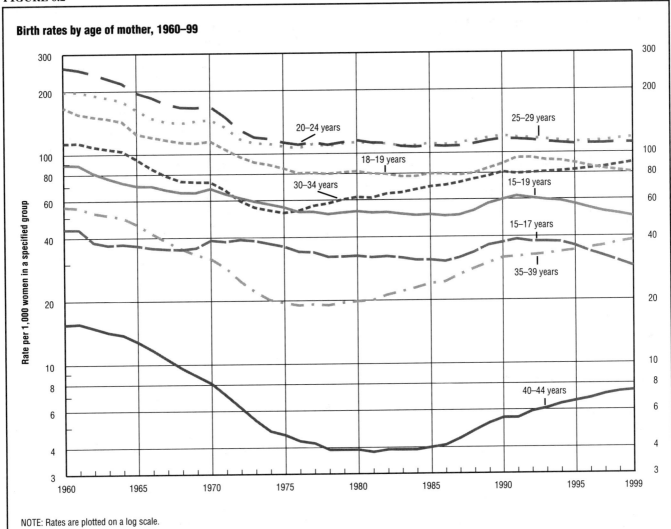

Birth rates by age of mother, 1960–99

NOTE: Rates are plotted on a log scale.

SOURCE: Stephanie J. Ventura, Joyce A. Martin, Sally C. Curtin, Fay Menacker, and Brady E. Hamilton, "Birth Rates by Age of Mother: United States, 1960–99," in "Births: Final Data for 1999," *National Vital Statistics Reports,* vol. 49, no. 1, April 17, 2001

in this age group, a result of the postwar baby boom. Birth rates for women aged 50 to 54 were not even calculated until 1997. Recent advances in reproductive technologies have enabled more women 50 and over to give birth. In 1999 there were 174 children born to women over 49, including 68 multiple births.

Racial and Ethnic Differences

The number of births increased in 2000 for all racial and ethnic groups. Hispanic women had by far the highest fertility rate at 105.9, up 4 percent from 1999 but below the high of 1992. Births to Hispanic women accounted for 20 percent of all births in the United States in 2000, compared to 14 percent in 1989. Hispanic 15- to 29-year-olds had higher birth rates than any other group of women. Non-Hispanic white women had the lowest fertility rate at 58.7. The other racial groups each had fertility rates of approximately 71. Fertility rates increased among non-Hispanic women

by about 2 percent in 2000, except among Asian and Pacific Islanders, whose fertility rate jumped 8 percent to its highest level since 1988. Asian and Pacific Islanders had the lowest birth rates among 10- to 24-year-olds and the highest among women 30 and over. (See Table 6.1.)

According to the Census Bureau, 12 percent of women of childbearing age were foreign-born (7.2 million in 1998). Foreign-born women had a higher fertility rate than native-born women; however, birth rates were not significantly different for women between 30 and 44. Whereas native-born women completed their childbearing years with an average of 1.8 children each, less than the replacement rate, foreign-born women had an average of 2.2 children each.

Childbearing among Teenagers

Both the number of births to teens and the birth rate among teenagers declined significantly for every age

TABLE 6.2

Births and birth rates for teenagers by age, 1991–2000

Year	Number of births			Birth rate		
	10–14 years	15–17 years	18–19 years	10–14 years	15–17 years	18–19 years
2000	8,561	157,661	312,845	0.9	27.5	79.5
1999	9,054	163,588	312,462	0.9	28.7	80.3
1998	9,462	173,231	311,664	1.0	30.4	82.0
1997	10,121	180,154	303,066	1.1	32.1	83.6
1996	11,148	185,721	305,856	1.2	33.8	86.0
1995	11,242	192,508	307,365	1.3	36.0	89.1
1994	12,901	195,169	310,319	1.4	37.6	91.5
1993	12,554	190,535	310,558	1.4	37.8	92.1
1992	12,220	187,549	317,866	1.4	37.8	94.5
1991	12,014	188,226	331,351	1.4	38.7	94.4
Percent change						
1991–2000	−28.7	−16.2	−5.6	−35.7	−28.9	−15.8

NOTE: Data for 2000 are preliminary.

SOURCE: Stephanie J. Ventura, T.J. Mathews, and Brady E. Hamilton, "Table A. Birth and Birth Rates for Teenagers by Age: United States, 1991–2000," in "Births to Teenagers in the United States, 1940–2000," *National Vital Statistics Reports,* vol. 49, no. 10, September 25, 2001

FIGURE 6.3

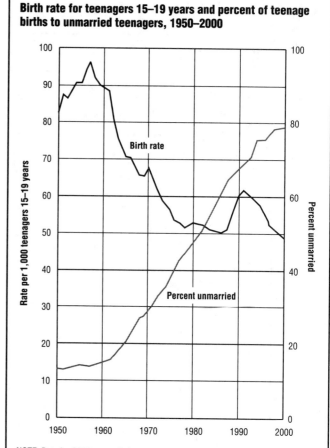

Birth rate for teenagers 15–19 years and percent of teenage births to unmarried teenagers, 1950–2000

NOTE: Data for 2000 are preliminary.

SOURCE: Stephanie J. Ventura, T.J. Mathews, and Brady E. Hamilton, "Figure 1. Birth Rate for Teenagers 15–19 Years and Percent of Teenage Births to Unmarried Teenagers: United States, 1950–2000," in "Births to Teenagers in the United States, 1940–2000," *National Vital Statistics Reports,* vol. 49, no. 10, September 25, 2001

group between 1991 and 2000. (See Table 6.2.) The number of teen births in 2000 was at its lowest point since 1987, despite an increase in the number of teenagers. Among very young teens aged 10 to 14 the rate declined from 1.4 in 1994 to an all-time low of 0.9 in 1999 and 2000. In 1999 there were 9,054 live births to girls aged 10 to 14, the lowest number since 1967, in spite of a significant increase in the number of females in this age group. The number of births in this age group declined another 5 percent in 2000. Non-Hispanic whites and Asian and Pacific Islanders had the lowest birth rates in this age group in 2000; blacks had the highest. (See Table 6.1.)

Among teens aged 15 to 19 the birth rate also declined throughout the 1990s, to its lowest point ever in 2000. (See Figure 6.3.) At its peak in 1957 the rate was 96.3 per 1,000, almost twice the rate of 48.7 in 2000. Despite a decrease in the number of teenagers, the birth rate increased 24 percent between 1986 and 1991, when it was 62.1. The birth rate in 2000 was 22 percent lower than in 1991, but it was only 3 percent lower than in 1986. Although the birth rates for all ages over 19 increased in 2000, the rate for teens 15 to 19 decreased 2 percent from 1999. Younger teens accounted for most of the decline. Between 1991 and 2000 the birth rate for 15- to 17-year-olds declined 28.9 percent. (See Table 6.2.)

Although birth rates for black teenagers declined steeply in the 1990s, blacks and Hispanics continued to have the highest teen birth rates. (See Figure 6.4.) The birth rate for black teenagers declined 31 percent between 1991 and 2000, to its lowest rate since data was first collected in 1960. The birth rate for Hispanic teens declined 13 percent from 1994 to 1999 but rose 1 percent in 2000.

Birth rates for non-Hispanic white teenagers fell 24 percent between 1991 and 2000, and birth rates for both American Indian and Asian and Pacific Islander teens fell 20 percent. Asian and Pacific Islander teenagers had the lowest birth rate. In each racial/ethnic group, the rates fell more sharply among teens 15 to 17 than among teens 18 and 19. Of teen mothers with one child, 17 percent had a second child in 2000, compared to 22 percent in 1991.

Education and Income

In 1998 women with at least one year of college but without a degree had the lowest fertility rate (54.6), and those with a graduate or professional degree had the highest (76.2), according to the Census Bureau. The fertility rate was highest for those with family incomes between $20,000 and $24,999 and lowest for those with incomes of $75,000 or more. Women who were not in the labor force had the highest fertility rate (90.5), and unemployed women in the labor force had a higher fertility rate than employed women (73.6 versus 47.6). Women who lived outside of metropolitan areas had a higher fertility rate than those living in cities and suburbs.

Family Size and Marital Status

Families are becoming smaller. According to the Census Bureau, 24 percent of women aged 15 to 44 had two children in 2000. Only 0.3 percent had seven or more children. The percentage of women with two or more children increased with age, and most women have completed their childbearing by the age of 44. In 1998 there were 1,877 children per 1,000 women aged 40 to 44, compared to 3,091 children per 1,000 women of that age in 1976. In 1976 the largest percentage of women aged 40 to 44 (36 percent) had four or more children, whereas in 1998, 36 percent had two children and only 10 percent had four or more. Among Hispanic women aged 40 to 44, 13 percent had four children in 2000. Only 6 percent of native-born women aged 40 to 44 had four children, compared to almost 9 percent of foreign-born women, and 7 percent of foreign-born women had five or six children, compared to less than 2 percent of native-born women.

Among women aged 35 to 39, 35 percent had two children and 7 percent had four children, although 9 percent of African American women in this age group had four. As Table 6.1 shows, women between the ages of 30 and 39 had the highest birth rates for their second child, and women between 40 and 44 had the highest birth rate for their fourth or more.

Although the fertility rate was highest for women who have been married (73.5 births per 1,000 women age 15 to 44), as of October 2000 the fertility rate for never-married women was 41.3, according to the Census Bureau. The birth rate for all unmarried women in 1999 was 44.4, up from 26.4 in 1970 but down from the high of 46.9 in 1994. (See Table 6.3.) Unmarried Hispanic women had the highest birth rate at 93.4, compared to 27.9 for non-Hispanic white women. The birth rate for unmarried women between the ages of 20 and 24 was 72.9. In 2000 the fertility rate for unmarried women increased another 2 percent, to 45.2 births per 1,000 women aged 15 to 44. The number of births to unmarried women was the highest ever, up 3 percent from 1999.

According to the Census Bureau, although most (78 percent) of never-married women aged 15 to 44 had no children, 12 percent had one child and 6 percent had two in 1998. Very few never-married women had more than two children.

Multiple Births

One of the most striking developments in childbearing has been the increase in multiple births in recent years. (See Table 6.4.) Between 1989 and 1999 the num-

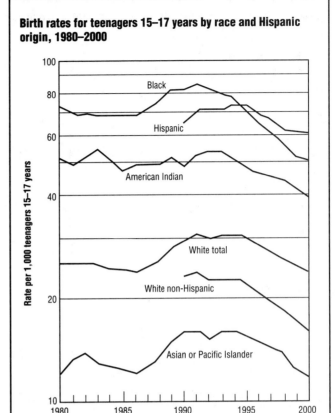

FIGURE 6.4

Birth rates for teenagers 15–17 years by race and Hispanic origin, 1980–2000

NOTES: Data for 2000 are preliminary. Rates are plotted on a log scale.

SOURCE: Stephanie J. Ventura, T.J. Mathews, and Brady E. Hamilton, "Figure 4. Birth Rate for Teenagers 15–17 Years by Race and Hispanic Origin: United States, 1980–2000," in "Births to Teenagers in the United States, 1940–2000," *National Vital Statistics Reports,* vol. 49, no. 10, September 25, 2001

ber of twin births rose 67 percent and the twin birth rate (twin births per 1,000 live births) rose 53 percent. In the past twin birth rates were always highest for women in their 30s, since twin birth rates increase steadily with maternal age. Thus, in 1999 the rates were highest for mothers aged 50 to 54. In this age group 34 percent of births were twins. Between 1990 and 1999 the twin birth rate rose 80 percent for mothers aged 40 to 44 and almost 600 percent for mothers aged 45 to 49. (See Figure 6.5.) The rate rose only 6 percent for mothers under age 20. The number of triplet and higher-order multiple births also increased dramatically since 1980, although the rate declined slightly from 1998 to 1999.

Although the multiple birth rate is increasing among all major racial and ethnic groups, it has increased the most among non-Hispanic white women. Among non-Hispanic white women aged 45 to 54 there were 227.7 multiple births per 1,000 live births in 1999.

Increasing maternal age is a factor in the number of multiple births, since, as women age, they often begin to

TABLE 6.3

Nonmarital childbearing by race, Hispanic origin, maternal age, and birth rate, selected years 1970–99

Race, Hispanic origin of mother, and maternal age	1970	1975	1980	1985	1990	1993	1994	1995	1996	1997	1998	1999
					Percent of live births to unmarried mothers							
All races	10.7	14.3	18.4	22.0	28.0	31.0	32.6	32.2	32.4	32.4	32.8	33.0
White	5.5	7.1	11.2	14.7	20.4	23.6	25.4	25.3	25.7	25.8	26.3	26.8
Black	37.5	49.5	56.1	61.2	66.5	68.7	70.4	69.9	69.8	69.2	69.1	68.9
American Indian or Alaska Native	22.4	32.7	39.2	46.8	53.6	55.8	57.0	57.2	58.0	58.7	59.3	58.9
Asian or Pacific Islander	- - -	- - -	7.3	9.5	13.2	15.7	16.2	16.3	16.7	15.6	15.6	15.4
Chinese	3.0	1.6	2.7	3.0	5.0	6.7	7.2	7.9	9.2	6.5	6.4	6.9
Japanese	4.6	4.6	5.2	7.9	9.6	10.0	11.2	10.8	11.4	10.1	9.7	9.9
Filipino	9.1	6.9	8.6	11.4	15.9	17.7	18.5	19.5	19.4	19.5	19.7	21.1
Hawaiian and part Hawaiian	- - -	- - -	32.9	37.3	45.0	47.8	48.6	49.0	49.9	49.1	51.1	50.4
Other Asian or Pacific Islander	- - -	- - -	5.4	8.5	12.6	16.1	16.4	16.2	16.5	15.6	15.2	14.5
Hispanic origin[1,2]	- - -	- - -	23.6	29.5	36.7	40.0	43.1	40.8	40.7	40.9	41.6	42.2
Mexican	- - -	- - -	20.3	25.7	33.3	37.0	40.8	38.1	37.9	38.9	39.6	40.1
Puerto Rican	- - -	- - -	46.3	51.1	55.9	59.4	60.2	60.0	60.7	59.4	59.5	59.6
Cuban	- - -	- - -	10.0	16.1	18.2	21.0	22.9	23.8	24.7	24.4	24.8	26.4
Central and South American	- - -	- - -	27.1	34.9	41.2	45.2	45.9	44.1	44.1	41.8	42.0	43.7
Other and unknown Hispanic	- - -	- - -	22.4	31.1	37.2	38.7	43.5	44.0	43.5	43.6	45.3	45.8
White, non-Hispanic[1]	- - -	- - -	9.6	12.4	16.9	19.5	20.8	21.2	21.5	21.5	21.9	22.1
Black, non-Hispanic[1]	- - -	- - -	57.3	62.1	66.7	68.9	70.7	70.0	70.0	69.4	69.3	69.1
					Number of live births, in thousands							
Live births to unmarried mothers	399	448	666	828	1,165	1,240	1,290	1,254	1,260	1,257	1,294	1,309
Maternal age					Percent distribution of live births to unmarried mothers							
Under 20 years	50.1	52.1	40.8	33.8	30.9	29.7	30.5	30.9	30.4	30.7	30.1	29.3
20–24 years	31.8	29.9	35.6	36.3	34.7	35.4	34.8	34.5	34.2	34.9	35.6	36.4
25 years and over	18.1	18.0	23.5	29.9	34.4	34.9	34.6	34.7	35.3	34.4	34.3	34.3
					Live births per 1,000 unmarried women 15–44 years of age[3]							
All races and origins	26.4	24.5	29.4	32.8	43.8	45.3	46.9	45.1	44.8	44.0	44.3	44.4
White[4]	13.9	12.4	18.1	22.5	32.9	35.9	38.3	37.5	37.6	37.0	37.5	38.1
Black[4]	95.5	84.2	81.1	77.0	90.5	84.0	82.1	75.9	74.4	73.4	73.3	71.5
Hispanic origin[1,2]	- - -	- - -	- - -	- - -	89.6	95.2	101.2	95.0	93.2	91.4	90.1	93.4
White, non-Hispanic	- - -	- - -	- - -	- - -	- - -	- - -	28.5	28.2	28.3	27.0	27.4	27.9

- - - Data not available.

[1] Trend data for Hispanics and non-Hispanics are affected by expansion of the reporting area for an Hispanic-origin item on the birth certificate and by immigration. These two factors affect numbers of events, composition of the Hispanic population, and maternal and infant health characteristics. The number of States in the reporting area increased from 22 in 1980, to 23 and the District of Columbia (DC) in 1983–87,30 and DC in 1988, 47 and DC in 1989, 48 and DC in 1990, 49 and DC in 1991–92, and 50 and DC in 1993 and later years.

[2] Includes mothers of all races.

[3] Rates computed by relating births to unmarried mothers, regardless of age of mother, to unmarried women 15-44 years of age. Population data for American Indian or Alaska Native and Asian or Pacific Islander women not available for rate calculations.

[4] For 1970 and 1975, birth rates are by race of child.

NOTES: National estimates for 1970 and 1975 for unmarried mothers based on births occurring in States reporting marital status of mother. The race groups, white, black, American Indian or Alaska Native, and Asian or Pacific Islander, include persons of Hispanic and non-Hispanic origin. Conversely, persons of Hispanic origin may be of any race. In 1995 procedures implemented in California to more accurately identify the marital status of Hispanic mothers account for some of the decline in measures of nonmarital childbearing for women of all races, white women, and Hispanic women between 1994 and 1995. Other reporting changes implemented in California, Nevada, New York City, and Connecticut in 1997 and 1998 have affected trends for all groups.

SOURCE: "Table 9. Nonmarital Childbearing according to Detailed Race and Hispanic Origin of Mother, and Maternal Age and Birth Rates for Unmarried Women by Race and Hispanic Origin of Mother: United States, Selected Years 1970–99," in *Health, United States, 2001*, National Center for Health Statistics, Hyattsville, MD, 2001

release multiple eggs during a single ovulation. However, most of the increase in triplet and higher-order births results from assisted reproductive techniques and ovulation-inducing (fertility) drugs. Ovulation-inducing drugs often result in women releasing multiple eggs for fertilization during a single cycle. Assisted reproductive techniques, such as in vitro fertilization, involve the implantation of multiple embryos into the mother's uterus.

Multiple births pose increased risks for mothers and children. Mothers suffer more ante- and postpartum complications. On average, twins weigh one-third less at birth than single newborns, and triplets weigh one-half as much as singletons. Multiple infants are more likely to be in neonatal intensive care and are less likely to survive their first year. In addition, multiple births may take a major toll on the financial and emotional well-being of families. In 1999 the American College of Obstetricians and Gynecologists and the American Society of Reproductive Medicine issued new recommendations for preventing triplet and higher-order births because of the high risk they pose to the fetuses and infants. Recent improvements in assisted reproductive techniques also may help to lower the incidence of multiple births.

TABLE 6.4

Numbers of twin, triplet, quadruplet, and quintuplet and other higher order multiple births, 1989–99

Year	Twins	Triplets	Quadruplets	Quintuplets and other higher order multiples[1]
1999	114,307	6,742	512	67
1998	110,670	6,919	627	79
1997	104,137	6,148	510	79
1996	100,750	5,298	560	81
1995	96,736	4,551	365	57
1994	97,064	4,233	315	46
1993	96,445	3,834	277	57
1992	95,372	3,547	310	26
1991	94,779	3,121	203	22
1990	93,865	2,830	185	13
1989	90,118	2,529	229	40

[1] Quintuplets, sextuplets, and higher order multiple births are not differentiated in the national data set.

SOURCE: Stephanie J. Ventura, Joyce A. Martin, Sally C. Curtin, Fay Menacker, and Brady E. Hamilton, "Table J. Numbers of Twin, Triplet, Quadruplet, and Quintuplet and Other Higher Order Multiple Births: United States, 1989–99," in "Births: Final Data for 1999," *National Vital Statistics Reports*, vol. 49, no. 1, April 17, 2001

UNMARRIED CHILDBEARING

Since the 1970s increasing percentages of women of all ages, races, and ethnicities have been giving birth outside marriage. (See Table 6.3.) In 1970 only 10.7 percent of births were to unmarried women, compared to 18.4 percent in 1980. Between 1994 and 1999, 32.6 to 33 percent of births were to unmarried mothers. Four out of every 10 first births in 1999 (1.3 million) were to unmarried women. Among women under age 25, two-thirds of those having their first baby were unmarried. According to the Census Bureau, 29 percent of all women aged 15 to 50 who gave birth in 2000 were unmarried. Most of these women were between 20 and 34 years old.

Pregnant women no longer feel that they have to marry, and the likelihood that a pregnant woman will marry before giving birth has declined sharply since the early 1960s. According to the Census Bureau, in the early 1960s three out of five single pregnant women under the age of 30 married before the baby was born; by the mid-1990s fewer than one in four married. There are several reasons for this change. Unmarried women are more sexually active than in the past, and many of them have put their education and careers ahead of marriage. The stigma that was formerly attached to unmarried motherhood has largely disappeared. In addition, many women feel that being single is preferable to living in an unhappy, unstable, or abusive marriage, and some women prefer to raise their children by themselves. Furthermore, many women who are having children without being married live with their partners in families that may be traditional in every

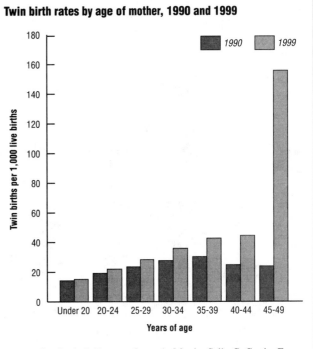

FIGURE 6.5

Twin birth rates by age of mother, 1990 and 1999

SOURCE: Stephanie J. Ventura, Joyce A. Martin, Sally C. Curtin, Fay Menacker, and Brady E. Hamilton, "Figure 10. Twin Birth Rates by Age of Mother: United States, 1990 and 1999," in "Births: Final Data for 1999," *National Vital Statistics Reports*, vol. 49, no. 1, April 17, 2001

way except for the marriage license. Some unmarried mothers are lesbians who have chosen to conceive a child with a male friend or by artificial insemination with sperm from a sperm bank. Finally, part of the increase in unmarried childbearing is attributable to the decrease in the birth rate for married women and to the increasing proportion of unmarried women of childbearing age.

Age and Race

Between 1980 and 1999 the percentage of births to unmarried mothers increased in every age group. (See Figure 6.6.) In 1970, 50.1 percent of births to unmarried mothers were to teenagers. (See Table 6.3.) In 1999 only 29.3 percent of births to unmarried mothers were to women under 20, compared to 36.4 percent to women aged 20 to 24 and 34.3 percent to women 25 and over. Nevertheless, the vast majority of teenage mothers were unmarried, as were nearly 50 percent of mothers between the ages of 20 and 24. (See Figure 6.6.)

In 1999 unmarried women accounted for 68.9 percent of all births to black mothers and 58.9 percent of all births to Native Americans, compared to 42.2 percent of births to Hispanic women and 22.1 percent to non-Hispanic white women. Among Hispanics 59.6 percent of Puerto Rican births were to unmarried mothers, compared to 26.4 percent to Cuban mothers. Only 15.4 percent of

FIGURE 6.6

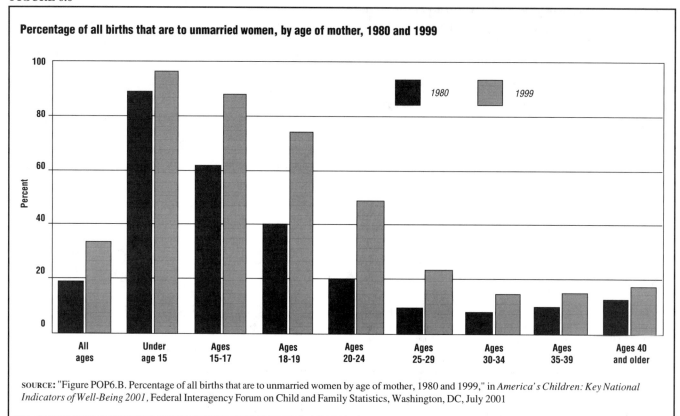

Percentage of all births that are to unmarried women, by age of mother, 1980 and 1999

SOURCE: "Figure POP6.B. Percentage of all births that are to unmarried women by age of mother, 1980 and 1999," in *America's Children: Key National Indicators of Well-Being 2001*, Federal Interagency Forum on Child and Family Statistics, Washington, DC, July 2001

Asian and Pacific Islander births were to unmarried mothers. Within this group 50.4 percent of Hawaiian births were to unmarried mothers, compared to only 6.9 percent of births to Chinese women. (See Table 6.3.)

Never-Married Mothers

According to the Census Bureau, mothers who have never been married tend to be younger and less able to support themselves and their children than other groups of unmarried mothers who may be divorced or widowed. In 1998, 23 percent of mothers (5.5 million women) had never married. Among never-married women in their 30s, 40 percent had given birth, as had one-third of those between the ages of 40 and 44, as compared to only 8 percent of never-married teenagers. Among never-married African American women, 48 percent had given birth, as had one-third of Hispanic women and 13 percent of white non-Hispanic women. Among never-married foreign-born women aged 40 to 44, 12 percent had four children, compared to only 5 percent of never-married native-born women in that age group.

TEENAGE MOTHERHOOD

Although the teenage birth rate has been declining steadily, there were 479,067 births to teens under 20 in 2000, and the birth rate remains much higher for American teens than for teens in other developed countries. Further-

more, the proportion of teen births to unmarried mothers increased steadily from 14 percent in 1957 to 79 percent in 1999 and 2000, although the birth rate for unmarried teens had declined since 1994. This reflects the overall trend toward nonmarital childbearing. In 2000, 72 percent of all births to unmarried mothers were to women aged 20 and over, compared to 50 percent in the mid-1970s.

Sexually Active Teenagers

According to the NCHS, after increasing steadily for 20 years, the proportion of sexually active teenagers stabilized in the mid-1990s. The Alan Guttmacher Institute (AGI), a nonprofit organization devoted to sexual and reproductive health research, policy analysis, and public education, reports that most adolescents begin having sexual intercourse in their middle to late teens. Child Trends, a nonpartisan research organization that conducts an annual statistical analysis of teen childbearing, found that in 2001, 25 percent of teenage girls and 27 percent of teenage boys were sexually active by age 15. Interestingly, teenagers guessed that 38 percent of their peers were sexually active by that age, and adults thought that 69 percent of teens were having sexual intercourse by that age.

Early sexual activity results in many unintended pregnancies. According to the NCHS, however, in addition to the teen birth rate, the teen pregnancy rate, which is based on the number of live births, induced abortions, and fetal losses, declined by 19 percent between 1991 and 1997 (the latest year for which statistics are available). Although there has been a strong movement in recent years to promote abstinence among teenagers, the major reason for the drop in the teen pregnancy rate appears to be increased use of contraception, particularly condoms. Many teenagers also are using implantable or injectable contraceptives, which may be particularly well suited for sexually active teens.

Health Risks of Teen Pregnancy

Figure 6.7 shows that mothers under age 20 were less likely to receive first trimester prenatal care, were more likely to smoke during pregnancy, were more likely to have a preterm birth, and were more likely to have a low-birth-weight baby. Teenage mothers were more likely to defer prenatal care until the third trimester or not get any prenatal care. During the late 1990s, as smoking rates were dropping for older women, they were increasing for pregnant teens. Low-birth-weight babies are at higher risk for serious and long-term illness, developmental delays, and infant mortality. Teenagers are usually emotionally, psychologically, and financially unprepared for parenthood, and their children may suffer from lack of attention and stimulation.

Social Consequences of Teen Childbearing

According to the Census Bureau, 60 percent of women without a high school diploma who gave birth in 1998 were unmarried, compared to only 3 percent of women with at least a bachelor's degree. Unmarried mothers, particularly teenagers, often have their educational plans disrupted, sometimes permanently. Not only are teenage mothers less likely to finish high school, but, according to the Federal Interagency Forum on Child and Family Statistics, their children are also less likely to graduate from high school.

Teenage mothers are more likely to depend on their families and on public assistance than are older mothers. Prior to 1996 as many as three-quarters of unmarried adolescent mothers received Aid to Families with Dependent Children (AFDC). However, the Personal Responsibility and Work Opportunity Reconciliation Act of 1996 (PRWORA) abolished the 60-year-old AFDC program and established the Temporary Assistance for Needy Families (TANF) block grant program. To qualify for TANF benefits, unmarried minor parents are required to remain in high school or its equivalent and to live at home or in an adult-supervised setting. PRWORA provided for the establishment of homes for teen parents and their children. These homes require that all residents either enroll in school or participate in a job-training program. They also provide parenting and life-skills classes, counseling, and support services. However, most teenage mothers under age 18 continue to live with one or both of their parents.

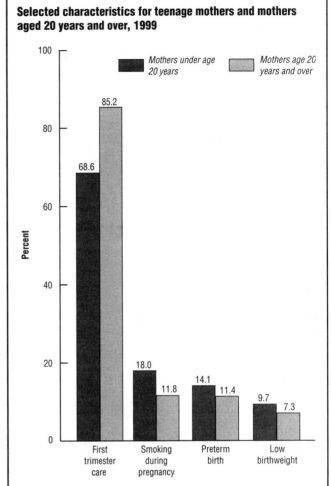

FIGURE 6.7

Selected characteristics for teenage mothers and mothers aged 20 years and over, 1999

NOTE: Smoking data exclude information for California and South Dakota.

SOURCE: Stephanie J. Ventura, T.J. Mathews, and Brady E. Hamilton, "Figure 7. Selected Characteristics for Teenage Mothers and Mothers Aged 20 Years and Over: United States, 1999," in "Births to Teenagers in the United States, 1940–2000," *National Vital Statistics Reports,* vol. 49, no. 10, September 25, 2001

HEALTH ISSUES DURING PREGNANCY, CHILDBIRTH, AND INFANCY

Smoking, Alcohol, and Illegal Drugs

In *Health, United States. 2001,* the NCHS reported that almost 22 percent of all women 18 and over smoked cigarettes in 1997–99. (See Table 6.5.) Among non-Hispanic white women aged 18 to 24, 31.8 percent smoked, as did 28.2 percent of those between 24 and 44. Smaller percentages of African American and Hispanic women between the ages of 18 and 34 smoked. However, the highest proportions of female smokers were in their peak childbearing years.

Although the overall smoking rate during pregnancy declined steadily between 1989 and 1999, smoking by pregnant teenagers increased 2 percent in 1999, for the

TABLE 6.5

Current cigarette smoking by females, according to race, Hispanic origin, age, and education, average annual 1990–92, 1993–95, and 1997–99

[Data are based on household interviews of a sample of the civilian noninstitutionalized population]

Characteristic	Female		
	1990–92	1993–95	1997–99
18 years of age and over, age adjusted[1]	Percent of persons		
All persons[2]	23.7	22.8	21.9
White	24.3	23.6	22.8
Black	23.1	21.9	21.4
American Indian or Alaska Native	36.7	32.7	31.7
Asian or Pacific Islander	6.3	7.3	10.2
White, non-Hispanic	25.2	24.7	24.0
Black, non-Hispanic	23.2	22.1	21.4
Hispanic[2]	15.8	13.8	13.1
Mexican	14.8	12.2	11.5
18 years of age and over, crude			
All persons[2]	23.6	22.7	21.8
White	24.1	23.3	22.4
Black	23.3	22.0	21.5
American Indian or Alaska Native	37.3	35.4	33.5
Asian or Pacific Islander	6.3	7.5	10.4
White, non-Hispanic	24.8	24.2	23.4
Black, non-Hispanic	23.3	22.2	21.5
Hispanic[2]	16.6	14.4	13.3
Mexican	15.0	12.6	11.5
18–24 years:			
White, non-Hispanic	28.7	29.1	31.8
Black, non-Hispanic	10.8	9.4	11.5
Hispanic[2]	12.8	13.2	12.2
25–34 years:			
White, non-Hispanic	30.9	30.7	28.2
Black, non-Hispanic	29.2	25.8	20.8
Hispanic[2]	19.2	15.1	12.7
35–44 years:			
White, non-Hispanic	27.3	27.9	28.2
Black, non-Hispanic	31.3	30.8	29.7
Hispanic[2]	19.9	19.5	16.3
45–64 years:			
White, non-Hispanic	26.1	24.5	22.2
Black, non-Hispanic	26.1	24.5	25.4
Hispanic[2]	17.1	12.9	13.9
65 years and over:			
White, non-Hispanic	12.3	11.3	11.3
Black, non-Hispanic	10.7	12.6	12.0
Hispanic[2]	6.6	*7.1	8.2

TABLE 6.5

Current cigarette smoking by females, according to race, Hispanic origin, age, and education, average annual 1990–92, 1993–95, and 1997–99 [CONTINUED]

[Data are based on household interviews of a sample of the civilian noninstitutionalized population]

Characteristic	Female		
	1990–92	1993–95	1997–99
Education[3], race, and Hispanic origin	Percent of persons		
25 years of age and over, age adjusted[4]			
No high school diploma or GED:			
White, non-Hispanic	40.4	40.8	40.7
Black, non-Hispanic	31.3	31.7	30.1
Hispanic[2]	15.8	13.9	12.8
High school diploma or GED:			
White, non-Hispanic	28.4	28.6	28.7
Black, non-Hispanic	25.4	25.0	25.3
Hispanic[2]	18.4	16.4	14.4
Some college or more:			
White, non-Hispanic	18.1	17.4	17.2
Black, non-Hispanic	22.8	20.1	18.9
Hispanic[2]	14.3	10.0	13.3

[1] Estimates are age adjusted to the year 2000 standard using five age groups: 18–24 years, 25–34 years, 35–44 years, 45–64 years, 65 years and over. For age groups where percent smoking is 0 or 100, the age adjustment procedure was modified to substitute the percent smoking from the previous 3-year period.
[2] The race groups white, black, American Indian or Alaska Native, and Asian or Pacific Islander include persons of Hispanic and non-Hispanic origin; persons of Hispanic origin may be of any race.
[3] Education categories shown are for 1997 and subsequent years. GED stands for general equivalency diploma. In 1990–92 the following categories based on number of years of school completed were used: less than 12 years, 12 years, 13 years or more.
[4] Estimates are age adjusted to the year 2000 standard using four age groups: 25–34 years, 35–44 years, 45–64 years, 65 years and over.
NOTE: The definition of current smoker was revised in 1992 and 1993.

SOURCE: Adapted from "Table 62. Current Cigarette Smoking by Adults, according to Sex, Race, Hispanic Origin, Age, and Education: United States, Average Annual 1990–92, 1993–95, and 1997–99," in *Health, United States, 2001*, National Center for Health Statistics, Hyattsville, MD, 2001

fifth year in a row. Smoking also increased among pregnant women aged 20 to 24. Smoking during pregnancy has been linked to miscarriages, premature births, stillbirths, low birth weight, infant mortality, and sudden infant death syndrome. Although some women stop smoking during pregnancy and resume smoking after they give birth, their children may still be exposed to dangerous secondhand smoke.

More women are becoming aware of the dangers of alcohol consumption during pregnancy. Nevertheless, many women continue to drink while they are pregnant. There is no level of alcohol consumption that is deemed to be safe during pregnancy. Alcohol consumption during pregnancy has been associated with low birth weight and minor birth defects. Excessive consumption of alcohol by pregnant women can lead to fetal alcohol syndrome, a condition that may include mental retardation and growth deficiencies in the child.

According to the Substance Abuse and Mental Health Services Administration's *National Household Survey on Drug Abuse* (1999, 2000), over 3 percent of pregnant women aged 15 to 44 had used an illicit drug in the past month. Marijuana and hashish were the most common drugs and were used by 2.5 percent of pregnant women.

Prenatal Care

As Table 6.6 shows, 83.2 percent of women received prenatal care during the first trimester of their pregnancies in 1999 and 2000. Non-Hispanic white women were more likely to receive first-trimester prenatal care than either black or Hispanic women. Overall, nearly 4 percent of women did not receive prenatal care until the third trimester of their pregnancies or received no prenatal care. Black and Hispanic women were most likely to receive care only late in their pregnancies or not at all.

TABLE 6.6

Total births and percent of births with selected demographic and health characteristics, by race and Hispanic origin of mother, final 1999 and preliminary 2000

Characteristic	All races[1]		White, total[2]		White, non-Hispanic		Black[2]		Hispanic[3]	
	2000	1999	2000	1999	2000	1999	2000	1999	2000	1999
	Number									
Births	4,064,948	3,959,417	3,202,932	3,132,501	2,370,778	2,346,450	619,970	605,970	815,778	764,339
	Percent									
Births to mothers under 20 years	11.8	12.3	10.6	10.9	8.8	9.2	19.8	20.7	16.2	16.7
Births to unmarried mothers	33.1	33.0	27.1	26.8	22.1	22.1	68.5	68.9	42.5	42.2
Low birthweight[4]	7.6	7.6	6.5	6.6	6.6	6.6	12.9	13.1	6.4	6.4
Very low birthweight[5]	1.42	1.45	1.13	1.15	1.13	1.15	3.05	3.14	1.14	1.14
Births delivered by cesarean	22.9	22.0	22.8	21.9	23.0	22.1	24.3	23.2	22.1	21.2
Prenatal care beginning in first trimester	83.2	83.2	85.0	85.1	88.5	88.4	74.2	74.1	74.4	74.4
Prenatal care beginning in third trimester or no care	3.9	3.8	3.3	3.2	2.3	2.3	6.7	6.6	6.4	6.3

Note: Figures for 2000 are based on weighted data rounded to the nearest individual.
[1] Includes races other than white and black.
[2] Race and Hispanic origin are reported separately on the birth certificate. Data for persons of Hispanic origin are included in the data for each race group according to the mother's reported race.
[3] Includes all persons of Hispanic origin of any race.
[4] Birthweight of less than 2,500 grams (5 pounds 8 ounces).
[5] Birthweight of less than 1,500 grams (3 pounds 4 ounces).

SOURCE: Joyce A. Martin, Brady E. Hamilton, and Stephanie J. Ventura, "Table A. Total Births and Percent of Births with Selected Demographic and Health Characteristics, by Race and Hispanic Origin of Mother: United States, Final 1999 and Preliminary 2000," in "Births: Preliminary Data for 2000," *National Vital Statistics Reports,* vol. 49, no. 5, July 24, 2001

Between 1989 and 1999 the proportion of women receiving early prenatal care rose almost 75 percent. Early prenatal care for African American and Hispanic women increased by more than 20 percent in the 1990s. The proportion of women receiving only late prenatal care, or no care at all, decreased 6 percent between 1989 and 2000.

Preterm and Cesarean Births

According to the NCHS, the overall rate of preterm births increased 11 percent between 1990 and 1999 to 12 percent of all births. Although the percentage of cesarean births steadily decreased between 1989 and 1996, the percentage increased for four straight years between 1997 and 2000 among all racial, ethnic, and age groups. This increase was the result of both an increase in the rate of cesarean first births and a decrease in the rate of vaginal births following a previous cesarean delivery. Black women were somewhat more likely to have cesarean deliveries. (See Table 6.6.)

Low Birth Weight

In 1999 and 2000, 7.6 percent of all babies born were low birth weight and 1.4 percent were very low birth weight. (See Table 6.6.) The overall percentage of low-birth-weight babies (less than 5.5 pounds) decreased slightly between 1970 and 1999. (See Table 6.7.) However, the percentages of low-birth-weight babies actually increased among most racial groups in 1999. The percentage of very low birth-weight babies (under 3.3 pounds) also increased among every other racial and ethnic group

between 1970 and 2000. Although the overall percentages increased among Asians and Pacific Islanders, the percentage of low-birth-weight babies decreased among Chinese, Japanese, and Filipinos and very low birth-weight babies decreased among Chinese and Japanese. Among non-Hispanic white women, some of the increase in low-birth-weight infants resulted from the increase in multiple births among these women, since about one-half of all multiple births are low birth weight.

The percentage of low and very low birth-weight babies increased among both smokers and nonsmokers but was significantly higher for mothers who smoked. (See Table 6.7.)

Breast-feeding

The Office on Women's Health of the U.S. Department of Health and Human Services (DHHS) has declared breast-feeding of infants to be a priority issue. Extensive research has shown that human breast milk is superior to infant formulas. Breast-fed infants experience fewer and less severe cases of both infectious and noninfectious diseases, including diarrhea and respiratory and ear infections. This is because of the transfer of immunological agents from mother to child. In addition, human breast milk provides the most balanced nutrition for infants. Mothers who breast-feed experience less postpartum bleeding, earlier return to prepregnancy weight, and are at lowered risk for ovarian and premenopausal breast cancers. Furthermore, infant formulas are quite expensive, and breast-feeding may promote mother-infant bonding.

TABLE 6.7

Low-birthweight live births, according to the mother's detailed race, Hispanic origin, and smoking status, selected years, 1970–99

[Data are based on the National Vital Statistics System]

Birthweight, race Hispanic origin of mother, and smoking status of mother	1970	1975	1980	1985	1990	1993	1994	1995	1996	1997	1998	1999
Low birthweight (less than 2,500 grams)					**Percent of live births[1]**							
All races	7.93	7.38	6.84	6.75	6.97	7.22	7.28	7.32	7.39	7.51	7.57	7.62
White	6.85	6.27	5.72	5.65	5.70	5.98	6.11	6.22	6.34	6.46	6.52	6.57
Black	13.90	13.19	12.69	12.65	13.25	13.34	13.24	13.13	13.01	13.01	13.05	13.11
American Indian or Alaska Native	7.97	6.41	6.44	5.86	6.11	6.42	6.45	6.61	6.49	6.75	6.81	7.15
Asian or Pacific Islander	- - -	- - -	6.68	6.16	6.45	6.55	6.81	6.90	7.07	7.23	7.42	7.45
Chinese	6.67	5.29	5.21	4.98	4.69	4.91	4.76	5.29	5.03	5.06	5.34	5.19
Japanese	9.03	7.47	6.60	6.21	6.16	6.53	6.91	7.26	7.27	6.82	7.50	7.95
Filipino	10.02	8.08	7.40	6.95	7.30	6.99	7.77	7.83	7.92	8.33	8.23	8.30
Hawaiian and part Hawaiian	- - -	- - -	7.23	6.49	7.24	6.76	7.20	6.84	6.77	7.20	7.15	7.69
Other Asian or Pacific Islander	- - -	- - -	6.83	6.19	6.65	6.89	7.06	7.05	7.42	7.54	7.76	7.76
Hispanic origin[2,3]	- - -	- - -	6.12	6.16	6.06	6.24	6.25	6.29	6.28	6.42	6.44	6.38
Mexican	- - -	- - -	5.62	5.77	5.55	5.77	5.80	5.81	5.86	5.97	5.97	5.94
Puerto Rican	- - -	- - -	8.95	8.69	8.99	9.23	9.13	9.41	9.24	9.39	9.68	9.30
Cuban	- - -	- - -	5.62	6.02	5.67	6.18	6.27	6.50	6.46	6.78	6.50	6.80
Central and South American	- - -	- - -	5.76	5.68	5.84	5.94	6.02	6.20	6.03	6.26	6.47	6.38
Other and unknown Hispanic	- - -	- - -	6.96	6.83	6.87	7.51	7.54	7.55	7.68	7.93	7.59	7.63
White, non-Hispanic[2]	- - -	- - -	5.67	5.60	5.61	5.92	6.06	6.20	6.36	6.47	6.55	6.64
Black, non-Hispanic[2]	- - -	- - -	12.71	12.61	13.32	13.43	13.34	13.21	13.12	13.11	13.17	13.23
Cigarette smoker[4]	- - -	- - -	- - -	- - -	11.25	11.84	12.28	12.18	12.13	12.06	12.01	12.06
Nonsmoker[4]	- - -	- - -	- - -	- - -	6.14	6.56	6.71	6.79	6.91	7.07	7.18	7.21
Very low birthweight (less than 1,500 grams)												
All races	1.17	1.16	1.15	1.21	1.27	1.33	1.33	1.35	1.37	1.42	1.45	1.45
White	0.95	0.92	0.90	0.94	0.95	1.01	1.02	1.06	1.09	1.13	1.15	1.15
Black	2.40	2.40	2.48	2.71	2.92	2.96	2.96	2.97	2.99	3.04	3.08	3.14
American Indian or Alaska Native	0.98	0.95	0.92	1.01	1.01	1.05	1.10	1.10	1.21	1.19	1.24	1.26
Asian or Pacific Islander	- - -	- - -	0.92	0.85	0.87	0.86	0.93	0.91	0.99	1.05	1.10	1.08
Chinese	0.80	0.52	0.66	0.57	0.51	0.63	0.58	0.67	0.64	0.74	0.75	0.68
Japanese	1.48	0.89	0.94	0.84	0.73	0.74	0.92	0.87	0.81	0.78	0.84	0.86
Filipino	1.08	0.93	0.99	0.86	1.05	0.95	1.19	1.13	1.20	1.29	1.35	1.41
Hawaiian and part Hawaiian	- - -	- - -	1.05	1.03	0.97	1.14	1.20	0.94	0.97	1.41	1.53	1.41
Other Asian or Pacific Islander	- - -	- - -	0.96	0.91	0.92	0.89	0.93	0.91	1.04	1.07	1.12	1.09
Hispanic origin[2,3]	- - -	- - -	0.98	1.01	1.03	1.06	1.08	1.11	1.12	1.13	1.15	1.14
Mexican	- - -	- - -	0.92	0.97	0.92	0.97	0.99	1.01	1.01	1.02	1.02	1.04
Puerto Rican	- - -	- - -	1.29	1.30	1.62	1.66	1.63	1.79	1.70	1.85	1.86	1.86
Cuban	- - -	- - -	1.02	1.18	1.20	1.23	1.31	1.19	1.35	1.36	1.33	1.49
Central and South American	- - -	- - -	0.99	1.01	1.05	1.02	1.06	1.13	1.14	1.17	1.23	1.15
Other and unknown Hispanic	- - -	- - -	1.01	0.96	1.09	1.23	1.29	1.28	1.48	1.35	1.38	1.32
White, non-Hispanic[2]	- - -	- - -	0.86	0.90	0.93	1.00	1.01	1.04	1.08	1.12	1.15	1.15
Black, non-Hispanic[2]	- - -	- - -	2.46	2.66	2.93	2.99	2.99	2.98	3.02	3.05	3.11	3.18
Cigarette smoker[4]	- - -	- - -	- - -	- - -	1.73	1.77	1.81	1.85	1.85	1.83	1.87	1.91
Nonsmoker[4]	- - -	- - -	- - -	- - -	1.18	1.28	1.30	1.31	1.35	1.40	1.44	1.43

- - - Data not available.

[1] Excludes live births with unknown birthweight. Percent based on live births with known birthweight.

[2] Trend data for Hispanics and non-Hispanics are affected by expansion of the reporting area for an Hispanic-origin item on the birth certificate and by immigration. These two factors affect numbers of events, composition of the Hispanic population, and maternal and infant health characteristics. The number of states in the reporting area increased from 22 in 1980, to 23 and the District of Columbia (DC) in 1983–87,30 and DC in 1988, 47 and DC in 1989, 48 and DC in 1990, 49 and DC in 1991–92, and 50 and DC in 1993 and later years.

[3] Includes mothers of all races.

[4] Percent based on live births with known smoking status of mother and known birthweight. Includes data for 43 states and the District of Columbia (DC) in 1989, 45 states and DC in 1990, 46 states and DC in 1991–93, 46 states, DC, and New York City (NYC) in 1994–98, and 48 states, DC, and NYC in 1999. Excludes data for California and South Dakota (1989–99),Indiana and New York (1989–98),New York City (1989–93), Oklahoma (1989–90), and Louisiana and Nebraska (1989), which did not require the reporting of mother's tobacco use during pregnancy on the birth certificate.

NOTES: The race groups, white, black, American Indian or Alaska Native, and Asian or Pacific Islander, include persons of Hispanic and non-Hispanic origin. Conversely, persons of Hispanic origin may be of any race.

SOURCE: "Table 12. Low-Birthweight Live Births, According to Mother's Detailed Race, Hispanic Origin, and Smoking Status: United States, Selected Years 1970–99," in *Health, United States, 2001*, National Center for Health Statistics, Hyattsville, MD, 2001

Many more women are breast-feeding their infants than in previous years. According to the NCHS, in the years 1972–74 only 30 percent of all women and only 13 percent of African American women breast-fed their infants. Of infants who were breast-fed in those years, 62 percent were breast-fed for at least three months. In 1998, 64 percent of all American women, but only 45 percent of African American women, breast-fed their newborns. (See

TABLE 6.8

Racial and ethnic disparities in breastfeeding rates and Healthy People 2010 breastfeeding objectives[1]

Objective: Increase the proportion of mothers who breastfeed their babies	1998 Baseline Percent (%)	2010 Target
In early postpartum period		
All women	64	75
Black or African American	45	75
Hispanic or Latino	66	75
White	68	75
At 6 months		
All women	29	50
Black or African American	19	50
Hispanic or Latino	28	50
White	31	50
At 1 year		
All women	16	25
Black or African American	9	25
Hispanic or Latino	19	25
White	17	25

[1]Healthy People 2010 contains broad reaching national health goals for the new decade, focusing on two major themes: 1. Increase quality and years of healthy life, and 2. Eliminate health disparities.

SOURCE: "Box 3. Racial and Ethnic Disparities in Breastfeeding Rates and Healthy People 2010 Breastfeeding Objectives for the Nation," in *HHS Blueprint for Action on Breastfeeding,* Office on Women's Health, Department of Health and Human Services, Washington, DC, Fall 2000

TABLE 6.9

Contraceptive use among women

Method	No. of users (in 000s)	% of users
Tubal sterilization	10,727	27.7
Pill	10,410	26.9
Male condom	7,889	20.4
Vasectomy	4,215	10.9
Withdrawal	1,178	3.0
Injectable	1,146	3.0
Periodic abstinence	883	2.3
Diaphragm	720	1.9
Other	670	1.8
Implant	515	1.3
IUD	310	0.8
TOTAL	**38,663**	**100.0**

SOURCE: : Reproduced with the permission of The Alan Guttmacher Institute from Dailard C, Challenges facing family planning clinics and Title X. *The Guttmacher Report*, 2001, 4(2):8–11.

Table 6.8.) Only 19 percent of African American mothers continued breast-feeding past six months, compared to 29 percent of all women. Only 16 percent of all women and 9 percent of African American women were still breast-feeding their babies after one year. Women in the western United States are significantly more likely to breast-feed than women in other parts of the country. Older mothers and those with more education are more likely than other women to breast-feed. The DHHS hopes to significantly increase the numbers of women who breast-feed by 2010.

Unfortunately breast-feeding can be difficult for working mothers. Some employers are beginning to address this issue by providing lactation rooms where mothers can pump their breasts to store milk for their babies. Employees with on-site child care may be able to breast-feed their babies throughout the work day.

ALTERNATIVES TO CHILDBEARING

Contraceptive Use

Contraceptive use rose significantly during the 1990s. According to the AGI, 64 percent of American women between the ages of 15 and 44 practice contraception. An additional 31 percent of women do not need contraception because they are pregnant, have just had a baby, are trying to become pregnant, are infertile, or are not sexually active. Nine out of 10 fertile, sexually active women practice contraception. During the 1990s, 76 percent of women used contraception at their first intercourse, compared with 50 percent prior to 1980.

Among women who practice contraception, 61 percent use reversible methods such as condoms or birth control pills. The single most widely used form of contraception (28 percent of contraceptive users) is surgery to block the fallopian tubes (tubal ligation or tubal sterilization). (See Table 6.9.) Sterilization is most likely to be used by women over 34, those who have been married, those with less than a high school education, and low-income women. African American and Hispanic women are most likely to have undergone sterilization, whereas white women are more likely to use oral contraceptives. Although most medical plans cover prenatal care, delivery, abortion, and sterilization, most do not cover the costs of contraception other than sterilization.

Among women aged 40 to 44 who practice contraception, 50 percent have been sterilized and 20 percent have male partners who have had a vasectomy. Of the 2.7 million teenage women who use contraception, 44 percent use birth control pills and 37 percent use condoms.

Almost half of all pregnancies in the United States are unintended. Among fertile women who do not use contraception, 85 percent will become pregnant within a year. As of 1998 there were 3 million unintended pregnancies in the United States every year, 53 percent among contraceptive users and 47 percent among women who did not use contraception. Most contraception failures were the result of inconsistent or improper use of the contraceptive. The highest failure rate was among those who used periodic abstinence or a cervical cap (9 percent annually if used perfectly). The lowest failure rate was with an implantable contraceptive (0.05 percent annually if used perfectly). Vasectomies and birth control pills had failure rates of 0.1 percent annually if used perfectly. Of unintended pregnancies, 44 percent resulted in births, 13 percent ended in miscarriage, and 43 percent ended in abortion.

TABLE 6.10

Legal abortion ratios, according to selected characteristics, selected years 1973–98

[Data are based on reporting by State health departments and by hospitals and other medical facilities]

Characteristic	1973	1975	1980	1985	1990	1992	1993	1994	1995	1996	1997	1998[1]
					Abortions per 100 live births[2]							
Total	19.6	27.2	35.9	35.4	34.5	33.5	33.4	32.1	31.1	31.4	30.6	26.2
Age												
Under 15 years	123.7	119.3	139.7	137.6	84.4	79.0	74.4	70.4	66.7	72.3	72.9	74.5
15–19years	53.9	54.2	71.4	68.8	51.5	44.0	44.0	41.5	39.9	41.5	40.7	38.8
20–24years	29.4	28.9	39.5	38.6	37.7	37.6	38.4	36.4	34.9	35.5	34.5	32.7
25–29years	20.7	19.2	23.7	21.7	22.0	22.2	22.7	22.2	22.1	22.7	22.4	21.5
30–34years	28.0	25.0	23.7	19.9	19.1	18.3	18.0	17.2	16.5	16.5	16.1	15.7
35–39years	45.1	42.2	41.0	33.6	27.3	25.6	24.8	23.4	22.4	22.0	20.9	19.7
40 years and over	68.4	66.8	80.7	62.3	50.1	45.4	43.0	41.2	38.7	37.6	35.2	33.3
Race												
White[3]	32.6	27.7	33.2	27.7	25.8	23.6	23.1	21.7	20.4	20.2	19.4	18.8
Black[4]	42.0	47.6	54.3	47.2	52.1	51.8	55.2	53.8	53.4	55.5	54.3	52.6
Hispanic origin[5]												
Hispanic	- - -	- - -	- - -	- - -	- - -	30.7	28.9	27.8	26.5	28.1	26.8	28.9
Non-Hispanic	- - -	- - -	- - -	- - -	- - -	32.6	30.9	29.0	28.0	28.3	27.2	26.3
Marital status												
Married	7.6	9.6	10.5	8.0	8.9	8.4	8.4	7.9	7.6	7.8	7.4	7.0
Unmarried	139.8	161.0	147.6	117.4	87.9	79.0	78.9	68.9	65.0	65.5	65.9	62.1
Previous live births[6]												
0	43.7	38.4	45.7	45.1	35.8	32.7	32.5	30.9	28.6	28.7	26.9	25.3
1	23.5	22.0	20.2	21.6	23.0	22.9	22.8	22.3	22.1	22.3	22.1	21.2
2	36.8	36.8	29.5	29.9	31.7	31.9	31.8	30.9	30.9	31.1	30.9	29.8
3	46.9	47.7	29.8	18.2	30.2	30.8	31.2	30.8	31.0	31.5	31.3	30.2
4 or more[7]	44.7	43.5	24.3	21.5	27.1	25.5	23.5	23.3	24.1	24.9	24.6	24.1

- - - Data not available.
[1] Preliminary data. In 1998 California, Alaska, New Hampshire, and Oklahoma did not report abortion data.
[2] For calculation of ratios according to each characteristic, abortions with the characteristic unknown have been distributed in proportion to abortions with the characteristic known.
[3] For 1989 and later years, white race includes women of Hispanic ethnicity.
[4] Before 1989 black race includes races other than white.
[5] Includes data for 20–22 States, the District of Columbia (DC), and New York City (NYC) in 1991–95, 22 States and NYC in 1996, 26 States, DC, and NYC in 1997, and 23 States, DC, and NYC in 1998. States with large Hispanic populations that are not included are California, Florida, and Illinois.
[6] For 1973–75 data indicate number of living children
[7] For 1975 data refer to four previous live births, not four or more. For five or more previous live births, the ratio is 47.3.
NOTES: For each year from 1973–1997the Centers for Disease Control and Prevention has compiled total abortion data from 50 States, DC, and NYC. Beginning in 1998, abortion data are available from only 46 States, DC, and NYC. The number of areas reporting adequate data (less than or equal to 15 percent missing) for each characteristic varies from year to year. For 1998, the number of areas reporting each characteristic was as follows: age, 45 States, DC, and NYC; race, 37 States, DC, and NYC; marital status, 37 States and NYC; previous live births, 39 States and NYC.

SOURCE: "Table 16. Legal Abortion Ratios, according to Selected Patient Characteristics: United States, Selected Years 1973–98," in *Health, United States, 2001*, National Center for Health Statistics, Hyattsville, MD, 2001

Abortion

DECLINING ABORTION RATES. Abortion has been a legal option for American women since the Supreme Court ruling in *Roe v. Wade* (410 U.S. 113, 1973). The number of abortions increased steadily until reaching a high in 1990, when the Centers for Disease Control and Prevention (CDC) reported 1.4 million abortions and the AGI estimated that there were 1.6 million. Since then the number of legal abortions in the United States has steadily declined. There were 878,000 abortions in 1998. The ratio of legal abortions to live births dropped from a high in 1980 of 35.9 abortions per 100 live births to 26.2 abortions per 100 births in 1998. (See Table 6.10.) The drop occurred among women in every age group and of every race/ethnicity and marital status.

Most young pregnant teenagers under 15 choose abortion (74.5 abortions per 100 live births in 1998).

Among teens aged 15 to 19 there were 38.8 abortions per 100 live births in 1998, down from 71.4 in 1980. The ratio of abortions to live births declined with age up to ages 35 to 39. Among women aged 40 and over there are 33.3 abortions per 100 live births, compared to 80.7 abortions per 100 live births among women over 39 in 1980. Women in their 40s may be concerned about increased health risks for the mother and child because of maternal age, although the development of methods such as amniocentesis that enable physicians to test the fetus for abnormalities associated with maternal age has alleviated some of these concerns. In addition, women over 40 may not want to begin raising children, particularly if they already have older children. According to the National Abortion Federation (NAF), an organization of abortion providers, by the age of 45, 43 percent of American women will have had an abortion.

TABLE 6.11

Women 15–44 years of age who have not had at least one live birth, selected years 1960–2000

[Data are based on the National Vital Statistics System]

Year [1]	15–19 years	20–24 years	25–29 years	30–34 years	35–39 years	40–44 years
			Percent of women			
1960	91.4	47.5	20.0	14.2	12.0	15.1
1965	92.7	51.4	19.7	11.7	11.4	11.0
1970	93.0	57.0	24.4	11.8	9.4	10.6
1975	92.6	62.5	31.1	15.2	9.6	8.8
1980	93.4	66.2	38.9	19.7	12.5	9.0
1985	93.7	67.7	41.5	24.6	15.4	11.7
1986	93.8	68.0	42.0	25.1	16.1	12.2
1987	93.8	68.2	42.5	25.5	16.9	12.6
1988	93.8	68.4	43.0	25.7	17.7	13.0
1989	93.7	68.4	43.3	25.9	18.2	13.5
1990	93.3	68.3	43.5	25.9	18.5	13.9
1991	93.0	67.9	43.6	26.0	18.7	14.5
1992	92.7	67.3	43.7	26.0	18.8	15.2
1993	92.6	66.7	43.8	26.1	18.8	15.8
1994	92.6	66.1	43.9	26.2	18.7	16.2
1995	92.5	65.5	44.0	26.2	18.6	16.5
1996	92.5	65.0	43.8	26.2	18.5	16.6
1997	92.8	64.9	43.5	26.2	18.4	16.6
1998	93.1	65.1	43.0	26.1	18.3	16.5
1999	93.4	65.5	42.5	26.1	18.1	16.4
2000	93.7	66.0	42.1	25.9	17.9	16.2

[1]As of January 1.
Notes: Data are based on cohort fertility. Percents are derived from the cumulative childbearing experience of cohorts of women, up to the ages specified. Data on births are adjusted for underregistration and population estimates are corrected for underregistration and misstatement of age. Beginning in 1970 births to persons who were not residents of the 50 States and the District of Columbia are excluded.

SOURCE: "Table 4. Women 15–44 Years of Age Who Have Not Had at least 1 Live Birth, by Age: United States, Selected Years 1960–2000," in *Health, United States, 2001*, National Center for Health Statistics, Hyattsville, MD, 2001

Among unmarried women the ratio of abortions to live births declined from 161 per 100 births in 1975 to 62.1 in 1998, reflecting the increasing trend toward childbearing among unmarried women. Among women with three or more children, the ratio of abortions to live births also declined from highs in 1973 and 1975. (See Table 6.10.)

A number of factors have contributed to the dropping abortion rate. The teen pregnancy rate has dropped significantly, and more women of all age groups are using contraception. The growing acceptance of unmarried childbearing and single motherhood has affected the abortion rate. Pressure from anti-abortion groups and increased legal restrictions on abortions also may have contributed to the drop. For some women access to abortion services has been reduced in recent years.

According to the CDC, most women (54 percent) who chose abortion in 1998 had not had a previous abortion. Only 8 percent of women had their fourth or more abortion in 1998. The majority of abortions (56 percent) were performed when the fetus was less than nine weeks old. Only 1 percent of abortions occurred after 20 weeks of gestation.

ABORTION DRUGS. Mifepristone, formerly known as RU 486, is an abortion-inducing drug that has been used in Europe and China since the late 1980s. In September 2000, the U.S. Food and Drug Administration approved mifepristone for use in the United States. When used in combination with the drug misoprostol, it is 95 percent effective in inducing abortion up to 49 days after the start of the last menstrual period. According to the NAF, many women are now choosing this method of abortion.

ABORTION RIGHTS. Judicial rulings since *Roe v. Wade* have weakened abortion rights in at least some states. As of 2001 states were not required to fund abortions through Medicaid, unless the pregnancy resulted from rape or incest or the woman's life was in danger. The U.S. Supreme Court has upheld the right of states to require parental consent before a minor can obtain an abortion, provided that the minor has the right to appeal in court. This, in addition to mandatory waiting periods, has made it more difficult for some women to obtain abortions.

Childlessness

With the development of fertility drugs and assisted reproductive techniques, many previously infertile couples are now able to have children. Nevertheless, as is apparent from Table 6.11, not only are women postponing childbearing, but increasing numbers of women are choosing not to have children. In 2000 among women aged 40 to 44, 16.2 percent had not had at least one live birth, compared to 15.1 percent of women in that age group in 1960 and only about 9 percent in 1975 and 1980. Between 1995 and 2000 the number of women 40 and over who had not given birth reached highs of 16 to 17 percent. Whereas 15 percent of Hispanic women aged 40 to 44 were childless in 1998, 20 percent of white non-Hispanic women were childless. The rate of childlessness among women aged 40 to 44 in 1998 was about the same as in 1900, even though women today have more options for giving birth.

The percentage of women aged 35 to 39 who had not had at least one live birth remained at about 18 percent from 1997 to 2000, down from a high of nearly 19 percent between 1990 and 1996 and up from only 9 percent in 1970. (See Table 6.11.)

Although fewer women are marrying, more unmarried women are having children and more married women are choosing not to have children. According to the Census Bureau in 2000, 67 percent of never-married women and 14 percent of ever-married women between the ages of 40 and 44 had never had children. In 1980, 79 percent of never-married women in that age group were childless, compared to only 7 percent of ever-married women.

Among non-Hispanic white women aged 40 to 44, 86 percent of never-married and 15 percent of ever-married women were childless in 2000. Among ever-married women of other race/ethnicities, 11 to 12 percent were childless. Among Asian and Pacific Islanders 89 percent of never-married women aged 40 to 44 were childless. Only 45 percent of Hispanic and 34 percent of African American never-married women in that age group were childless. Among native-born never-married women, 69 percent were childless, compared to 48 percent of foreign-born women aged 40 to 44.

According to the National Adoption Information Clearinghouse (NAIC), a service of the Children's Bureau of the DHHS, about one-third of all infertile, childless, married women are between 35 and 44. The number of women who are infertile or who report impaired fecundity (difficulty conceiving or carrying a child to term) has increased in recent years, primarily as a result of the postponement of childbearing and of the large numbers of baby boomer women in their reproductive years. There are no significant differences in the racial or ethnic background of infertile women or those with impaired fecundity; however, women using infertility services tend to be white, older, college-educated, of higher income, and never-married, and have never given birth. Of infertile adoptive parents, approximately one-half were treated for infertility for an average of three years before adopting.

Adoption

No public agency or private organization collects current, comprehensive adoption statistics. In part this is because, at least until recent years, it was widely believed that adoptions should be kept forever secret. Legal records of adoptions are sealed, and in the past many children were never even told that they were adopted. Birth mothers never again heard of their children after relinquishing them for adoption.

According to Adam Pertman (*Adoption Nation: How the Adoption Revolution Is Transforming America,* Basic Books, New York, 2000), there are estimated to be 5 to 6 million adoptees in the United States. This is far higher than previous estimates. The NAIC estimates that during the 1990s there were about 120,000 adoptions per year, up from a low of about 40,000 adoptions in 1944 and down from a high of about 175,000 in 1970. As of 1993 there were estimated to be 1 million adopted children in the United States, with 2 to 4 percent of American families having at least one adopted child. According to data from the NCHS in 1999, 9.9 million women had considered adopting a child. Of the 16 percent of these women who pursued the possibility, 31 percent actually adopted a child.

Although the demand for adoption has remained stable, the adoption rate has fallen significantly since 1973. This is because there are far fewer infants available for adoption in the United States—at least healthy white infants—than in the past. The decline in the pregnancy rate, particularly among teenagers, the availability of abortion, and the increased numbers of unmarried women who are choosing to bear and raise children have all contributed to the reduced number of infants being placed for adoption.

Unmarried women are not being pressured into relinquishing their babies, at least to the extent that they were in the past. Prior to 1993, 8.7 percent of all never-married mothers, 19.3 percent of never-married white mothers, and 1.5 percent of never-married black mothers relinquished their children for adoption. Between 1989 and 1996 the rate fell to 0.9 percent of all never-married mothers and 1.7 percent of never-married white mothers. In 1999 less than 3 percent of white unmarried mothers and about 2 percent of all unmarried mothers placed their children for adoption. The percentage of African American and Hispanic unmarried mothers who relinquish their children for adoption has remained consistently under 2 percent.

According to the NAIC, about one-half of all adoptions are by relatives or stepparents of the adopted children, and these types of adoptions have been increasing in recent years. About 8 percent of all adoptions, including international adoptions, are interracial, meaning that the child is of a different race than the adoptive parents.

FOSTER CARE ADOPTIONS. About 15 to 20 percent of adoptions are through public child welfare systems. In 1992 (the last year for which statistics are available) 38 percent of adoptions were through private independent agencies. The majority of public adoptions involve children with "special needs." Special-needs children may be older, minority children with physical, mental, or psychological problems.

The Adoption and Safe Families Act of 1997 included provisions for collecting state data on children in foster care and public adoptions. Between 1986 and 1995 there was a 72 percent increase in the number of children in foster care; however, public agencies are beginning to place more children in the homes of relatives, and in many cases the relatives adopt these children. In January 2000 it was estimated that 520,000 children were in foster care in the United States. Most children in foster care were under age 10, and 46 percent were between one and five years old. Slightly more boys than girls were in foster care, and 46 percent were African American. About 23 percent of these children were eligible for adoption. In fiscal year (FY) 1998, 36,000 children were adopted from public foster care. Of these, 65 percent were adopted by former foster parents and 15 percent by relatives. Married couples adopted 66 percent of these children, and single parents adopted 33 percent. About 15 percent of adoptions from foster care were interracial.

INTERNATIONAL ADOPTION. International adoptions first became common after the Korean War, when Americans began adopting South Korean children who had been fathered by American G.I.'s. Most international adoptions were from South Korea until the 1990s, when China began allowing the foreign adoption of girls. With the breakup of the Soviet Union, Americans began adopting Russian children in large numbers. The number of children adopted by Americans from foreign countries increased from 6,336 in 1992 to 16,396 in 1999. Of these children 27 percent were from Russia, 25 percent from China, 12 percent from South Korea, 6 percent from Guatemala, and 5 percent from Romania. In FY 1998, 64 percent of these children were female and 46 percent were under one year of age. Another 43 percent were between the ages of one and four.

ADOPTION BY SINGLE MOTHERS. Both domestic and international adoptions by single parents increased steadily from 0.5 to 4 percent in the 1970s to an estimated 8 to 34 percent in the 1980s. This increase continued into the 1990s. Most single adoptive parents are women who have not been foster parents. Single women are more likely to adopt older "special needs" children. Many adoptive mothers are lesbians who may adopt on their own or with their female partners.

CHANGING ATTITUDES TOWARD ADOPTION. Since 1997 adoptive families have been able to take a federal tax credit to help cover adoption expenses. More employers are offering adoption benefits to their employees, often in the form of cash to help cover medical costs for the birth mother and legal and other adoption fees. Employers are also beginning to grant the same leaves to new adoptive parents that they grant to birth parents.

"Open adoptions" have become increasingly common since the 1970s. These arrangements vary from the sharing of information to the establishment of an ongoing relationship between the birth mother/family and the adoptive family. In addition, thousands of people who were adopted as infants—and the mothers and fathers who relinquished them—are finding each other. Six states allow all adopted adults to have access to their original birth certificates, and other states allow access under limited circumstances. In the past many people turned to private investigators to find their children or birth parents; however, the World Wide Web has streamlined this process. Sometimes the search is motivated by the need to diagnose and treat diseases. For example, a genetically related individual may be required for an organ or bone marrow transplant, and many adopted children want to know about diseases or conditions that they may have inherited. Many more children and birth parents hope to find each other to fulfill emotional and psychological needs.

FAMILY AND WORK ARRANGEMENTS FOR MOTHERS AND CHILDREN

Single Mothers

Of the 12 million single-parent American families in 2000, 83 percent were single-mother families. (See Table 6.12.) Single-mother families were more likely than single-father families to include more than one child and to live below the poverty level. Single mothers were more likely than single fathers to never have been married (43 percent versus 34 percent, respectively). Divorced mothers were more likely to be older, to have more education, and to have higher incomes than never-married mothers. Among black single mothers, 65 percent had never been married, as compared with 44 percent of Hispanic single mothers and 30 percent of non-Hispanic white single mothers. Black and Hispanic single mothers (18 and 22 percent, respectively) were more likely than non-Hispanic white single mothers (14 percent) to live with other members of their families. White single mothers were much more likely than black or Hispanic single mothers to live outside of central cities.

In 2000, 22 percent of American children lived with their mothers only, compared to 18 percent in 1980. (See Table 6.13.) Among non-Hispanic white children in 2000, 16 percent lived with their mothers only, compared to 49 percent of black children and 25 percent of Hispanic children. These percentages were higher than those in 1980 but down from the highs of 1996. Furthermore, a significant number of these children were living in families that included the mother's unmarried partner who may or may not be the child's father.

Grandmothers

According to the Census Bureau, about one-half of children who did not live with a parent in 2000 lived with

TABLE 6.12

Single parents by sex and selected characteristics, March 2000

(In thousands)

	Single fathers					Single mothers				
		Race and ethnicity					Race and ethnicity			
Characteristic	Total	White	White non-Hispanic	Black	Hispanic (of any race)	Total	White	White non-Hispanic	Black	Hispanic (of any race)
All single parents	2,044	1,622	1,331	335	313	9,681	6,216	4,766	3,060	1,565
Type of family group										
Family household	1,786	1,429	1,202	280	246	7,571	4,869	3,815	2,409	1,145
Related subfamily	201	140	87	50	55	1,633	995	665	550	347
Unrelated subfamily	57	53	42	5	11	477	352	286	101	73
Presence of children										
With own children under 18	2,044	1,622	1,331	335	313	9,681	6,216	4,766	3,060	1,565
With own children under 12	1,441	1,145	900	225	260	7,337	4,558	3,459	2,484	1,190
With own children under 6	819	647	466	138	189	4,115	2,519	1,855	1,459	720
With own children under 3	511	393	269	95	129	2,319	1,396	1,027	846	409
With own children under 1	196	152	103	38	51	824	499	372	307	141
Number of own children under 18										
1 child	1,300	1,016	849	233	182	5,239	3,544	2,819	1,493	774
2 children	543	441	364	74	80	2,954	1,848	1,423	983	463
3 children	146	126	91	12	37	1,013	592	390	377	223
4 or more children	55	39	27	16	13	475	232	134	207	105
Marital status										
Never married	693	497	333	164	168	4,181	2,039	1,422	1,984	686
Married spouse absent[1]	350	236	184	84	61	1,716	1,146	782	474	386
Divorced	913	824	757	71	74	3,392	2,748	2,369	524	394
Widowed	88	65	56	17	10	391	283	193	79	99
Poverty status										
Below poverty level	326	225	135	84	99	3,305	1,817	1,190	1,344	678
At or above poverty level	1,718	1,397	1,196	251	214	6,376	4,399	3,576	1,716	887
Metropolitan residence										
Metropolitan	1,635	1,278	1,014	289	282	8,047	5,005	3,647	2,727	1,464
In central cities	631	421	282	169	146	3,790	1,906	1,115	1,727	865
Outside central cities	1,004	857	732	120	136	4,257	3,099	2,532	1,000	599
Nonmetropolitan	409	344	317	47	31	1,634	1,211	1,119	333	101

[1]Married spouse absent, includes separated.

SOURCE: Jason Fields and Lynne M. Casper, "Table 4. Single Parents by Sex and Selected Characteristics: March 2000," in *America's Families and Living Arrangements: March 2000,* Current Population Reports, P20-537, U.S. Census Bureau, Washington, DC, June 2001

grandparents instead. An additional one-fourth of such children lived with other relatives, and the final one-quarter lived with nonrelatives, including foster families. In 2000 an estimated 5.6 million grandparents had grandchildren under 18 living with them. Among these grandparents, 42 percent had responsibility for their grandchildren, 23 percent of whom were under one year of age and 24 percent between the ages of one and two. Grandmothers accounted for 62 percent of grandparents who were responsible for their grandchildren. Thus, large numbers of older women are raising children for a second time.

Working Mothers

The majority of American mothers are in the labor force. Figure 6.8 shows that 62.2 percent of mothers with children under three were in the labor force in 1998, compared to 39.4 percent in 1978. Among mothers with children under six, 65.2 percent were in the labor force in 1998, compared to 44 percent in 1978.

According to the Census Bureau, between 1994 and 2000 the labor force participation rate for unmarried mothers increased almost 12 percent. Between 1994 and 1998 the labor force participation rate for unmarried mothers with children under one year increased 13 percent. The labor force participation rate for married mothers with children under one year decreased for the third straight year in 2000.

In 2000, 56.8 percent of all mothers with children under age three were employed, and 68 percent of these women were employed full-time. (See Table 6.14.) Of mothers with children under one year, 51 percent were employed, and 67 percent of these mothers were employed full-time. Among mothers with children under one year, married women were about as likely as single women to be working; however, among those with children aged one or two, a higher proportion of single mothers than married mothers were employed.

TABLE 6.13

Percent of children under age 18 by presence of parents in household, race, and Hispanic origin, selected years, 1980–2000

Race, Hispanic origin, and family type	1980	1985	1990	1995	1996	1997	1998	1999	2000
Total									
Two parents[a]	77	74	73	69	68	68	68	68	69
Mother only[b]	18	21	22	23	24	24	23	23	22
Father only[b]	2	2	3	4	4	4	4	4	4
No parent	4	3	3	4	4	4	4	4	4
White, non-Hispanic									
Two parents[a]	–	–	81	78	77	77	76	77	77
Mother only[b]	–	–	15	16	16	17	16	16	16
Father only[b]	–	–	3	3	4	4	5	4	4
No parent	–	–	2	3	3	3	3	3	3
Black									
Two parents[a]	42	39	38	33	33	35	36	35	38
Mother only[b]	44	51	51	52	53	52	51	52	49
Father only[b]	2	3	4	4	4	5	4	4	4
Noparent	12	7	8	11	9	8	9	10	9
Hispanic[c]									
Two parents[a]	75	68	67	63	62	64	64	63	65
Mother only[b]	20	27	27	28	29	27	27	27	25
Father only[b]	2	2	3	4	4	4	4	5	4
No parent	3	3	3	4	5	5	5	5	5

– = not available

[a] Excludes families where parents are not living as a married couple.

[b] Because of data limitations, includes some families where both parents are present in the household, but living as unmarried partners.

[c] Persons of Hispanic origin may be of any race.

NOTE: Family structure refers to the presence of biological, adoptive, and stepparents in the child's household. Thus, a child with a biological mother and stepfather living in the household is said to have two parents.

SOURCE: "Table POP5.A. Family Structure and Children's Living Arrangements: Percentage of Children under Age 18 by Presence of Parents in Household, Race, and Hispanic Origin, Selected Years 1980–2000," in *America's Children: Key National Indicators of Well-Being 2001*, Federal Interagency Forum on Child and Family Statistics, Washington, DC, July 2001

In 1998 the unemployment rate for mothers with children under one year was higher than for mothers with older children. (See Table 6.15.) Older mothers were much more likely to be employed than younger mothers, regardless of the number of children they had. Mothers between the ages of 15 and 24 were most likely to be unemployed. Among mothers who had a child in the past year, non-Hispanic white mothers were most likely to be employed full-time; however, among mothers with older children, black mothers were most likely to be employed full-time. Among both groups of mothers, blacks were most likely to be unemployed. Separated, divorced, or widowed mothers were more likely to be employed full-time, and never-married mothers were least likely to be employed full-time. There was a corre-lation between a mother's educational attainment and the likelihood that she was employed full-time. Among mothers with graduate or professional degrees and children under one year, 63.2 percent were employed full-time, compared to 13.6 percent of those with only a high school diploma.

Older and more educated women are more likely to have greater career commitments and to have salaries that justify continuing to work outside the home. Child care may be more accessible and more affordable for these women. However, women with more than one child are less likely to be employed. Not only is it more difficult to raise multiple children while working, but arranging and affording child care for more than one child may be an obstacle.

FIGURE 6.8

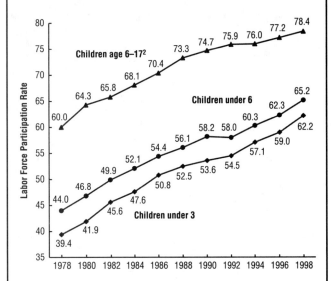

Labor force participation rates of mothers with children under age 18 by children's age, 1978–98[1]

[1]Includes single women, married women with spouse present, and widowed, divorced and separated women.
[2]None younger than six.

Note: In 1978, it was not the norm for a mother with a child under six to work, and even less common if her child was a toddler (under three). But by 1998, nearly two in every three mothers with children under six, and more than three in five with toddlers, were in the workforce.

SOURCE: "Figure 4-12. Labor Force Participation Rates of Mothers with Children under 18 by Children's Age, 1978–1998," in *The American Woman 2001–2002: Getting to the Top,* ed. by Cynthia B. Costello and Anne J. Stone, Women's Research and Education Institute, Washington, DC, 2001

TABLE 6.14

Employment status of mothers with own children under 3 years old by single year of youngest child and by marital status, annual averages 1999–2000

(Numbers in thousands)

| Characteristic | Civilian noninstitutional population | Total | Percent of population | Civilian labor force | | | | | |
| | | | | Employed | | | | Unemployed | |
				Total	Percent of population	Full-time workers (1)	Part-time workers (2)	Number	Percent of labor force
1999									
TOTAL MOTHERS									
With own children under 3 years old	9,339	5,742	61.5	5,389	57.7	3,692	1,697	353	6.1
2 years	2,890	1,888	65.3	1,788	61.9	1,257	530	101	5.3
1 year	3,283	2,062	62.8	1,934	58.9	1,298	635	128	6.2
Under 1 year	3,166	1,792	56.6	1,668	52.7	1,137	531	124	6.9
Married, spouse present									
With own children under 3 years old	7,089	4,224	59.6	4,078	57.5	2,744	1,334	147	3.5
2 years	2,175	1,356	62.4	1,316	60.5	898	419	40	2.9
1 year	2,522	1,532	60.8	1,477	58.6	964	513	56	3.6
Under 1 year	2,392	1,336	55.8	1,285	53.7	882	403	51	3.8
Other marital status(3)									
With own children under 3 years old	2,251	1,517	67.4	1,311	58.3	949	362	206	13.6
2 years	715	532	74.4	472	65.9	360	112	61	11.4
1 year	761	529	69.5	457	60.0	334	123	72	13.7
Under 1 year	774	456	58.8	383	49.5	255	128	73	16.0
2000									
TOTAL MOTHERS									
With own children under 3 years old	9,356	5,653	60.4	5,311	56.8	3,614	1,697	342	6.0
2 years	2,803	1,807	64.5	1,712	61.1	1,193	519	95	5.3
1 year	3,300	2,069	62.7	1,939	58.8	1,310	629	130	6.3
Under 1 year	3,253	1,777	54.6	1,660	51.0	1,112	548	117	6.6
Married, spouse present									
With own children under 3 years old.	7,056	4,090	58.0	3,940	55.8	2,613	1,327	150	3.7
2 years	2,096	1,276	60.9	1,233	58.9	823	411	42	3.3
1 year	2,499	1,503	60.1	1,448	57.9	953	495	55	3.6
Under 1 year	2,461	1,312	53.3	1,259	51.1	837	421	53	4.1
Other marital status(3)									
With own children under 3 years old.	2,300	1,563	67.9	1,371	59.6	1,002	370	191	12.2
2 years	707	531	75.1	478	67.6	370	108	53	9.9
1 year	801	566	70.7	491	61.3	357	134	75	13.2
Under 1 year	792	465	58.8	402	50.7	275	127	64	13.7

[1]Usually work 35 hours or more a week at all jobs.
[2]Usually work less than 35 hours a week at all jobs.
[3]Includes never-married, divorced, separated, and widowed persons.
NOTE: Own children include sons, daughters, step-children and adopted children. Not included are nieces, nephews, grandchildren, and other related and unrelated children. Data for 2000 are not strictly comparable with data for 1999 and earlier years because of the introduction of revised population controls in the household survey in January 2000. Detail may not sum to totals due to rounding

SOURCE: "Employment Status of Mothers with Own Children Under 3 Years Old by Single Year of Age of Youngest Child and by Marital Status, 1999–2000 Annual Averages," in *Employment Characteristics of Families in 2000*, [Online] ftp://146.142.4.23/pub/news.release/famee.txt [accessed September 29, 2001]

TABLE 6.15

Labor force participation among mothers 15 to 44 years old by fertility status and selected characteristics, June 1998

(Numbers in thousands. Limited to women with at least one child ever born)

| | Mothers who had a child in the last year | | | | | Mothers who did not have a child in the last year | | | | |
| | | Percent in labor force | | | | | Percent in labor force | | | |
Characteristic	Number of mothers	Total	Full-time	Part-time	Unem-ployed	Number of mothers	Total	Full-time	Part-time	Unem-ployed
Total	3,671	58.7	35.8	17.3	5.6	31,303	72.8	51.8	17.0	4.0
Age										
15 to 19 years	460	43.2	9.0	21.9	12.3	483	57.4	24.4	20.8	12.3
20 to 24 years	864	56.4	31.9	15.3	9.3	2,306	66.1	38.8	17.9	9.5
25 to 29 years	950	61.9	40.5	17.2	4.2	4,387	69.3	50.3	14.8	4.1
30 to 44 years	1,397	63.0	43.7	17.1	2.2	24,127	74.4	53.8	17.3	3.2
Births to Date and Age of Woman										
First birth	1,490	60.8	38.3	16.2	6.3	9,188	76.9	57.3	14.9	4.6
15 to 19 years	280	48.4	12.6	22.9	12.9	360	58.3	23.9	20.9	13.5
20 to 24 years	444	54.8	30.8	16.1	7.9	1,443	68.9	44.4	16.6	8.0
25 to 29 years	395	68.5	49.3	14.8	4.4	1,824	75.8	58.6	13.8	3.4
30 to 44 years	370	69.3	54.9	12.9	1.4	5,562	80.5	62.5	14.4	3.6
Second or higher order birth	2,181	57.3	34.0	18.0	5.2	22,115	71.1	49.5	17.9	3.7
15 to 19 years	180	35.2	3.4	20.5	11.3	124	54.9	25.8	20.4	8.7
20 to 24 years	420	58.2	33.0	14.5	10.7	863	61.5	29.6	20.0	11.9
25 to 29 years	555	57.3	34.3	18.9	4.0	2,563	64.6	44.4	15.5	4.7
30 to 44 years	1,026	60.7	39.7	18.6	2.4	18,565	72.5	51.2	18.2	3.1
Race and Ethnicity										
White	2,947	58.4	36.3	17.5	4.6	24,647	72.1	50.4	18.6	3.1
White non-Hispanic	2,374	61.6	38.9	19.2	3.5	20,690	73.7	51.3	19.7	2.6
Black	554	63.0	33.5	17.9	11.6	5,079	77.5	58.4	10.8	8.4
Asian and Pacific Islander	138	49.9	34.7	11.0	4.2	1,250	67.6	50.3	14.4	2.9
Hispanic (of any race)	618	45.7	26.1	11.2	8.4	4,182	64.5	46.3	12.7	5.5
Marital Status										
Married, husband present	2,469	60.0	39.3	17.4	3.3	21,121	70.7	49.1	19.1	2.5
Separated[1], divorced or widowed	202	64.5	50.2	9.3	5.0	5,731	82.1	65.2	12.0	4.9
Never married	1,000	54.4	24.2	18.6	11.6	4,451	70.8	46.9	14.0	9.9
Educational Attainment										
Not a high school graduate	793	37.7	13.6	13.5	10.6	4,871	56.3	35.4	12.9	7.9
High school graduate	1,034	58.4	33.5	17.0	7.9	11,511	73.8	52.8	16.5	4.5
College, 1 or more years	1,844	67.9	46.6	19.1	2.2	14,920	77.4	56.3	18.8	2.2
No degree	690	66.4	39.8	22.1	4.4	6,329	75.8	56.4	16.7	2.6
Associate degree	288	69.7	50.4	17.3	2.0	2,664	81.5	57.5	21.1	2.9
Bachelor's degree	627	66.5	45.8	19.9	0.8	4,509	76.3	54.0	20.8	1.4
Graduate or professional degree	239	73.6	63.2	10.4	—	1,418	80.6	61.1	17.5	2.1
Family Income										
Under $10,000	413	41.8	14.4	13.8	13.6	3,179	56.7	26.0	16.8	13.8
$10,000 to $19,999	514	49.5	26.4	15.2	7.8	3,763	69.8	48.5	15.7	5.6
$20,000 to $24,999	301	58.8	35.4	12.9	10.5	2,024	71.2	52.5	14.5	4.2
$25,000 to $29,999	236	57.2	36.6	12.0	8.5	2,013	75.2	55.7	14.8	4.7
$30,000 to $34,999	230	54.8	26.0	24.7	4.1	2,006	76.2	56.7	16.1	3.4
$35,000 to $49,999	522	67.3	41.1	24.3	1.8	5,080	76.7	58.0	16.3	2.5
$50,000 to $74,999	663	69.6	46.7	21.2	1.7	5,634	80.1	58.4	20.0	1.6
$75,000 and over	484	66.9	48.3	16.2	2.4	4,526	75.1	53.0	20.9	1.2
Income not reported	308	49.9	34.7	9.8	5.5	3,078	66.9	51.9	12.7	2.4

— Represents zero or rounds to zero.
[1] Includes married, husband absent.

SOURCE: Amara Bachu and Martin O'Connell, "Table F. Labor Force Participation Among Mothers 15 to 44 Years Old by Fertility Status and Selected Characteristics: June 1998," in *Fertility of American Women June 1998: Population Characteristics,* Current Population Reports, P20-526, U.S. Census Bureau, Washington, DC, September 2000

CHAPTER 7

CHILD CARE AND ELDER CARE

Far more women than ever before, including mothers with infants and small children, have entered the labor force and are working full-time outside of the home. Many more women than ever before are pursuing education and embarking on careers that may require long hours and extensive travel. More women than ever before are raising children on their own, at a time when there are fewer extended families to help out. The Personal Responsibility and Work Opportunity Reconciliation Act of 1996 (PRWORA) has moved low-income women off welfare and into the labor force, schools, and job-training programs. However, one element has not changed: women remain the primary caregivers for children and elderly family members.

WORKING MOTHERS

In 2000, 72.3 percent of women with children under the age of 18 were in the labor force, and all but 4.3 percent of them were employed. Overall, 69.2 percent of American women with children under 18 were working, 75 percent of them full-time. (See Table 7.1.) Among women with children under 18 who did not live with a spouse, 73 percent were employed, 83 percent of them full-time. Among all mothers with children under the age of six, 61 percent were employed and 71 percent of them worked full-time. In 2000, 56.8 percent of all mothers with children under age three were employed, and 68 percent of these women were employed full-time. (See Table 6.14.) In 1978 only 44 percent of mothers with children under six and 39.4 percent of mothers with children under three were in the labor force. (See Figure 6.8.) Of mothers with children under one year in 2000, 51 percent were employed, and 67 percent of these mothers were employed full-time. (See Table 6.14.)

Child-care arrangements are a major concern for working mothers, at least until their children reach about the age of 12, since full-time working mothers may need before- and after-school care for their school-age children. Part-time workers and those with irregular working hours require child-care arrangements that fit their work schedules and may need to make last-minute arrangements on a near-daily basis. Child-care arrangements must be made for school closures and vacations. Leaving work to give birth, to care for a newborn, or to nurse a sick child may cost a mother her job. According to a December 2000 report by the Institute for Women's Policy Research, many states do not consider lack of child care to be a "good cause" for leaving a job; so mothers who are forced to quit work to care for a child may not be eligible for unemployment insurance.

According to a 2000 report by the National Center for Children in Poverty, *Better Strategies for Babies: Strengthening the Caregivers and Families of Infants and Toddlers,* the number of infants and toddlers in child care increased significantly in the 1990s, particularly among low-income working families and those transitioning from welfare.

Infant care poses special challenges for working mothers, particularly those who are breast-feeding their infants. In 1998 mothers of infants were more likely to be unemployed than other mothers; however, 50 percent of divorced, separated, or widowed women who had given birth in the previous year were employed full-time, compared to 39.3 percent of married mothers and 24.2 percent of never-married mothers with infants. (See Table 6.15.) Never-married women in the labor force were more likely to be unemployed, in part because they were more likely to be without child care and/or job training. Women with more education returned to work more quickly after giving birth and were more likely to return to work full-time. These women tend to work later into their pregnancies and may have stronger job commitments than less-educated women. Furthermore, they tend to have higher incomes than other women, making quality child care more

TABLE 7.1

Employment status of the population by sex, marital status, and presence and age of own children under 18, 2000 annual average

(Numbers in thousands)

Characteristic	2000 Total	Men	Women
WITH OWN CHILDREN UNDER 18 YEARS			
Civilian noninstitutional population	63,267	27,673	35,595
Civilian labor force	51,944	26,202	25,742
Participation rate	82.1	94.7	72.3
Employed	50,259	25,622	24,637
Employment-population ratio	79.4	92.6	69.2
Full-time workers[1]	43,365	24,922	18,443
Part-time workers[2]	6,894	699	6,195
Unemployed	1,685	581	1,104
Unemployment rate	3.2	2.2	4.3
Married, spouse present			
Civilian noninstitutional population	51,415	25,540	25,874
Civilian labor force	42,361	24,290	18,072
Participation rate	82.4	95.1	69.8
Employed	41,357	23,816	17,541
Employment-population ratio	80.4	93.2	67.8
Full-time workers[1]	35,793	23,212	12,581
Part-time workers[2]	5,564	604	4,960
Unemployed	1,004	474	531
Unemployment rate	2.4	2.0	2.9
Other marital status[3]			
Civilian noninstitutional population	11,853	2,132	9,720
Civilian labor force	9,583	1,913	7,670
Participation rate	80.8	89.7	78.9
Employed	8,902	1,806	7,096
Employment-population ratio	75.1	84.7	73.0
Full-time workers[1]	7,572	1,710	5,862
Part-time workers[2]	1,330	96	1,234
Unemployed	681	107	574
Unemployment rate	7.1	5.6	7.5
WITH OWN CHILDREN 6 TO 17 YEARS, NONE YOUNGER			
Civilian noninstitutional population	34,737	15,165	19,572
Civilian labor force	29,576	14,178	15,398
Participation rate	85.1	93.5	78.7
Employed	28,744	13,877	14,868
Employment-population ratio	82.7	91.5	76.0
Full-time workers[1]	25,042	13,513	11,529
Part-time workers[2]	3,703	364	3,339
Unemployed	832	302	530
Unemployment rate	2.8	2.1	3.4
WITH OWN CHILDREN UNDER 6 YEARS			
Civilian noninstitutional population	28,530	12,508	16,022
Civilian labor force	22,368	12,024	10,344
Participation rate	78.4	96.1	64.6
Employed	21,515	11,745	9,770
Employment-population ratio	75.4	93.9	61.0
Full-time workers[1]	18,323	11,410	6,914
Part-time workers[2]	3,191	335	2,856
Unemployed	853	279	574
Unemployment rate	3.8	2.3	5.6
WITH NO OWN CHILDREN UNDER 18 YEARS			
Civilian noninstitutional population	145,199	71,825	73,374
Civilian labor force	88,014	48,140	39,874
Participation rate	60.6	67.0	54.3
Employed	84,058	45,781	38,278
Employment-population ratio	57.9	63.7	52.2
Full-time workers[1]	68,046	39,136	28,910
Part-time workers[2]	16,012	6,645	9,367
Unemployed	3,956	2,359	1,596
Unemployment rate	4.5	4.9	4.0

[1]Usually work 35 hours or more a week at all jobs.
[2]Usually work less than 35 hours a week at all jobs.
[3]Includes never-married, divorced, separated, and widowed persons.

SOURCE: Adapted from "Table 5. Employment status of the population by sex, marital status, and presence and age of own children under 18, 1999–2000 annual averages," in *Employment Characteristics of Families in 2000*, U.S. Department of Labor, Bureau of Labor Statistics, Washington, DC, April 19, 2001 [Online] http://stats.bls.gov/news.release/famee.nr0.htm [accessed October 11, 2001]

affordable. In 1998 there were no significant differences between the employment rates of mothers with single infants and mothers with both an infant and older children. In contrast, in 1995 the labor force participation rate of women with an infant and one or more older children was 10 percent less than that of women with just an infant.

CHILD-CARE ARRANGEMENTS

Types of Arrangements

Parents want their children to be cared for in a safe, stable, and attentive environment. The choice of child-care arrangements depends on availability, work schedules, transportation, affordability, and, in particular, on the age of the child. Child care is categorized as parental or nonparental. Parental care means that the child is cared for on a regular basis only by the parents. Nonparental care may be child care by relatives, by nonrelatives, or in a child-care center. Many children (22 percent of three- to six-year-olds in 1999) have more than one type of regular nonparental care, according to the Federal Interagency Forum on Child and Family Statistics.

According to an October 1999 study by the Center for Law and Social Policy, the majority of families who left welfare for work relied on friends and relatives for child care. Lack of child care was consistently identified as one of the reasons for unemployment among parents who had left welfare. Child-care arrangements also appeared to affect the type of job that the parent could accept, the hours worked, and absences from work.

PARENTAL CARE. As Table 7.2 shows, 46 percent of children from birth through the third grade received regular care only from their parents in 1999, compared to 49 percent in 1995. In each age group the percentage of children receiving only parental care declined between 1995 and 1999.

In general, younger children are more likely to receive parental care only. Among children under age three, 49 percent received only parental care, compared to 23 percent of children from age three up to kindergarten. (See Table 7.2.) According to the National Center for Education Statistics (NCES), 31 percent of three-year-olds, 18 percent of four-year-olds, and 14 percent of five-year-olds had parental care only in 1999.

Hispanic children were most likely to have only parental care, and black children were least likely. Although children living below the poverty level were more likely than others to have parental care only, even among these children 50 percent were cared for in other situations at least part of the time. In general, the more educated the mother, the more likely she was to be in the workforce and the less likely her children were to receive only parental care. Although some working mothers are able to arrange schedules with their spouses to accommodate child care,

TABLE 7.2

Percent of children by type of care arrangement for children from birth through third grade by child and family characteristics, 1995 and 1997

	Parental care only		Type of nonparental care arrangement							
			Total in nonparental care[b]		Care in a home[a]				Center-based program[c]	
					By a relative		By a nonrelative			
Characteristic	1995	1999	1995	1999	1995	1999	1995	1999	1995	1999
Total	49	46	51	54	20	22	15	14	23	27
Age/grade in school										
Ages 0-2	51	49	50	51	23	24	19	17	12	16
Ages 3-6, not yet in kindergarten	26	23	74	77	19	23	17	16	55	60
Kindergarten	56	52	44	48	18	20	14	13	16	22
1st-3rd grade	62	57	38	43	18	21	10	9	13	18
Race and Hispanic origin										
White, non-Hispanic	49	48	51	53	17	19	17	16	24	28
Black, non-Hispanic	40	34	60	66	31	33	10	11	27	35
Hispanic[d]	58	52	42	48	23	24	10	11	13	19
Other	49	43	51	57	22	29	11	11	25	28
Poverty status										
Below poverty	56	50	44	50	23	27	9	10	18	22
At or above poverty	46	45	54	55	19	21	17	15	25	29
Mother's highest level of education[e]										
Less than high school graduate	67	59	33	41	18	21	6	9	13	16
High school graduate/GED	51	49	49	51	22	27	13	11	19	23
Vocational/technical or some college	44	43	56	57	22	23	17	16	25	29
College graduate	40	43	60	57	14	15	22	17	34	35
Mother's employment status[e]										
35 hours or more per week	22	22	78	78	32	33	25	22	33	37
Less than 35 hours per week	42	45	58	55	25	25	19	17	24	26
Looking for work	64	62	36	38	15	19	4	5	20	21
Not in the labor force	76	75	24	25	7	7	4	4	15	17

[a] Relative and nonrelative care can take place in either the child's own home or another home.

[b] Some children participate in more than one type of nonparental care arrangement. Thus, details do not sum to the total percentage of children in nonparental care.

[c] Center-based programs include day care centers, prekindergartens, nursery schools, Head Start programs, and other early childhood education programs.

[d] Persons of Hispanic origin may be of any race.

[e] Children without a mother in the home are excluded from estimates of mother's highest level of education and mother's employment status.

SOURCE: "Table POP7. Child Care: Percentage of Children by Type of Care Arrangement for Children from Birth through Third Grade by Child and Family Characteristics, 1995 and 1999," in *America's Children: Key National Indicators of Well-Being 2001*, Federal Interagency Forum on Child and Family Statistics, Washington, DC, July 2001.

only 22 percent of children whose mothers worked full-time received only parental care, compared to 62 percent of those whose mothers were looking for work and 75 percent of those whose mothers were not in the labor force. (See Table 7.2.)

According to a 2001 report by The Urban Institute, *Who's Caring for Our Youngest Children? Child Care Patterns of Infants and Toddlers,* among children of employed mothers, 33 percent of those under one year were cared for primarily by their parents, compared to 25 percent of one-year-olds and 26 percent of two-year-olds. Infants and toddlers of single parents spent more time in care than children from two-parent families (34 hours versus 23 hours per week), and more children of single parents were in care full-time (60 percent versus 34 percent).

HOME-BASED CHILD CARE BY RELATIVES. Relatives provided 22 percent of nonparental child care in 1999, up from 20 percent in 1995. Grandparents, older siblings, or other family members may care for children in their home

or in the child's home. The most common type of nonparental care arrangement for infants and toddlers, Hispanic children, and children living below the poverty line was child care by a relative. Although 33 percent of black children were cared for by a relative, 35 percent were in center-based programs, compared to only 19 percent of Hispanic children. Furthermore, 23 percent of preschoolers aged three to six in nonparental care were cared for by a relative, as were 20 percent of kindergarteners. (See Table 7.2.)

According to the report from The Urban Institute, among children of employed mothers, 32 percent of those under one year were cared for by a relative, as were 27 percent of one-year-olds and 23 percent of two-year-olds. The majority of these infants and toddlers (51 percent) were being cared for by relatives who also provided care to at least one other child.

HOME-BASED CHILD CARE BY NONRELATIVES. In 1999, 14 percent of children from birth through the third grade in nonparental care were cared for in a home by nonrelatives, down from 15 percent in 1995. (See Table 7.2.) Some working parents can afford to hire a babysitter or nanny to care for children in their own home, and some parents rely on their friends for child care. Groups of parents may form a child-care cooperative, using parent volunteers or a hired caregiver or preschool teacher. However, most home-based or family day care is provided by an adult, usually a mother, who cares for several children in her home. These home-based day-care businesses may or may not be licensed by the state and often are more affordable than center-based day care.

Younger children are more likely than older children to have family-based day care by nonrelatives. According to The Urban Institute report, small home-based child-care providers cared for 13 percent of infants under one year with employed mothers, 16 percent of one-year-olds, and 21 percent of two-year-olds. Less than 10 percent of children under three were cared for by nannies or babysitters while their mothers were at work.

CHILD-CARE CENTERS. Nearly 20 million children received regular nonparental care in 1999. Among children from birth through the third grade, 27 percent were cared for in a center-based program, up from 23 percent in 1995. These center-based programs include day-care centers, nursery schools, preschools, Head Start programs, and other early childhood education programs such as prekindergartens. (See Table 7.2.) These child-care facilities may operate as commercial businesses, private nonprofit organizations, or publicly funded programs such as Head Start. Some businesses have child-care facilities for their employees, and many schools and universities have child-care facilities for students and staff. Some centers care for only one age group of children; others care for all children from infancy through school age.

As Table 7.2 shows, 60 percent of preschoolers aged three to six were in center-based programs, and 22 percent of kindergarteners also attended a child-care center in 1999. Children under three in nonparental care were least likely to be in a center in 1999 (16 percent, up from 12 percent in 1995.) However, The Urban Institute report found that two-year-old children of employed mothers were more likely to be in a child-care center than in other types of nonparental arrangements. In that study 15 percent of children under the age of one with employed mothers were in child-care centers, as were 23 percent of one-year-olds and 27 percent of two-year-olds.

Among children with nonparental care, black and non-Hispanic white children were most likely to be at a center. There was a correlation between a mother's education and the likelihood that her children had center-based care. In 1999, 35 percent of children in nonparental care whose mothers were college graduates were in child-care centers, compared to only 16 percent of those whose mothers had less than a high school diploma. Full-time working mothers also were more likely to utilize center-based child care. (See Table 7.2.)

PRESCHOOLS. Early childhood education programs improve the likelihood of a child's success in school, according to the Federal Interagency Forum on Child and Family Statistics. Studies have shown that high-quality preschool education improves school achievement in the short term and increases the likelihood that low-income minority children will complete school.

According to the Census Bureau, 7.8 million three- to five-year-olds were enrolled in nursery school and kindergarten in 1998, up from 4.1 million in 1970. Approximately equal numbers were enrolled in public and private nursery schools, although 82 percent of kindergarteners were in public schools.

According to the NCES, 60 percent of three- to five-year-olds with nonparental care were enrolled in early childhood care and education programs in 1999 (76 percent of five-year-olds, 69 percent of four-year-olds, and 46 percent of three-year-olds), up from 53 percent in 1993. African American children were most likely to be enrolled in such programs (73 percent, compared to 60 percent of non-Hispanic white children and 44 percent of Hispanic children).

Between 1993 and 1999 preschool enrollment increased among all races/ethnicities, including those living in poverty and those whose mothers were not in the labor force. However, children living in poverty were less likely than others to be enrolled in preschool programs (52 versus 62 percent). Among children whose mothers had completed college, 74 percent attended preschools, compared to only 40 percent of those whose mothers had less than a high school education. Among children not living with both parents, 62 percent were enrolled in preschools, compared to 54 percent in 1993.

SCHOOL-AGE CHILDREN. Since the average workday is longer than the average school day, many mothers need to find before- and after-school care. Figure 7.1 shows that although 52 percent of children in kindergarten through the eighth grade were regularly in the care of their parents, and 12 percent (primarily in sixth grade and above) cared for themselves, 19 percent attended center-based programs in 1999. Very few children under the age of 11 cared for themselves. An additional 19 percent of school-age children were cared for by a relative (sometimes an older sibling) and 8 percent by a nonrelative.

Child-Care Breakdowns

Mothers who work nonstandard hours or weekends, or are called into work unexpectedly, may struggle to find child care. Working mothers also must arrange for child care during school closures and vacations. Centers may have extended hours for working parents and extra staff to cover for absent employees; but mothers who depend on relatives or home-based day care may have to find alternative arrangements if their regular caregiver becomes ill or is otherwise unavailable. Married working women may be able to rely on their husbands when child care breaks down or if a child becomes ill and cannot go to school or to a regular caregiver. However, single mothers may have to stay home from work under such circumstances. Any disruption of the normal child-care routine can result in loss of working hours and productivity for mothers.

According to a Census Bureau survey, about 10 percent of employed, unmarried women with children under 15, particularly those with younger children, lost time from work because of failures in child-care arrangements. Married women were nearly four times more likely than their husbands to lose work time. Women with children in organized day care lost more time from work than did women with children who were cared for in their own homes. Children in group-care arrangements are more likely pick up minor illnesses, and most child-care facilities cannot accommodate sick children. In their *1998 Business Work-Life Study (BWLS),* the Families and Work Institute reported that 83 percent of employed mothers said they were more likely than their children's fathers to take time off work for a sick child.

Child-Care Workers

According to the Census Bureau, there were 51,656 child day-care services in the United States in 1998, with 644,111 paid employees and an annual payroll of $7.5 billion. One-third of establishments (36 percent) had five to nine employees. About 40 percent of child-care workers are self-employed home-care providers, according to the Bureau of Labor Statistics (BLS).

In 2000 almost 98 percent of child-care workers were women, as were almost 99 percent of prekindergarten and kindergarten teachers. Child care is an occupation that requires a high degree of skill, patience, and energy. Many child-care workers have degrees in early childhood education. Nevertheless, most of America's child-care workers are members of the working poor, with median weekly earnings of only $264, just 54 percent of the median weekly earnings for all full-time women workers.

According to a January 1999 Working Paper by The Foundation for Child Development, *Child Care Employment: Implications for Women's Self Sufficiency and for Child Development,* child care is viewed as a major job opportunity for women coming off welfare, despite the low pay and sometimes poor working conditions. Child-care workers are subjected to physical strain and frequent illness, yet less than one-third of them have fully paid health insurance. About one-third of child-care workers leave their jobs each year because of low pay, long hours, and stressful conditions.

FIGURE 7.1

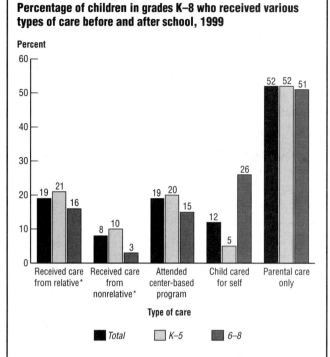

Percentage of children in grades K–8 who received various types of care before and after school, 1999

NOTE: The survey asked parents or guardians about the type of care the child received on a regular basis before or after school. "Received care from a relative" includes care received from someone other than the parent or guardian. Percentages may not add to 100 because children can be included in more than one type of care arrangement.
*Care received from a relative or nonrelative may be provided inside or outside of the child's home.

SOURCE: John Wirt, et al., "Before and After School Care: Percentage of children in grades K–8 who received various types of care before and after school: 1999," in *The Condition of Education 2001,* U.S. Department of Education, National Center for Education Statistics, Washington, DC, June 2001

A study of comparatively high-quality child-care centers by the Center for the Child Care Workforce and the Institute of Industrial Relations at the University of California at Berkeley, published in April 2001, confirmed that the child-care industry was losing educated, experienced teachers and administrators at a very high rate. These workers were being replaced with less-educated and less-experienced personnel. Furthermore, between 1994 and 2000 child-care wages did not keep up with the cost of living. According to an April 2000 report by the W. E. Upjohn Institute for Employment Research, the high turnover rate among child-care workers both lowered the quality of child care and increased the costs.

Child-Care Costs

According to a December 2000 study by The Urban Institute, about one-half of all working families with children under 13 and about 60 percent of all working families with children under 5 paid for child care. For many working families, child care is the fourth largest expense after food, housing, and taxes. Families in The Urban

Institute study paid an average of 10 percent of their earnings for child care. Among single-parent working families, 50 percent paid for child care, averaging 16 percent of their earnings. In some states low-income working families paid an average of 20 percent or more of their earnings for child care. Working families earning below the poverty level paid an average of 23 percent of their earnings for child care. Child-care costs may determine whether a mother can afford to go to work and, if she does, what quality of child care is affordable.

According to the Census Bureau, in 1999 married-couple families with incomes of less than $36,800 spent $860 annually on child care and education for their three- to five-year-olds and $760 per year for child care for children under two. Families with higher incomes spent substantially more on child care. Child-care costs are generally higher for infants and younger children. The parents of these children are often young themselves, just beginning their careers or working in relatively low-paying jobs. Child care could account for as much as 30 percent of these families' budgets. When a family has more than one child cared for by the same provider, the costs were approximately 25 percent lower per child.

The General Accounting Office (GAO) reported that the supply of infant care, care for children with special needs, and nonstandard-hours care was much more limited than overall child care. Lower-income areas had less of all types of child care than higher-income areas. Among families living at or below 200 percent of the poverty level, 40 percent paid for child care, spending an average of 16 percent of their annual earnings; 27 percent paid more than 20 percent of their annual earnings for child care. Higher-income families spent on average only 6 percent of their annual earnings on child care. Families receiving child-care subsidies are required to pay some of the cost, which may amount to between 4 and 17 percent of a family's monthly income.

CHILD-CARE ASSISTANCE

Employee Benefits

FAMILY LEAVE. On February 5, 1993, President Bill Clinton signed the Family and Medical Leave Act (FMLA) (PL 103-3), providing for up to 12 weeks of unpaid leave annually for illness, the birth or adoption of a child or a foster care placement, or to care for a seriously ill child or spouse. The law applies to companies with 50 or more employees and to employees who worked 1,250 hours in the previous year. Employers are required to maintain the employee's health coverage and to reinstate the returning employee in the same or an equivalent job. The FMLA applies to about 46 percent of the private-sector workforce.

A 1999 study by the Department of Labor found that family leave coverage, particularly paternity leave,

increased after the passage of the FMLA among those employers and employees covered by the act. Among those not covered by the FMLA, increases in family leave coverage since 1993 were much smaller. Likewise, employer-provided child-care benefits changed very little during the 1990s.

The Families and Work Institute's 1998 *BWLS* surveyed 1,057 for-profit and not-for-profit companies with more than 100 employees. Although many companies provided more than the required 12 weeks of leave, 7 to 10 percent of the companies with more than 100 employees did not provide 12 weeks, although the *BWLS* concluded that most of these companies were not out of compliance with the letter of the FMLA. Many of the companies (53 percent) provided at least some replacement pay during maternity leave, but only 13 percent provided paid paternity leave and only 12.5 percent provided paid adoption/foster care leave. Almost half of the companies (49 percent) allowed employees paid time off to care for a mildly ill child, although they were not required by law to do so. Among the companies surveyed, 81 percent allowed parents to return to work gradually following childbirth or adoption. Larger companies were more likely than smaller companies to provide long maternity, paternity, and adoption leaves, paid maternity leave, flexible hours, and child-care and elder-care resources.

ASSISTANCE WITH CHILD CARE. Among other policies to accommodate family responsibilities, the most common (68 percent of companies) was to allow employees to periodically change their work hours, although only 24 percent allowed changing hours on a daily basis. More than half of the companies allowed employees to switch back and forth between full- and part-time work and to occasionally work at home; however, only 37.5 percent allowed job sharing and only 33 percent allowed employees to work at home on a regular basis. However, 88 percent of the companies allowed employees time off for school or child-care functions.

The *BWLS* survey found that only 9 percent of companies provided on-site child care and only 5 percent provided child-care subsidies to employees. However, 50 percent provided dependent care assistance plans (DCAPs) that enable employees to pay for child care with pretax dollars. Only a small percentage of the companies provided sick child, school vacation, or backup child care, or reimbursed employees for child care when they worked late or were traveling on business. Only 5 percent of the companies were involved in child-care programs in their communities, and only 7 percent had parent education and support programs.

ON-SITE CHILD CARE. In 1998 the human resources consulting firm William M. Mercer, Inc., surveyed almost 25,000 employees at nine large national companies. When questioned about benefits that would influence their choice of an employer, 35 percent of the respondents said that they would be greatly influenced by the availability of on-site child care and 47 percent said that they would be somewhat influenced. On-site child care was much more important to employees than child-care resource and referral services, backup child care, or child-care vouchers or subsidies. Of the female respondents, 30 percent said they would use on-site child care, compared to 23 percent of the men, and equal numbers of men and women said they might need it someday. Lower-income respondents were more likely to want on-site child care than those making over $75,000 per year.

BACKUP CHILD CARE. The December 2000 study by the Institute for Women's Policy Research reported that 64 percent of single parents with children under six could not take paid time off when their child was sick. Although some hospitals and physician groups have set up "sick day care" centers, these arrangements tend to be considerably more expensive than regular day care.

Some employers are beginning to establish backup care programs for the children of workers whose regular child-care arrangements break down. In response to employee suggestions, Chase Manhattan Bank initiated a backup child-care program in 1999. Employees receive up to 20 days of free child care annually to cover school holidays and to care for mildly ill children. Newborns and newly adopted children of employees are eligible for up to eight consecutive weeks of free care. According to one Chase Manhattan employee, "[It's] like insurance. You're always glad you have it, because when you need it, you really need it."

ChildrenFirst, Inc. began operating employer-sponsored backup child-care facilities in 1992. It now serves 35,000 children and their families from more than 250 companies across the country. Bright Horizons Family Solutions, a Massachusetts-based company that provides child-care facilities for businesses, hospitals, universities, and government offices, has expanded its offerings with family centers that include backup care, care for school-age children into their teens, and summer camps.

RESOURCE AND REFERRAL SERVICES. The BLS found that in 2000 only 13.8 percent of civilian workers had access to employer-provided child-care resource and referral services. (See Table 7.3.) However, 17 percent of state and local government employees had these services, as did 45.8 percent of those in establishments with 5,000 or more employees. Workers in the western United States were most likely to have child-care resource services. The *BWLS* survey found that 36 percent of companies provided child-care resource services to their employees. Although 56 percent of the companies had an Employee Assistance Program to help with various types of prob-

lems, only 24 percent provided workshops or seminars on parenting, child development, elder care, or other work-family issues.

PROGRAMS FOR TEENAGERS. The *BWLS* survey found that only 12 percent of companies provided any type of program for the teenage children of employees and only 0.5 percent had after-school programs for teens. Information and referral services, scholarships, and education assistance for teens were provided by 1 percent of the companies, and 3 percent offered counseling services for teens.

UNION-MANAGEMENT PARTNERSHIPS. The Department of Labor's 1998 report, *Meeting the Needs of Today's Workforce: Best Child Care Practices,* cited 40 models for on-site, backup, school-age, sick child, and nonstandard hours child care, as well as family leave, child-care discounts and reimbursements, assistance for trainees and low-wage workers, and children-in-the-workplace programs. The report cited a partnership between the United Auto Workers (UAW) and General Motors in Flint, Michigan as one of the models for improving child-care practices.

As a result of 1999 contract negotiations between the UAW and Ford Motor Company, focusing on "Bargaining for Families," a union-management program called the Family Service and Learning Center was formed. The program called for the establishment of 13 child-care centers by 2003, each serving over 220 children and operating up to 24 hours per day, providing full- and part-time, backup, school-age, and sick child services. The initiative established programs for after-school care, preteen and teenage programs, summer camps, and vacation programs. It also established a network to assist child-care providers with accreditation.

MILITARY CHILD CARE. The military has the largest employer-sponsored child-care program in the country, offering full- and part-time child care, drop-in and extended-hours child care, and before- and after-school programs. The Military Child Care Act of 1989 made the Department of Defense (DOD) Child Development Program a leader in training and compensating child-care workers. However, with 173,522 spaces in its centers, the DOD meets only 58 percent of its child-care requirements. Therefore, the DOD program provides training and certification for the family-care homes that provide about one-third of the military's child care. Child-care costs to families are on a sliding scale that depends on family income. The average of $7,200 per year per child is shared equally by the parents and the government. A GAO study found that the DOD child-care costs were about 7 percent higher than civilian costs, primarily because of higher pay for workers, accreditation of the centers, and the large numbers of infants and toddlers served by the military centers.

TABLE 7.3

Child care resource and referral services by industry, establishment size, and region, June 2000

Category	Total	With child care resource and referral services				Without child care resource and referral services
		Total	Service contracted out	Provided internally	Other[2]	
Percent of workers						
Civilian workers	100.0	13.8	8.0	4.5	1.3	86.2
State and local governments	100.0	17.0	5.3	10.1	1.6	83.0
Private Industry	100.0	13.3	8.5	3.6	1.2	86.7
Goods producing	100.0	14.7	10.4	1.5	2.8	85.3
Service producing	100.0	12.8	7.9	4.3	0.7	87.2
Establishment size						
1–99 workers	100.0	4.5	2.6	1.5	0.4	95.5
100–499 workers	100.0	14.6	8.5	5.2	1.0	85.4
500–999 workers	100.0	23.9	15.8	6.0	2.1	76.1
1,000–4,999 workers	100.0	32.3	20.2	8.9	3.3	67.7
5,000 workers or more	100.0	45.8	20.1	19.5	6.2	54.2
Region[3]						
Northeast	100.0	16.0	9.3	5.9	0.8	84.0
South	100.0	10.3	6.4	3.5	0.5	89.7
Midwest	100.0	13.5	7.2	4.0	2.2	86.5
West	100.0	17.7	10.5	5.2	2.0	82.3
Percent of establishments						
All industries	100.0	3.0	1.7	1.1	0.1	97.0
State and local governments	100.0	13.5	6.7	–	–	86.5
Private Industry	100.0	2.7	1.6	1.0	0.1	97.3
Goods producing	100.0	1.9	1.4	–	0.1	98.1
Service producing	100.0	2.9	1.6	1.1	0.1	97.1
Establishment size						
1–99 workers	100.0	2.5	1.4	1.0	0.1	97.5
100–499 workers	100.0	14.0	7.6	5.7	0.7	86.0
500–999 workers	100.0	25.5	18.5	4.9	2.1	74.5
1,000–4,999 workers	100.0	33.9	24.4	6.6	2.9	66.1
5,000 workers or more	100.0	44.4	20.0	14.3	10.1	55.6
Region[3]						
Northeast	100.0	2.5	1.7	0.7	–	97.5
South	100.0	2.8	1.7	1.2	([4])	97.2
Midwest	100.0	2.2	0.9	1.2	0.1	97.8
West	100.0	4.6	2.8	1.4	0.4	95.4

[1] Incidence refers to the percent of workers eligible for child care resource and referral services and the percent of establishments that provide this service.

[2] "Other" refers to establishments that provide child care resource and referral services both internally and by contractors. For example, an establishment provides these services internally to non-management workers and contracts the services for management workers.

[3] The regional breakout is as follows: Northeast: Connecticut, Maine, Massachusetts, New Hampshire, New Jersey, New York, Pennsylvania, Rhode Island, and Vermont. South: Alabama, Arkansas, Delaware, District of Columbia, Florida, Georgia, Kentucky, Louisiana, Maryland, Mississippi, North Carolina, Oklahoma, South Carolina, Tennessee, Texas, Virginia, and West Virginia. Midwest: Illinois, Indiana, Iowa, Kansas, Michigan, Minnesota, Missouri, Nebraska, North Dakota, Ohio, South Dakota, and Wisconsin. and the West: Alaska, Arizona, California, Colorado, Hawaii, Idaho, Montana, Nevada, New Mexico, Oregon, Utah, Washington, and Wyoming.

[4] Less than 0.05 percent.

NOTE: Because of rounding, sums of individual items may not equal totals. Dashes indicate that data did not meet publication criteria.

SOURCE: "Table 1. Incidence of Child Care Resource and Referral Services by Industry, Establishment Size, and Region, June 2000," in *Pilot Survey on the Incidence of Child Care Resource and Referral Services in June 2000*, Bureau of Labor Statistics, Washington DC, November 2000 [Online] http://www.bls.gov/ncs2/ncrp0002.pdf [accessed October 2, 2001]

Government Benefits

In 1976 changes to the federal tax code granted a tax credit for child-care expenses for working families. However, additional federal child-care assistance to working families has been slow in coming.

In 2001 President George W. Bush signed into law a tax-cut package that included a 25 percent business tax credit to help cover the costs of establishing and operating worksite child care, including backup care facilities. The credit is also available to businesses that subsidize off-site child care for employees and includes a 10 percent tax credit to employers who offer child-care resource and referral services.

CHILD CARE AND DEVELOPMENT FUND. PRWORA recognized that moving single mothers off welfare and into the workforce would increase the need for affordable child care. The act established the Child Care and Development Fund (CCDF), to be administered by the Child Care Bureau of the Department of Health and Human Services (DHHS). It provided for more than $20 billion in block grants to the states between 1997 and 2002. A portion of the money was to be used to increase the quality and availability of child care for all families. In fiscal year (FY) 2001, the CCDF provided $4.5 billion to assist with child care for low-income families, families receiving Temporary Assistance for Needy Families (TANF) benefits, and those in transition from welfare to work.

In FY 1999 the CCDF served 1.8 million children in over 1 million families. Most of the children (79 percent) were cared for while their parents worked. Another 10 percent of the children's parents were in education or training programs. Most of CCDF assistance (83 percent) was in the form of certificates or vouchers to parents to help cover child-care expenses. Another 11 percent of the assistance was in the form of contracts with child-care centers, and 6 percent was cash assistance to parents. Most CCDF-assisted child care (56 percent) occurred in centers; 31 percent was for care in a family home, and 10 percent was for care in the child's home.

In addition to administering CCDF funds, states may use TANF funds for child care. A February 2001 study by the GAO found that between FY 1994–95 and FY 1999–2000, state spending on child care for low-income families increased significantly. (See Table 7.4.) Some states gave preference to families transitioning from welfare, whereas other states gave all low-income families equal access to CCDF funds. In the seven states studied by the GAO, there were not enough funds to serve the child-care needs of all low-income families, even though states had unspent CCDF and TANF funds. California and Texas had waiting lists for child-care subsidies. A 1998 DHHS study found that in one-fifth of all states, less than 10 percent of eligible families were receiving child-care assistance.

A 2001 study by the Center on Budget and Policy Priorities found that even though almost all former welfare recipients were eligible for child-care assistance, less than one-third of them received such assistance because of lack of information, high copayments, or lack of available child care for nonstandard work hours. Overall, less than 15 percent of eligible low-income families were receiving child-care assistance. On the other hand, since 1995 some states have increased the amount of TANF funds spent on child care, have increased income eligibility to 250 percent of the poverty line, have lowered copayments, and have increased payments to centers to cover off-hours child care. Some states also have established a child-care tax credit.

EARLY HEAD START. In 1995 the Administration of Children, Youth, and Families of the DHHS initiated Early Head Start. By 2001 there were more than six hundred programs to help meet the parenting needs of 45,000 low-income pregnant women and families with infants and toddlers. A January 2001 report by the DHHS indicated that the program had a positive impact on child development and parenting skills and had helped to reduce stress and conflict in the families. Other programs are directed at improving the quality of infant and toddler care by home-based and family caregivers.

TABLE 7.4

Selected states' child care expenditures of federal and state funds, fiscal years 1995–2000

1997 constant dollars in millions

State	1994–95	1998–99	1999–2000	Percent increase for 1994–95 to 1999–2000
California	$661	$1,443	$1,755	166
Connecticut	87	173	170	95
Maryland	87	117	122	40
Michigan	453	835	885	95
Oregon	64	79	77	20
Texas	396	544	692	75
Wisconsin	$58	$169	$166	186

SOURCE: "Table 2: Selected States' Child Care Expenditures of Federal and State Funds, Fiscal Years 1995 to 2000," in *Child Care: States Increased Spending on Low-Income Families,* U.S. General Accounting Office, Washington, DC, February 2001

ELDER CARE

If the creation of high-quality, affordable child care has not kept up with the needs of a changing workforce, issues surrounding elder care are only now starting to be recognized. The American population is aging rapidly, and people with chronic diseases are living longer. By the year 2010 the Census Bureau projects that 13 percent of the population, almost 40 million people, will be aged 65 or older. By 2050, 20 percent of the population, almost 82 million people, will be in this age group. Those 85 years and older are expected to be the fastest growing group, with the population increasing from 4.4 million in 2001 to over 19 million in 2050. Family members, primarily women, have traditionally cared for elderly relatives.

According to a March 2000 study by The Urban Institute, *Parental Care at Midlife: Balancing Work and Family Responsibilities Near Retirement,* most elder care is provided informally in the home. Spouses or adult children accounted for 57 percent of primary caregivers to impaired individuals aged 70 and over. Adult children were the primary caregivers for 42 percent of the unmarried elderly. As the older population grows, so will the numbers of elderly people needing care; however, there will be fewer adult children to take on these responsibilities.

Older Americans may suffer from failing vision or hearing, infirmity, loneliness, financial difficulties, and general loss of control over their lives. The elderly may need a wide variety of services, and their needs are constantly changing. Whereas children require less care as they get older, the elderly usually need more care. Most elderly prefer to remain at home and avoid institutionalization, putting the burden of care on nearby relatives, often a daughter or daughter-in-law.

The "Sandwich Generation"

A July 2001 study by AARP (formerly known as the American Association of Retired Persons) found that members of the "sandwich generation," baby boomers between the ages of 45 and 55, often had both child-care and elder-care responsibilities:

• Seventy percent had at least one living parent.

• Forty percent had children living at home: 32 percent had children under 21, and 7 percent had adult children at home.

• Asian Americans were most likely to have both children at home and aging parents, since many Asian Americans postponed having children.

• Almost 20 percent reported that their elder caregiving had caused strain between themselves and their spouses or siblings.

• African Americans tended to feel the most overwhelmed by these family responsibilities.

Among the elder-care providers, AARP found that:

• Eighty percent provided social interaction

• Forty-six percent provided transportation

• Forty-five percent performed housework

• Forty-four percent shopped

• Thirty-six percent talked to doctors

• Thirty-three percent handled paperwork or bills

• Seventeen percent hired nurses or aides

• Twelve percent handled intimate care

• Twenty-seven percent helped with expenses

AARP found that among women aged 45 to 55, 44 percent had both children under 21 and living parents and/or in-laws; 54 percent were caring for children, parents, or both; 22 percent were caring only for a parent or in-law. Of the survey respondents who provided elder care, nearly 30 percent said that they timed vacations around their parents' needs. More than 20 percent had moved or changed their retirement savings plans to accommodate their elder-care responsibilities.

Racial/Ethnic Differences among Elder-Care Providers

The AARP survey found that non-Hispanic whites were least likely to be caring for an elderly family member. Only 19 percent of non-Hispanic whites between the ages of 45 and 55 were providing care or financial support to an elderly parent, in-law, or other relative, compared to 28 percent of African Americans, 34 percent of Hispanics, and 42 percent of Asian Americans. Furthermore, only 20 percent of non-Hispanic whites wanted their children to care for them in their later years, compared to 30 to 40 percent of other racial/ethnic groups. Asian Americans reported the most care-related stress, as well as the most guilt over not providing more care.

Women as Caregivers for the Elderly

According to the National Older Women's League (OWL), more than 80 percent of family caregivers for chronically ill elders are women, and the average American woman will spend 18 years caring for an elderly parent. Furthermore, more than 90 percent of paid long-term care workers are women who, like child-care workers, perform a wide range of duties for low pay and few employee benefits. About 25 percent of caregivers to the elderly report health problems related to their responsibilities.

WORKING WOMEN. According to The Urban Institute study, the cost of caring for elderly parents in the home can be very high, particularly if it requires reducing work hours or retiring early. Women in the study were 75 percent more likely than men to help parents. Only 15 percent of the men helped parents with personal activities, errands, or chores. Whereas employed women were almost as likely as other women to care for a parent, employed men were much less likely than other men to care for a parent (14 percent versus 20 percent). Many more middle-aged women caregivers than male caregivers were in the workforce. Among the women in the study between the ages of 53 and 55, 44 percent cared for parents and 69 percent were employed. Employed women with elder-care responsibilities spent an average of almost 11 hours per week providing assistance. Although most women did not quit their jobs, about one-third reduced their work hours or took time off from work to provide care. Others rearranged their work hours or hired care for their elderly relative. Women between the ages of 53 and 65 who spent two or more hours per week helping a parent were employed 43 percent fewer hours than other women. Furthermore, among women whose parent could not be left alone, only 48 percent worked for pay. Likewise, nearly one-fifth of the elder-care providers in the AARP study had reduced their own hours of employment. The Urban Institute study concluded that time devoted to parental care substantially reduced the labor supply of both women and men and that informal elder care may be incompatible with the full-time employment of middle-aged caregivers.

Business Involvement

As baby boomers join the ranks of the middle-aged, elder care is emerging as the next challenge for employees trying to balance work and family. According to Andrew

Scharlach, professor of aging at the University of California at Berkeley, by 2020 an estimated one in three American workers will have elder-care obligations. He estimates that elder care costs companies $17 billion a year, or $2,500 per caregiver per year, in missed work and the cost of replacing employees who quit work to care for relatives.

In 1998 nearly one-third of companies with more than 1,000 employees offered some services to elder-care providers, up from just 1 percent of companies in 1988. This assistance included resource and referral services, seminars, support groups, or long-term care insurance. Approximately 15 percent of medium-size firms with 80 to 500 employees provided some assistance. However, only 25 percent of workers nationwide had access to employer-sponsored elder-care resource and referral services. Scharlach estimates that within 10 to 15 years every large American company and many small to mid-sized firms will offer elder-care benefits.

The 1998 *BWLS* survey found that although 21 percent of the companies with 100 or more employees offered elder-care resource and referral services, only 9 percent offered long-term care insurance for family members. Only 5 percent provided financial support to elder-care programs in their communities.

The American Business Collaboration for Quality Dependent Care is a $100 million national initiative to improve dependent-care programs in 68 communities. The 2001 projects are being managed by WFD, a Boston-based consulting firm that specializes in work-life issues. In the Portland, Oregon-Vancouver, Washington, metro area, Bank of America, IBM, and Hewlett-Packard have invested $112,000 in projects that include recruiting and training family child-care providers to improve infant and toddler care. The companies also are sponsoring two Elder Care Fairs where employees can learn about elder-care options in the community. In Philadelphia, Aetna U.S. Health Care, Deloitte & Touche, and IBM are investing $223,500 in projects that are aimed at improving the quality of child care and summer camp programs and expanding in-home and transportation services for the elderly.

CHAPTER 8
WOMEN IN AMERICAN POLITICS

On August 26, 1920, Tennessee became the 36th state to ratify the Nineteenth Amendment to the Constitution. With three-quarters of the states having ratified the amendment, all American women were granted the right to vote. On the advice of his mother, Henry Thomas Burn cast the deciding vote in the Tennessee House of Representatives. Previously he had sided with the antisuffragists, who were opposed to women voting. Allegedly, the antisuffragists were so angry at Burn that they chased him from the chamber, forcing him to climb out a window of the Capitol and inch along a ledge to safety.

The passage of the Nineteenth Amendment marked the end of a long and bitter struggle for the suffragists, led by Susan B. Anthony, Elizabeth Cady Stanton, and Lucretia Mott. Between 1838 and 1910, 25 states passed laws allowing women to vote on school issues. In 1893 Colorado became the first state to allow women's suffrage, and by 1920, 30 states, primarily in the West and Midwest, had already granted women full suffrage. In the years since 1920, American women have exercised their right to vote, helped to elect their government, influenced legislation, and helped determine the direction of the nation.

As more women enter American politics, their influence continues to grow. Nevertheless, fewer women than men are politically active. According to 1998 data reported by the Center for American Women and Politics (CAWP) of the Eagleton Institute of Politics at Rutgers, the State University of New Jersey, only 13.9 percent of first-year female college students believed that it was essential or very important for them to influence the political structure of the United States, compared to 18.5 percent of male college students. Only approximately 31 percent of women, compared to 43 percent of men, had e-mailed Congress in the previous year, and only about 19 percent of women, compared to 30 percent of men, had visited campaign Web sites.

WOMEN VOTERS

Registration and Voter Turnout

In 2000 American women were 51.9 percent of the voting-age population. (See Table 8.1.) Men outnumbered women only among 18- to 24-year-olds. Women made up 58 percent of the population over age 64 and outnumbered voting-age men in every racial/ethnic group and in every state except Alaska and Nevada. About 93 percent of voting-age U.S. residents are citizens and therefore eligible to vote. The voting-age population does not include U.S. citizens living abroad who may vote.

Not only do women outnumber men in the voting-age population, but a higher proportion of women than men register to vote. In 1998, 67.1 percent of U.S. citizens aged 18 and over were registered to vote, 68.4 percent of eligible women and 65.7 percent of eligible men. (See Table 8.2.) According to CAWP, 62.1 million women were registered to vote in 1984, compared to only 54 million men. Between 1984 and 1998 the number of registered females increased 5.3 percent, and the number of registered males, 6.9 percent.

NONPRESIDENTIAL ELECTIONS. In the 1998 congressional elections 43.7 million women voted, compared to 39.4 million men. A higher proportion of eligible women than eligible men voted (45.7 percent compared to 44.9 percent), but among registered voters, men were more likely than women to vote (68.3 percent, compared to 66.8 percent). (See Table 8.2.) Among the voting-age population in 1998 a higher proportion of women than men aged 18 to 64 voted; however, a higher proportion of men than women over age 64 voted. (See Table 8.3.)

Among the population of citizens aged 18 and over, non-Hispanic whites were most likely to be registered and to have voted in 1998. (See Table 8.2.) Non-Hispanic Asian and Pacific Islanders were least likely to be registered and were least likely to vote. Non-Hispanic blacks

TABLE 8.1

Projection of the population of the voting age, by race, Hispanic origin, and sex, November 7, 2000

(In thousands. Population 18 years and over.)

State, race, and Hispanic origin	Total, 18 years and over	Male Total, 18 years and over	18 to 24 years	25 to 44 years	45 to 64 years	65 years and over	Female Total, 18 years and over	18 to 24 years	25 to 44 years	45 to 64 years	65 years and over
UNITED STATES											
Total	205,813	98,947	13,687	40,718	30,008	14,534	106,865	13,135	41,368	31,952	20,409
White	171,380	83,014	10,951	33,375	25,752	12,935	88,366	10,370	33,162	26,808	18,025
Black	24,635	11,336	2,021	5,177	2,978	1,161	13,299	2,038	5,792	3,686	1,784
American Indian and Alaska Native	1,629	796	148	373	203	71	833	148	366	221	97
Asian and Pacific Islander	8,169	3,802	567	1,793	1,076	366	4,368	579	2,048	1,237	503
Hispanic (of any race)	21,305	10,583	2,094	5,278	2,380	831	10,722	1,938	5,062	2,583	1,140
White non-Hispanic	151,957	73,354	9,032	28,569	23,586	12,166	78,603	8,603	28,567	24,459	16,973

SOURCE: Adapted from "Table 1. Projections of the Population by Voting Age, for States, by Race, Hispanic Origin, Sex, and Selected Ages: November 7, 2000," in *Projections of the Voting-Age Population for States: November 2000 Tables,* [Online] http://www.census.gov/population/socdemo/voting/proj00/tab01.txt [accessed October 7, 2001]

were more likely than Hispanics to have registered and to have voted. However, within every racial/ethnic group women were more likely than men to be registered and to have voted. In particular, 66.2 percent of eligible black women were registered in 1998 and 43.7 percent voted, compared to only 60.6 percent of eligible black men who were registered and 39.6 percent who voted.

In 1972 the voting age was lowered from 21 to 18 nationwide, thereby increasing the voting-age population. Between 1966 and 1998 the numbers of women voting in nonpresidential (congressional) elections increased 37.4 percent, whereas the numbers of voting men increased 28.0 percent. (See Table 8.3.) However, in 1966, 53.0 percent of the female voting-age population voted, compared to only 42.4 percent in 1998. The percentage of the male voting-age population who voted decreased from 58.2 percent in 1966 to 41.4 percent in 1998. Between 1966 and 1982 a higher proportion of men than women voted in nonpresidential elections. Since 1986 a higher proportion of voting-age women have voted in nonpresidential elections. The Census Bureau credits women's increased education and labor force participation for the increase in women voters, since both education and employment correlate positively with voting behavior.

PRESIDENTIAL ELECTIONS. Voter turnout is usually lower for nonpresidential elections, and voter turnout was at an all-time low of 41.9 percent in 1998. In every presidential election between 1980 and 1996 a higher proportion of eligible women than men voted. Higher percentages of African American, white, and Hispanic eligible women voted in presidential elections as compared with men. Prior to 1980 higher proportions of men than women voted in presidential elections. Still, the number of women voters has exceeded the number of male voters in every presidential election since 1964.

According to the Census Bureau, 52.8 percent of voting-age men voted in the 1996 presidential election between incumbent President Bill Clinton and Senator Robert Dole, compared to 55.5 percent of voting-age women. Almost 68 million women (67.3 percent of all women 18 years and older) and nearly 60 million men (64.4 percent) were registered to vote. In the 1992 presidential election between incumbent President George Bush and Governor Clinton, 62.3 percent of voting-age women and 60.2 percent of voting-age men actually voted.

The Political Gender Gap

THE OPINION GAP. Differences in the political opinions of men and women may reflect differences in their lives. Since women generally earn less than men, have fewer employee benefits than men, and live longer than men, they tend to be more concerned about health-care reform, Social Security, and other social programs. As the primary caregivers for children and the elderly, women are more likely to support programs that would help these groups. CAWP examined the gender gap in political attitudes using polls on various issues from a number of sources. They found that women, in comparison with men, were:

• Less militaristic on issues of war and peace

• More often opposed to the use of force in nonmilitary situations

• More likely to favor measures to protect the environment and to check the growth of nuclear power.

• More supportive of programs designed to meet basic human needs such as quality health care.

• More supportive of efforts to achieve racial equality

• More supportive of feminist positions on some women's issues

TABLE 8.2

Reported rates of voting and registration by race and sex, November 1998

[Numbers in thousands]

Characteristics	Total population					Total citizen		
	Total population	Reported registered		Reported voted		Total citizen	Percent registered	Percent voted
		Number	Percent	Number	Percent			
Total, 18 years and over	198,228	123,104	62.1	83,098	41.9	183,450	67.1	45.3
Sex								
Male	95,187	57,659	60.6	39,391	41.4	87,713	65.7	44.9
Female	103,042	65,445	63.5	43,706	42.4	95,738	68.4	45.7
Non-Hispanic White, total	146,501	99,510	67.9	68,068	46.5	143,651	69.3	47.4
Male	70,624	47,256	66.9	32,786	46.4	69,290	68.2	47.3
Female	75,876	52,254	68.9	35,282	46.5	74,361	70.3	47.5
Non-Hispanic Black, total	22,603	13,773	60.9	9,044	40.0	21,613	63.7	41.9
Male	10,047	5,789	57.6	3,781	37.6	9,555	60.6	39.6
Female	12,557	7,984	63.6	5,263	41.9	12,058	66.2	43.7
Non-Hispanic Asian and Pacific Islander, total	7,327	2,133	29.1	1,404	19.2	4,344	49.1	32.3
Male	3,477	992	28.5	647	18.6	2,079	47.7	31.1
Female	3,851	1,141	29.6	757	19.7	2,265	50.4	33.4
Hispanic, total[1]	20,321	6,843	33.7	4,068	20.0	12,395	55.2	32.8
Male	10,327	3,235	31.3	1,942	18.8	6,090	53.1	31.9
Female	9,994	3,608	36.1	2,126	21.3	6,305	57.2	33.7

[1]Hispanics may be of any race.

SOURCE: Adapted from Jennifer C. Day and Avalaura L Gaither, "Table C. Reported Rates of Voting and Registration by Selected Characteristics: November 1998," in *Voting and Registration in the Election of November 1998,* Current Population Reports, P20-523RV, U.S. Census Bureau, Washington, DC, August 2000

EMILY's List, a donor network for Democratic women candidates, conducted a survey of 1,034 women and 501 men who voted in the November 2000 election, *The Women's Vote and the 2000 Elections* (December 14, 2000). Nearly two-thirds of the women surveyed reported that their choice for president was strongly influenced by the candidate's support for working families and plans for improving education, although a strong economy also was very important to women voters. Other determining issues reported by approximately one-half of the women included:

- Health care

- Accountability of health maintenance organizations

- Social Security

- Prescription drug coverage for seniors

- Abortion

Abortion was a much more important issue for women than it was for men. Many more men than women were influenced by the candidates' positions on foreign policy and national defense. Far more women than men supported additional gun controls.

THE VOTING GAP. The political opinion gap between men and women is reflected in their voting patterns. Women are more likely than men to vote for Democratic candidates. Although the 2000 presidential election was the closest in history, the voting gender gap was very large. The EMILY's List survey found a 22-point gender gap: 54 percent of women voted for Vice-President Al Gore, a Democrat, and only 43 percent voted for the Republican governor George W. Bush, whereas 53 percent of men voted for Bush and only 42 percent for Gore. In the 1996 presidential election there was a 17-point gender gap: 16 percent more women voted for the Democratic president Clinton than for Senator Dole, a Republican, and 1 percent more men voted for Dole than for Clinton. In the 1992 election there was only a five-point gender gap: 8 percent more women voted for Governor Clinton than for Republican president George Bush, and 3 percent more men voted for Clinton.

EMILY's List also reported a gender gap in votes for third-party presidential candidates and congressional candidates. In the 2000 presidential election, 4 percent of men but only 2 percent of women voted for Ralph Nader. Likewise, in the 1992 and 1996 elections more men than women voted for Ross Perot. Women favored Democratic congressional candidates by 11 percentage points in 2000, whereas men favored Republican candidates by 6 points. This was approximately same gap as in the 1996 election.

Unmarried women, working women, lower-income women, union women, suburban women, and those from the Midwest were all much more likely to have voted for Vice-President Gore in 2000. Hispanic, African American, and white Catholic women were all more likely to have voted for Gore. Religious women, homemakers,

TABLE 8.3

Voter turnout in non-presidential elections, 1966–98

Non-presidential Election Year	% of Voting Age Population Who Reported Voting		Number Who Reported Voting (in millions)	
	Women	Men	Women	Men
1998	42.4	41.4	43.7	39.3
1994	45.3	44.7	44.9	40.7
1990	45.4	44.6	43.3	38.7
1986	46.1	45.8	42.2	37.7
1982	48.4	48.7	42.3	38.0
1978	45.3	46.6	36.3	33.3
1974	43.4	46.2	32.5	30.7
1970	52.7	56.8	33.8	32.0
1966	53.0	58.2	31.8	30.7

1988	% of Voting Age Population Who Reported Voting		Number Who Reported Voting (in millions)	
	Women	Men	Women	Men
18-24 yrs.	35.0	29.8	4.3	3.6
25-44 yrs.	51.5	46.9	21.8	19.2
45-64 yrs.	65.1	63.7	18.0	16.5
65-74 yrs.	68.1	72.6	6.8	5.9
75 yrs. up	59.4	68.2	5.0	3.5
1994				
18-24 yrs.	21.5	18.6	2.7	2.3
25-44 yrs.	40.2	38.6	16.9	15.7
45-64 yrs.	56.6	56.8	14.8	13.9
65-74 yrs.	62.1	67.4	6.3	5.4
75 yrs. up	51.8	64.9	4.1	3.1

Note: Since 1986, the proportion of eligible female adults who voted has exceeded the proportion of eligible male adults who voted, reversing the historical pattern of higher turnout rates for men than for women. Among younger citizens (18-44), a higher proportion of women than men voted in 1998 and 1994; the pattern is reversed among older voters (65 and up).

SOURCE: "Voter Turnout in Non-Presidential Elections," in *Sex Differences in Voter Turnout,* Center for American Women and Politics, Eagleton Institute of Politics, Rutgers, The State University of New Jersey, New Brunswick, NJ, 2000 [Online] http://www.cawp.rutgers.edu/pdf/sexdiff.pdf [accessed October 7, 2001]

women from small towns or rural areas, and wealthier women were more likely to have voted for Governor Bush. Among independents men were much more likely than women to have voted for Governor Bush. Many more women than men cited character and values as their reasons for supporting Bush. Many more men cited taxes and foreign policy issues as their reasons for supporting him.

In exit polls conducted on Election Day 1998, Voter News Service (VNS) found a gender gap of at least four percentage points in 47 out of 65 races (72.3 percent). There were gender gaps in 23 out of 33 gubernatorial races and 24 out of 32 U.S. Senate races. In 44 of the 47 races with gender gaps, female voters were more likely than male voters to support Democratic candidates.

In 13 races in 1998 a majority of women voted for a different candidate than did the majority of men. (See Table 8.4.) Five Democratic candidates won because of women voters and eight Republican candidates won because of male voters. Of the seven races with a gender gap of at least 10 percentage points, women voters elected

Democratic senators in New York and North Carolina and a Democratic governor in Maryland and male voters elected Republican governors in Colorado, Florida, Massachusetts, and Ohio.

WOMEN AS ELECTED OFFICIALS

The number of women holding elective office at all levels of government has increased spectacularly in the past two decades. In 2001 the U.S. Congress was 14 percent women, up from about 12 percent in 1999 and 3 percent in 1979. (See Table 8.5.) Women held 27 percent of statewide elective offices, down from about 28 percent in 1999 but up from only about 11 percent in 1979. Women accounted for 22 percent of state legislators in 2001, down from about 23 percent in 1999 but up from 10 percent in 1979. The majority of female elected officials are Democrats.

Women in Congress

Many more women served in the U.S. Congress in 2001 than ever before. (See Table 8.6.) Women held 73 of the 535 seats in the 107th Congress (2001–2003). Since 1917 only the 66th Congress (1919–1921) had no female representation. According to CAWP, as of 2001, 206 women had served in Congress, 135 Democrats and 71 Republicans (135D, 71R)—7 women (5D, 2R) had served in both houses of Congress, 24 women in the Senate only (15D, 9R), and 175 in the House of Representatives only (115D, 60R). As of 2001 California had sent the most women to Congress (27), but six states (Alaska, Delaware, Iowa, Mississippi, New Hampshire, and Vermont) had never been represented by a congresswoman. Overall, eight women senators and 37 representatives first went to Congress after being elected or appointed to fill the seats of their deceased husbands.

SENATORS. Out of the 100 senators in 2001 there were 13 women, 10 Democrats and 3 Republicans, representing 10 states. Both of the senators from three states—California, Washington, and Maine—were women. In the November 2000 election, for the first time in history, all six women who ran for the Senate as major-party candidates won their elections. Three women—Hillary Rodham Clinton, a Democrat from New York (D-NY), Debbie Stabenow (D-MI), and Maria Cantwell (D-WA)—were elected for the first time, and one Democrat and two Republicans were reelected. Jean Carnahan (D-MO) was appointed to the Senate in 2001 to fill her husband's seat after he was elected posthumously.

As of 2001 a total of 31 women had served in the Senate, 20 Democrats and 11 Republicans. The 102nd Congress (1991–1993) was the first to include more than two women senators. (See Table 8.6.) The first woman senator was Rebecca Latimer Felton (D-GA) who was appointed in 1922 and served for one day. In 1931 Hattie Wyatt Caraway (D-AR) was appointed to

TABLE 8.4

Races where female and male voters made different choices, 1998

State	Office	Candidates	Seat	Won/Lost	Vote Counts		Exit Polls		Winner Elected By
					Votes	% Votes	% Women	% Men	
CO	Gov.	Gail Schoettler (D)	Open	Lost	639,214	49	55	41	
		Bill Owens (R)	Open	Won	646,997	50	43	55	Men
FL	Gov.	Buddy MacKay (D)	Open	Lost	1,660,107	45	52	42	
		Jeb Bush (R)	Open	Won	2,062,227	55	47	58	Men
IL	US Sen.	Carol Moseley-Braun (D)	Incum	Lost	1,566,955	47	50	43	
		Peter Fitzgerald (R)	Chall	Won	1,698,092	51	47	55	Men
KY	US Sen.	Scotty Baesler (D)	Open	Lost	561,294	50	54	46	
		Jim Bunning (R)	Open	Won	568,380	50	46	54	Men
MA	Gov.	Scott Harshbarger(D)	Chall	Lost	898,788	48	54	41	
		A. Paul Cellucci (R)	Incum	Won	961,099	51	45	56	Men
MD	Gov.	Parris Glendening (D)	Incum	Won	826,609	56	60	50	Women
		Ellen Sauerbrey (R)	Chall	Lost	662,554	44	40	50	
NE	Gov.	Bill Hoppner (D)	Lost	Lost	237,237	46	50	41	
		Mike Johanns (R)	Won	Won	277,985	54	50	59	Men
NV	Gov.	Jan Laverty Jones (D)	Open	Lost	181,921	43	48	41	
		Kenny Guinn (R)	Open	Won	223,428	52	46	53	Men
NY	US Sen.	Charles Schumer (D)	Chall	Won	2,358,112	55	59	49	Women
		Alfonse D'Amato (R)	Incum	Lost	1,937,108	45	40	50	
NC	US Sen.	John Edwards (D)	Chall	Won	1,008,098	52	59	43	Women
		Lauch Faircloth (R)	Incum	Lost	923,824	47	40	55	
OH	Gov.	Lee Fisher (D)	Open	Lost	1,467,688	45	49	41	
		Robert Taft (R)	Open	Won	1,645,649	50	45	55	Men
SC	US Sen.	Ernest Hollings (D)	Incum	Won	553,362	53	55	48	Women
		Bob Inglis (R)	Chall	Lost	483,322	46	42	50	
WI	US Sen.	Russell Feingold (D)	Incum	Won	879,300	51	52	49	Women
		Mark Neumann (R)	Chall	Lost	842,197	49	46	50	

SOURCE: *Gender Gap Evident in Numerous 1998 Races*, Center for American Women and Politics, Eagleton Institute of Politics, Rutgers, The State University of New Jersey, New Brunswick, NJ, 1999

TABLE 8.5

Percentage of women in elective offices, 1979–2001

Level of Office	1979	1981	1983	1985	1987	1989	1991	1993	1995	1997	1999	2001
U.S. Congress	3%	4%	4%	5%	5%	5%	6%	10%	10%	11%	12%	14%
Statewide Elective	11%	11%	11%	14%	14%	14%	18%	22%	26%	26%	28%	27%
State Legislatures	10%	12%	13%	15%	16%	17%	18%	21%	21%	22%	23%	22%

SOURCE: "Percentage of Women in Elective Offices," in *Women in Elective Office 2001*, Center for American Women and Politics, Eagleton Institute of Politics, Rutgers, The State University of New Jersey, New Brunswick, NJ, 2001 [Online] http://www.cawp.rutgers.edu/pdf/elective.pdf [accessed October 7, 2001]

her husband's seat following his death and subsequently won three more Senate races. Margaret Chase Smith, a Republican from Maine, was the first woman to enter the Senate via an election, although she had been elected first to her deceased husband's seat in the House. Smith was the first woman to serve in both houses of Congress. As of 2001, 12 women had first entered the Senate through appointments to unexpired terms, and 6 women had won special elections to fill unexpired terms. Of the 14 women who first entered the Senate via regular elections, Cantwell and Stabenow in 2000 were the first to defeat incumbents in a general election, although Carol Moseley-Braun (D-IL) defeated the incumbent in a 1992 primary election. The other 11 women won open Senate seats.

REPRESENTATIVES. Of the 435 seats in the House of Representatives in 2001, 42 were held by Democratic women and 18 by Republican women, representing 27 states. (See Table 8.6.) In addition, the House of Representatives included Democratic women delegates from the Virgin Islands and Washington, D.C. According to CAWP, a record number of women, 122 (80D, 42R), were major-party candidates for regular House seats in 2000. Of the 56 women serving in the House in 2000, 4 did not run for reelection. All 52 incumbents (37D, 15R) were reelected. In addition, five women ran for open seats (2D, 3R), and two Democrats defeated incumbents.

The first woman elected to Congress was Jeanette Rankin (R-MT), who served in the House of Representatives

TABLE 8.6

Women in the U.S. Congress, 1917-2001[1]

CONGRESS	DATES	WOMEN IN SENATE	WOMEN IN HOUSE	TOTAL WOMEN
65th	1917-1919	0 (0D, 0R)	1 (0D, 1R)	1 (0D, 1R)
66th	1919-1921	0 (0D, 0R)	0 (0D, 0R)	0 (0D, 0R)
67th	1921-1923	1 (1D, 0R)	3 (0D, 3R)	4 (1D, 3R)
68th	1923-1925	0 (0D, 0R)	1 (0D, 1R)	1 (0D, 1R)
69th	1925-1927	0 (0D, 0R)	3 (1D, 2R)	3 (1D, 2R)
70th	1927-1929	0 (0D, 0R)	5 (2D, 3R)	5 (2D, 3R)
71st	1929-1931	0 (0D, 0R)	9 (5D, 4R)	9 (5D, 4R)
72nd	1931-1933	1 (1D, 0R)	7 (5D, 2R)	8 (6D, 2R)
73rd	1933-1935	1 (1D, 0R)	7 (4D, 3R)	8 (5D, 3R)
74th	1935-1937	2 (2D, 0R)	6 (4D, 2R)	8 (6D, 2R)
75th	1937-1939	2 (1D, 1R)[2]	6 (5D, 1R)	8 (6D, 2R)
76th	1939-1941	1 (1D, 0R)	8 (4D, 4R)	9 (5D, 4R)
77th	1941-1943	1 (1D, 0R)	9 (4D, 5R)	10 (5D, 5R)
78th	1943-1945	1 (1D, 0R)	8 (2D, 6R)	9 (3D, 6R)
79th	1945-1947	0 (0D, 0R)	11 (6D, 5R)	11 (6D, 5R)
80th	1947-1949	1 (0D, 1R)	7 (3D, 4R)	8 (3D, 5R)
81st	1949-1951	1 (0D, 1R)	9 (5D, 4R)	10 (5D, 5R)
82nd	1951-1953	1 (0D, 1R)	10 (4D, 6R)	11 (4D, 7R)
83rd	1953-1955	2 (0D, 2R)	11 (5D, 6R)[3]	13 (5D, 8R)[3]
84th	1955-1957	1 (0D, 1R)	16 (10D, 6R)[3]	17 (10D, 7R)[3]
85th	1957-1959	1 (0D, 1R)	15 (9D, 6R)	16 (9D, 7R)
86th	1959-1961	2 (1D, 1R)	17 (9D, 8R)	19 (10D, 9R)
87th	1961-1963	2 (1D, 1R)	18 (11D, 7R)	20 (12D, 8R)
88th	1963-1965	2 (1D, 1R)	12 (6D, 6R)	14 (7D, 7R)
89th	1965-1967	2 (1D, 1R)	11 (7D, 4R)	13 (8D, 5R)
90th	1967-1969	1 (0D, 1R)	11 (6D, 5R)	12 (6D, 6R)
91st	1969-1971	1 (0D, 1R)	10 (6D, 4R)	11 (6D, 5R)
92nd	1971-1973	2 (1D, 1R)	13 (10D, 3R)	15 (11D, 4R)
93rd	1973-1975	0 (0D, 0R)	16 (14D, 2R)	16 (14D, 2R)
94th	1975-1977	0 (0D, 0R)	19 (14D, 5R)	19 (14D, 5R)
95th	1977-1979	2 (2D, 0R)	18 (13D, 5R)	20 (15D, 5R)
96th	1979-1981	1 (0D, 1R)	16 (11D, 5R)	17 (11D, 6R)
97th	1981-1983	2 (0D, 2R)	21 (11D, 10R)	23 (11D, 12R)
98th	1983-1985	2 (0D, 2R)	22 (13D, 9R)	24 (13D, 11R)
99th	1985-1987	2 (0D, 2R)	23 (12D, 11R)	25 (12D, 13R)
100th	1987-1989	2 (1D, 1R)	23 (12D, 11R)	25 (13D, 12R)
101st	1989-1991	2 (1D, 1R)	29 (16D, 13R)	31 (17D, 14R)
102nd	1991-1993	4 (3D, 1R)[5]	28 (19D, 9R)[4]	32 (22D, 10R)[4]
103rd	1993-1995	7 (5D, 2R)[6]	47 (35D, 12R)[4]	54 (40D, 14R)[4]
104th	1995-1997	9 (5D, 4R)[7]	48 (31D, 17R)[4]	57 (36D, 21R)[4]
105th	1997-1999	9 (6D, 3R)	54 (37D, 17R)[8]	63 (43D, 20R)[8]
106th	1999-2001	9 (6D, 3R)	56 (39D, 17R)[9]	65 (45D, 20R)[9]
107th	2001-2003	13 (10D, 3R)	60 (42D, 18R)[9]	73 (52D, 21R)[9]

[1] Table shows maximum number of women elected or appointed to serve in that Congress at one time. Some filled out unexpired terms and some were never sworn in.

[2] A total of three (2D, 1R) women served in the Senate in the 75th Congress, but no more than two served together at any one time. Part of the time two Democrats served together, and part of the time one Democrat and one Republican served together.

[3] Does not include a Republican Delegate to the House from pre-statehood Hawaii.

[4] Does not include a Democratic Delegate to the House from Washington, DC.

[5] On election day in 1992, three women served in the Senate; two were elected and one was appointed. On November 3rd, Dianne Feinstein won a special election to complete two years of a term; she was sworn in on November 10, 1992.

[6] Includes Kay Bailey Hutchison (R-TX), who won a special election on June 5, 1993 to serve out the remaining year and one half of a term.

[7] Includes Sheila Frahm (R-KS), who was appointed on June 11, 1996 to fill a vacancy caused by resignation. She was defeated in her primary race to complete the full term.

[8] Does not include two Democratic Delegates from the Virgin Islands and Washington, DC. Also does not include Susan Molinari (R-NY) who resigned 8/1/97. Includes 4 women (2 Democrats and 2 Republicans) who won special elections in March, April, and June 1998.

[9] Does not include two Democratic Delegates from the Virgin Islands and Washington, DC.

SOURCE: "Women in the U.S. Congress 1917–2001," in *Women in the U.S. Congress 2001*, Center for American Women and Politics, Eagleton Institute of Politics, Rutgers, The State University of New Jersey, New Brunswick, NJ, 2001 [Online] http://www.cawp.rutgers.edu/pdf/cong.pdf [accessed October 7, 2001]

from 1917 to 1919 and again from 1941 to 1942. In 1970 only 25 women (15D, 10R) ran for House seats. In 1976, 5 Republican women and 13 Democratic women won seats in the House.

MINORITY WOMEN IN CONGRESS. According to CAWP, among the women of the 107th Congress (2001–2003), 13 representatives and the delegate from Washington, D.C., were African American, 6 representatives were Latina, and the delegate from the Virgin Islands was Caribbean American. Patsy Takemoto Mink (D-HI), the first Asian/Pacific Islander woman in Congress, served in the House from 1965 until 1977, was reelected in 1990, and continued to serve in the 107th Congress. Ileana Ros-Lehtinen (R-FL) was the first Cuban American and the first Hispanic woman to serve in Congress. She was elected to the House in a special August 1989 election and remained the only Republican woman of color in Congress in 2001.

Shirley Chisholm (D-NY) was the first African American woman in Congress. She was elected to the House in 1968 and served until 1983. In 1992 Carol Moseley-Braun (D-IL) became the first African American woman to win a major-party Senate nomination and the first woman of color to be elected to the Senate. She lost her bid for reelection in 1998. As of 2001, 19 African American women, six Latinas, and two Asian/Pacific Islander women had served in Congress, all but Moseley-Braun in the House. In 1998 Tammy Baldwin (D-WI) became the first openly lesbian woman elected to Congress, and she continued to serve in the House in 2001.

CONGRESSIONAL POSITIONS OF POWER. In the 107th Congress women held more leadership positions and committee chairs than ever before, according to CAWP. Five women held leadership roles in the Senate in 2001, including Patty Murray (D-WA), who chaired the Democratic Senate Campaign Committee. In the 104th Congress (1995–1997) only two women senators held positions of leadership. Nancy Kassebaum (R-KS) became the first woman to chair a major Senate committee when she became head of the Labor and Human Resources Committee of the 104th Congress. The only previous female senate committee chair was Hattie Caraway, who chaired the committee on Enrolled Bills from 1933 to 1945.

On October 10, 2001, Nancy Pelosi (D-CA) was elected House minority whip, the highest position ever held by a woman in Congress. Five other women representatives in the 107th Congress held leadership roles, compared to only two women in the 103rd Congress (1993–1995). However, the last woman to chair a House committee was Jan Meyers (R-KS), who headed the Committee on Small Business for the 104th Congress (1995–1997).

State Executive Offices

In 2001, 88 women held statewide elective executive posts, 27.3 percent of the 322 posts. (See Table 8.7.) Of these women, 44 were Democrats, 40 were Republicans, 3 held nonpartisan offices, and the Minnesota lieutenant governor represented the Independence Party. In 1969, 23 women (14D, 9R) held statewide elective executive offices (6.6 percent).

There were two Democratic and three Republican women governors in 2001. Puerto Rico also elected its first woman governor, Sila Calderón, former mayor of San Juan and a member of the Popular Democratic Party. Ruth Ann Minner, the Democratic governor of Delaware, began her long career as a receptionist in the governor's office. Christina Todd Whitman served as the Republican governor of New Jersey from 1994 until 2001, when she

TABLE 8.7

Women in statewide elective executive offices, 2001

GOVERNORS -- 5 (2D, 3R)[1]	Attorney General - 8 (5D, 3R)
Jane Dee Hull (R-AZ)	Secretary of State - 13 (6D, 7R)
Judy Martz (R-MT)	
Ruth Ann Minner (D-DE)	State Treasurer - 11 (7D, 4R)
Jeanne Shaheen (D-NH)	
Jane Swift (R-MA)	State Comptroller - 4 (2D, 2R)
LIEUTENANT GOVERNORS -- 17	State Auditor - 6 (4D, 2R)
(7D, 9R, 1IP)[2]	
Fran Ulmer (D-AK)	Chief Agricultural Official - 3 (2D, 1R)
M. Jodi Rell (R-CT)	(title varies from state to state)
Mazie K. Hirono (D-HI)	Chief State Education Official - 10
Sally Pederson (D-IA)	(4D, 3R, 3NP)[2]
Corrine Wood (R-IL)	(title varies from state to state)
Kathleen Blanco (D-LA)	
Kathleen Kennedy Townsend (D-MD)	Commissioner of Elections - 1R
Mae Schunk (IP-MN)[2]	Commissioner of Insurance - 2 (1D, 1R)
Amy Tuck (D-MS)	
Beverly Perdue (D-NC)	Commissioner of Labor - 2R
Lorraine Hunt (R-NV)	Corporation Commissioner - 1R
Mary O. Donohue (R-NY)	
Maureen O'Connor (R-OH)	Public Regulatory Commissioner - 1D
Mary Fallin (R-OK)	
Carole Hillard (R-SD)	Public Service Commissioner - 3 (2D, 1R)
Olene S. Walker (R-UT)	Public Utilities Commissioner - 1D
Margaret Farrow (R-WI)	

[1] In addition, Sila Calderón serves as Puerto Rico's first woman governor.
[2] IP = Independence Party; NP = election was nonpartisan.
Note: In 2001, 88 women hold statewide elective executive offices across the country; women hold 27.3% of the 322 available positions. Among these women, 44 are Democrats, 40 are Republicans, 1 is a member of Independence Party, and 3 were elected in nonpartisan races.

SOURCE: "Statewide Elective Executive Offices," in *Women in Elective Office 2001*, Center for American Women and Politics, Eagleton Institute of Politics, Rutgers, The State University of New Jersey, New Brunswick, NJ, 2001 [Online] http://www.cawp.rutgers.edu/pdf/elective.pdf [accessed October 7, 2001]

resigned to become administrator of the Environmental Protection Agency (EPA).

Of the five state gubernatorial races that included women in 2000, Ruth Ann Minner and Judy Martz (R-MT) won open seats. Incumbent governor Jeanne Shaheen (D-NH) won reelection. Two women candidates lost elections: a Democrat running for an open seat in North Dakota and a Republican challenger in Vermont. All of the women candidates ran against men.

A total of 19 women have served as state governors, 13 Democrats and 6 Republicans. Of these women, 12 were first elected in their own right, 4 became governors by constitutional succession, and 3 replaced their husbands as governor. Nellie Tayloe Ross served as the Democratic governor of Wyoming from 1925 to 1927, replacing her deceased husband following a special election. Miriam "Ma" Ferguson (D-TX), who served from 1925 to 1927 and again from 1933 to 1936, and Lurleen Wallace (D-AL), who served in 1967–68, were elected in place of their husbands, who could not succeed themselves. Ella Grasso (D-CT) was the first woman governor

TABLE 8.8

Women in state legislatures, 2001

Year	Women Legislators	% of Total Legislators	Year	Women Legislators	% of Total Legislators
1969	301	4.0	1989	1,270	17.0
1971	344	4.5	1991	1,368	18.3
1973	424	5.6	1993	1,524	20.5
1975	604	8.0	1995	1,532	20.6
1977	688	9.1	1996	1,539	20.7
1979	770	10.3	1997	1,605	21.6
1981	908	12.1	1998	1,617	21.8
1983	991	13.3	1999	1,664	22.4
1985	1,103	14.8	2000	1,670	22.5
1987	1,170	15.7	2001	1,663	22.4

THE PARTY BREAKDOWN FOR WOMEN SERVING IN STATE LEGISLATURES

	Total Legislators		State Senators		State Reps.	
	#	%	#	%	#	%
Democrats	1,007	60.6	245	61.9	762	60.1
Republicans	645	38.8	141	35.6	504	39.8
Nonpartisans*	9	0.5	9	2.3	---	---
Progressives	1	0.1	---	---	1	0.1
Independents	1	0.1	1	0.3	---	---
Total	1,663	100.1	396	100.1	1,267	100.0

THE TEN STATES WITH THE HIGHEST PERCENTAGES OF WOMEN STATE LEGISLATORS

State	% Women	State	% Women
Washington	38.8	Kansas	32.7
Arizona	35.6	New Mexico	31.3
Nevada	34.9	Maine	30.1
Colorado	34.0	Connecticut	29.9
Oregon	33.3	New Hampshire	29.3

THE TEN STATES WITH THE LOWEST PERCENTAGES OF WOMEN STATE LEGISLATORS

State	% Women	State	% Women
Alabama	7.9	Arkansas	13.3
Oklahoma	10.1	Pennsylvania	13.4
South Carolina	10.6	New Jersey	15.0
Kentucky	10.9	South Dakota	15.2
Mississippi	12.6	Wyoming	15.6

* In Nebraska, where the legislature is unicameral, legislators are elected on a nonpartisan basis.

Note: In 2001, 1,663 or 22.4% of the 7,424 state legislators in the United States are women. Women currently hold 396, or 20.0%, of the 1,984 state senate seats and 1,267, or 23.3%, of the 5,440 state house or assembly seats. Since 1969, the number of women serving in state legislatures has increased more than five-fold.

SOURCE: "Women in State Legislatures 2001," in *Women in State Legislative Office,* Center for American Women and Politics, Eagleton Institute of Politics, Rutgers, The State University of New Jersey, New Brunswick, NJ, 2001 [Online] http://www.cawp.rutgers.edu/pdf/stleg.pdf [accessed October 7, 2001]

dently of the governor. In 2001, 13 women served as secretaries of state (6D, 7R), 11 as state treasurers (7D, 4R), and 10 as state education heads. In statewide elections eight women were chosen attorneys general (5D, 3R) and two additional female attorneys general were elected by their state legislatures.

Only five women of color held statewide elective executive offices in 2001. Denise Nappier, an African American, was the Democratic state treasurer of Connecticut, and Mazie K. Hirono, an Asian American/Pacific Islander, was the Democratic lieutenant governor of Hawaii. Patricia Madrid and Rebecca Vigil-Giron, both Latina Democrats, served as attorney general and secretary of state, respectively, of New Mexico. Native American Lynda Lovejoy was the Democratic Public Regulatory commissioner of New Mexico.

State Legislators

Women accounted for 22.4 percent of state legislators in 2001. (See Table 8.8.) These 1,663 women held 396 (20.0 percent) of the state senate seats and 1,267 (23.3 percent) of the state house or assembly seats. The majority (60.6 percent) were Democrats, compared to 38.8 percent Republicans. In Nebraska the nine women state senators were elected on a nonpartisan basis, and there was one Progressive Party state representative in Vermont and one Independent state senator in Maine. The Washington State legislature had the highest percentage of women (38.8 percent) and Alabama had the lowest (7.9 percent).

In the 2000 election there were 2,228 major-party female candidates for state legislatures, of which 1,387 were elected. Another 269 female legislators were not up for reelection. Democrats constituted 60.2 percent of the candidates, 59.6 percent of the winners, and 65.4 percent of the holdovers. In 1992 there were 2,373 women candidates, of which 1,374 won election. In 1976 there were 1,258 candidates.

The first women state legislators were three Republicans elected to the Colorado House of Representatives in 1894. The first female state senator was a Utah Democrat elected in 1896. In 1969 there were only 301 female state legislators (4.0 percent). (See Table 8.8.)

According to CAWP, among the women in state legislatures, 182 (181D, 1R) were African American, including 46 senators and 136 representatives in 36 states. Asian American/Pacific Islander women (16D, 3R) held 7 senate and 12 representative seats in California, Hawaii, Oregon, and Washington. Latinas (52D, 3R) accounted for 19 senators and 36 representatives in 15 states. Native American women (9D, 1R) accounted for 1 senator and 9 representatives in five states. An additional Native American woman, representing the Penobscot Nation, was first elected as a nonvoting member of the Maine legislature in 1997.

elected in her own right. She was elected in 1974 and reelected in 1978 for a second four-year term. She resigned in 1980 for health reasons. West Virginia and Maine are the only states that have never elected a woman to an executive office; however, in Maine the governor is the only statewide elected office.

Of the female 17 lieutenant governors in 2001, 7 were Democrats, 9 were Republicans, and Mae Schunk of Minnesota was a member of the Independence Party. (See Table 8.7.) Three of these women were elected indepen-

In 2001 women held 12.5 percent of the leadership positions in state legislatures, 16 in senates and 20 in houses. Seven women served as state senate presidents or presidents pro tempore. Moira K. Lyons (D-CT) was speaker of the state house, and six other women were speakers pro tempore of state houses. The Kansas legislature had the highest proportion of women in leadership positions (50 percent); however, 20 states had no women legislators in leadership positions. As of 2001, 13 women had served as presidents of state senates and 22 as state house speakers.

Women chaired 18.8 percent of the standing committees in state legislatures in 2001. Women chaired committees in 44 state senates and in all but one state house. Democratic women chaired 20.9 percent of the committees and Republican women chaired 16.7 percent. The Colorado legislature had the highest percentage of women committee chairs (45.0 percent), and the South Carolina legislature had the lowest (3.8 percent).

Municipal Offices

In 1889 Susanna Salter of Argonia, Kansas, became the first elected woman mayor in the United States; her salary was one dollar per year. In June 2001, 13 of the 100 largest American cities had women mayors. (See Table 8.9.) Portland, Oregon, was the largest city in the country with a woman mayor. Mayor Sharon Sayles Belton of Minneapolis was African American, and Heather Fargo, mayor of Sacramento, was a Latina. Of the 231 mayors of cities with over 100,000 people, 19 percent were women, including two African Americans and six Latinas. Of the 985 mayors of cities over 30,000, 21.2 percent were women in 2001. Since June 2001, Jane Campbell of Cleveland and Shirley Franklin, an African American, of Atlanta were sworn in as mayors.

Financing Women's Political Campaigns

Political campaigns are becoming increasingly expensive, and political action committees (PACs) are a major source of campaign financing. Lack of campaign funds has been an obstacle for women candidates. According to CAWP, there were 46 PACs or donor networks, 11 national and 35 state or local, that either gave money primarily to women candidates or received the majority of their donations from women. In addition, PACs that raise money for specific issues of concern to women, such as abortion rights, may donate to women candidates who support those issues.

EMILY stands for "early money is like yeast,"—it makes the "dough" rise. EMILY's List is a 68,000-member donor network founded in 1985 with the goal of electing more Democratic congresswomen and women governors who supported abortion rights. The network raises money for women candidates, helps with their cam-

TABLE 8.9

Women municipal officials, 2001

City	Mayor	Rank
Portland, OR	Vera Katz	28th
Long Beach, CA	Beverly O'Neill	35th
Kansas City, MO	Kay Barnes	37th
Virginia Beach, VA	Meyera E. Oberndorf	39th
Sacramento, CA	Heather Fargo	43rd
Tulsa, OK	Susan Savage	46th
Minneapolis, MN	Sharon Sayles Belton	49th
Colorado Springs, CO	Mary Lou Makepeace	50th
Lexington, KY	Pam Miller	75th
Glendale, AZ	Elaine M. Scruggs	83rd
Madison, WI	Susan J.M. Bauman	87th
Scottsdale, AZ	Mary Manross	91st
Lubbock, TX	Windy Sitton	94th

Note: As of June 2001, among the 100 largest cities in the U.S., 13 have women mayors. One is African American (Sharon Sayles Belton, Minneapolis) and one is Latina (Heather Fargo, Sacramento). In order of city population.[1]
Note: Of the 231 mayors of U.S. cities with populations over 100,000, 44 or 19.0% were women, including two African Americans and six Latinas. Of the 985 mayors of U.S. cities with populations over 30,000, 209, or 21.2%, were women.[2]

[1] According to data from the U.S. Bureau of the Census.
[2] Source: CAWP. Information was compiled using the United States Conference of Mayors' June 2001 directory, "The Mayors of America's Principal Cities," as the primary reference.

SOURCE: "Municipal Officials," in *Women in Elective Office 2001*, Center for American Women and Politics, Eagleton Institute of Politics, Rutgers, The State University of New Jersey, New Brunswick, NJ, 2001 [Online] http://www.cawp.rutgers.edu/pdf/elective.pdf [accessed October 7, 2001]

paigns, and encourages women to vote. EMILY's list has become the largest financial resource for minority women seeking election to federal office.

PRESIDENTIAL AND VICE-PRESIDENTIAL CANDIDATES

Although several First Ladies, including Eleanor Roosevelt and Hillary Rodham Clinton, played important political roles during their husbands' presidencies, no woman has yet served as president of the United States. However, at least 21 women have made a bid for the presidency. In 1872 Victoria Claflin Woodhull ran against Ulysses S. Grant and Horace Greeley as the candidate of the suffragist Equal Rights Party. Belva Ann Bennett Lockwood was the Equal Rights Party presidential candidate in 1884 and 1888. She was also the first woman lawyer to practice before the U.S. Supreme Court.

In 1964 Margaret Chase Smith (R-ME) became the first woman to run in presidential primary elections. In 1972 Shirley Chisholm became the first African American woman to run in the presidential primaries. In 1988 Patricia S. Schroeder (D-CO) became the first woman to initiate a serious bid for the presidency, although she dropped out before the primaries because of lack of money. In 1996 three women Democrats and six women Republicans entered presidential primaries. Elizabeth Hanford Dole initiated a bid for the Republican Party presidential nomination in 1999 but dropped out of the race before the primaries. Lenora Fulani ran as the New Alliance Party presidential candidate in the 1992 general election, and in 1996 women representing the Socialist Party, the Reform Party, and the Workers World Party ran for the presidency in the general election.

Two women have sought major party vice-presidential nominations. The first, Frances "Sissy" Farenthold, received 400 votes at the 1972 Democratic National Convention. In 1984 Geraldine Anne Ferraro became the only woman to run for vice-president on a major-party ticket when Walter F. Mondale picked her as his running mate. The Mondale-Ferraro ticket lost to Ronald Reagan and Dan Quayle in a landslide election.

PRESIDENTIAL CABINETS

The first woman to serve in a cabinet post was Frances Perkins, appointed by President Franklin D. Roosevelt as secretary of labor in 1933. She remained in that post until 1945, one of only two cabinet members to serve throughout the entire Roosevelt administration. Perkins was instrumental in the design and implementation of the New Deal legislation. As of 2001, 29 women had been appointed by presidents to cabinet or cabinet-level posts. Three Democratic presidents appointed 16 of these women and five Republican presidents appointed 13.

President Dwight D. Eisenhower named Oveta Culp Hobby as secretary of health, education and welfare in 1953, and President Gerald Ford named Carla Anderson Hills as secretary of Housing and Urban Development (HUD) in 1975. Since then many more women have been named to cabinet-level positions. Patricia Roberts Harris was appointed secretary of HUD by President Jimmy Carter in 1977 and secretary of Health and Human Services (DHHS) in 1979. She was the first African American woman to serve in a presidential cabinet. Carter also appointed Shirley M. Hufstedler as secretary of education. President Ronald Reagan had three women cabinet members, including Elizabeth Dole, who was secretary of

transportation under Reagan and secretary of labor under President George Bush. Reagan also named Jeane J. Kirkpatrick as United Nations ambassador and Carla Hills as special trade representative.

Approximately 37 percent of President Bill Clinton's first five hundred appointees were women. Hazel R. O'Leary served as energy secretary, Carol M. Browner was head of the EPA, Janet Reno was attorney general and head of the Justice Department, Donna E. Shalala was secretary of DHHS, and Alexis Herman was secretary of labor. Madeleine K. Albright served Clinton first as U.N. Ambassador and then as secretary of state, the highest-ranking woman in the U.S. government. Clinton also named women as chairs of the National Economic Council and the Council of Economic Advisors, U.S. trade representative, and director of the Office of Personnel Management. Clinton appointed Alice M. Rivlin as director of the Office of Management and Budget (OMB) in 1994 and named her to the Federal Reserve Board in February 1996. Aida Alvarez became administrator of the Small Business Administration in 1997, the first Hispanic woman to hold a cabinet-level position.

In 2001 George W. Bush appointed Elaine Chao as secretary of labor, the first Asian American woman to hold a cabinet-level post. Bush also named Gale Norton as secretary of interior, Condoleezza Rice as national security advisor, Anne Veneman as secretary of agriculture, and Christine Todd Whitman as administrator of the EPA.

As of 2001, six women had headed the Departments of Labor, and DHHS had had three women heads. Women had never been appointed heads of the Defense, Treasury, or Veterans Affairs Departments. Among the cabinet-level appointees, 12 women were attorneys and 10 were from academia. Twenty women had held other federal offices prior to being named to cabinet-level posts. Margaret M. Heckler, Reagan's secretary of DHHS and later ambassador to Ireland, and Lynn Morley Martin, secretary of labor from 1991 to 1993, were former congresswomen.

CHAPTER 9
WOMEN AS VICTIMS

VICTIMS OF CRIMES

Falling Crime Rates

There were about 25.9 million violent and property victimizations in the United States in 2000, according to the Bureau of Justice Statistics (BJS), down from 28.8 million in 1999 and 44 million in 1973. Both violent victimization and property crime rates were at their lowest levels since 1973. Approximately 75 percent of all victimizations in 2000 were household property crimes: theft, burglary, and motor vehicle theft. About one-quarter of victimizations were nonfatal violent crimes against individuals age 12 and over (rape, sexual assault, robbery, and simple and aggravated assault). About 1 percent of victimizations were personal thefts including pocket picking and purse snatching.

Violent crime rates have been dropping since 1994. (See Figure 9.1.) Between 1999 and 2000 violent crime rates fell about 15 percent. This was the largest annual percent drop since the BJS began its annual National Crime Victimization Survey (NCVS) in 1973. The rate of violent victimizations in 2000 was 28 per 1,000 persons age 12 and over, down 15.2 percent from the rate of 33 per 1,000 in 1999 and down 44.0 percent from the rate of 50 per 1,000 in 1993. The violent crime rate fell in 2000 because of decreases in simple assault and rape/sexual assault, as well as a slight fall in the rate of aggravated assault.

The property crime rate fell steadily between 1974 and 2000. Between 1999 and 2000 the rate fell 10.1 percent, from 198 to 178 per 1,000 households, the lowest level since 1974. A decrease in theft and a small decrease in motor vehicle theft contributed to the falling property crime rate.

Female Victims of Violent Crime

Fewer women than men are victims of violent crime. (See Figure 9.1.) The rate of violent crimes against males

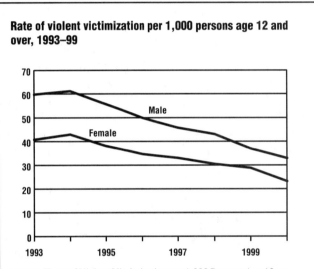

FIGURE 9.1

Rate of violent victimization per 1,000 persons age 12 and over, 1993–99

SOURCE: "Rate of Violent Victimization per 1,000 Persons Age 12 or Over," in *Criminal Victimization 2000: Changes 1999–2000 with Trends 1993–2000,* Bureau of Justice Statistics, Washington, DC, June 2001

was 41.8 percent higher than against females in 2000. Between 1999 and 2000 there was a drop of 19.4 percent in the number of violent crimes against females, from 28.8 per 1,000 persons age 12 and older in 1999 to 23.2 per 1,000 in 2000. (See Table 9.1.) The number of violent crimes against males declined 11.1 percent over the same period. The violent victimization rate for females was 40.7 per 1,000 in 1993.

Assaults were the most common crime committed against both males and females, although the rate of aggravated assault was 159.4 percent higher for males than females in 2000. Far more females than males were raped or sexually assaulted (2.1 per 1,000), and females experienced more personal theft (1.4 victimizations per 1,000). Far more males than females were robbed in 2000. (See Table 9.1.)

TABLE 9.1

Rates of violent crime and personal theft, 2000

Characteristic of victim	Population	Victimizations per 1,000 persons age 12 or older						Per-sonal theft
		Violent crimes						
		All	Rape/ sexual assault	Robbery	Assault			
					Total	Aggra-vated	Simple	
Gender								
Male	109,816,970	32.9	0.1*	4.5	28.3	8.3	19.9	1.0
Female	116,987,650	23.2	2.1	2.0	19.0	3.2	15.8	1.4

Note: The National Crime Victimization Survey includes as violent crime rape, sexual assault, robbery, and assault. Because the NCVS interviews persons about their victimizations, murder and manslaughter cannot be included.
* Based on 10 or fewer sample cases.

SOURCE: Adapted from "Table 2. Rates of Violent Crime and Personal Theft, by Gender, Age, Race, and Hispanic Origin, 2000," in *Criminal Victimization 2000: Changes 1999–2000 with Trends 1993–2000*, Bureau of Justice Statistics, Washington, DC, June 2001

Regardless of race or gender, victims of robbery and assault tend to be young, and the rates for these crimes decline sharply among older age groups. (See Table 9.2.) Among black males and females 12- to 15-year-olds had the highest rates of violent victimizations, whereas for white males the highest rate was among 16- to 19-year-olds, and for white females the highest rate was among 20- to 24-year-olds. According to the BJS, there were 66.7 violent victimizations per 1,000 females aged 16 to 19 in 1999—41.2 attempted or threatened acts of violence and 25.5 completed violent crimes. There were 12.4 threatened or completed rapes and sexual assaults per 1,000 females aged 16 to 19. However, more females aged 20 to 24 were assault victims in 1999, 10.1 aggravated assaults and 40.6 simple assaults per 1,000. Female victims of robbery and assault were more likely than male victims to be injured (26.4 percent versus 23.2 percent).

In most age groups victimization rates were higher for black females than for white females. (See Table 9.2.) In particular, the rates were higher for black females aged 12 to 15. According to the BJS, Hispanic women were less likely to be victims of violent crime than non-Hispanic women. In 1999 there were 43 victims of personal crime per 1,000 African American females, compared to 27.8 per 1,000 white females. There were 25.2 victimizations per 1,000 Hispanic females, compared to 29 per 1,000 non-Hispanic females. Although Hispanic women were less likely than non-Hispanic women to experience completed or attempted rape/sexual assault, completed robbery, or simple assault, they were more likely to experience attempted robbery, aggravated assault, and purse snatching/pocket picking.

Self-Protection

According to the NCVS, 67 percent of violent crime victims did not face an armed offender. Robbery victims (about 55 percent) were most likely to face an armed person, whereas only 6 percent of rape/sexual assault victims

faced an armed offender. However, women victims were more likely than men to take self-protective action (in 72.4 percent of violent victimizations versus 70.5 percent). Women were somewhat less likely than men to take protective action in the face of threatened or attempted violence, but they were much more likely than men to take self-protective measures in the face of completed violence (79.3 percent versus 66.9 percent of victimizations.) Most women (85.3 percent) took self-protective action when faced with rape or sexual assault, and 69.6 percent of women took protective action in the face of robbery, compared to 62.0 percent of men. Similar numbers of men and women took self-protective measures in the face of assault.

The most commonly used self-protective measure for both men and women was to resist or capture the offender (22.4 percent of male victims and 17.9 percent of females). Women were less likely than men to threaten or attack the offender but more likely than men to scare or warn the offender, get help, or give alarm or scream.

Victim-Offender Relationship

Most violent crimes against women are not committed by strangers. In 2000 only 33 percent of violent crimes against women were committed by a stranger, compared to 54 percent of violent crimes against men. (See Table 9.3). Strangers committed 60 percent of robberies of females and 74 percent of robberies of males. Strangers committed only 34 percent of all rape/sexual assault crimes against women, 41 percent of aggravated assaults, and 27 percent of simple assaults.

Among crimes against females committed by non-strangers, 56 percent were committed by a friend or acquaintance and 31.1 percent were committed by an intimate of the victim. The latter accounted for 21 percent of all violent crimes against women. The intimates were current or former spouses, boyfriends, or girlfriends. In con-

TABLE 9.2

Number of victimizations and victimization rates for persons age 12 and over, by race, gender, and age of victims and type of crime, 1999

Race, gender, and age	Total population	Crimes of violence[a]		Robbery		Aggravated assault		Simple assault	
		Number	Rate	Number	Rate	Number	Rate	Number	Rate
White									
Male									
12-15	6,421,490	549,960	85.6	67,900	10.6	94,060	14.6	383,030	59.6
16-19	6,558,010	594,970	90.7	69,910	10.7	149,410	22.8	361,330	55.1
20-24	7,299,160	566,320	77.6	71,170	9.8	189,110	25.9	298,230	40.9
25-34	15,480,610	620,300	40.1	68,270	4.4	167,290	10.8	382,190	24.7
35-49	26,837,760	720,120	26.8	76,460	2.8	122,600	4.6	518,780	19.3
50-64	16,556,390	277,900	16.8	34,820	2.1	27,340*	1.7*	213,690	12.9
65 and over	12,365,040	68,740	5.6	14,610*	1.2*	15,620*	1.3*	36,250	2.9
Female									
12-15	6,067,050	305,440	50.3	5,200*	0.9*	53,220	8.8	213,180	35.1
16-19	6,253,540	395,330	63.2	31,290	5.0	37,340	6.0	247,970	39.7
20-24	7,240,630	463,040	63.9	24,050*	3.3*	68,450	9.5	317,850	43.9
25-34	15,564,550	518,890	33.3	35,930	2.3	84,070	5.4	345,430	22.2
35-49	26,811,250	638,990	23.8	44,210	1.6	105,280	3.9	456,020	17.0
50-64	17,471,040	214,720	12.3	22,810*	1.3*	28,380*	1.6*	156,530	9.0
65 and over	16,649,480	45,360	2.7	8,810*	0.5*	16,580*	1.0*	19,960*	1.2*
Black									
Male									
12-15	1,327,180	121,800	91.8	18,020*	13.6*	39,510	29.8	64,280	48.4
16-19	1,190,240	98,530	82.8	17,740*	14.9*	38,450	32.3	42,340	35.6
20-24	1,134,500	86,080	75.9	27,880*	24.6*	13,510*	11.9*	44,690	39.4
25-34	2,423,130	62,020	25.6	29,950	12.4	19,020*	7.8*	13,050*	5.4*
35-49	3,651,290	107,930	29.6	25,100*	6.9*	32,950	9.0	46,790	12.8
50-64	1,750,970	43,260	24.7	11,940*	6.8*	7,010*	4.0*	24,310*	13.9*
65 and over	1,068,940	3,600*	3.4*	0*	0.0*	0*	0.0*	3,600*	3.4*
Female									
12-15	1,343,470	171,330	127.5	10,540*	7.8*	22,100*	16.5*	113,840	84.7
16-19	1,158,440	108,450	93.6	11,710*	10.1*	25,130*	21.7*	59,540	51.4
20-24	1,391,580	79,500	57.1	13,800*	9.9*	17,250*	12.4*	38,720	27.8
25-34	2,931,090	128,700	43.9	14,280*	4.9*	34,850	11.9	68,580	23.4
35-49	4,288,650	116,780	27.2	30,280	7.1	33,650	7.8	41,870	9.8
50-64	2,229,480	15,840*	7.1*	0*	0.0*	7,540*	3.4*	8,310*	3.7*
65 and over	1,650,880	1,850*	1.1*	0*	0.0*	0*	0.0*	1,850*	1.1*

Note: Excludes data on persons of "Other" races.
* Estimate is based on about 10 or fewer sample cases.
[a] Includes data on rape and sexual assault, not shown separately.

SOURCE: "Table 10. Number of Victimizations and Victimization Rates for Persons Age 12 and Over, by Race, Gender, and Age of Victims and Type of Crime," in *Criminal Victimization in United States, 1999 Statistical Tables* [Online] http://www.ojp.usdoj.gov/bjs/abstract/cvusst.htm [accessed October 12, 2001]

---

trast, only 3 percent of crimes against males were committed by an intimate of the victim. Friends or acquaintances of the victims committed 42 percent of rape/sexual assault crimes against women. (See Table 9.3.)

In general, the likelihood of a violent crime being committed by a stranger increased with the age of the female victim. (See Table 9.4.) For example, in 1999, 100.0 percent of completed or threatened rape/sexual assaults of women aged 50 to 64 were committed by strangers, as compared to only 17.2 percent of rape/sexual assaults against females aged 12 to 15. Essentially all robberies (100.0 percent) of women over 64 were committed by strangers as compared with 0.0 percent of robberies of girls aged 12 to 15. Among female victims aged 65 and over, 68.8 percent of aggravated assaults were committed

by strangers as compared with only 20.5 percent of simple assaults. As noted on Table 9.4 these numbers are based on about 10 or fewer sample cases.

According to the BJS, in 1999, 9.1 violent crimes per 1,000 females aged 12 and over were committed by strangers, compared to 10.1 per 1,000 females that were committed by a person well known to the victim. There were 4.6 violent crimes per 1,000 females committed by casual acquaintances and 4.0 per 1,000 committed by relatives. The rate of aggravated assaults against women by strangers (1.9 per 1,000) was slightly higher than the rate committed by someone well known to the victim (1.5 per 1,000), but simple assaults were somewhat more likely to have been committed by a well-known person (6.6 per 1,000) than by a stranger (5.4 per 1,000).

TABLE 9.3

Victim and offender relationship, 2000

Relationship with victim	Violent crime		Rape or sexual assault		Robbery		Aggravated assault		Simple assault	
	Number	Percent	Number	Percent	Number	Percent	Number	Percent	Number	Percent
All victims										
Total	6,322,730	100%	260,950	100%	731,780	100%	1,292,510	100%	4,037,500	100%
Nonstranger	3,376,520	53%	162,160	62%	203,630	28%	550,190	43%	2,460,530	61%
Intimate	655,350	10	45,100	17	38,000	5	66,350	5	505,900	13
Other relative	339,930	5	4,730	2*	20,650	3*	67,610	5	246,940	6
Friend/acquaintance	2,381,240	38	112,330	43	144,980	20	416,230	32	1,707,690	42
Stranger	2,829,840	45%	89,180	34%	507,170	69%	720,940	56%	1,512,540	38%
Relationship unknown	116,380	2%	9,600	4%*	20,970	3%*	21,380	2%*	64,420	2%
Male victims										
Total	3,612,390	100%	14,770	100%*	494,650	100%	915,970	100%	2,187,000	100%
Nonstranger	1,585,130	44%	9,260	63%*	113,430	23%	329,190	36%	1,133,250	52%
Intimate	98,850	3	0	0*	0	0*	18,380	2*	80,470	4
Other relative	107,970	3	0	0*	2,310	1*	36,930	4	68,730	3
Friend/acquaintance	1,378,310	38	9,260	63*	111,110	23	273,870	30	984,060	45
Stranger	1,945,980	54%	5,510	37%*	365,730	74%	565,410	62%	1,009,340	46%
Relationship unknown	81,280	2%	0	0%*	15,500	3%*	21,380	2%*	44,400	2%
Female victims										
Total	2,710,340	100%	246,180	100%	237,130	100%	376,540	100%	1,850,500	100%
Nonstranger	1,791,390	66%	152,900	62%	90,210	38%	221,010	59%	1,327,280	72%
Intimate	556,500	21	45,100	18	38,000	16	47,970	13	425,430	23
Other relative	231,960	9	4,730	2*	18,340	8*	30,680	8	178,220	10
Friend/acquaintance	1,002,930	37	103,070	42	33,870	14	142,360	38	723,630	39
Stranger	883,860	33%	83,680	34%	141,450	60%	155,530	41%	503,200	27%
Relationship unknown	35,090	1%	9,600	4%*	5,470	2%*	0	0%*	20,020	1%*

Note: Percentages may not total to 100% because of rounding.
* Based on 10 or fewer sample cases.

SOURCE: "Table 4. Victim and Offender Relationship, 2000," in *Criminal Victimization 2000: Changes 1999–2000 with Trends 1993–2000,* Bureau of Justice Statistics, Washington, DC, June 2001

White women were more likely than African American women to be the victim of a violent crime by a stranger in 1999 (35.5 percent versus 30.4 percent). Only 12.8 percent of rape/sexual assault crimes against African American women were committed by strangers as compared with 34.2 percent of rape/sexual assaults against white women.

CRIME REPORTING

According to the NCVS, 47.9 percent of violent crimes, 35.0 percent of personal thefts, and 35.7 percent of property crimes were reported to police in 2000, a significant increase over 1999. However, the reporting rates for most types of crimes did not increase significantly between 1993 and 2000. Higher percentages of violent crimes against females (54.4 percent) than against males (42.9 percent) were reported to the police in 2000. White, African American, and Hispanic females were all more likely to report violent crimes than were their male counterparts. However, women of different race/ethnicities were all about equally likely to report violent victimizations. Similar percentages of males and females of all race/ethnicities reported property crimes in 2000.

Crimes in which the victim was injured were much more likely to be reported than those in which no injuries occurred. (See Table 9.5.) Whereas 89.1 percent of attempted robberies of females in which an injury occurred were reported, only 31.5 percent of rape/sexual assault crimes against women were reported.

Women victims were more likely than male victims to report violent crimes committed by either strangers or nonstrangers. Female victims reported 49.7 percent of violent crimes committed by nonstrangers and 48.4 percent of crimes committed by strangers, whereas male victims reported only 34.1 percent of violent crimes committed by nonstrangers and 43.1 percent of crimes committed by strangers. Female victims reported 41.3 percent of rape/sexual assault crimes committed by strangers but only 27.2 percent of those committed by nonstrangers. Likewise, they reported 100 percent of robbery attempts by strangers in which injury occurred and 75.4 percent of such crimes without injury, but only 84.9 percent of robbery attempts with injury committed by nonstrangers and 20.6 percent of those without injury committed by nonstrangers.

In 1999, 48.7 percent of all personal crimes against females were reported to the police, compared to 39

TABLE 9.4

Percent of victimizations involving strangers, by gender and age of victims and type of crime, 1999

| | | | | Percent of victimizations involving strangers | | |
| Gender and age | Crimes of violence | Rape/ Sexual assault[a] | Robbery | Assault | | |
				Total	Aggravated	Simple
Both gender	**48.6 %**	**33.9 %**	**70.9 %**	**46.6 %**	**53.7 %**	**44.3 %**
12-15	37.2	15.8 *	63.1	35.8	47.2	32.9
16-19	50.2	45.0	60.8	49.4	55.9	47.0
20-24	54.6	23.2 *	67.2	55.2	61.7	52.5
25-34	49.5	39.8 *	70.1	47.3	58.2	43.2
35-49	46.5	30.8 *	77.1	43.1	46.9	42.1
50-64	57.6	100.0 *	84.3	52.7	36.1 *	55.5
65 and over	57.7	0.0 *	100.0 *	48.8	59.0 *	43.1 *
Male	**59.7 %**	**61.5 %***	**79.8 %**	**56.5 %**	**60.5 %**	**54.9 %**
12-15	45.1	0.0 *	74.1	41.0	46.2	39.5
16-19	61.3	100.0 *	82.3	57.4	63.3	54.5
20-24	68.4	38.2 *	81.2	66.6	65.5	67.3
25-34	67.5	100.0 *	78.5	65.5	66.8	64.9
35-49	55.3	42.3 *	79.5	51.9	55.8	50.9
50-64	63.3	100.0 *	80.3	60.0	60.9 *	59.9
65 and over	61.2	0.0 *	100.0 *	53.8	50.0 *	55.5 *
Female	**35.3 %**	**30.7 %**	**52.4 %**	**34.2 %**	**42.3 %**	**32.1 %**
12-15	26.3	17.2 *	0.0 *	28.6	49.1	24.1
16-19	35.0	36.8	16.9 *	36.5	33.5 *	37.2
20-24	38.3	21.6 *	33.1 *	41.4	53.0	38.5
25-34	31.1	37.4 *	54.9	28.1	45.8	22.9
35-49	37.0	29.5 *	73.7	33.3	37.1	32.3
50-64	49.9	100.0 *	92.0 *	43.3	12.4 *	49.6
65 and over	52.3 *	0.0 *	100.0 *	41.4 *	68.8 *	20.5 *

* Estimate is based on about 10 or fewer sample cases.
[a] Includes verbal threats of rape and threats of sexual assault.

SOURCE: "Table 29. Percent of Victimizations Involving Strangers, by Gender and Age of Victims and Type of Crime," in *Criminal Victimization in United States, 1999 Statistical Tables* [Online] http://www.ojp.usdoj.gov/bjs/abstract/cvusst.htm [accessed October 12, 2001]

percent of all personal crimes against males. More purse snatchings/pocket pickings of females were reported (30.1 percent) than of males (21.5 percent).

RAPE AND SEXUAL ASSAULT

Although men are sometimes raped, particularly in prison, rape is primarily a crime against women. Although rape was once believed to be a crime of sexual passion, it is now recognized as a crime of anger and hate, driven by the desire for power over others. The Violence Against Women Act (PL 103-322), passed in 1994, categorized rape as a gender-based hate crime, punishable under federal civil rights laws as well as state criminal statutes. The act increased penalties for violence against women and provided funding to police, prosecutors, and the courts to help protect women from violence.

The rape/sexual assault category of the NCVS covers a variety of crimes ranging from completed or attempted rape to verbal threats of sexual assault. Sexual assault ranges from grabbing or fondling a victim to attempted sexual intercourse. Rape/sexual assault includes the use of psychological coercion as well as physical force. In about 84 percent of all rape/sexual assaults the offender does not have a weapon.

There were 260,950 rape/sexual assaults in 2000 for a rate of 1.2 per 1,000 persons age 12 or older, down 29.4 percent from 1999. Sexual assaults accounted for 43.7 percent of these crimes, attempted rape accounted for 25.3 percent, and rape accounted for 35.2 percent. In 2000, 94.3 percent of all rape/sexual assault victims were female. (See Table 9.3.)

The Uniform Crime Reporting Program of the Federal Bureau of Investigation (FBI) defines forcible rape as "the carnal knowledge of a female forcibly and against her will." It includes assaults or attempts to commit rape by force or threat of force but does not include rape without force or other sexual offenses. Both the number and the rate of reported forcible rapes declined dramatically between 1995 and 1999. (See Figure 9.2.) The number of forcible rapes declined 4.3 percent to 89,107 from 1998 to 1999. The rate declined from 34.5 per 100,000 people to 32.7. The Uniform Crime Reporting Program defines all rape victims as female, so the total forcible rape rate just among females is an estimated 64 per 100,000. The highest rates of forcible rape were in metropolitan areas; however, between 1989 and 1999 the rate declined by about 25 percent in metropolitan areas, whereas it increased about 2 to 3 percent outside of metropolitan areas. From 1998 to 1999 there was

TABLE 9.5

Percent of victimizations reported to the police, by type of crime, victim-offender relationship and gender of victims, 1999

| | Percent of all victimizations reported to the police | | | | | | | | |
| | All victimizations | | | Involving strangers | | | Involving nonstrangers | | |
Type of crime	Both gender	Male	Female	Both gender	Male	Female	Both gender	Male	Female
Crimes of violence	**43.9%**	**39.5%**	**49.3%**	**44.9%**	**43.1%**	**48.4%**	**43.0%**	**34.1%**	**49.7%**
Completed violence	57.5	54.7	60.4	64.1	64.4	63.4	52.4	41.2	59.1
Attempted/threatened violence	37.8	33.4	43.6	37.4	35.0	42.4	38.2	31.1	44.2
Rape/Sexual assault[a]	28.3	0.0*	31.5	33.6	0.0*	41.3	25.6	0.0*	27.2
Robbery	61.2	55.1	74.1	62.0	55.8	81.4	59.4	52.0	66.0
Completed/property taken	66.3	61.5	75.7	70.0	65.9	83.2	59.0	48.0	69.0
With injury	72.0	63.2	84.4	79.7	75.6	91.8 *	62.6	34.6*	80.7
Without injury	63.1	60.7	68.9	66.0	61.9	79.3	55.7	56.6	54.5*
Attempted to take property	51.7	43.4	70.6	49.4	40.1	78.6	60.9	65.8*	57.0*
With injury	61.6	48.6*	89.1*	51.7	44.9*	100.0*	87.4*	100.0*	84.9*
Without injury	47.9	41.4	62.9	48.6	38.1	75.4	44.6*	60.1*	20.6*
Assault	42.6	37.4	49.1	41.9	40.8	44.4	43.2	33.1	51.6
Aggravated	55.3	54.7	56.4	55.3	58.9	46.6	55.3	48.1	63.5
With injury	73.0	69.7	79.5	79.7	82.6	70.7	66.9	53.8	84.2
Threatened with weapon	47.8	47.8	47.6	46.4	49.5	39.5	49.4	45.0	54.3
Simple	38.5	30.9	47.3	36.7	33.2	43.6	40.0	28.1	49.0
With minor injury	54.5	43.5	64.1	55.9	54.7	57.8	53.8	33.9	66.0
Without injury	34.2	28.0	41.8	32.9	29.2	40.5	35.3	26.4	42.5

Note: Detail may not add to total shown because of rounding.
* Estimate is based on about 10 or fewer sample cases.
a Includes verbal threats of rape and threats of sexual assault.

SOURCE: "Table 93. Percent of Victimizations Reported to the Police, by Type of Crime, Victor-Offender Relationship and Gender of Victims," in *Criminal Victimization in United States, 1999 Statistical Tables* [Online] http://www.ojp.usdoj.gov/bjs/abstract/cvusst.htm [accessed October 12, 2001]

approximately an 8 percent decrease in the nationwide arrest rate for forcible rape.

More than two-thirds of the rapes and sexual assaults of women measured by the NCVS went unreported. Women are often psychologically devastated by rape. They may be unwilling to talk about it, may feel responsible for it, or believe that even if they do report it, nothing will happen to the offender.

Friends or acquaintances of the victim committed 42 percent of all rape/sexual assaults. An additional 18 percent were committed by intimates of the victim and 2 percent by another relative of the victim. (See Table 9.3.) In 1999 females reported 27.2 percent of rape/sexual assaults involving nonstrangers, compared to 41.3 percent of rape/sexual assaults involving strangers.

Sexual Victimization on College Campuses

It has been recognized for some time that college women are particularly vulnerable to sexual assault. In December 2000 the BJS and the National Institute of Justice (NIJ) published *The Sexual Victimization of College Women* (NCWSV), a survey of 4,446 college women. The survey was conducted between February and May of 1997 and covered the period since the fall of 1996. Of the women surveyed, 2.8 percent had experienced either a completed rape (1.7 percent) or an attempted rape (1.1

percent), for a rate of 27.7 rapes per 1,000 female students. Of the 123 victims, 22.8 percent experienced multiple rapes. The study found that there were 19.3 completed rapes and 16 attempted rapes per 1,000 female students per academic year. Of the attempted rapes committed by a single offender, 43.5 percent were committed by a classmate of the victim, as were 35.5 percent of the completed rapes. (See Figure 9.3.) Most of the other rapes and attempted rapes were committed by a friend, a boyfriend, or an ex-boyfriend of the victim.

The survey found that in 65.1 percent of the completed rapes and 91.5 percent of the attempted rapes, the victim tried to protect herself. Most women also tried to protect themselves from sexual coercion, sexual contact with or without force, and from sexual threats with or without force. Physical force against the assailant was the most common self-defense, used by 69.2 percent of victims of attempted rape and 55.4 percent of victims of completed rape. Women also pleaded with the offender to stop, screamed, attempted to negotiate with the offender, ran away, or attempted to avoid the offender.

Almost none of the incidents in the NCWSV survey had been reported to the police, including 95.2 percent of completed rapes, 95.8 percent of attempted rapes, 100 percent of completed or attempted sexual coercion, and 99.2 percent of completed sexual contact with force or threat of force. The most common reasons given for not

FIGURE 9.2

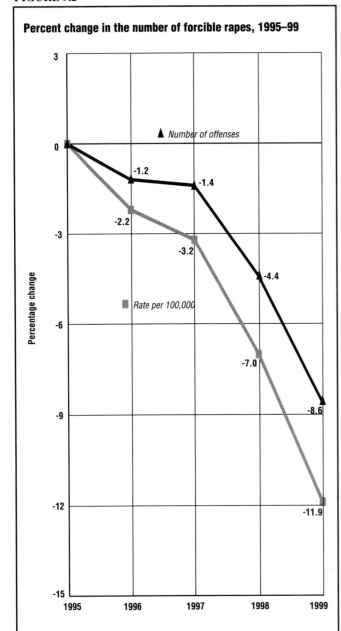

Percent change in the number of forcible rapes, 1995–99

SOURCE: "Figure 2.8. Forcible Rape: Percent Change from 1995," in *Crime in the United States—1999*, Federal Bueau of Investigation, Washington, DC, n.d. [Online] http://www.fbi.gov/ucr/Cius_99/99crime/99c2_01.pdf [accessed November 2001]

FIGURE 9.3

Victim-offender relationship for rape victimizations committed by single offenders against college women, 1996–97

SOURCE: Bonnie S. Fisher, Francis T. Cullen, and Michael G. Turner, "Exhibit 8. Victim-Offender Relationship for Rape Victimizations Committed by Single Offenders," in *The Sexual Victimization of College Women*, National Institute of Justice and Bureau of Justice Statistics, Washington, DC, December 2000

reporting the crimes were that the women did not want other people to know (46.9 percent of victims of completed rape), the women did not want their families to know (44.4 percent of the rape victims), and lack of proof (42.0 percent of the rape victims). In addition, 24.7 percent of the victims of completed rape were afraid that the police would treat them with hostility. About one-half of the victims of all types of victimizations, including threats, said that they were not sure if a crime had been committed or if harm was intended. This included 44.4 percent of the victims of completed rapes, 58.1 percent of the victims of completed sexual coercion, and nearly 40 percent of vic-

tims of attempted or completed sexual coercion or contact that involved force. Approximately 30 percent of the victims did not believe that the police would think that the incident was serious enough to report.

HOMICIDE

According to the FBI, there were 3,085 female homicide victims in 1999, 24.4 percent of total murder victims. (See Table 9.6.) Most victims (81.9 percent) were age 18 or over. Among single female victim/single offender homicides in 1999, 55.3 percent of the victims were white and 40.0 percent were African American. Males committed 88.3 percent of these homicides. Only 13.8 percent of female murders were committed during the course of a felony, usually a robbery. (See Table 9.7.) Other circumstances, primarily arguments or brawls, accounted for 58.2 percent of the murders. Approximately 32 percent of the female homicide victims were murdered by their husbands or boyfriends. In 1999, 542 women were murdered by their husbands and 432 by another intimate partner. In addition, 99 mothers were murdered by their son or daughter, 224 daughters were murdered by a parent, and 26 women were murdered by a sibling.

TABLE 9.6

Murder victims, by age and sex, 1999

Age	Total	Male	Female	Unknown
		Sex		
Total	12,658	9,558	3,085	15
Percent distribution[1]	100.0	75.5	24.4	.1
Under 18[2]	1,449	953	496	–
Under 22[2]	3,322	2,551	771	–
18 and over[2]	10,997	8,464	2,528	5
Infant (under 1)	205	102	103	–
1 to 4	280	142	138	–
5 to 8	95	43	52	–
9 to 12	79	40	39	–
13 to 16	447	337	110	–
17 to 19	1,286	1,103	183	–
20 to 24	2,258	1,896	362	–
25 to 29	1,793	1,476	316	1
30 to 34	1,385	1,044	339	2
35 to 39	1,289	915	374	–
40 to 44	1,064	754	310	–
45 to 49	706	523	182	1
50 to 54	456	327	128	1
55 to 59	291	216	75	–
60 to 64	208	149	59	–
65 to 69	181	123	58	–
70 to 74	142	75	67	–
75 and over	281	152	129	–
Unknown	212	141	61	10

[1] Because of rounding, the percentages may not add to total.
[2] Does not include unknown ages.

SOURCE: Adapted from "Table 2.5. Murder Victims, by Age, Sex, and Race, 1999," in *Crime in the United States—1999,* Federal Bueau of Investigation, Washington, DC, n.d. [Online] http://www.fbi.gov/ucr/Cius_99/99crime/99c2_01.pdf [accessed November, 2001]

TABLE 9.7

Murder circumstances, by sex of victim, 1999

Circumstances	Total murder victims[1]	Male	Female	Unknown
Total[1]	12,658	9,558	3,085	15
Felony type total:	2,137	1,710	425	2
Rape	46	1	45	–
Robbery	1,010	872	138	–
Burglary	79	46	33	–
Larceny–theft	14	10	4	–
Motor vehicle theft	13	12	1	–
Arson	63	37	26	–
Prostitution and commercialized vice	7	6	1	–
Other sex offenses	19	8	11	–
Narcotic drug laws	564	519	45	–
Gambling	17	17	–	–
Other–not specified	305	182	121	2
Suspected felony type	64	52	12	–
Other than felony type total:	6,678	4,879	1,796	3
Romantic triangle	133	97	36	–
Child killed by babysitter	32	18	14	–
Brawl due to influence of alcohol	187	169	18	–
Brawl due to influence of narcotics	111	85	26	–
Argument over money or property	211	176	35	–
Other arguments	3,391	2,450	940	1
Gangland killings	116	111	5	–
Juvenile gang killings	579	548	31	–
Institutional killings	11	11	–	–
Sniper attack	4	3	1	–
Other–not specified	1,903	1,211	690	2
Unknown	3,779	2,917	852	10

[1] Total number of murder victims for whom supplemental homicide data were received.

SOURCE: "Table 2.15. Murder Circumstances by Victim Sex, 1999," in *Crime in the United States—1999,* Federal Bueau of Investigation, Washington, DC, n.d. [Online] http://www.fbi.gov/ucr/Cius_99/99crime/99c2_01.pdf [accessed November, 2001]

According to the BJS, the 1,320 women murdered by an intimate in 1998 accounted for about 33 percent of all female homicides. This percentage had not changed significantly since 1976. In contrast, only about 4 percent of male homicide victims were murdered by their wives or girlfriends in 1998. Between 1976 and 1998 intimate partner homicides decreased among African American and white males and African American females. Homicides of African American women by intimates decreased approximately 45 percent during that period. However, homicides of white women by intimates did not decrease substantially during that period, and between 1997 and 1998 the number of white females murdered by intimate partners increased by 15 percent. Between 1976 and 1998 the number of male victims of intimate partner homicide fell an average of about 4 percent per year, compared to an average fall of 1 percent per year for female victims. Among the 1,830 intimate partner homicides in 1998, approximately 72 percent of the victims were female, compared to just over one-half of the 3,000 intimate partner murder victims in 1976.

INTIMATE PARTNER CRIME

The Extent of Domestic Violence

Aside from homicides, it has been very difficult to estimate the extent of domestic and intimate partner violence.

The majority of victims of domestic violence are women who are abused by their intimate partners. The American Medical Association (AMA) and the National Coalition Against Domestic Violence (NCADV) characterize domestic violence as a pattern of behavior that may include physical and/or sexual assault, psychological abuse, intimidation, and social isolation. The abuse is usually recurrent and escalates in frequency and severity, as the abuser attempts to dominate the victim and control her activities.

NATIONAL CRIME VICTIMIZATION SURVEYS. The BJS, in its May 2000 report based on the NCVS, *Intimate Partner Violence,* found that in 1998 about 1 million violent crimes were committed against current or former spouses, boyfriends, or girlfriends. Women were the victims of approximately 85 percent of these crimes. Between 1993 and 1998 about 22 percent of the violent crimes against women were committed by intimate partners, whereas only about 3 percent of the violent crimes against men were committed by intimate partners.

Between 1993 and 1998 the rate of intimate partner violence against women fell 21.4 percent, from 9.8 to 7.7 per 1,000 women; the rate of violence against males remained between 1.5 and 1.6 per 1,000 men over that period. (See Figure 9.4.). The number of female victims of intimate violence declined from about 1.1 million in 1993 to about 876,340 in 1998, for a rate of 766.8 per 100,000 persons. In both 1993 and 1998 men were the victims of about 160,000 violent crimes by intimates, for a rate of 146.2 per 100,000.

The great majority of intimate partner violent crimes were simple assaults, the least serious form of violence. However, between 1993 and 1998 females were injured in 50.3 percent of intimate partner violent incidents, and 9.3 percent of the injuries were serious. Broken bones were the most common injuries. Furthermore, between 1993 and 1998 about 63 percent of intimate partner violence against women took place in the victim's home, and about 45 percent of the households had children under age 12.

NATIONAL VIOLENCE AGAINST WOMEN SURVEY. In July 2000 the NIJ and the Centers for Disease Control and Prevention (CDC) published *Extent, Nature, and Consequences of Intimate Partner Violence,* which included findings from the National Violence Against Women (NVAW) survey. This survey of 8,000 women and 8,000 men found that about 24.8 percent of women aged 18 and over had been raped and/or physically assaulted by a spouse, ex-spouse, cohabiting partner, or date at some point in their lives. Within the past 12 months 1.5 percent of the women had been raped and/or assaulted by an intimate. During their lifetimes 7.7 percent of women, 7.8 million, had been raped by an intimate partner, and 0.2 percent, or 201,394 women, had been raped in the past 12 months. During their lifetimes 22.1 percent of women (22.3 million) had been physically assaulted by an intimate partner, and 1.3 percent (1.3 million) women had been assaulted in the past 12 months.

In contrast, 7.6 percent of men in the survey had been raped and/or physically assaulted by an intimate partner at some point in their lives, and 0.9 percent had been raped and/or assaulted in the past 12 months. The study estimated that 1.5 million women and 834,732 men are raped and/or assaulted annually by an intimate partner. Since many individuals are victimized repeatedly, the total number of estimated victimizations is much higher.

The NVAW survey also examined stalking as a form of intimate partner victimization. Stalking was defined as "a course of conduct directed at a specific person involving repeated visual or physical proximity; nonconsensual communication; verbal, written, or implied threats; or a combination thereof that would cause fear in a reasonable person." "Repeated" was defined as two or more occasions. The survey found that the incidence of stalking was

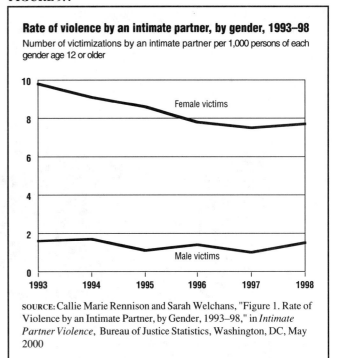

FIGURE 9.4

Rate of violence by an intimate partner, by gender, 1993–98

Number of victimizations by an intimate partner per 1,000 persons of each gender age 12 or older

SOURCE: Callie Marie Rennison and Sarah Welchans, "Figure 1. Rate of Violence by an Intimate Partner, by Gender, 1993–98," in *Intimate Partner Violence,* Bureau of Justice Statistics, Washington, DC, May 2000

much higher than previously believed. During their lifetimes 4.8 percent of women had been victims of intimate partner stalking incidents in which they felt a high degree of fear. Over the previous 12 months 0.5 percent of the surveyed women had been stalked by a current or former intimate partner. Among men, 0.6 percent had been stalked by a current or former intimate partner during their lifetime, and 0.2 percent had been stalked within the previous 12 months.

In total, 25.5 percent of women, 25.7 million, had been victimized by an intimate partner during their lifetime, and 1.8 percent of women, 1.8 million, had been victimized in the previous 12 months.

The NVAW survey confirmed that intimate violence against women is usually chronic. Among women victims 51.2 percent reported having been raped multiple times by their partner and 65.5 percent reported being physically assaulted multiple times. On average, women victims were raped by their partners 1.6 times per year and physically assaulted 3.4 times. The most common forms of physical assault were pushing, grabbing, or shoving (18.1 percent) and slapping or hitting (16.0 percent). Only 0.09 percent of the assaults involved a knife, although 0.7 percent involved a gun.

HIGHER ESTIMATES. Some studies suggest that intimate partner violence against women is even more widespread than indicated by the Department of Justice surveys and that perhaps 2 million to almost 4 million women are assaulted by their partners every year. According to the AMA:

FIGURE 9.5

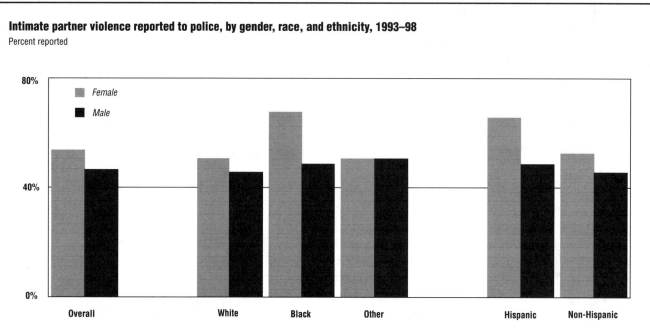

Intimate partner violence reported to police, by gender, race, and ethnicity, 1993–98

Percent reported

SOURCE: "Figure 10. Percent of Intimate partner victimization reported to police, by gender race, and ethnicity, 1993-1998," in *Intimate Partner Violence*, Bureau of Justice Statistics, Washington, DC, May 2000

- 47 percent of men who assault their wives do so at least three times per year

- More than one-half of nonfatal intimate partner assaults result in injury and 10 percent require medical treatment

- Between 19 and 30 percent of women seen in hospital emergency departments are victims of intimate partner violence

- 75 percent of medically identified victims of domestic violence go on to suffer further abuse

- 25 percent of women who attempt suicide are victims of domestic violence

- 23 percent of pregnant women seeking prenatal care are victims of domestic violence

- 45 to 59 percent of the mothers of abused children are themselves victims of domestic violence

- 50 percent of women over 30 who have been raped are victims of domestic violence

- 14 percent of women who have ever been married have been raped by current or former husbands, and rape is a major form of abuse in 54 percent of violent marriages

MARITAL RAPE. One of the reasons for the wide disparity in estimates of intimate partner violence is that women may have difficulty recognizing or admitting that they have been victimized. This is particularly true for rape. Just as almost half of the college women who had been raped in the NCWSV survey were unsure if a crime had been committed or if harm was intended, many women may not identify their experiences with an intimate partner as rape or assault. Only recently has American society begun to accept that sexual relations must be consensual even in marriage.

Various research carried out through the 1990s showed that women who were raped by their husbands suffered from the same range of physical and psychological trauma as women who were raped by acquaintances or strangers and that marital rape may be just as violent as other rapes. However, although a woman now has the right to prosecute her husband for marital rape, it remains very difficult to prove in court.

Reporting and Prosecuting Domestic Violence

Women are somewhat more likely than men to report intimate partner victimizations to the police. (See Figure 9.5.) About 67 percent of black women reported intimate partner violence, compared to about 50 percent of white women. About 65 percent of Hispanic females reported the violence, compared to about 52 percent of non-Hispanic women. The percent of intimate partner violence against women that was reported to police increased from about 48 percent in 1993 to 59 percent in 1998.

Among both men and women the most common reason for not reporting intimate partner violence was that they considered it to be a private or personal matter. (See

TABLE 9.8

Reasons intimate partner violence not reported to police, by gender of victim, 1993–98

Reasons for not reporting to police	Female average annual		Male average annual	
	Number	Percent	Number	Percent
Total victimizations not reported	480,060		85,400	
Private or personal matter	151,900	35%*	39,690	52%
Afraid of reprisal	83,090	19	—	—
Minor crime	29,270	7*	11,480	15
Police will not bother	25,440	6	—	—
Protect offender	13,580	3*	8,400	11
Police biased	12,200	3%	—	—
Inconvenient	14,190	3	—	—
Reported to another official	11,910	3	—	—
Police ineffectiveness	15,290	4	—	—
Not clear a crime occurred	7,010	2	—	—
Don't know why I did not report it	7,100	2%	—	—
Other reason given	109,070	25	14,500	19

Note: Detail may not add to total because victims may have reported more than one reason and because of values not shown in instances in which the sample cases were fewer than 10.
—Based on 10 or fewer sample cases.
* The difference in male and female percentages is significant at the 95%-confidence level.

SOURCE: "Table 8. Reasons Intimate Partner Violence Was Not Reported to the Police, by Gender of Victim, 1993-98," in *Intimate Partner Violence,* Bureau of Justice Statistics, Washington, DC, May 2000

Table 9.8.) However, about 19 percent of women cited fear of reprisal as the reason for not reporting the violence.

In the NVAW survey 26.7 percent of female assault victims and 51.9 percent of female stalking victims reported the incident to police. In contrast, only 17.2 percent of female rape victims reported their most recent rape to police. Most reports were made by the victim herself within 24 hours.

The overwhelming reason given by female victims in the NVAW survey for not reporting their victimization was that the police could not do anything. Among women who did not report, 100 percent of the stalking victims, 99.7 percent of the assault victims, and 13.2 percent of the rape victims said that the police could not do anything. Among female rape victims, 21.2 percent were afraid their partner would retaliate if they reported the rape, 20.3 percent believed it to be a minor, one-time incident, and 16.1 percent were ashamed and wanted to keep it private. Among female assault victims, 61.3 percent said that the police would not believe them, 37.9 percent said it was a minor incident, and 34.8 percent wanted to protect the attacker, the relationship, or children. In addition, 32 percent of the female assault victims did not want the police or court involved, 11.7 percent were afraid of the perpetrator, and 10.4 percent were ashamed and/or wanted to keep it quiet. Among female stalking victims who did not report to the police, 98.2 percent said the police would not believe them, 38.2 percent were afraid of the stalker, and 61.8 percent were ashamed and wanted to keep it quiet.

Among the violent incidents against women that were reported to the police in the NVAW survey, police reports were taken in the majority of cases. However, less than half of the reports resulted in the arrest or detention of the perpetrator (47.4 of rapes, 36.4 percent of assaults, and 28.7 percent of stalkings). Among rape cases, 10.5 percent were referred to the prosecutor or court, compared to 33 percent of assault cases and 28.1 percent of stalkings. Approximately one-quarter of the female assault and stalking victims were referred to services or given advice on self-protection.

The NVAW survey found that only 7.5 percent of perpetrators of rape against intimate female partners were prosecuted. Of these, 41.9 percent were convicted, and 69.2 percent of the convicted were sentenced to jail or prison. Among perpetrators of physical assault, only 7.3 percent were prosecuted, 47.9 percent of whom were convicted and 35.6 percent sentenced to jail or prison. In contrast, 14.6 percent of stalkers were prosecuted; 40 percent were convicted, and 56.3 percent of the convicted were sentenced to jail or prison.

Women victims of assault by an intimate were much more likely than male victims to obtain a protective or restraining order (17.1 percent of women versus 3.5 percent of men). Among female stalking victims, 36.6 percent obtained a restraining order, as did 16.4 percent of rape victims. More than half of all female victims who obtained restraining orders reported that the orders were violated.

The Victims of Domestic Violence

According to the BJS, between 1993 and 1998 the highest rates of intimate partner violence against women were among those aged 16 through 24 with household incomes of less than $7,500. Women who were divorced, separated, or never married had higher rates of intimate partner violence than did married women. Intimate partner violence against African American women was 35 percent higher than against white women and about 2.5 times higher than against women of other races. Women living in rental housing and in urban areas were at slightly higher risk than women in rural areas and at much higher risk than suburban women.

The NVAW Survey also found that, as a group, non-white females and males experience significantly more intimate partner violence than do white females and males. Native American women reported the highest rate of intimate partner violence, and Asian/Pacific Islander women reported far lower rates.

The NVAW survey found that married women living apart from their husbands were almost four times more likely to have been raped, assaulted, or stalked by their husbands than women living with their husbands. Rape and physical assaults of females occurred either before or both before and after the relationship ended. Very few first rapes or assaults occurred after the end of the relationship. In contrast, 42.8 percent of the stalking incidents against female victims first occurred after the relationship ended.

When comparing same-sex and opposite-sex intimate partners, the NVAW survey found that 30.4 percent of women with a woman partner had been victimized by a male partner during their lifetime, compared to 20.3 percent of women living with an opposite-sex partner. Only 11.4 percent of women with a same-sex partner had ever been victimized by a female partner.

Perpetrators of Domestic Violence

According to the NCADV, behaviors and characteristics of an abusive partner may include:

• Embarrassing or ridiculing a partner in front of others

• Intimidating or humiliating talk or behavior

• Grabbing, pushing, shoving, or hitting

• Abuse of alcohol or other drugs

• Sexual pressure

• Limiting a partner's activities or personal relationships

• Holding traditional ideas of a partner's role

• Moodiness, including extreme kindness at some times and extreme anger at other times

• Making demands of a partner and becoming enraged if they are not met

• A history of violence

Indications that a woman may be in an abusive relationship include:

• Fear of her partner

• Making excuses for her partner's behavior

• Feeling that she is the one who must change

• Avoiding conflict at all costs

• Avoiding angering her partner

• Trying to always do what her partner wants

• The presence of weapons in the home

• Fear of leaving the relationship

The AMA has identified certain additional factors that may put a woman at risk for intimate partner violence:

• Alcohol or drug abuse by the woman and/or her partner

• Pregnancy

• Excessive jealousy or possessiveness by the partner

• A partner's exposure to violence as a child

Why Women Don't Leave

The NCADV has identified factors that prevent women from leaving violent domestic relationships:

• Lack of resources, including employment, cash, and access to bank accounts and credit

• Fear of losing their children

• Lack of shelters for battered women

• Lack of support from clergy, counselors, police, and prosecutors

• Belief that it is their responsibility to save the relationship

• Reluctance to take children from their fathers

• Belief that the abusive behavior will change

Legislation

Many states now require arrests when police are summoned during domestic disputes. The Family Violence Prevention and Services Act of 1992 (PL 102-295) provided funds for women's shelters and other services for victims of family violence. The law made it legal to evict batterers from their homes.

SEXUAL HARASSMENT

Sexual harassment is pervasive in American society, and at one time or another essentially all women experience uninvited and unwanted attention of a sexual nature. However, both men and women define sexual harassment in individual ways. Sexual harassment of a woman may range from being looked at on the street to losing her job for refusing to have sex with her boss. Stalking, sexual coercion, sexual assault, and rape are particularly severe forms of sexual harassment.

Scott Lindquist, in *The Date Rape Prevention Book: The Essential Guide for Girls and Women* (Sourcebooks, Inc., Naperville, IL, 2000), defines sexual harassment, in part, as:

- Catcalls, leering, ogling, whistling

- Suggestive or insulting gestures or noises

- Sexual innuendos or suggestive, offensive, or derogatory comments

- Jokes about sex or gender-specific traits

- Offensive remarks about physical characteristics, clothing, or sexual activity

- Sexual insults

- Requests or demands for sex

- Unwanted physical contact

- Physical assault or coerced sexual activity

Awareness of sexual harassment has increased in recent years, in part because of complaints and class-action lawsuits against large corporations and in part because of high-profile accusations of sexual harassment against such public officials as President Bill Clinton and Supreme Court Justice Clarence Thomas.

The Law

The government and the courts have focused primarily on issues of sexual harassment in the workplace. The U.S. Equal Employment Opportunity Commission defines sexual harassment as unwelcome sexual advances, requests for sexual favors, and other verbal or physical conduct of a sexual nature that becomes a condition of employment or the basis for employment decisions such as promotion, or that creates an intimidating, hostile, or offensive work environment.

MERITOR SAVINGS BANK V. VINSON. The U.S. Supreme Court, in *Meritor Savings Bank v. Vinson* (477 U.S. 57, 1986), ruled that sexual harassment was a violation of Title VII of the Civil Rights Act of 1964, which prohibited sexual discrimination. Mechelle Vinson claimed that her supervisor harassed her at work and outside of work and raped her. She did not file a complaint until a year after the harassment had ceased for fear of jeopardizing her employment. A lower court ruled against her, finding that sexual favors had not been a condition of her employment. The Supreme Court reversed the decision, ruling that "Title VII affords employees the right to work in an environment free from discriminatory intimidation, ridicule, and insult."

THE EMPLOYER'S RESPONSIBILITY. In 1998 the Supreme Court ruled that (1) employers could be held liable when a supervisor threatened to demote or take other action against an employee who refused a supervisor's sexual demands, even when the threats were not carried out (*Burlington Industries v. Ellerth* [66 LW 4643]), and (2) that companies were liable for the misconduct of their employees even though the company was unaware of the behavior (*Faragher v. Boca Raton* [118 S. Ct. 2275, 1998]). The Court's majority decision (seven to two) stated that employers could generally avoid liability for sexual harassment by showing that they had strong antiharassment programs, that the programs were communicated to all employees, and that systems were in place for submitting and reviewing complaints. Following these rulings, many companies reexamined their sexual harassment policies and revised them to meet the Court's tougher standards.

College Women

The NCWSV report found that 54.3 percent of the college women in their survey had been exposed to general sexist remarks, at a rate of 7,070.2 remarks per 1,000 female students. (See Table 9.9.) Catcalls, whistles, and sexually suggestive noises were also common forms of harassment. This type of verbal victimization was much more common than visual victimization such as exposure to pornography. Verbal and visual victimizations occurred both on and off campuses; however, exposure to pornography, obscene phone calls, false sexual rumors, and nonconsensual taping of sex or nudity were much more likely to happen on campus. Catcalls, whistling, noises, and inappropriate questions about sex, as well as sexual exposure from another person and other forms of visual victimization, were somewhat more likely to occur off campus.

The NCWSV survey examined the prevalence of stalking by asking whether the respondent had been watched, followed, telephoned, or e-mailed in a way that seemed obsessive and made them afraid. The report found that since the beginning of the academic year, 13.1 percent of the women had been stalked, for a rate of 156.5 stalkings per 1,000 female students. Four out of five victims knew their stalker and, in 42.5 percent of the cases, it was a boyfriend or ex-boyfriend. On average the stalkings lasted for 60 days. In 15.3 percent of the incidents, the stalker threatened or attempted harm, and in 10.3 percent of the stalkings the perpetrator attempted or forced sexual contact. Only 17 percent of the incidents were reported to police. The study found that Native American women were at the greatest risk for being stalked and Asian/Pacific Islander women were at the lowest risk.

Harassment in the Military

During the 1990s it became increasingly clear that sexual harassment of women was rampant throughout the military and that it was condoned and even perpetrated by high-ranking officers.

TABLE 9.9

Extent of verbal and visual sexual victimization among college women, 1996–97

	Percentage and number of victims for sample	Total number of victimizations[1]	Rate per 1,000 female students	Number of victimizations per victim	Percentage and number of victimizations on campus	Percentage and number of victimizations off campus
Type of verbal victimization						
General sexist remarks in front of you	54.3% (2,398)	31,434	7,070.2	13.0	50.6% (15,894)	49.4% (15,540)
Cat calls, whistles about your looks, or noises with sexual overtones	48.2 (2,129)	29,609	6,660.0	13.9	38.6 (11,423)	61.4 (18,186)
Obscene telephone calls or messages	21.9 (973)	4,885	1,099.0	5.0	59.8 (2,922)	40.2 (1,963)
Asked questions about sex or romantic life when clearly none of their business	19.0 (844)	4,694	1,055.8	5.6	41.2 (1,933)	58.8 (2,761)
False rumors about sex life with them or other people	9.7 (431)	1,166	262.3	2.7	59.7 (696)	40.3 (470)
Type of visual victimization						
Someone exposed you to pornographic pictures or materials when you did not agree to see them	6.1 (272)	865	194.6	3.2	59.9 (518)	40.1 (347)
Someone exposed their sexual organs to you when you did not agree to see them	4.8 (214)	568	127.8	2.7	34.0 (193)	66.0 (375)
Anyone, without your consent, observed or tried to observe you while you were undressing, nude, or in a sexual act	2.4 (105)	302	67.9	2.9	44.0 (133)	56.0 (169)
Anyone, without your consent, showed other people or played for other people photographs, videotapes, or audiotapes having sex or in a nude or seminude state	0.3 (15)	18	4.0	1.2	44.4 (8)	55.6 (10)
Anyone, without your consent, photographed, videotaped, or audiotaped you having sex or in a nude or seminude state	0.2 (8)	9	2.0	1.1	77.8 (7)	22.2 (2)

[1] The distributions for the number of victimization variables are right censored because they include the value "97 or more."

SOURCE: Bonnie S. Fisher, Francis T. Cullen, and Michael G. Turner, "Exhibit 14. The Extent of Verbal and Visual Victimization," in *The Sexual Victimization of College Women,* National Institute of Justice and Bureau of Justice Statistics, Washington, DC, December 2000

As a result of charges brought against male drill sergeants by female recruits at Aberdeen Proving Ground in Maryland in 1996, the army began an investigation of 59 military installations around the world. Investigators found that sexual harassment was pervasive throughout the army and that the army leadership was, in large part, to blame. A 1997 army survey found that about 47 percent of females had experienced unwanted sexual attention, 15 percent had experienced sexual coercion, and 7 percent had been victims of sexual assault. Most female soldiers were afraid to report sexual misconduct. Only 12 percent of recent sexual harassment victims had filed a formal complaint. Many female soldiers reported that they believed their commanders had little interest in enforcing the army's rules against sexual harassment.

A survey by the Department of Veterans Affairs (VA) Health Services Research and Development Service, reported in the December 13, 1999, issue of *Mental Health Weekly,* found that 23 percent of 3,600 female outpatients at VA medical facilities reported being forced into sexual relations during their service in the military. Of the women who had been sexually assaulted, 60 percent suffered symptoms of depression and 7 percent reported current alcohol abuse.

A study by the University of Iowa and the Iowa City VA Medical Center was reported in *USA Today* in August 2001. The researchers interviewed 537 women veterans who had served in the military from the Vietnam era through the Persian Gulf War. Among these women, about 79 percent reported having been sexually harassed during their military service: 54 percent were subjected to unwanted sexual contact, 23 percent were physically assaulted, and 21 percent were subjected to physical violence while being raped. Some women reported as many as 20 incidents of physical assault. Women who worked in military environments where sexual harassment occurred were five times more likely than other military women to have been physically assaulted. Women whose superior officers had made sexually demeaning comments or who tolerated such comments were three times more likely to have been victims of physical assault.

Harassment in Prison

For several years Amnesty International, a worldwide human rights organization, has been drawing attention to the sexual harassment and sexual abuse of women prisoners in the United States. As a result of the "war on drugs" and mandatory minimum sentences, the number of women in U.S. prisons has tripled over the past decade. Many of these women are at the mercy of male guards and correctional officers. In a June 1999 report, *Women in Prison—Sexual Misconduct by Correctional Staff,* the U.S. General Accounting Office admitted that sexual abuse of women prisoners does occur. The report examined the three largest female correctional systems—the Federal Bureau of Prisons and the state systems in California and Texas—as well as the District of Columbia correctional system.

In their 1999 report *"Not Part of My Sentence": Violations of the Human Rights of Women in Custody,* Amnesty International found widespread sexual abuse of women prisoners throughout the United States. Their follow-up 2001 study, *Abuse of Women in Custody: Sexual Misconduct and Shackling of Pregnant Women,* found that no state granted women prisoners full protection from sexual mistreatment by custodians. Most states allowed pat-down searches of women prisoners by male guards, and in some states cross-gender pat-down searches were routine.

Hate Crimes

In addition to sexual harassment, women may be the victims of hate crimes because of their race, sexual orientation, ethnicity, religion, or disability. In its report on hate crimes between 1997 and 1999 the BJS found that white females were the victims of about 25 percent of all hate crimes, 22 percent of violent hate crimes, and 33 percent of property hate crimes. Black females were the victims of approximately 12 percent of hate crimes, 13 percent of violent hate crimes, and 10 percent of property hate crimes. Women of other races were the victims of about 1 percent of hate crimes. Hate crimes directed against lesbians accounted for 65 incidents between 1997 and 1999, or 2.2 percent of total hate crimes.

CHAPTER 10
WOMEN AS CRIMINALS

Women commit only about one out of every five crimes and even fewer violent crimes. In centuries past, crimes by women were often committed out of desperation—for example, stealing to feed their starving children. During the Middle Ages and up into the 17th and 18th centuries millions of women were tried and executed for the crime of witchcraft. These "witches" were scapegoats for the ills that befell society: infant deaths, disease, plague, crop failures, famine, and war. Pregnancy outside of marriage also was viewed as a crime that could be punishable by banishment or death.

Violent crimes by women are often sensationalized. This is particularly true of mothers who murder their children. On October 24, 1994, Susan Smith of Union, South Carolina, strapped her two young sons in their car seats and then rolled her car into a lake. The little boys drowned. On June 6, 1996, Darlie Routier from Rowlett, Texas, allegedly stabbed two of her sons to death. She was tried and found guilty for the death of one of the boys. On June 20, 2000, Andrea Yates, a housewife in Houston, Texas, called the police and told them that she had just drowned each of her five children in the bathtub. Yates was said to be suffering from a psychotic form of postpartum depression.

Because women are the traditional caregivers and nurturers, acts such as these may be perceived as crimes against nature and, as such, are considered far more shocking than equivalent crimes committed by men.

ARRESTS OF WOMEN

There were almost 2 million female arrests in 1999, 21.8 percent of total arrests. (See Table 10.1.) Women 18 and over accounted for 78.4 percent of these arrests. Property crimes accounted for 323,118 female arrests, and violent crimes accounted for 71,468 arrests. In 1999 females were arrested for 190,342 assaults other than aggravated assault and for 177,542 drug violations (8.9 percent of all

female arrests). There were 148,490 female arrests for driving under the influence. Larceny-theft accounted for 14.1 percent of all female arrests. Larceny-theft is the taking of property without force, violence, or fraud, and includes shoplifting and pocket picking.

According to the Federal Bureau of Investigation (FBI), in 1999 females were arrested for 17 percent of all violent crimes and 29.6 percent of all property crimes. Females accounted for 11.4 percent of all murder and nonnegligent manslaughter arrests but only 1.3 percent of arrests for forcible rape. They accounted for 49.2 percent of all arrests for embezzlement, 60.8 percent of all arrests for prostitution and commercialized vice, and 59.2 percent of arrested runaways. Women accounted for only 7.8 percent of arrests for weapons violations.

More Women Are Being Arrested

Although crime rates have dropped significantly in recent years, more women than ever before are being arrested. (See Table 10.2.) Between 1990 and 1999 total arrests of males fell 5.0 percent, although arrests of males under age 18 rose 4.7 percent. In contrast, total female arrests rose 17.9 percent over the same period, and arrests of females under 18 rose 31.8 percent. Although between 1990 and 1999 the crime index total fell 7.3 percent for all females, during the same period it fell 26.1 percent for all males and 27.3 percent for males under 18. The crime index total rose 5.7 percent for females under 18.

Despite this increase in female arrests and the decrease in male arrests, males accounted for 80.7 percent of all arrests in 1999, about the same percentage as in 1990. In 1999 males accounted for 72.6 percent of all arrests of those under 18, compared to 76.9 percent in 1990. Females under 18 accounted for 21.8 percent of all female arrests in 1999, compared to 19.5 percent in 1990. Males under 18 accounted for 16.2 percent of all male arrests in 1999, up from 14.7 percent in 1990. (See Table 10.2.)

TABLE 10.1

Arrests of females, by age, 1999

[8,546 AGENCIES; 1999 ESTIMATED POPULATION 171,831,000]

Offense charged	Total all ages	Ages under 15	Ages under 18	Ages 18 and over	Under 10	10-12	13-14	15	16	17	18	19	20	21
TOTAL	1,997,270	152,721	431,697	1,565,573	4,478	30,456	117,787	90,117	98,257	90,602	87,468	86,702	77,836	66,393
Percent distribution[1]	100.0	7.6	21.6	78.4	.2	1.5	5.9	4.5	4.9	4.5	4.4	4.3	3.9	3.3
Murder and nonnegligent manslaughter	1,105	12	70	1,035	—	3	9	11	22	25	57	46	51	31
Forcible rape	238	28	62	176	—	11	17	15	8	11	6	7	9	11
Robbery	7,405	474	1,627	5,778	4	88	382	366	381	406	441	400	346	261
Aggravated assault	62,720	3,853	10,085	52,635	94	850	2,909	2,008	2,055	2,169	2,226	2,244	2,257	2,213
Burglary	24,909	3,110	7,289	17,620	178	817	2,115	1,370	1,414	1,395	1,419	1,227	975	800
Larceny-theft	281,974	35,539	88,884	193,090	1,158	9,159	25,222	16,820	18,546	17,979	15,921	13,142	10,688	8,879
Motor vehicle theft	14,675	1,772	5,429	9,246	9	197	1,566	1,347	1,278	1,032	862	720	538	520
Arson	1,560	451	665	895	56	152	243	104	60	50	35	33	37	29
Violent crime[2]	71,468	4,367	11,844	59,624	98	952	3,317	2,400	2,466	2,611	2,730	2,697	2,663	2,516
Percent distribution[1]	100.0	6.1	16.6	83.4	.1	1.3	4.6	3.4	3.5	3.7	3.8	3.8	3.7	3.5
Property crime[3]	323,118	40,872	102,267	220,851	1,401	10,325	29,146	19,641	21,298	20,456	18,237	15,122	12,238	10,228
Percent distribution[1]	100.0	12.6	31.7	68.3	.4	3.2	9.0	6.1	6.6	6.3	5.6	4.7	3.8	3.2
Crime Index total[4]	394,586	45,239	114,111	280,475	1,499	11,277	32,463	22,041	23,764	23,067	20,967	17,819	14,901	12,744
Percent distribution[1]	100.0	11.5	28.9	71.1	.4	2.9	8.2	5.6	6.0	5.8	5.3	4.5	3.8	3.2
Other assaults	190,342	19,858	46,112	144,230	502	4,665	14,691	9,181	9,009	8,064	7,271	7,090	6,521	6,505
Forgery and counterfeiting	26,820	202	1,637	25,183	8	33	161	280	464	691	1,247	1,303	1,482	1,197
Fraud	98,413	428	2,305	96,108	16	73	339	351	596	930	2,381	3,692	4,235	4,180
Embezzlement	5,518	24	527	4,991	1	—	23	22	165	316	374	358	317	283
Stolen property; buying, receiving, possessing	12,595	767	2,450	10,145	24	141	602	489	554	640	766	663	575	504
Vandalism	27,888	4,399	9,162	18,726	316	1,283	2,800	1,509	1,658	1,596	1,447	1,239	1,126	994
Weapons; carrying, possessing, etc.	8,927	1,097	2,599	6,328	33	273	791	506	503	493	385	353	291	294
Prostitution and commercialized vice	38,849	63	470	38,379	5	7	51	66	120	221	801	1,087	1117	1,059
Sex offenses (except forcible rape and prostitution)	4,263	420	810	3,453	44	123	253	143	130	117	140	157	136	165
Drug abuse violations	177,542	4,044	18,535	159,007	46	519	3,479	3,365	4,861	6,265	8,107	7,842	6,917	6,200
Gambling	872	4	35	837	—	—	4	9	7	15	20	19	17	20
Offenses against the family and children	20,484	900	2,291	18,193	153	176	571	483	472	436	571	587	624	658
Driving under the influence	148,490	89	2,354	146,136	13	14	62	155	673	1,437	3,224	3,941	4,245	5,469
Liquor laws	94,343	4,694	32,204	62,139	53	380	4,261	5,859	9,345	12,306	16,426	15,199	10,752	1,808
Drunkenness	55,547	609	2,755	52,592	14	56	539	573	680	893	1,357	1,403	1,256	1,596
Disorderly conduct	96,971	13,248	31,748	65,223	259	2,828	10,161	6,898	6,241	5,361	4,552	3,926	3,548	3,584
Vagrancy	3,715	79	305	3,410	3	13	63	66	69	91	137	130	104	97
All other offenses (except traffic)	498,511	22,562	69,258	429,253	788	3,807	17,967	14,954	16,261	15,481	17,259	19,849	19,626	18,993
Suspicion	1,019	85	254	765	2	19	64	50	52	67	36	45	46	43
Curfew and loitering law violations	34,787	10,838	34,787	—	188	1,571	9,079	8,205	9,229	6,515	—	—	—	—
Runaways	56,988	23,072	56,988	—	511	3,198	19,363	14,912	13,404	5,600	—	—	—	—

TABLE 10.1

Arrests of females, by age, 1999 [CONTINUED]

[8,546 AGENCIES; 1999 ESTIMATED POPULATION 171,831,000]

Offense charged	22	23	24	25–29	30–34	35–39	40–44	45–49	50–54	55–59	60–64	65 and over
TOTAL	60,996	54,338	53,201	253,089	254,070	250,682	165,563	83,708	37,219	16,337	7,875	10,096
Percent distribution¹	3.1	2.7	2.7	12.7	12.7	12.6	8.3	4.2	1.9	.8	.4	.5
Murder and nonnegligent manslaughter	42	45	46	187	170	150	88	57	32	14	12	7
Forcible rape	8	5	11	35	29	23	21	4	5	2	–	–
Robbery	268	210	200	994	1,016	856	511	166	61	21	17	10
Aggravated assault	2,159	1,978	1,860	9,044	9,176	8,729	5,668	2,773	1,267	521	235	285
Burglary	702	663	636	2,899	2,821	2,511	1,585	762	383	124	55	58
Larceny-theft	7,713	6,728	6,490	29,440	27,678	25,702	18,174	10,272	5,548	2,795	1,575	2,345
Motor vehicle theft	473	350	323	1,746	1,602	1,118	655	234	55	26	8	16
Arson	22	23	29	112	167	156	131	71	28	8	6	8
Violent crime²	2,477	2,238	2,117	10,260	10,391	9,758	6,288	3,000	1,365	558	264	302
Percent distribution¹	3.5	3.1	3.0	14.4	14.5	13.7	8.8	4.2	1.9	.8	.4	.4
Property crime³	8,910	7,764	7,478	34,197	32,268	29,487	20,545	11,339	6,014	2,953	1,644	2,427
Percent distribution¹	2.8	2.4	2.3	10.6	10.0	9.1	6.4	3.5	1.9	.9	.5	.8
Crime Index total⁴	11,387	10,002	9,595	44,457	42,659	39,245	26,833	14,339	7,379	3,511	1,908	2,729
Percent distribution¹	2.9	2.5	2.4	11.3	10.8	9.9	6.8	3.6	1.9	.9	.5	.7
Other assaults	6,216	5,504	5,368	24,887	23,920	23,459	14,393	6,946	3,173	1,376	688	913
Forgery and counterfeiting	1,090	993	1,017	4,776	4,463	3,653	2,305	986	435	138	50	48
Fraud	4,243	3,910	3,923	18,870	16,702	14,564	9,277	5,183	2,570	1,179	575	624
Embezzlement	260	220	253	838	680	650	350	226	105	42	18	17
Stolen property; buying, receiving, possessing	437	404	445	1,839	1,675	1,364	865	351	144	59	22	32
Vandalism	884	815	738	3,162	2,842	2,547	1,574	704	311	132	69	142
Weapons; carrying, possessing, etc.	299	265	220	1,035	932	982	654	316	134	82	39	47
Prostitution and commercialized vice	1,045	964	1,127	7,244	8,709	8,243	4,652	1,735	422	96	34	44
Sex offenses (except forcible rape and prostitution)	148	135	109	614	598	577	378	161	71	40	10	14
Drug abuse violations	5,544	4,955	4,793	24,884	28,409	29,547	19,377	8,344	2,747	828	274	239
Gambling	11	13	9	68	80	85	94	203	66	69	23	40
Offenses against the family and children	636	691	754	3,477	3,514	3,249	1,837	793	358	174	91	179
Driving under the influence	5,196	4,543	4,472	21,409	23,088	27,746	20,585	11,660	5,551	2,579	1,291	1,137
Liquor laws	1,126	876	742	3,014	3,076	3,510	2,608	1,583	698	352	147	222
Drunkenness	1,399	1,296	1,207	6,597	8,555	11,332	8,611	4,631	1,919	815	342	276
Disorderly conduct	3,093	2,571	2,493	10,107	9,887	9,556	6,166	2,973	1,425	656	286	400
Vagrancy	93	81	56	482	673	660	493	225	92	43	20	24
All other offenses (except traffic)	17,855	16,062	15,858	75,204	73,488	69,584	44,451	22,312	9,605	4,162	1,980	2,965
Suspicion	34	38	22	125	120	129	60	37	14	4	8	4
Curfew and loitering law violations	–	–	–	–	–	–	–	–	–	–	–	–
Runaways	–	–	–	–	–	–	–	–	–	–	–	–

¹ Because of rounding, the percentages may not add to total.

² Violent crimes are offenses of murder, forcible rape, robbery, and aggravated assault.

³ Property crimes are offenses of burglary, larceny-theft, motor vehicle theft, and arson.

⁴ Includes arson.

SOURCE: "Table 40. Arrests, Females, by Age, 1999," in *Crime in the United States–1999*, Federal Bureau of Investigation, Washington, DC, n.d. [Online] http://www.fbi.gov/ucr/Cius_99/99crime/99c4_06.pdf [accessed January 18, 2002]

TABLE 10.2

Ten-year arrest trends, by sex, 1990–99

[6,364 AGENCIES; 1999 ESTIMATED POPULATION 140,836,000; 1990 ESTIMATED POPULATION 128,207,000]

	Males						Females					
	Total			Under 18			Total			Under 18		
Offense charged	1990	1999	Percent change	1990	1999	Percent change	1990	1999	Percent change	1990	1999	Percent change
TOTAL[1]	6,092,905	5,788,285	-5.0	897,082	939,176	+4.7	1,382,203	1,629,304	+17.9	269,578	355,337	+31.8
Murder and nonnegligent manslaughter	9,741	5,880	-39.6	1,397	616	-55.9	1,129	719	-36.3	81	49	-39.5
Forcible rape	19,774	14,535	-26.5	2,814	2,450	-12.9	214	169	-21.0	57	48	-15.8
Robbery	72,993	53,465	-26.8	16,580	13,784	-16.9	6,770	6,123	-9.6	1,516	1,354	-10.7
Aggravated assault	229,471	208,264	-9.2	29,667	28,147	-5.1	33,839	50,312	+48.7	5,068	7,948	+56.8
Burglary	215,967	137,505	-36.3	72,290	47,618	-34.1	22,979	21,246	-7.5	6,778	6,229	-8.1
Larceny-theft	575,614	425,314	-26.1	178,745	135,989	-23.9	273,421	234,755	-14.1	71,384	75,632	+6.0
Motor vehicle theft	102,851	60,118	-41.5	43,600	20,908	-52.0	11,851	11,176	-5.7	5,593	4,234	-24.3
Arson	8,938	7,603	-14.9	4,070	4,341	+6.7	1,267	1,224	-3.4	406	555	+36.7
Violent crime[2]	331,979	282,144	-15.0	50,458	44,997	-10.8	41,952	57,323	+36.6	6,722	9,399	+39.8
Property crime[3]	903,370	630,540	-30.2	298,705	208,856	-30.1	309,518	268,401	-13.3	84,161	86,650	+3.0
Crime Index total[4]	1,235,349	912,684	-26.1	349,163	253,853	-27.3	351,470	325,724	-7.3	90,883	96,049	+5.7
Other assaults	457,158	517,385	+13.2	61,770	83,116	+34.6	89,614	153,361	+71.1	18,994	36,576	+92.6
Forgery and counterfeiting	32,473	34,994	+7.8	2,683	2,401	-10.5	17,930	21,819	+21.7	1,401	1,410	+.6
Fraud	98,579	90,558	-8.1	2,993	3,298	+10.2	84,173	75,855	-9.9	1,524	1,685	+10.6
Embezzlement	4,450	4,911	+10.4	353	478	+35.4	3,258	4,781	+46.7	210	440	+109.5
Stolen property; buying, receiving, possessing	78,345	52,472	-33.0	22,266	13,467	-39.5	10,764	9,698	-9.9	2,413	2,012	-16.6
Vandalism	154,711	127,384	-17.7	64,701	56,400	-12.8	18,740	22,569	+20.4	5,982	7,681	+28.4
Weapons; carrying, possessing, etc.	107,563	80,497	-25.2	20,850	19,356	-7.2	8,409	6,830	-18.8	1,343	1,935	+44.1
Prostitution and commercialized vice	23,158	19,655	-15.1	427	309	-27.6	36,146	29,921	-17.2	482	376	-22.0
Sex offenses (except forcible rape and prostitution)	54,862	47,307	-13.8	8,367	8,210	-1.9	4,492	3,521	-21.6	494	653	+32.2
Drug abuse violations	488,454	660,104	+35.1	38,005	85,226	+124.2	101,490	144,920	+42.8	5,208	15,126	+190.4
Gambling	7,537	4,069	-46.0	383	397	+3.7	1,176	650	-44.7	28	25	-10.7
Offenses against the family and children	40,193	59,130	+47.1	1,287	2,992	+132.5	7,504	16,770	+123.5	637	1,687	+164.8
Driving under the influence	893,756	629,889	-29.5	9,478	9,158	-3.4	127,997	119,565	-6.6	1,553	1,866	+20.2
Liquor laws	286,026	277,294	-3.1	58,613	60,692	+3.5	64,082	78,467	+22.4	22,021	27,304	+24.0
Drunkenness	500,375	330,902	-33.9	12,692	9,628	-24.1	54,492	47,332	-13.1	2,252	2,265	+.6
Disorderly conduct	290,239	242,822	-16.3	47,475	62,755	+32.2	67,907	75,124	+10.6	12,267	24,673	+101.1
Vagrancy	21,426	13,520	-36.9	1,949	1,053	-46.0	3,600	3,336	-7.3	367	247	-32.7
All other offenses (except traffic)	1,244,366	1,580,872	+27.0	119,742	164,551	+37.4	261,843	410,738	+56.9	34,403	55,004	+59.9
Suspicion	9,150	3,144	-65.6	2,175	794	-63.5	1,592	856	-46.2	515	230	-55.3
Curfew and loitering law violations	33,890	68,927	+103.4	33,890	68,927	+103.4	12,729	30,456	+139.3	12,729	30,456	+139.3
Runaways	39,995	32,909	-17.7	39,995	32,909	-17.7	54,387	47,867	-12.0	54,387	47,867	-12.0

[1] Does not include suspicion.
[2] Violent crimes are offenses of murder, forcible rape, robbery, and aggravated assault.
[3] Property crimes are offenses of burglary, larceny-theft, motor vehicle theft, and arson.

SOURCE: "Table 33. Ten-Year Arrest Trends by Sex, 1990-1999," in *Crime in the United States—1999*, Federal Bureau of Investigation, Washington, DC, n.d. [Online] http://www.fbi.gov/ucr/Cius_99/99crime/99c2_01.pdf [accessed November, 2001]

According to the FBI, between 1995 and 1999 arrests of all males declined 4.7 percent and arrests of females under 18 declined 1.1 percent. Total female arrests increased 3.7 percent over the five-year-period. However, between 1998 and 1999 female arrests decreased 4.5 percent and arrests of females under 18 decreased 7.2 percent. Male arrests decreased even more than female arrests. Between 1998 and 1999 there were fewer female arrests for all crimes except embezzlement, prostitution and commercial vice, gambling, driving under the influence, liquor laws, and suspicion. However, among females under 18, there were more arrests for arson, sex offenses other than forcible rape and prostitution, and drug violations in 1999 as compared with 1998.

VIOLENT CRIME ARRESTS. Between 1990 and 1999 arrests of females for violent crimes (murder and nonnegligent manslaughter, forcible rape, robbery, and aggravated assault) rose 36.6 percent. Arrests rose 39.8 percent for females under 18. This increase was accounted for solely by the large increase in arrests for aggravated assault, a 48.7 percent increase for all females and a 56.8 percent increase for females under 18. In contrast, arrests for violent crime fell 15.0 percent for all males and 10.8 percent for males under 18. Male arrests for aggravated assault dropped 9.2 percent. The number of arrests for all other types of violent crime dropped significantly over the 10-year period, although the drop in male arrests was significantly higher than the drop in female arrests. (See Table 10.2.)

PROPERTY CRIME ARRESTS. Arrests for property crimes (burglary, larceny-theft, motor vehicle theft, and arson) dropped among both males and females between 1990 and 1999, although less for females than for males (13.3 percent versus 30.2 percent). Property crime arrests rose 3.0 percent for females under 18, compared to a drop of 30.1 percent for males under 18. Arrests for burglary and motor vehicle theft fell for girls under 18, but there was a 6.0 percent rise in arrests for larceny-theft and a 36.7 percent increase in arrests for arson. (See Table 10.2.)

OTHER TYPES OF CRIME. The numbers of female arrests for the majority of other offenses rose between 1990 and 1999, particularly for girls under 18. Arrests for assault other than aggravated assault rose 71.1 percent for all females and 92.6 percent for females under 18. Arrests for embezzlement rose 46.7 percent for all females and 109.5 percent for girls under 18. Female arrests for curfew and loitering violations rose 139.3 percent. Arrests for drug abuse violations rose 190.4 percent for females under 18 and 124.2 percent for males under 18, compared to increases of 42.8 percent for all females and 35.1 percent for all males. Arrests for disorderly conduct rose 101.1 percent for females under 18. (See Table 10.2.)

Although males accounted for 77.9 percent of all arrests for offenses against family and children, including nonsupport, neglect, desertion, or abuse, male arrests for such offenses rose 47.1 percent, compared to a rise of 123.5 percent in female arrests. Arrests of females under 18 for such offenses rose 164.8 percent, compared to a 132.5 percent increase in arrests of males under 18. (See Table 10.2.)

Prostitution and commercialized vice and runaways were the only crimes for which more females than males were arrested in 1999. Runaways are limited to juveniles taken into protective custody under local statutes. Between 1990 and 1999 prostitution and commercialized vice arrests of females decreased 17.2 percent, with a 22.0 percent drop among females under 18. (See Table 10.2.) In part this decrease may be due to changing attitudes toward prostitution. Many people believe that sex between consenting adults, regardless of whether money is exchanged, is a victimless crime and does not warrant the expenditure of law enforcement resources. However, many teenage runaways, both male and female, turn to prostitution to support themselves or to buy drugs. This can contribute to the spread of HIV/AIDS and other sexually transmitted diseases.

Federal Arrests

According to the Bureau of Justice Statistics (BJS), between October 1, 1998, and September 30, 1999, females accounted for 15 percent of all federal arrests and 9.6 percent of federal arrests for violent crimes. They accounted for 29.5 percent of arrests for fraudulent prop-

erty crimes and 26.3 percent of arrests for other property crimes. Females accounted for 15.4 percent of drug arrests and 14.6 percent of arrests as material witnesses.

During the same one-year period, Drug Enforcement Administration (DEA) agents arrested 6,540 women, 17.4 percent of all DEA arrests. Of these female drug arrests, 29.3 percent involved methamphetamines, 20.8 percent involved cocaine powder, 20.5 percent were for marijuana, 13.7 percent were for crack cocaine, and 7.7 percent were for opiates. Only 2.6 percent of the arrested women were armed, compared to 4.5 percent of arrested males. Of the armed females, 84.6 percent had handguns and 30.8 percent had a shotgun or rifle, according to the BJS.

VIOLENT CRIMES COMMITTED BY WOMEN

According to the BJS, in 1999 women committed 19.1 percent of all single-offender violent crimes, 17.9 percent of completed violent crimes, and 19.5 percent of attempted or threatened violence. Females committed 20.8 percent of attempted robberies resulting in injury and 20.7 percent of assaults, but only 5.4 percent of rape/sexual assaults.

Among multiple-offender violent victimizations in 1999, 9.1 percent were committed by two or more women and 14.5 percent were committed by women and men acting together. Females were involved in no multiple-offender rapes or sexual assaults. Multiple females committed 13.3 percent of simple assaults and 12.9 percent of robberies that resulted in injuries. Males and females acting together committed 17.1 percent of threatened or attempted violence and 17.4 percent of all assaults.

Hate Crimes

Among serious hate crimes committed between 1997 and 1999, about 11 percent were committed by white women, including 10 percent of violent hate crimes and 15 percent of property crimes. (See Table 10.3.) Black females committed about 5 percent of all serious hate crimes, 6 percent of violent hate crimes, and 2 percent of property crimes. Among racially motivated hate crimes, about 11 percent were committed by white females and 6 percent by African American females.

Murder

According to the FBI, of the 14,112 murders committed in 1999, 1,046, or 7.4 percent, were known to have been committed by females. Most murders were committed by females between the ages of 17 and 44. In 1999 females under age 18 committed 98 murders, and 264 murders were committed by females under age 22.

Among single-victim/single-offender murders in 1999, 497 women murdered males and 196 females murdered other women. According to the FBI, 343 of the

TABLE 10.3

Offender characteristics, by most serious offense type, 1997–99

Offender characteristic	Most serious offense		
	All offenses	Violent	Property
Total	100%	100%	100%
Age			
0-12	4%	4%	6%
13-17	29	27	40
18-24	29	29	25
25-34	17	18	12
35-44	13	13	11
45 or older	9	9	6
Gender/race			
White male	62%	60%	69%
Black male	20	21	12
Other male	2	2	1
White female	11	10	15
Black female	5	6	2
Other female	1	1	1

Note: Unit of count is known offenders (n=3,072). Offender age was missing in 19% and gender/race in 14% of data. In an additional 812 incidents the offender was listed as unknown.

SOURCE: Kevin J. Strom, "Table 8. Offender Characteristics, by Most Serious Offense Type, 1997-99," in *Hate Crimes Reported in NIBRS, 1997-99*, Bureau of Justice Statistics, Washington, DC, September 2001

murder victims were white and 328 were African American. There were 22 victims of other races. In 1999 about 3 percent of male murder victims were killed by their wives or girlfriends. There were 156 husbands killed by their wives, almost all of them in the course of an argument or brawl.

Intimate Partner Crime

In the vast majority of intimate partner crime and violence, the victim is female and the perpetrator is male. Nevertheless, a significant portion of intimate partner crime is committed by females. In July 2000 the National Institute of Justice and the Centers for Disease Control and Prevention published *Extent, Nature, and Consequences of Intimate Partner Violence*, which included findings from the National Violence Against Women survey. This survey of 8,000 women and 8,000 men found that about 2.9 million physical assaults were committed against men annually by an intimate partner—a current or former spouse, cohabiting partner, boyfriend, or girlfriend. Furthermore, 0.6 percent of men had been stalked by a current or former intimate in their lifetime, and 0.2 percent had been stalked in the previous 12 months. However, the survey found that men living with male intimate partners experienced more intimate partner violence than men living with female partners. Among men living with a male partner, 15.4 percent had been raped, physically assaulted, or stalked by a male cohabitant. In contrast, only 7.7 percent of men living with women had been vic-

timized by a woman intimate partner. The survey also found that 11.4 percent of women cohabiting with another woman had been victimized by a woman intimate partner at some point in their lives.

WOMEN IN PRISON

The first female prison in the United States was Mount Pleasant Prison in New York, established in the 1830s. However before the end of the century men were being imprisoned there to alleviate overcrowding at Sing Sing Prison. Until the 1930s, when more gender-segregated prisons were built, most female arrests were for prostitution, public drunkenness, vagrancy, and petty theft. However, over the past 70 years, women have been committing a much greater range of crimes.

As of June 30, 2000, there were 156,200 female inmates in state and federal prisons and local jails, for a rate of 110 per 100,000 female residents. (See Table 10.4.) Non-Hispanic black women (380 per 100,000) were three times more likely than Hispanic women (117 per 100,000) and six times more likely than white women (63 per 100,000) to be incarcerated. These racial disparities held across all age groups. The highest rate of incarceration was among non-Hispanic black females between the ages of 30 and 34 (1,409 per 100,000). This rate was almost as high as the highest rate among white males (1,861 per 100,000). Among each race/ethnicity, the number of female inmates increased steadily with age until ages 30 to 34 and then steadily declined.

State and Federal Prisoners

According to the BJS Bulletin, *Prisoners in 2000* (August 2001), the number of females incarcerated in state and federal prisons increased 1.2 percent in 2000 to 91,612, compared to 1,290,280 men. Of these women prisoners, 83,668 had sentences of more than one year, up 1.5 percent from 1999. Between 1990 and 2000 the number of female state and federal prisoners increased by an average of 7.6 percent annually, compared to an average annual increase of 5.7 percent for men. At the end of 2000, women accounted for 6.6 percent of all state and federal prisoners, up from 5.7 percent in 1990.

Between December 31, 1990, and June 30, 2000, the female prison population more than doubled, increasing 110.3 percent. (See Table 10.5.) Over the same period the male prison population increased 77.1 percent. As of June 30, 2000, there were 92,688 women prisoners in state and federal correctional facilities, a 3.6 percent increase over July 1, 1999. The incarceration rate (the number of prisoners with sentences of more than one year per 100,000 U.S. residents) increased from 32 to 66 women between 1990 and 2000 and from 572 to 961 men. The numbers of both male and female prisoners who were under age 18

TABLE 10.4

Number of inmates in state or federal prisons and local jails, by gender, race, Hispanic origin, and age, 2000

	Number of inmates in state or federal prisons or local jails							
	Male				Female			
Age	Total[1]	White[2]	Black[2]	Hispanic	Total[1]	White[2]	Black[2]	Hispanic
Total	1,775,700	663,700	791,600	290,900	156,200	63,700	69,500	19,500
18-19	81,300	26,200	36,700	15,600	3,900	1,900	1,400	500
20-24	310,100	99,500	142,800	60,000	19,600	8,300	7,400	3,500
25-29	329,900	104,900	160,200	58,400	30,000	11,200	13,500	4,000
30-34	334,000	125,000	149,700	54,800	39,100	15,000	19,400	4,100
35-39	294,100	116,200	136,100	39,600	30,700	12,500	14,400	3,300
40-44	198,300	81,300	83,400	31,200	17,000	7,200	7,500	1,900
45-54	164,500	77,900	62,200	22,200	12,100	5,600	4,500	1,700
55 or older	51,300	29,500	13,300	7,800	2,700	1,800	800	200

Note: Estimates were rounded to the nearest 100.

[1] Includes American Indians, Alaska Natives, Asians, Native Hawaiians, and other Pacific Islanders.
[2] Excludes Hispanics.

SOURCE: Allen J. Beck and Jennifer C. Karberg, "Table 12. Number of inmates in State or Federal prisons and local jails, by gender, race, Hispanic origin, and age, June 30, 2000," in *Prison and Jail Inmates at Midyear 2000*, Bureau of Justice Statistics, Washington, DC, March 2001

TABLE 10.5

Prisoners under the jurisdiction of state or federal correctional authorities, by gender, 1990, 1999, and 2000

	Men	Women
All inmates		
6/30/00	1,292,804	92,688
6/30/99	1,265,275	89,507
12/31/90	729,840	44,065
Percent change		
1999-2000	2.2%	3.6%
Average annual,		
1990-2000	6.2%	8.1%
Sentenced to more than 1 year		
6/30/00	1,239,317	85,108
12/31/90	699,416	40,564
Incarceration rate*		
6/30/00	961	66
12/31/90	572	32

*The total number of prisoners with a sentence of more than 1 year per 100,000 U.S. residents.

SOURCE: Allen J. Beck and Jennifer C. Karberg, "Table 4. Prisoners under the jurisdiction of State or Federal correctional authorities, by gender, 1990, 1999, and 2000," in *Prison and Jail Inmates at Midyear 2000*, Bureau of Justice Statistics, Washington, DC, March 2001

TABLE 10.6

Number of inmates under age 18 held in state and federal prisons, by gender, 1990, 1995, and 1998–2000

	Inmates under age 18		
Year	Total	Male	Female
1990*	3,600	—	—
1995*	5,309	—	—
1998	4,863	4,668	195
1999	4,194	4,027	167
2000	3,915	3,741	174

Note: Federal prisons held 39 inmates under age 18 in 1990 but none in 1995, 1998, 1999, and 2000.

—Not available.

*Data for 1990 and 1995 were based on Census of State and Federal Correctional Facilities.

SOURCE: Allen J. Beck and Jennifer C. Karberg, "Table 6. Number of inmates under age 18 held in State and Federal prisons, by gender, June 30, 1990, 1995, and 1998-2000," in *Prison and Jail Inmates at Midyear 2000*, Bureau of Justice Statistics, Washington, DC, March 2001

declined between 1990 and 2000. In 1998 there were 195 female prisoners under 18, compared to 174 in 2000. (See Table 10.6.)

At the end of 2000 there were 59 female inmates with sentences of more than one year per 100,000 women residents, up from 32 per 100,000 in 1990. White women accounted for 41.2 percent of these prisoners, 44.7 percent were African American, and 12 percent were Hispanic. Thus, the rates of sentenced female state and federal prisoners in 2000 were 34 per 100,000 white females, 205

per 100,000 African American females, and 60 per 100,000 Hispanic females.

At midyear 2000, according to the BJS, almost four out of five female inmates were in federal prisons or in California or Texas systems. Texas had 12,714 female prisoners on June 30, 2000, California had 11,432 female prisoners, and federal prisons held 10,599 women. Florida was next with 4,019 female prisoners, and North Dakota had the lowest number with 67 female prisoners.

STATE PRISONERS. According to the BJS, of the 74,400 female sentenced prisoners under state jurisdiction in 1999, 29.0 percent had committed violent offenses: 6,600 murders and nonnegligent manslaughters, 5,400

TABLE 10.7

Sentenced prisoners under state jurisdiction, by offense and gender, 1990–99

	Total		Male		Female	
	Increase, 1990-99	Percent of total	Increase, 1990-99	Percent of total	Increase, 1990-99	Percent of total
Total	500,200	100%	462,600	100%	37,700	100%
Violent	254,100	51	243,600	53	10,500	28
Property	70,000	14	62,100	13	7,900	21
Drug	101,500	20	88,200	19	13,300	35
Public-order	74,800	15	68,900	15	5,900	16

SOURCE: Allen J. Beck and Paige M. Harrison, "Table 17. Partitioning the Total Growth of Sentenced Prisoners under State Jurisdiction, by Offense and Gender, 1990-99," in *Prisoners in 2000*, Bureau of Justice Statistics, Washington, DC, August 2001

assaults, 5,200 robberies, 1,800 manslaughters, 800 sexual assaults, and 300 rapes. Of the 26.3 percent of sentenced females in state prisons who had committed property offenses, 7,600 had committed fraud, 6,100 had committed larceny, 3,600 were guilty of burglary, and 700 had committed motor vehicle theft. Among female state prisoners in 1999, 33.7 percent had been convicted of drug offenses. An additional 10.5 percent had been convicted of public-order offenses such as weapons charges, drunk driving, court offenses, commercialized vice, morals and decency charges, and liquor law violations.

The number of female inmates under state jurisdiction increased by 37,700 women between 1990 and 1999. (See Table 10.7.) The number of male inmates increased by 462,600. Violent offenders accounted for 28 percent of the increase in female inmates and 53 percent of the increase in male inmates. Drug offenses accounted for 35 percent of the increase in female inmates but only 19 percent of the increase in male inmates. Property crimes accounted for 21 percent of the increase in female inmates. The remainder of the increase was the result of public-order offenses.

According to *Prisoners in 2000*, the state of Oklahoma had the highest female incarceration rate, with 138 sentenced female inmates per 100,000 female state residents. Mississippi had the second highest rate at 105, followed by Texas and Louisiana at 100 each. Massachusetts, with 7 sentenced female inmates per 100,000 female residents, had the lowest incarceration rate. Between 1990 and 2000, 17 states had at least a 10 percent average annual increase in female prisoners. Texas had the highest average annual increase at 18.7 percent, followed by Idaho with an average annual increase of 15.2 percent.

Women in Jails

LOCAL JAILS. According to the BJS, on June 30, 2000, there were 70,414 women inmates of local jails, compared to 37,198 at midyear 1990. Nearly 1 out of every 181 adult men and 1 out of every 1,509 adult women were held in local jails in 2000. In the 12-month period ending June 30, 2000, the female inmate population of local jails increased 4.3 percent, compared to a 2.7 percent increase in the number of male inmates. Women made up 11.4 percent of the local jail population in 2000, compared to 9.2 percent in 1990 and 6.0 percent in 1983. Between 1990 and 2000 the number of female inmates in local jails increased an average of 6.6 percent annually, compared to an annual increase in male inmates of about 4 percent. In 2000, 54.5 percent of female jail inmates had not been convicted of a crime, the same percentage as in 1983.

According to the BJS's 1999 *Census of Jails* (August 2001), the average daily adult female jail population in 1999 was 67,487, compared to 15,652 in 1983. In 1999, 1,671 female jail inmates were HIV positive, compared to 7,022 male inmates. Among these women, 31.9 percent had confirmed cases of AIDS and 19.4 percent were symptomatic. Over the 12-month period ending June 30, 1999, 85 female jail inmates died: 11.8 percent of AIDS, 48.2 percent of other natural causes, and 28.2 percent of suicide. One female inmate was a victim of homicide.

PRIVATE JAILS. The number of privately operated jails increased during the 1990s. According to the 1999 *Census of Jails*, of the 47 privately operated facilities, 30 held both men and women, 15 held only men, and 2 held only women. Privately operated jails held a total of 1,575 female inmates, compared to 12,239 male inmates, at midyear 1999.

FEDERAL JAILS. The Federal Bureau of Prisons maintains a small number of detention facilities that function as jails. According to the *Census of Jails*, in 1999 female inmates accounted for 6.7 percent of the population of the 11 federal jails.

Mothers in Prison

As of 1998 approximately 7 out of 10 women under correctional supervision had children under the age of 18, although of the 1.3 million affected children, 82.1 percent

TABLE 10.8

Children of women under correctional supervision, 1998

	Estimated number		
	Women offenders	Women offenders with minor children	Minor children
Probation	721,400	516,200	1,067,200
Jail	63,800	44,700	105,300
State prisons	75,200	49,200	117,100
Federal prisons	9,200	5,400	11,200
Total	**869,600**	**615,500**	**1,300,800**

Note: Only children under age 18 are counted.

SOURCE: Lawrence A. Greenfeld and Tracy L. Snell, "Children of women under correctional supervision, 1998," in *Women Offenders*, Bureau of Justice Statistics, Washington, DC, 1999

TABLE 10.9

Women under sentence of death, as of December 31, 1999

State	Women under sentence of death, 12/31/99		
	Total*	White	Black
Total	50	29	19
California	11	7	2
Texas	9	6	3
Florida	4	2	2
North Carolina	4	3	1
Oklahoma	3	2	1
Pennsylvania	3	0	3
Illinois	3	0	3
Tennessee	2	2	0
Alabama	2	1	1
Missouri	1	1	0
Arkansas	1	1	0
Georgia	1	1	0
Mississippi	1	1	0
Arizona	1	1	0
Idaho	1	1	0
Indiana	1	0	1
Louisiana	1	0	1
Nevada	1	0	1

*Total includes other races.

SOURCE: Tracy L. Snell, "Women under sentence of death, 12/31/99," in *Capital Punishment 1999*, Bureau of Justice Statistics, Washington, DC, December 2000

had mothers who were on probation. (See Table 10.8.) Approximately 58.9 percent of women in federal prisons had minor children, as did 65.4 percent of women in state prisons and 70.1 percent of women in local jails.

Some states have mother-infant programs within their prison systems to help prisoners care for their infants. The federal system has the Mothers and Infants Together (MINT) program to help pregnant women and mothers with infants. However, most mothers in prison rely on fathers or other family members to care for their children. Additionally, many children of women prisoners are in foster care.

Probation and Parole

According to the BJS, women accounted for about 22 percent of all adult probationers in 2000, up from 18 percent in 1990. Women accounted for 12 percent of all parolees in 2000, up from 8 percent in 1990.

SENTENCES OF DEATH

Women on Death Row

According to the BJS Bulletin *Capital Punishment 1999* (December 2000), 3,527 prisoners were under sentence of death in the federal prison system and in 37 states. During 1999 three women were sentenced to death and two were removed from death row, leaving a total of 50 women on death row in 18 states at the end of the year. These women included 29 whites, 19 blacks, and 2 women of other races. (See Table 10.9.) Four of the women on death row were Hispanics. At the end of 1999 California had 11 women on death row (7 whites and 2 blacks) and Texas had 9 women (6 whites and 3 blacks). Women spent an average of 6.6 years in prison following their death sentence, compared to 7.7 years for men.

According to a report by Victor L. Streib, professor of law at Ohio Northern University (*Death Penalty for Female*

Offenders January 1, 1973, to December 31, 2000), women account for only 1.7 percent of death penalties at the trial level and only 1.4 percent of death row inmates. Four women were sentenced to death in 1999 and 2000 for killing their husbands, and between 1998 and 2000 four women were sentenced to death for killing their children. As of year-end 2000, North Carolina had sentenced the most women to death (16), followed by Florida (15), California (14), and Texas (13). California had 12 women on death row, Texas had 7, and North Carolina had 6.

Executions

According to Professor Streib, 561 women were executed in the United States between 1632 and 2000. According to Amnesty International, seven women were executed between the reinstatement of the death penalty in 1977 and November 15, 2001, out of a total of 744 executions. The first woman to be executed in the modern era was Velma Barfield, put to death by the state of North Carolina in 1984. She had been convicted of poisoning her boyfriend with arsenic. During her trial it came out that she had also poisoned her mother and two other people who were in her care. While in prison she also admitted to causing the deaths of her first and second husbands.

Two women were executed in 1998. Karla Faye Tucker was executed in Texas for murdering two people with a pickax while on drugs. Judias Beunoano was the first female to be executed in Florida in 150 years. Known as the "Black Widow," she had poisoned her husband with arsenic, drowned her paralyzed son, and tried to blow up her fiancé.

In February 2000 Betty Lou Beets was put to death in Texas after being found guilty of murdering her fifth husband. On May 2, 2000, a mentally ill woman, Christina Riggs, was executed in Arkansas by lethal injection.

On January 11, 2001, Wanda Jean Allen was executed by lethal injection in Oklahoma. She was the first African American female to be executed in the United States since 1954. She had been convicted of murdering a childhood friend and later killing her lesbian lover. It has been suggested that she was mentally retarded. On May 1, 2001, Marilyn Plantz was executed by lethal injection in Oklahoma for the 1988 murder of her husband.

CHAPTER 11

WOMEN AND THEIR HEALTH

In 1999 the life expectancy at birth was 79.8 years for American females and 74.1 years for males. (See Table 1.3.) Females had a longer life expectancy than males within each racial and ethnic group. Asian women had the longest life expectancy (86.5 years) and African American women had the shortest (75.1 years). By the year 2100 the U.S. Census Bureau projects that female life expectancy at birth will be between 89.3 and 95.2 years.

Women are generally healthier than men. Women tend to take better care of themselves and smoke and drink less than men. Women are no longer likely to die from the complications of childbirth, as they so often did in the past. However, because more women than men survive into old age, they are more likely to suffer from chronic illnesses. Furthermore, because more women than men live in poverty, they may have less access to preventative medicine and advanced medical treatments.

The 2000 National Health Interview Survey (NHIS), conducted by the National Center for Health Statistics (NCHS) of the Centers for Disease Control and Prevention (CDC), found that males' assessment of their health and that of family members living in the same household was somewhat better than females' assessment of their health. (See Figure 11.1.) Among females, 35.1 percent assessed their health as excellent, 31.4 percent assessed their health as very good, and 23.5 percent assessed it as good, as compared to 38.9, 31.0, and 22.0 for males, respectively. Among females 7.2 percent assessed their health as fair and 2.3 percent as poor, compared to 6.0 and 2.1 percent for males, respectively. Among both males and females under age 18, 82.2 percent assessed their health as excellent, compared to 68.5 percent of those aged 18 to 64 and 37.6 percent of those aged 65 and older. Within each age group, similar percentages of men and women assessed their health as excellent or very good.

The health-care needs and the medical problems of women are often very different from those of men. From

FIGURE 11.1

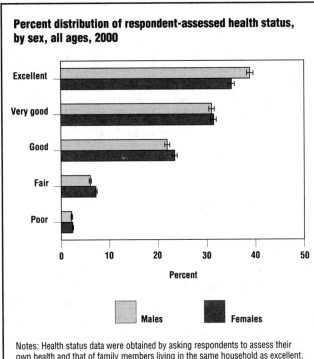

Percent distribution of respondent-assessed health status, by sex, all ages, 2000

Notes: Health status data were obtained by asking respondents to assess their own health and that of family members living in the same household as excellent, very good, good, fair, or poor. The analysis excluded 420 people with unknown health status. Brackets indicate 95% confidence intervals.

SOURCE: "Figure 11.2. Percent Distribution of Respondent-Assessed Health Status, by Sex: All Ages, United States, 2000," in *National Health Interview Survey*, [Online] http://www.cdc.gov/nchs/data/nhis/measure11.pdf [accessed October 8 , 2001]

the onset of menarche (the first menstrual period), usually between the ages of about 9 and 13, for the rest of their lives women's health issues may be focused on their reproductive systems. They may experience menstrual irregularities, amenorrhea (lack of menstruation), cramping and other side effects of menstruation, premenstrual syndrome (PMS), or other difficulties associated with their menstrual cycles. Women must deal with contraception,

FIGURE 11.2

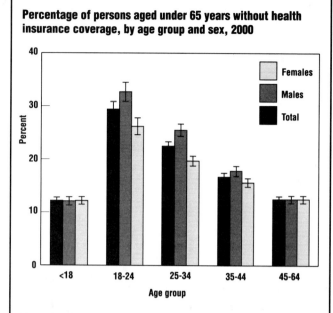

Percentage of persons aged under 65 years without health insurance coverage, by age group and sex, 2000

Notes: A person was defined as uninsured if he or she did not have any private health insurance, Medicaid, state-sponsored or other government-sponsored health plan, Medicare or military plan at the time of the interview. A person was also defined as uninsured if he or she had only Indian Health Service coverage, or had only a private plan that paid for one type of service such as accidents or dental care. The analysis excluded 1,153 people with unknown health insurance status. The data on health insurance status were electronically cleaned or edited using strategies of logical checking and keyword searching. The resulting estimates of persons not having health insurance coverage are generally 0.1% lower than those based on the final data files. Brackets indicate 95% confidence intervals (CI).

SOURCE: "Figure 1.2. Percentage of Persons Aged Under 65 Years Without Health Insurance Coverage, by Age Group and Sex: United States, 2000," in *National Health Interview Survey*, [Online] http://www.cdc.gov/nchs/data/nhis/measure01.pdf [accessed October 8 , 2001]

FIGURE 11.3

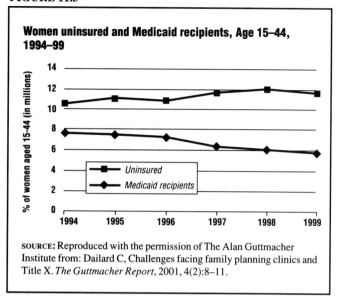

Women uninsured and Medicaid recipients, Age 15–44, 1994–99

SOURCE: Reproduced with the permission of The Alan Guttmacher Institute from: Dailard C, Challenges facing family planning clinics and Title X. *The Guttmacher Report*, 2001, 4(2):8–11.

fertility, abortion, pregnancy, and childbearing, as well as the possibility of postpartum depression and other complications. In their 40s or 50s women enter menopause, experiencing multiple symptoms and making decisions about possible treatments such as estrogen supplementation. Many women are affected by diseases or abnormalities of the reproductive system, and hundreds of thousands of women have hysterectomies (removal of the uterus) every year.

WOMEN'S ACCESS TO HEALTH CARE

Sources of Health Care

The 2000 NHIS found that women were more likely than men to have a regular source of medical care (89.7 percent versus 79.8 percent). Among both genders, individuals aged 18 to 24 were less likely than other age groups to have a regular source of health care. Hispanics were less likely than non-Hispanic whites and African Americans to have a regular source.

According to the NCHS compendium *Health. United States. 2001*, in 1998–99, 11.7 percent of women aged 18

to 64 had no usual source of health care, compared to 23.5 percent of men. In 1993–94, 13.9 percent of women had no usual source of health care. Women also made far more health-care visits than men. Only 12 percent of women made no visits in 1999, compared to 23.1 percent of men, and 15.9 percent of women made 10 or more visits. Women were somewhat more likely than men to have visited emergency departments in 1999: 18.2 percent of women had one or more visits and 6 percent had two or more. Women also had more hospitalizations than men in 1999: 116.7 discharges per 1,000 population compared to 77.9 for men.

Women were about as likely as men to have activity limitations due to a chronic condition (12.2 percent of women in 1999). According to the NCHS, in 1999, 1,091,700 women aged 65 and over were nursing home residents, up from 695,800 in 1973–74, for an age-adjusted rate of 49.8 per 1,000 population. This compared to 377,800 males over 64 who were nursing home residents, for an age-adjusted rate of 30.6 per 1,000. Furthermore, according to the Census Bureau, in 1998, 66.4 percent of all home health-care patients were female, as were 57.3 percent of those in hospice care.

Health Insurance

According to *Health. United States. 2001*, in 1999, 15 percent of women under 65 had no health-care coverage, compared to 13.6 percent in 1984. Males and females under 18 and over 44 were equally likely to be without health insurance. (See Figure 11.2.) In 2000, 12.2 percent of females under 18, 26.2 percent of those between 18 and 24, and 19.7 percent of those between 25 and 34 were without health insurance, as were 15.6 percent of women between 35 and 44 and 12.5 percent of those between 45 and 64.

According to the Alan Guttmacher Institute, a nonprofit organization devoted to sexual and reproductive health research, as the number of Medicaid recipients fell because of welfare reform, the number of women without health insurance rose. (See Figure 11.3.) The number of women of reproductive age receiving Medicaid fell about 24 percent between 1994 and 1999. During those years the number of uninsured women of reproductive age increased 1.2 million. The institute estimates that as many as 3 in 10 women in their 20s are uninsured. These are the peak years for both childbearing and the need for contraception. Many of these women are low-wage workers who are either not offered health insurance by their employers or cannot afford it because of high copayments and deductibles.

In May 2001 the Women's Research and Education Institute (WREI) published a study based on *The Commonwealth Fund 1999 Health Care Survey of Adults Ages 50–70*. The study, *Midlife Women: Insurance Coverage and Access*, found that although women between the ages of 50 and 64 were more likely than younger women to have health insurance, about 16 percent of women aged 50 to 64, as well as 6 percent of women aged 65 to 70, were uninsured, compared to 14 percent and 3 percent of men in those age groups, respectively. Furthermore, the study found that 23 percent of women aged 50 to 64 and 21 percent of women aged 65 to 70 had been uninsured at some point since age 50, compared to 20 percent and 17 percent of men, respectively. During their adult lives, 17 percent of women aged 50 to 64 and 16 percent of women aged 65 to 70 had never, rarely, or only sometimes had health insurance, compared to only 13 percent and 10 percent of men in those respective age groups. Women between 50 and 64 with annual incomes of $35,000 or less were twice as likely as women with higher incomes to be uninsured or to have had periods without insurance. Women between the ages of 50 and 70 were slightly more likely than men in that age group to have prescription drug coverage; however, fewer women with Medicare coverage had prescription drug coverage as compared with insured women between the ages of 50 and 64.

According to *Health. United States. 2001*, approximately equal percentages of men and women had private health insurance: 72.8 percent of women in 1999, down from 76.5 percent in 1984. In 1999, 66.9 percent of women had private insurance through the workplace, compared to 68.4 percent in 1984. Among women under 65, 10.4 percent had Medicaid coverage in 1999, compared to 7.7 percent of men. Among women aged 65 and over, 63.8 percent had private insurance in 1999, compared to 75.4 percent in 1989. In 1999, 26.3 percent of women 65 and over had only Medicare, compared to 16.2 percent in 1989.

Barriers to Obtaining Health Care

According to the 2000 NHIS, more women than men in all age groups had failed to obtain needed medical care

FIGURE 11.4

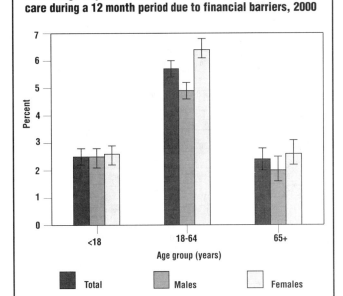

Percentage of persons who failed to obtain needed medical care during a 12 month period due to financial barriers, 2000

Notes: The analysis excluded 403 people with unknown success in obtaining needed medical care. Brackets indicate 95% confidence intervals (CI).

SOURCE: "Figure 3.2. Percentage of Persons Who Failed to Obtain Needed Medical Care during the Past 12 Months due to Financial Barriers, by Sex and Age Group: All Ages, United States, 2000," in *National Health Interview Survey*, [Online] http://www.cdc.gov/nchs/data/nhis/measure03.pdf [accessed October 8, 2001]

over the previous 12 months because of financial barriers. (See Figure 11.4.) In 2000 the cost of medical care prevented 2.6 percent of females under 18, 6.4 percent of those aged 18 to 64, and 2.6 percent of females over age 64 from obtaining needed medical care.

The WREI report found a strong correlation between lack of insurance and poor access to health care. Overall, about 25 percent of women compared to 19 percent of men aged 50 to 64 had problems with access to medical care because of cost. Even among insured women, gaps in coverage affected many women's access to health care. Among women aged 50 to 64, 20 percent had trouble paying their medical bills, compared to 15 percent of men in that age group, and 10 percent of women had had to significantly change their way of life to pay their medical bills. Even after women turned 65 and were eligible for Medicare, they continued to have problems. Among women aged 65 to 70, 17 percent had trouble paying medical bills, compared to 11 percent of men that age. Women were more likely than men to have not seen a doctor for a medical problem, to have had problems seeing a specialist, to have skipped a treatment or test, or to have failed to have a prescription filled.

According to a survey by the American Social Health Association released on October 10, 2001, about 55

FIGURE 11.5

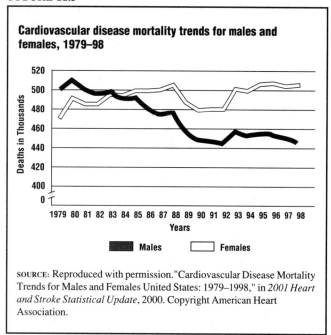

Cardiovascular disease mortality trends for males and females, 1979–98

SOURCE: Reproduced with permission."Cardiovascular Disease Mortality Trends for Males and Females United States: 1979–1998," in *2001 Heart and Stroke Statistical Update*, 2000. Copyright American Heart Association.

percent of women reported that they avoided routine gynecologic health care. About 24 percent of the women cited cost as a major reason. In addition, 20 percent of the women cited language and cultural barriers, 20 percent cited discomfort with physicians, 14 percent cited a fear of diagnosis, and 10 percent cited embarrassment.

LEADING CAUSES OF DEATH AMONG WOMEN

According to *Health. United States. 2001*, the age-adjusted death rate for females in 1999 was 743.7 per 100,000 people, compared to a male death rate of 1,061.8. Age-adjusted means that the rate is determined for a population with a standard age distribution, so that the rates for different years can be compared, even though the age distribution of the population may have changed. Thus, although the crude death rate may increase simply because the population has aged, the age-adjusted death rate may not have increased. In 1950 the female death rate from all causes was 1,236.0 per 100,000. Of female deaths in 1999, 95.8 percent were from natural causes, compared to 93.8 percent of male deaths. The remaining 4.2 percent of female deaths were from external causes such as unintentional injuries, motor-vehicle-related injuries, suicides, and homicides. Natural causes accounted for 95.3 percent of all female deaths in 1980.

Cardiovascular Disease

Cardiovascular disease (CVD) is the leading cause of death among American males and females of all races/ethnicities. CVD includes both diseases of the heart and cerebrovascular diseases such as stroke. According to the American Heart Association (AHA) publication, *2001*

Heart and Stroke Statistical Update, 503,927 women and 445,692 men died of some form of CVD in 1998. CVD accounted for 43 percent of white female deaths, 41.4 percent of African American female deaths, 35.7 percent of Asian/Pacific Islander female deaths, 28.1 percent of Native American female deaths, and 34.3 percent of Hispanic female deaths. Between 1979 and 1998 CVD mortality declined among men and rose among women. (See Figure 11.5.)

According to the AHA, women first experience cardiovascular events about 10 years later than men; however, this gender gap decreases with age as women's estrogen levels drop at menopause. Among non-Hispanic whites, the age-adjusted prevalence of CVD in women in 2000 was estimated to be 23.8 percent, compared to 30 percent for men; it was 39.6 percent for non-Hispanic African American women, very close to the 40.5 percent for non-Hispanic African American men; among Mexican Americans the prevalence of CVD was 26.6 percent for women and 28.8 percent for men. The AHA attributes these racial/ethnic differences to the early detection and superior treatment available to white women as compared with other groups.

Despite the similar numbers of men and women with CVD, men were much more likely than women to have cardiovascular operations requiring hospitalizations in 1998. (See Table 11.1.) Until recently CVD was believed to be more prevalent and more serious in men than in women. The Framingham Study, one of the most comprehensive and influential medical studies ever carried out, did not include older women. Since premenopausal women's production of estrogen appears to help protect them from CVD, the Framingham Study led researchers to believe that CVD was primarily a male problem.

Smoking, a diet high in fats, and lack of exercise are all risk factors for developing CVD. The use of oral contraceptives, combined with smoking, increases the risk factor for women.

DISEASES OF THE HEART. Heart disease was the leading cause of death among both American men and women in 1999, killing 373,483 women, 30.7 percent of all female deaths. (See Table 11.2.) Diseases of the heart were the leading cause of death among men and among women of all races/ethnicities except Asian/Pacific Islander females. Diseases of the heart were also the leading cause of death among women in 1980, accounting for 38.9 percent of all female deaths. The death rate in 1999 from heart disease was 220.8 per 100,000 females, compared to 327.9 per 100,000 males. In 1950 the female death rate from heart disease was 484.7 per 100,000.

According to the AHA, coronary heart disease (CHD) is the leading cause of death among both male and female Americans and accounts for more than one-half of all CVD

TABLE 11.1

Estimated inpatient cardiovascular operations, procedures, and patient data by sex, age, and region, 1998

(In thousands)

Operations/Procedures/Patients (ICD/9 Code		Sex			Age				Region†			
		Total	Male	Female	<15	15–44	45–64	65+	Northeast	Midwest	South	West
Angioplasty (36.0)	Procedures	926	594	332	—	60	410	456	174	246	327	176
PTCA(36.01, 36.02, 36.05) (a)	Procedures	539	346	193	—	27	235	269	95	144	185	113
	Patients	528	339	189	—	34	231	264	97	137	182	112
Stenting (36.06)	Procedures	376	241	135	—	25	168	182	75	102	137	62
Cardiac Revascularization (Bypass) (36.1–36.3) (b)	Procedures	553	396	158	—	14	234	304	126	136	200	91
	Patients	336	236	99	—	9	137	190	74	81	123	57
Diagnostic Cardiac Catheterizations (37.2) (a)	Procedures	1,291	770	522	16	107	530	638	256	294	548	193
Endarterectomy (38.12)	Procedures	121	69	52	—	—	28	93	24	29	49	20
Implantable Defibrillators (37.94–.99)	Procedures	26	19	7	—	—	9	13	6	8	7	—
Open-Heart Surgery (c)	Procedures	734	492	243	28	34	284	382	184	170	243	123
Pacemakers (37.8) (d)	Procedures	170	82	88	—	—	21	145	41	33	67	29
Valves (35.1, 35.2, 35.99)	Procedures	89	48	36	—	6	24	45	23	16	23	16
Total Vascular and Cardiac Surgery and Procedures (35–39)**		**5,791**	**3,364**	**2,427**	**171**	**547**	**2,033**	**3,040**	**1,276**	**1,316**	**2,154**	**1,045**

* Breakdowns are not available for some procedures, so entries for some categories don't add to totals. These data include codes where the estimated number of procedures is fewer than 5,000. Categories of such small numbers are considered unreliable by CDC/NCHS, and in some cases may have been omitted.

† Regions: Northeast — Connecticut, Maine, Massachusetts, New Hampshire, New Jersey, New York, Pennsylvania, Rhode Island, Vermont
Midwest — Illinois, Indiana, Iowa, Kansas, Michigan, Minnesota, Missouri, Nebraska, North Dakota, Ohio, South Dakota, Wisconsin
South — Alabama, Arkansas, Delaware, District of Columbia, Florida, Georgia, Kentucky, Louisiana, Maryland, Mississippi, North Carolina, Oklahoma, South Carolina, Tennessee, Texas, Virginia, West Virginia
West — Alaska, Arizona, California, Colorado, Hawaii, Idaho, Montana, Nevada, New Mexico, Oregon, Utah, Washington, Wyoming

(a) — Does not include procedures in the outpatient or other nonhospitalized setting; thus, excludes some cardiac catheterizations and PTCAs.
(b) — Some patients have both internal mammary artery grafts and saphenous vein grafts. These numbers represent a combination of code and vessel data. It's impossible from this (mixed) data to determine the average number of vessels per patient.
(c) — Includes valves, bypass and 92,000 "other" open-heart procedures. (Codes 35 [less 35.1–35.2, 35.4, 35.96, 35.99]; 36 [less 36.0–36.1]; 37.1, 37.3–37.5.)
(d) — There are additional insertions, revisions and replacements of pacemaker leads, including those associated with temporary (external) pacemakers.

** Totals include procedures not shown here.

SOURCE: Reproduced with permission. "Estimated* Inpatient Cardiovascular Operations, Procedures and Patient Data by Sex, Age and Region," in *2001 Heart and Stroke Statistical Update*, 2000. Copyright American Heart Association.

events in men and women under age 75. The lifetime risk of developing CHD after age 40 is 32 percent for women and 49 percent for men. Women of the same age are two to three times more likely to have CHD if they are post-menopausal. In 1998 CHD caused 226,467 female deaths, 49.2 percent of all deaths from CHD. The age-adjusted death rate in 1998 from CHD was 135 per 100,000 for white females and 154.7 for African American females.

According to the AHA, because women experience heart attacks at older ages than men, they are more likely to die within a few weeks. Within one year of their first recognized heart attack, about 38 percent of women and 25 percent of men die. Within six years of their first heart attack, 35 percent of women and 18 percent of men will have a second heart attack. Women are more than twice as likely as men to be disabled by heart failure. The age-adjusted death rate in 1998 for stroke was 56.6 per 100,000 white females and 75.3 per 100,000 African American females.

CEREBROVASCULAR DISEASES. In 1999 cerebrovascular diseases, including stroke, atherosclerosis, and high-blood pressure (hypertension), were the third leading cause of death among males and females of all races/ethnicities except Native American Indian/Alaska Natives. Among the latter they were the fifth leading cause of death. (See Table 11.2.) Cerebrovascular diseases were also the third leading cause of death among women in 1980. They accounted for 8.5 percent of all female deaths in 1999, compared to 11 percent in 1980. In 1999 the death rate from cerebrovascular diseases was 60.5 per 100,000 females and 62.4 per 100,000 males, compared to 175.8 females and 186.4 males per 100,000 in 1950.

According to the AHA, up to age 55 high blood pressure is more prevalent among men. Over age 55, high blood pressure is more prevalent among women. High blood pressure is two to three times more prevalent among women taking oral contraceptives, particularly older and obese women. Among those aged 20 and over, the age-adjusted prevalence of high blood pressure is 36.6 percent for non-Hispanic African American women and 20.5 percent for non-Hispanic white women.

TABLE 11.2

Leading causes of death and numbers of deaths in females, according to race and Hispanic origin, 1980 and 1999

[Data are based on the National Vital Statistics System]

Sex, race, Hispanic origin, and rank order	1980		Preliminary 1999†	
	Cause of death	Deaths	Cause of death	Deaths
White female				
	All causes	804,729	All causes	1,056,144
1	Diseases of heart	318,668	Diseases of heart	327,463
2	Malignant neoplasms	169,974	Malignant neoplasms	229,837
3	Cerebrovascular diseases	88,639	Cerebrovascular diseases	89,948
4	Unintentional injuries	27,159	Chronic lower respiratory diseases	57,735
5	Pneumonia and influenza	24,559	Influenza and pneumonia	32,410
6	Diabetes mellitus	16,743	Alzheimer's disease	29,268
7	Atherosclerosis	16,526	Unintentional injuries	29,215
8	Chronic obstructive pulmonary diseases	16,398	Diabetes mellitus	29,050
9	Chronic liver disease and cirrhosis	8,833	Nephritis, nephrotic syndrome and nephrosis	14,408
10	Certain conditions originating in the perinatal period	6,512	Septicemia	13,796
Black female				
	All causes	102,997	All causes	139,363
1	Diseases of heart	35,079	Diseases of heart	40,976
2	Malignant neoplasms	19,176	Malignant neoplasms	29,083
3	Cerebrovascular diseases	10,941	Cerebrovascular diseases	10,986
4	Unintentional injuries	3,779	Diabetes mellitus	7,167
5	Diabetes mellitus	3,534	Unintentional injuries	3,933
6	Certain conditions originating in the perinatal period	3,092	Nephritis, nephrotic syndrome and nephrosis	3,703
7	Pneumonia and influenza	2,262	Chronic lower respiratory diseases	3,407
8	Homicide	1,898	Septicemia	3,204
9	Chronic liver disease and cirrhosis	1,770	Influenza and pneumonia	3,038
10	Nephritis, nephrotic syndrome, and nephrosis	1,722	Human immunodeficiency virus (HIV) disease	2,393
American Indian or Alaska Native female				
	All causes	2,730	All causes	5,222
1	Diseases of heart	577	Diseases of heart	1,102
2	Malignant neoplasms	362	Malignant neoplasms	887
3	Unintentional injuries	344	Unintentional injuries	436
4	Chronic liver disease and cirrhosis	171	Diabetes mellitus	403
5	Cerebrovascular diseases	159	Cerebrovascular diseases	309
6	Diabetes mellitus	124	Chronic liver disease and cirrhosis	214
7	Pneumonia and influenza	109	Chronic lower respiratory diseases	209
8	Certain conditions originating in the perinatal period	92	Influenza and pneumonia	168
9	Nephritis, nephrotic syndrome, and nephrosis	56	Nephritis, nephrotic syndrome and nephrosis	115
10	Homicide	55	Septicemia	88

Cancer

Malignant neoplasms (cancers) were the second leading cause of death in 1999 among women and men of all races/ethnicities except Asian/Pacific Islander women. Among the latter, cancer was the leading cause of death. (See Table 11.2.) Cancer caused 21.7 percent of all female deaths in 1999. The age-adjusted death rates from cancer were 169.9 per 100,000 females and 251.6 males per 100,000 males in 1999, compared to 182.3 females and 208.1 males per 100,000 in 1950.

The American Cancer Society (ACS) estimated that 625,000 new cases of cancer would be diagnosed in women in 2001, compared to 643,000 newly diagnosed cases in men. (See Figure 11.6.) The ACS estimated that 267,300 women would die of cancer in 2001.

Breast cancer is the most common type of cancer in females, and prostate cancer is the most common form in males. (See Figure 11.6.) Cancer of the lung and bronchus are the second most common cancers among both men and women, followed by cancer of the colon and rectum.

BREAST CANCER. The ACS estimated that 192,200 new cases of invasive breast cancer would be diagnosed in American women in 2001, 31 percent of all newly diagnosed female cancers. (See Figure 11.6.) Women account for 99.2 percent of newly diagnosed breast cancers. During the 1980s the number of breast cancer cases increased by about 4 percent annually. In 2001 the number of cases continued to increase slightly among white women. The ACS predicted that there would be 46,400 new cases of in situ breast cancer in 2001. Removal of this cancerous tissue prevents the development of invasive breast cancer.

The ACS estimates that about one in eight American women will develop breast cancer at some point in their lives. Between the ages of 30 and 40, a woman's chance of being diagnosed with breast cancer is about one in 257; by the time she reaches age 81, a woman has a one in eight chance of being diagnosed with breast cancer.

TABLE 11.2

Leading causes of death and numbers of deaths in females, according to race and Hispanic origin, 1980 and 1999 [CONTINUED]

[Data are based on the National Vital Statistics System]

Sex, race, Hispanic origin, and rank order	1980		Preliminary 1999 †	
	Cause of death	Deaths	Cause of death	Deaths
Asian or Pacific Islander female				
	All causes	4,262	All causes	15,349
1	Diseases of heart	1,091	Malignant neoplasms	4,178
2	Malignant neoplasms	1,037	Diseases of heart	3,942
3	Cerebrovascular diseases	507	Cerebrovascular diseases	1,621
4	Unintentional injuries	254	Diabetes mellitus	625
5	Diabetes mellitus	124	Unintentional injuries	588
6	Certain conditions originating in the perinatal period	118	Chronic lower respiratory diseases	406
7	Pneumonia and influenza	115	Influenza and pneumonia	380
8	Congenital anomalies	104	Nephritis, nephrotic syndrome and nephrosis	281
9	Suicide	90	Essential (primary) hypertension and hypertensive renal disease	196
10	Homicide	60	Septicemia	195
Hispanic female				
	- - -	- - -	All causes	45,763
1	- - -	- - -	Diseases of heart	12,315
2	- - -	- - -	Malignant neoplasms	9,566
3	- - -	- - -	Cerebrovascular diseases	3,099
4	- - -	- - -	Diabetes mellitus	2,848
5	- - -	- - -	Unintentional injuries	2,070
6	- - -	- - -	Chronic lower respiratory diseases	1,311
7	- - -	- - -	Influenza and pneumonia	1,153
8	- - -	- - -	Certain conditions originating in the perinatal period	963
9	- - -	- - -	Chronic liver disease and cirrhosis	829
10	- - -	- - -	Nephritis, nephrotic syndrome and nephrosis	770

† The rank order of leading causes of death changed somewhat between 1998 and 1999, reflecting in part changes in the coding rules for selecting underlying cause of death. For example, for all persons, Influenza and pneumonia dropped from 6th to 7th, Alzheimer's disease rose from 12th to 8th, and Septicemia rose from 11th to 10th.
. . . Category not applicable.
- - - Data not available.

SOURCE: Adapted from "Table 32. Leading Causes of Death and Numbers of Deaths, according to Sex, Race, and Hispanic Origin: United States, 1980 and 1999," in *Health, United States, 2001*, National Center for Health Statistics, Hyattsville, MD, 2001

The ACS estimated that breast cancer would kill 40,200 American women in 2001, 15 percent of all female cancer deaths. The mortality from breast cancer declined significantly during the 1990s, particularly among younger white and African American women. According to the NCHS, the 1999 age-adjusted death rate from breast cancer was 27 per 100,000 women, compared to 31.9 per 100,000 in 1950. According to the AHA, the age-adjusted mortality rate for breast cancer in 1998 was 27.3 per 100,000 white females and 35.8 per 100,000 African American females.

The five-year-survival rate for breast cancer that has not yet spread is approximately 97 percent; if the cancer has spread locally, the survival rate drops to about 77 percent. If the cancer has metastasized (spread to other parts of the body), the survival rate drops to about 22 percent.

Breast cancer mortality rates declined significantly during the 1990s because of earlier detection and improved treatments. More women are examining their breasts regularly, having professional examinations, and receiving mammograms. A mammogram is a low-dose X-ray examination that can detect very small cancers. Mammography is useful for screening women for breast cancer and for diagnosing women with possible symptoms of breast cancer, such as a lump or discharge.

The percentage of women having mammograms increased steadily between 1987 and 1998, across all age groups over age 40, all race/ethnicities, poverty levels, and levels of educational attainment. (See Table 11.3.) In 1987 only 29.0 percent of women aged 40 and over had had a mammogram in the previous two years, compared to 67.0 percent in 1998. Among women aged 50 to 64, 73.7 percent had had a mammogram in 1998, compared to only 31.7 percent of women in that age group in 1987. In 1998 white women in all age groups were more likely than African American or Hispanic women to have had a mammogram, as were women who lived at or above the poverty level, compared to those below the poverty threshold. The likelihood of a woman having had a mammogram correlated with her educational attainment.

The government has acted to improve detection and treatment of breast cancer. In 1996 the Department of Health and Human Services expanded a program begun in 1992 to provide mammograms to women in all 50 states. The program is aimed at uninsured, older, and minority women, in particular. In 1998 Congress enacted legislation

FIGURE 11.6

Leading sites of new cancer cases* and deaths, 2001 estimates

Cancer Cases by Site and Sex

Male	Female
Prostate 198,100 (31%)	Breast 192,200 (31%)
Lung & bronchus 90,700 (14%)	Lung & bronchus 78,800 (13%)
Colon & rectum 67,300 (10%)	Colon & rectum 68,100 (11%)
Urinary bladder 39,200 (6%)	Uterine corpus 38,300 (6%)
Non-Hodgkin's lymphoma 31,100 (5%)	Non-Hodgkin's lymphoma 25,100 (4%)
Melanoma of the skin 29,000 (5%)	Ovary 23,400 (4%)
Oral cavity 20,200 (3%)	Melanoma of the skin 22,400 (4%)
Kidney 18,700 (3%)	Urinary bladder 15,100 (2%)
Leukemia 17,700 (3%)	Pancreas 15,000 (2%)
Pancreas 14,200 (2%)	Thyroid 14,900 (2%)
All Sites 643,000 (100%)	All Sites 625,000 (100%)

Cancer Deaths by Site and Sex

Male	Female
Lung & bronchus 90,100 (31%)	Lung & bronchus 67,300 (25%)
Prostate 31,500 (11%)	Breast 40,200 (15%)
Colon & rectum 27,700 (10%)	Colon & rectum 29,000 (11%)
Pancreas 14,100 (5%)	Pancreas 14,800 (6%)
Non-Hodgkin's lymphoma 13,800 (5%)	Ovary 13,900 (5%)
Leukemia 12,000 (4%)	Non-Hodgkin's lymphoma 12,500 (5%)
Esophagus 9,500 (3%)	Leukemia 9,500 (4%)
Liver 8,900 (3%)	Uterine corpus 6,600 (2%)
Urinary bladder 8,300 (3%)	Brain 5,900 (2%)
Kidney 7,500 (3%)	Stomach 5,400 (2%)
All Sites 286,100 (100%)	All Sites 267,300 (100%)

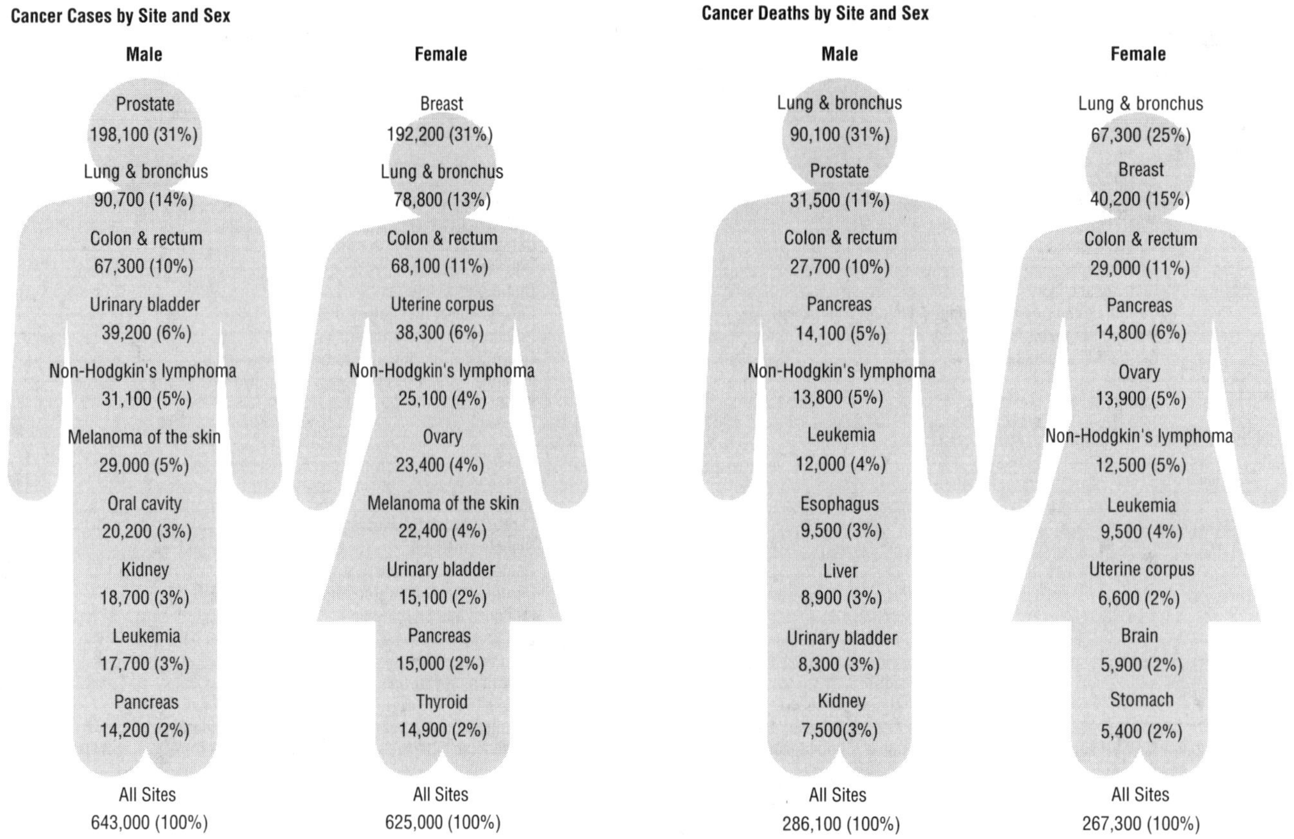

*Excludes basal and squamous cell skin cancers and in situ carcinomas except urinary bladder.

SOURCE: "Leading Sites of New Cancer Cases* and Deaths—2001 Estimates," in *Cancer Facts and Figures 2001*, American Cancer Society, Inc., Atlanta, GA, 2001

---

that required all insurers who cover mastectomies (removal of the breast and possibly adjacent tissue) to cover the cost of reconstructive breast surgery. Government agencies also have received increased appropriations for breast cancer research and detection.

According to the ACS, risk factors for breast cancer include a family history of breast cancer, early menarche and/or late menopause, childlessness or having a first child after age 30, use of oral contraceptives, lack of exercise, smoking, and alcohol consumption. Worldwide the incidence of breast cancer appears to correlate with dietary fat intake.

LUNG CANCER. Lung cancer is the leading cause of cancer deaths in women (25 percent, compared to 31 percent of male cancer deaths). (See Figure 11.6.) The ACS estimated that 67,300 women would die of cancers of the lung and bronchus in 2001 and that 78,800 women would be diagnosed with lung cancer, 13 percent of all newly diagnosed female cancers. According to the NCHS, the age-adjusted death rates for cancers of the trachea, bronchus, and lung were 40.8 per 100,000 females and 77.0 per 100,000 males in 1999, compared to 5.8 females and 24.6 males per 100,000 in 1950. According to the AHA, the age-adjusted death rate from lung cancer in 1998 was 43.2 per 100,000 white females and 42.2 per 100,000 African American females. Since 1987 more women have died each year from lung cancer than from breast cancer, which had been the leading cause of cancer deaths among women for 40 years.

The increase in lung cancers among women is primarily due to increased cigarette smoking among women in the second half of the 20th century. Smoking is the major cause of lung cancer. Other causes include exposure to industrial materials such as arsenic; some organic chemicals, radon, and asbestos, particularly among smokers; radiation; air pollution; tuberculosis; and environmental tobacco smoke (secondhand smoke).

TABLE 11.3

Use of mammography for women 40 years of age and over according to selected characteristics, selected years 1987–98

[Data are based on household interviews of a sample of the civilian noninstitutionalized population]

Characteristic	1987	1990	1991	1993	1994	1998
	Percent of women having a mammogram within the past 2 years[1]					
40 years and over, age adjusted[2,3]	29.0	51.7	54.7	59.7	61.0	67.0
40 years and over, crude[2]	28.7	51.4	54.6	59.7	60.9	66.9
Age						
40–49 years	31.9	55.1	55.6	59.9	61.3	63.4
50–64 years	31.7	56.0	60.3	65.1	66.5	73.7
65 years and over:	22.8	43.4	48.1	54.2	55.0	63.8
65–74 years	26.6	48.7	55.7	64.2	63.0	69.4
75 years and over	17.3	35.8	37.8	41.0	44.6	57.2
Race[4]						
40 years and over, crude:						
White	29.6	52.2	55.6	60.0	60.6	67.4
Black	24.0	46.4	48.0	59.1	64.3	66.0
Asian or Pacific Islander	*	46.0	45.9	55.1	55.8	60.2
Race and Hispanic origin						
40 years and over, crude:						
White, non-Hispanic	30.3	52.7	56.0	60.6	61.3	68.0
Black, non-Hispanic	23.8	46.0	47.7	59.2	64.4	66.0
Hispanic[4]	18.3	45.2	49.2	50.9	51.9	60.2
Age, race, and Hispanic origin						
40–49 years:						
White, non-Hispanic	34.3	57.0	58.1	61.6	62.0	64.4
Black, non-Hispanic	27.8	48.4	48.0	55.6	67.2	5.0
Hispanic[4]	*15.3	45.1	44.0	52.6	47.5	55.2
50–64 years:						
White, non-Hispanic	33.6	58.1	61.5	66.2	67.5	75.3
Black, non-Hispanic	26.4	48.4	52.4	65.5	63.6	71.2
Hispanic[4]	23.0	47.5	61.7	59.2	60.1	67.2
65 years and over:						
White, non-Hispanic	24.0	43.8	49.1	54.7	54.9	64.3
Black, non-Hispanic	14.1	39.7	41.6	56.3	61.0	60.6
Hispanic[4]	*	41.1	40.9	*35.7	48.0	59.0
Age and poverty status[5]						
40 years and over, crude:						
Below poverty	16.4	30.8	35.2	41.1	44.2	50.5
At or above poverty	31.3	54.1	57.5	61.8	63.4	69.3
40–49 years:						
Below poverty	23.0	32.2	33.0	36.1	43.0	44.9
At or above poverty	33.4	57.0	58.1	62.1	63.4	65.0
50–64 years:						
Below poverty	15.1	29.9	37.3	47.3	46.2	53.5
At or above poverty	34.3	58.5	63.0	66.8	68.8	76.7
65 years and over:						
Below poverty	13.6	30.8	35.2	40.4	43.9	52.3
At or above poverty	25.5	46.2	51.1	56.4	57.7	66.2

Other Leading Causes of Death in Women

Chronic lower respiratory diseases caused the deaths of 61,757 women in 1999 and a similar number of male deaths. (See Table 11.2.) They were the fourth leading cause of death among white females. The death rates from chronic lower respiratory diseases were 38.2 per 100,000 females and 58.1 per 100,000 males in 1999, compared to 14.9 females and 49.9 males per 100,000 in 1980.

Diabetes mellitus resulted in the deaths of 37,245 women in 1999, compared to 31,134 males. (See Table 11.2.) The age-adjusted death rate from diabetes was 23.3 females and 27.7 males per 100,000 in 1999, compared to 27.0 females and 18.8 males per 100,000 in 1950. According to the AHA, about 5.66 million American women had been diagnosed with diabetes and another 2.58 million had undiagnosed diabetes as of 2001. The age-adjusted prevalence of diabetes in adult women age 20 and over was 9.5 percent for non-Hispanic African Americans and 4.7 percent for non-Hispanic whites.

Alzheimer's disease killed 31,120 women in 1999, accounting for 2.8 percent of deaths among white women. (See Table 11.2.) Nephritis, nephrotic syndrome, and nephrosis (kidney disease), influenza and pneumonia, unintentional injuries, and septicemia were all among the top 10 causes of death among women in 1999. The age-adjusted death rates from influenza and pneumonia were 20.8 females and 28.0 males per 100,000 in 1999, compared to 41.9 females and 55.0 males per 100,000 in

TABLE 11.3

Use of mammography for women 40 years of age and over according to selected characteristics, selected years 1987–98 [CONTINUED]

[Data are based on household interviews of a sample of the civilian noninstitutionalized population]

Characteristic	1987	1990	1991	1993	1994	1998
Age and education[6]	\multicolumn{6}{c}{**Percent of women having a mammogram within the past 2 years[1]**}					
40 years and over, crude:						
No high school diploma or GED	17.8	36.4	40.0	46.4	48.2	54.5
High school diploma or GED	31.3	52.7	55.8	59.0	61.0	66.7
Some college or more	37.7	62.8	65.2	69.5	69.7	72.8
40–49 years of age:						
No high school diploma or GED	15.1	38.5	40.8	43.6	50.4	47.3
High school diploma or GED	32.6	53.1	52.0	56.6	55.8	59.1
Some college or more	39.2	62.3	63.7	66.1	68.7	68.3
50–64 years of age:						
No high school diploma or GED	21.2	41.0	43.6	51.4	51.6	58.8
High school diploma or GED	33.8	56.5	60.8	62.4	67.8	73.3
Some college or more	40.5	68.0	72.7	78.5	74.7	79.8
65 years of age and over:						
No high school diploma or GED	16.5	33.0	37.7	44.2	45.6	54.7
High school diploma or GED	25.9	47.5	54.0	57.4	59.1	66.8
Some college or more	32.3	56.7	57.9	64.8	64.3	71.3

* Estimates are considered unreliable. Data preceded by an asterisk have a relative standard error of 20–30 percent. Data not shown have a relative standard error greater than 30 percent.

[1] Questions concerning use of mammography differed slightly on the National Health Interview Survey across the years for which data are shown. In 1987 and 1990 women were asked to report when they had their last mammogram. In 1991 women were asked whether they had a mammogram in the past 2 years. In 1993 and 1994 women were asked whether they had a mammogram within the past year, between 1 and 2 years ago, or over 2 years ago. In 1998 women were asked whether they had a mammogram a year ago or less, more than 1 year but not more than 2 years, or more than 2 years ago.

[2] Includes all other races not shown separately, unknown poverty status, and unknown education.

[3] Estimates are age adjusted to the year 2000 standard using four age groups: 40–49 years, 50–64 years, 65–74 years, and 75 years and over

[4] The race groups white, black, and Asian or Pacific Islander include persons of Hispanic and non-Hispanic origin; persons of Hispanic origin may be of any race.

[5] Prior to 1998 poverty status is based on family income and family size using Bureau of the Census poverty thresholds. Beginning in 1998 poverty status is based on family income, family size, number of children in the family, and for families with two or fewer adults the age of the adults in the family. Missing family income data were imputed for 13–16 percent of adults in the sample in 1990–94. Poverty status was unknown for 25 percent of persons in the sample in 1998.

[6] Education categories shown are for 1998. GED stands for general equivalency diploma. In years prior to 1998 the following categories based on number of years of school completed were used: less than 12 years, 12 years, 13 years or more.

NOTES: Estimates for American Indian or Alaska Native women are not shown due to instability of single year estimates.

SOURCE: "Table 82. Use of Mammography for Women 40 Years of Age and Over according to Selected Characteristics: United States, Selected Years 1987–98," in *Health, United States, 2001*, National Center for Health Statistics, Hyattsville, MD, 2001

1950. Chronic liver disease and cirrhosis were the sixth leading cause of death among Native American women and the ninth leading cause of death among Hispanic women in 1999.

According to the NCHS, the death rate from unintentional injuries fell from 54.5 females and 102.2 males per 100,000 in 1950 to 22.6 females and 50.3 males per 100,000 in 1999. In 1980 unintentional injuries were the fourth leading cause of death among females.

Childbearing

For centuries childbearing was a major cause of death among women. Conditions arising from childbearing were the eighth leading cause of death among Hispanic women in 1999. (See Table 11.2.) Conditions arising from childbearing were the 10th leading cause of death among all American women in 1980 and the 6th leading cause of death among black and Asian/Pacific Islander women. In 1950, 2,960 women died from complications of pregnancy, childbirth, or post-childbirth, compared to 281 women in 1998. (See Table 11.4.) The age-adjusted maternal death rate per 100,000 live births was 6.1 in 1998, compared to 73.7 in 1950. Among

women age 20 and over, the maternal death rate rose with age up to 14.5 per 100,000 live births for women 35 and over in 1998. The rate was 222.0 per 100,000 births among women over 34 in 1950. Black women of all ages were significantly more likely than white women to suffer maternal mortality in 1998.

HIV/AIDS

Women Who Get AIDS

AIDS (acquired immune deficiency syndrome) caused by the human immunodeficiency virus (HIV) was the 10th leading cause of death among black women in 1999. (See Table 11.2.) The incidence of AIDS among women increased steadily between 1986 and 1993. (See Figure 11.7.) Between 1993 and 1996 the number of new female AIDS cases remained at about 13,000 annually and then began to decline, primarily because of treatment of HIV-positive women with new antiviral drugs. Between 1996 and midyear 2000 approximately 10,500 new AIDS cases were diagnosed in women annually. In the first half of 2000, women accounted for about 26 percent of newly diagnosed cases of AIDS.

TABLE 11.4

Maternal mortality for complications of pregnancy, childbirth, and the puerperium, according to race, Hispanic origin, and age, selected years, 1950–98

[Data are based on the National Vital Statistics System]

Race, Hispanic origin, and age	1950[1]	1960[1]	1970	1980	1990	1995	1996	1997	1998
					Number of deaths				
All persons	2,960	1,579	803	334	343	277	294	327	281
White	1,873	936	445	193	177	129	159	179	158
Black	1,041	624	342	127	153	133	121	125	104
American Indian or Alaska Native	- - -	- - -	- - -	3	4	1	6	2	2
Asian or Pacific Islander	- - -	- - -	- - -	11	9	14	8	21	17
Hispanic[2]	- - -	- - -	- - -	- - -	47	43	39	57	42
White, non-Hispanic[2]	- - -	- - -	- - -	- - -	125	84	114	121	116
All persons					**Deaths per 100,000 live births**				
All ages, age adjusted	73.7	32.1	21.5	9.4	7.6	6.3	6.4	7.6	6.1
All ages, crude	83.3	37.1	21.5	9.2	8.2	7.1	7.6	8.4	7.1
Under 20 years	70.7	22.7	18.9	7.6	7.5	3.9	*	5.7	*
20–24 years	47.6	20.7	13.0	5.8	6.1	5.7	5.0	6.6	5.0
25–29 years	63.5	29.8	17.0	7.7	6.0	6.0	6.6	7.9	6.7
30–34 years	107.7	50.3	31.6	13.6	9.5	7.3	7.6	8.3	7.5
35 years and over[3]	222.0	104.3	81.9	36.3	20.7	15.9	19.0	16.1	14.5
White									
All ages, age adjusted	53.1	22.4	14.4	6.7	5.1	3.6	4.1	5.2	4.2
All ages, crude	61.1	26.0	14.3	6.6	5.4	4.2	5.1	5.8	5.1
Under 20 years	44.9	14.8	13.8	5.8	*	*	*	*	*
20–24 years	35.7	15.3	8.4	4.2	3.9	3.5	*	4.2	3.1
25–29 years	45.0	20.3	11.1	5.4	4.8	4.0	4.0	5.4	4.9
30–34 years	75.9	34.3	18.7	9.3	5.0	4.0	5.0	5.4	4.9
35 years and over[3]	174.1	73.9	59.3	25.5	12.6	9.1	14.9	11.5	11.0
Black									
All ages, age adjusted	- - -	92.0	65.5	24.9	21.7	20.9	19.9	20.1	16.1
All ages, crude	- - -	103.6	60.9	22.4	22.4	22.1	20.3	20.8	17.1
Under 20 years	- - -	54.8	32.3	13.1	*	*	*	*	*
20–24 years	- - -	56.9	41.9	13.9	14.7	15.3	15.1	15.3	12.7
25–29 years	- - -	92.8	65.2	22.4	14.9	21.0	25.5	24.3	17.2
30–34 years	- - -	150.6	117.8	44.0	44.2	31.2	28.6	32.9	27.7
35 years and over[3]	- - -	299.5	207.5	100.6	79.7	61.4	49.9	40.4	37.2
Hispanic[2,4]									
All ages, age adjusted	- - -	- - -	- - -	- - -	7.4	5.4	4.8	7.6	5.2
All ages, crude	- - -	- - -	- - -	- - -	7.9	6.3	5.6	8.0	5.7
White, non-Hispanic[2]									
All ages, age adjusted	- - -	- - -	- - -	- - -	4.4	3.3	3.9	4.4	4.0
All ages, crude	- - -	- - -	- - -	- - -	4.8	3.5	4.8	5.2	4.9

- - - Data not available.
* Based on fewer than 20 deaths.
[1] Includes deaths of persons who were not residents of the 50 States and the District of Columbia.
[2] Excludes data from States lacking an Hispanic-origin item on their death and birth certificates. See Appendix I, National Vital Statistics System.
[3] Rates computed by relating deaths of women 35 years and over to live births to women 35–49 years.
[4] Age-specific maternal mortality rates are not calculated because rates based on fewer than 20 deaths are unreliable.

NOTES: Rates are age adjusted to the 1970 distribution of live births by mother's age in the United States. For data years shown, the code numbers for cause of death are based on the then current *International Classification of Diseases*. The race groups, white, black, Asian or Pacific Islander, and American Indian or Alaska Native, include persons of Hispanic and non-Hispanic origin. Conversely, persons of Hispanic origin may be of any race. For 1950 and 1960, rates are based on live births by race of child; for all other years, rates are based on live births by race of mother. Rates are not calculated for American Indian or Alaska Native and Asian or Pacific Islander mothers because rates based on fewer than 20 deaths are unreliable.

SOURCE: "Table 44. Maternal Mortality for Complications of Pregnancy, Childbirth, and the Puerperium, according to Race, Hispanic Origin, and Age: United States, Selected Years 1950–98," in *Health, United States, 2001*, National Center for Health Statistics, Hyattsville, MD, 2001

According to the NCHS, among those aged 13 and over, there were a total of 119,454 AIDS cases among females reported as of June 30, 2000, compared to 601,471 male cases and 8,401 cases among children under 13. As of the 12-month period ending June 30, 2000, the incidence of AIDS was 8.9 females and 29.9 males per 100,000 female or male population.

Black non-Hispanic women accounted for 63 percent of female AIDS cases reported in 2000. (See Table 11.5.) The rate for non-Hispanic black females was 46 per 100,000, compared to 14 for Hispanics, 8 for American Indian/Alaska Native females, 2 for non-Hispanic white females, and 2 for Asian/Pacific Islanders. Among African American women in the

FIGURE 11.7

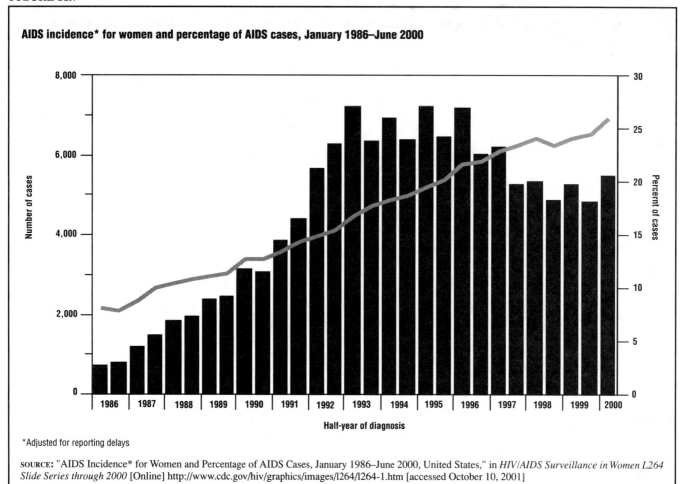

AIDS incidence* for women and percentage of AIDS cases, January 1986–June 2000

Half-year of diagnosis

*Adjusted for reporting delays

SOURCE: "AIDS Incidence* for Women and Percentage of AIDS Cases, January 1986–June 2000, United States," in *HIV/AIDS Surveillance in Women L264 Slide Series through 2000* [Online] http://www.cdc.gov/hiv/graphics/images/l264/l264-1.htm [accessed October 10, 2001]

northeast United States the rate was 83.3 per 100,000 in 2000.

According to the NCHS, the age at which women were first diagnosed with AIDS rose steadily up to the ages of 30 to 39. That age group accounted for 44.8 percent of all female AIDS cases through 2000. Above age 39 the diagnosis of AIDS in females declined steadily.

The age-adjusted death rates from HIV disease in 1999 were 2.6 females per 100,000, compared to 8.3 males per 100,000. The female death rate from AIDS declined after 1995, when it peaked at 5.3 per 100,000. The death rates were highest for women aged 35 to 44, at 6.7 per 100,000, and for African Americans at 13.3 per 100,000. Among African American women between the ages of 25 and 44, the death rate was 27.2 per 100,000. Death rates were lowest among non-Hispanic white women at 0.7 per 100,000.

How Women Are Infected

As of June 2000 the NCHS reported that 41.5 percent of all female AIDS patients had acquired HIV through intravenous drug use and 39.4 percent through heterosexual contact, 15.5 percent of those through sex with an intravenous drug user. Among women diagnosed with AIDS between July 1999 and June 2000, the CDC estimated that about 62 percent acquired HIV through heterosexual contact: 45 percent through sexual contact with either HIV-infected men or men at high-risk for HIV infection (bisexual men or hemophiliacs who may have received a transfusion of infected blood) and 17 percent through sexual contact with an intravenous drug user. (See Figure 11.8.) The CDC estimated that an additional 35 percent of the women contracted HIV through intravenous drug use and 2 percent through transfusions received prior to March 1985.

Thus, women who have sex with high-risk men, such as those who inject drugs, and are themselves intravenous drug users are in double jeopardy for contracting HIV. Furthermore, women may transmit HIV to their newborns during childbirth. However, planned cesarean deliveries combined with antiviral drug therapy throughout pregnancy lowers the chances of delivering an HIV-positive baby.

OTHER SEXUALLY TRANSMITTED DISEASES

In addition to AIDS a number of other sexually transmitted diseases (STDs) are of particular concern to

TABLE 11.5

AIDS cases and rates in adult/adolescent women, by race/ethnicity, reported in 2000

Race/Ethnicity	Number	Percent	Rate per 100,000
White, not Hispanic	1,895	18	2
Black, not Hispanic	6,545	63	46
Hispanic	1,855	18	14
Asian/Pacific Islander	77	1	2
American Indian/ Alaska Native	68	1	8
Total*	10,459	100	9

*Includes19 women of unknown race/ethnicity

SOURCE: "AIDS Cases and Rates in Adult/Adolescent Women, by Race/Ethnicity, Reported in 2000, United States," in *HIV/AIDS Surveillance in Women L264 Slide Series through 2000* [Online] http://www.cdc.gov/hiv/graphics/images/l264/l264-2.htm [accessed October 10, 2001]

FIGURE 11.8

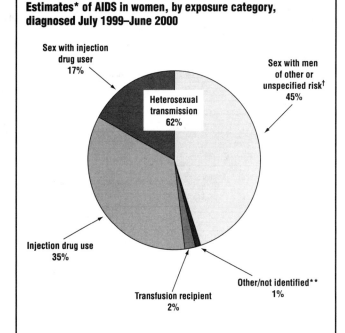

Estimates* of AIDS in women, by exposure category, diagnosed July 1999–June 2000

*Data adjusted for reporting delays and estimated proportional redistribution of cases initially reported without risk. Data reported through December 2000.

**Includes patients whose medical record review is pending; patients who died, were lost to follow-up, or declined interview; and patients with other or undetermined modes of exposure.

† Includes sex with a bisexual male, a person with hemophilia, a transfusion recipient with HIV infection, or an HIV-infected person with an unspecified risk

SOURCE: "Estimates* of AIDS in Women, by Exposure Category Diagnosed July 1999–June 2000, United States," in *HIV/AIDS Surveillance in Women L264 Slide Series through 2000* [Online] http://www.cdc.gov/hiv/graphics/images/l264/l264-4.htm [accessed October 10, 2001]

women. According to the American Social Health Association, although women account for about half of all STD infections, they are more vulnerable to STDs than men. Genital infections, including HIV, are more easily passed from men to women than from women to men. Women may have less control than men over whether to have sex and whether to use a condom. Women are less likely than men to have noticeable symptoms of STD, and they are more likely than men to have long-term consequences, including infertility, tubal pregnancy, and cervical cancer. Essentially every STD can be passed from a woman to her fetus or newborn, sometimes with tragic consequences.

Chlamydia and Gonorrhea

In 1999 women accounted for 81.4 percent of all reported cases of *Chlamydia trachomatis*, a vaginal bacterial infection. (See Table 11.6.). This STD affected over one-half million women in 1999. Reported cases of chlamydial infection among women have increased steadily since the late 1980s, when public programs were instituted for detecting and treating the infection in women. The number of reported cases among males has also increased with better screening.

Women accounted for approximately one-half of all reported cases of gonorrhea in 1999. (See Table 11.6.) Between 1997 and 1999 the gonorrhea rate in women increased more than 9 percent, from 109 per 100,000 to 129.9 per 100,000. The incidences of chlamydia and gonorrhea were highest among women between the ages of 15 and 24, particularly among females aged 15 to 19. In 1999 the gonorrhea rate among non-Hispanic white women aged 15 to 19 was 198.3 per 100,000. It was 178.4 per 100,000 women aged 20 to 24. Among African American women it was 3,691.0 and 3,273.1 per 100,000 in those age groups, respectively. In 1999 there were 131,572 cases of gonorrhea reported among African

American women, 73.2 percent of all reported cases among women.

Most women with chlamydia (about 70 percent) and about 50 percent of women with gonorrhea have no symptoms, so screening for infection is essential. If not adequately treated, 20 to 40 percent of women infected with chlamydia and 10 to 40 percent of women infected with gonorrhea develop pelvic inflammatory disease (PID), which can lead to infertility and other reproductive complications. According to Planned Parenthood, one in five women with PID becomes infertile. PID also is a major cause of ectopic or tubal pregnancy. The rate of ectopic pregnancy increased fivefold in the last two decades of the 20th century. Ectopic pregnancies account for about 9 percent of all pregnancy-related deaths in the United States. Chlamydial and gonorrheal infections during pregnancy can result in blindness and pneumonia in the newborn infants.

TABLE 11.6

Reported cases of sexually transmitted disease, by gender and reporting source, 1999

Disease	Non-STD Clinic			STD Clinic			Total[1]		
	Male	Female	Total	Male	Female	Total	Male	Female	Total
Total *Chlamydia Trachomatis*	65,297	426,550	493,829	54,773	110,410	165,545	120,094	537,003	659,441
Chlamydial PID[2]	NA	2,555	2,558	NA	478	479	NA	3,033	3,037
Ophthalmia Neonatorum	115	152	267	11	16	28	126	168	295
Total Gonorrhea	80,506	126,471	207,803	99,038	53,051	152,241	179,564	179,534	360,076
Gonococcal PID	NA	2,360	2,362	NA	1,379	1,381	NA	3,739	3,743
Ophthalmia Neonatorum	15	21	36	3	2	5	18	23	41
Total Syphilis	NA	NA	NA	NA	NA	NA	18,771	16,803	35,628
Primary	645	215	860	1,156	295	1,452	1,801	510	2,312
Secondary	974	1,144	2,120	1,080	1,142	2,224	2,055	2,286	4,345
Early Latent	2,915	3,166	6,087	2,893	2,697	5,590	5,808	5,863	11,677
Late and Late Latent[4]	4,884	4,766	9,657	3,947	3,129	7,081	8,831	7,895	16,738
Neurosyphilis[3]	227	93	320	16	5	21	243	98	341
Congenital <1 year[5]	NR	NR	NR	NR	NR	NR	276	249	556
Chancroid	21	25	46	69	26	95	91	51	143
Granuloma Inguinale	1	0	1	14	4	18	15	4	19
Lymphogranuloma Venereum	6	12	18	33	11	44	39	23	62
Genital Herpes[6]	858	2,515	3,389	3,605	3,154	6,763	4,463	5,669	10,149
Other and Nonspecified PID	NA	1,042	1,042	NA	1,880	1,880	NA	2,922	2,922
Nonspecific Urethritis in Men	2,704	NA	2,704	26,027	NA	26,027	28,731	NA	28,731

NA = Not applicable. NR = No report.
[1] Totals include unknown gender and reporting source.
[2] PID = Pelvic inflammatory disease.
[3] Neurosyphilis cases are not included with Total Syphilis cases but are included in the late and late latent syphilis cases.
[4] Cases of unknown duration for syphilis are included in late and late latent syphilis.
[5] Cases of congenital syphilis <1 year of age are obtained using reporting from CDC 73.126. Clinic reporting source is not available from that form.
[6] Genital herpes data are only available for a limited number of states.

SOURCE: "Table 2. Reported cases of sexually transmitted disease by gender and reporting source: United States, 1999," in *Sexually Transmitted Disease Surveillance 1999*, Centers for Disease Control and Prevention, Atlanta, GA, September, 2000

Other STDs

Women accounted for slightly less than one-half of new syphilis cases in 1999. (See Table 11.6.) African American women had the highest rates of syphilis among females. Infection with gonorrhea, chlamydia, and syphilis make women two to five times more vulnerable to HIV infection.

Women also accounted for 55.9 percent of reported cases of genital herpes. (See Table 11.6.) Trichomoniasis, caused by a microscopic parasite, affects both men and women. Genital infections with certain types of human papillomavirus (HPV) are associated with the development of cervical cancer. Other types of HPV cause genital warts, which can infect newborns. The hepatitis B virus also can be sexually transmitted. Hepatitis B can lead to severe liver damage.

Risks

According to the Alan Guttmacher Institute, one-third of all sexually active women are at risk of infection from STDs because either they or their partners have had multiple partners within the past year. Unmarried women and women aged 18 to 19 have the highest risk of STDs because of multiple partnerships (both are at over 60 percent risk). Married women have about a 10 percent risk of STDs because of multiple partnerships. Women in monogamous relationships may be at risk if their partner has an incurable STD from a previous relationship.

Consistent and careful use of condoms is the best protection from HIV and other STDs. Among sexually active women aged 15 to 44, teenagers and never-married women were most likely to report using condoms, according to the Alan Guttmacher Institute. Over 30 percent of never-married women and teens aged 15 to 19 reported using condoms.

OSTEOPOROSIS

Osteoporosis and arthritis are chronic diseases that affect large numbers of older women and can restrict their mobility. Osteoporosis, the loss of bone mass and deterioration of bone tissue, puts women at risk for debilitating bone fractures. According to the National Osteoporosis Foundation, as of 2001 about 10 million Americans had this disease and 18 million more had low bone mass, placing them at risk for osteoporosis; 80 percent of these people were female. About 15 percent of women in their 50s have osteoporosis, increasing to 50 percent of women in their 80s. Although white and Asian women are at the greatest risk for osteoporosis, about 10 percent of African American women over age 50 have the disease and an additional 30 percent have low bone mass. One in two white women over age 50 will have an osteoporosis-related bone fracture at some point in her life, and it is estimated that approximately 80 percent of hip fractures are the result of osteoporosis.

Osteoporosis is associated with the drop in estrogen production at menopause. Thin, small-boned women of northern European descent are at the highest risk for the disease. Menstruation at an early age, smoking, alcohol consumption, and certain medications can increase the risk of osteoporosis. Weight-bearing exercise, such as running, and consumption of adequate levels of calcium, Vitamin D, and magnesium reduce the risk of osteoporosis.

MENTAL HEALTH

According to the National Institute of Mental Health (NIMH), about twice as many women as men suffer from depression. (See Table 11.7.) About 12 percent of women, compared to only about 6.6 percent of men, will experience a depressive disorder within a one-year period. Anxiety disorders affect two to three times more women than men. Women also are much more at risk for developing post-traumatic stress disorder (13 percent of women versus 6 percent of men).

Depression

Hormonal factors including menstrual cycle changes, PMS, pregnancy, miscarriage, the postpartum period, premenopause, and menopause can bring about depression in women. Furthermore, women may experience more emotional stress than men from balancing home, family, and work responsibilities. Reproductive hormones and stress hormones have been linked to depression in women.

Types of depression include:

- Major depression

- Dysthymia, a long-term chronic but less severe depression

- Seasonal affective disorder (SAD)

- Bipolar disorder (manic-depressive illness), which is characterized by extreme highs and extreme lows

Major depression occurs in episodes, one in a lifetime or recurrent. Women seem to be especially susceptible to SAD, a depression that usually occurs in the fall and winter and subsides in the spring. Men and women are equally at risk for bipolar disorder.

Causes of depression include:

- Heredity, particularly for bipolar disorder

- Upbringing

- Brain biochemistry

- Hormone production

TABLE 11.7

Symptoms of depression and mania

Depression
- Persistent sad, anxious, or "empty" mood
- Feelings of hopelessness, pessimism
- Feelings of guilt, worthlessness, helplessness
- Loss of interest or pleasure in hobbies and activities that were once enjoyed, including sex
- Decreased energy, fatigue, being "slowed down"
- Difficulty concentrating, remembering, making decisions
- Insomnia, early-morning awakening, or oversleeping
- Appetite and/or weight loss or overeating and weight gain
- Thoughts of death or suicide; suicide attempts
- Restlessness, irritability
- Persistent physical symptoms that do not respond to treatment, such as headaches, digestive disorders, and chronic pain

Mania
- Abnormal or excessive elation
- Unusual irritability
- Decreased need for sleep
- Grandiose notions
- Increased talking
- Racing thoughts
- Increased sexual desire
- Markedly increased energy
- Poor judgment
- Inappropriate social behavior

SOURCE: Margaret Strock, "Symptoms of Depression and Mania," in *Depression,* National Institute of Mental Health, Bethesda, MD, 2000

- Emotional stress, such as loss of a loved one, relationship difficulties, or financial problems

- Physical illness

About one-third of people with any type of depressive disorder also exhibit some form of substance abuse.

Treatments for depression include:

- A wide variety of medications, including antidepressants

- Psychotherapy

- Counseling

Eating Disorders

The most common eating disorders are anorexia nervosa and bulimia nervosa. Anorexia is severe weight loss to at least 15 percent below normal body weight. Anorexics see themselves as overweight even when they are dangerously thin. Bulimics may binge-eat (eat large amounts of food in a short period of time) and then force themselves to vomit and/or abuse laxatives.

According to a NIMH 2001 report on eating disorders, 85 to 95 percent of those with anorexia or bulimia are women, as are about 65 percent of those with binge-eating disorder. It is estimated that 0.5 to 3.7 percent of females suffer from anorexia and 1.1 to 4.2 percent of females suffer from bulimia at some point in their lives. According to Anorexia Nervosa and Related Eating

FIGURE 11.9

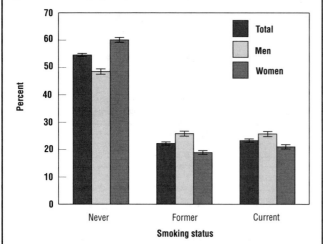

Percent distribution of smoking status among adults aged 18 years and older, by sex, 2000

Note: Current smokers were defined as those who smoked more than 100 cigarettes in their lifetime and now smoke every day or some days. The analysis excluded 301 people with unknown smoking status. Brackets indicate 95% confidence intervals (CI).

SOURCE: "Figure 8.2. Percent Distribution of Smoking Status Among Adults Aged 18 Years and Older, by Sex: United States, 2000," in *National Health Interview Survey*, [Online] http://www.cdc.gov/nchs/data/nhis/measure08.pdf [accessed October 8, 2001]

Disorders, Inc. (ANRED), research suggests that about 1 percent of adolescent females have anorexia and about 4 percent of college-aged women have bulimia. According to the National Association for Anorexia Nervosa and Associated Disorders (ANAD), eating disorders affect about 7 million American women. About 86 percent of eating disorders first appear before the age of 20.

The mortality rate for people with anorexia has been estimated at 0.56 percent annually, or 12 times higher than the annual death rate from all other causes for females aged 15 to 24 in the general population. The most common causes of death are cardiac arrest, electrolyte imbalance, and suicide. Less severe consequences of anorexia may include a cessation in menstruation, lowered pulse and blood pressure, heart irregularities, anemia (low red blood cell count), swollen joints, hair loss, osteoporosis, and depression.

According to ANRED about 20 percent of people with untreated serious eating disorders die. With treatment, only 2 to 3 percent die and approximately 60 percent recover.

PREVENTION

Smoking

During the first half of the 20th century, most cigarette smokers were men. By 1955 more than 50 percent of men smoked and more and more women had taken up smoking. By the time the U.S. Surgeon General's first report on the health hazards of smoking was released in 1964, smoking rates among men had already begun to decline but smoking among women was on the increase.

In 1997–99, 21.8 percent of females 18 and over smoked cigarettes, compared to 26.6 percent of males, down from 23.6 percent of females in 1990–92 and 33.9 percent in 1965. (See Table 6.5.) Among American Indian/Alaska Native women in 1997–99, 33.5 percent smoked, compared to only 10.4 percent of Asian/Pacific Islander women. Non-Hispanic white women were more likely to smoke than non-Hispanic black women (23.4 versus 21.5 percent). Only 13.3 percent of Hispanic women smoked.

Among non-Hispanic white women smoking decreased with age, from 31.8 percent among 18- to 24-year-olds to 11.3 percent among those over 64. However among non-Hispanic black women smoking increased with age, peaking at 29.7 percent for ages 35 to 44, and then decreasing to 12.0 percent for women over 64. Among non-Hispanic black and white women, smoking decreased with increasing educational attainment. (See Table 6.5.)

As of 2000 a higher percentage of women than men had never smoked (60.1 percent versus 48.5 percent) and a higher percentage of men than women were current smokers (25.7 percent versus 21.0 percent) or former smokers (25.8 percent versus 18.9 percent). (See Figure 11.9.) More men than women in every age group smoked; however, among those aged 65 and over the difference was not significant. In 2000, among women aged 18 to 44, 24.6 percent smoked compared to 29.4 percent of men. Among women aged 45 to 64, 21.6 percent smoked, compared to 26.4 percent of men. Among women 65 and older, 9.3 percent smoked, compared to 10.2 percent of men. In 1965, 43.7 percent of all females aged 25 to 44 smoked.

According to the AHA in 1999, 39.1 of non-Hispanic white female high school students had smoked cigarettes in the past 30 days, compared to 17.7 percent of non-Hispanic African American girls and 31.5 percent of Hispanic girls. More males than females smoked among African American and Hispanic high school students, but slightly fewer white males than females smoked. Far more boys than girls used smokeless tobacco, which is also a health hazard.

The rise in smoking among women has led to large increases in the death rates from smoking-related illnesses. According to the National Center on Addiction and Substance Abuse (CASA) at Columbia University, about half of women who smoke (47 percent) will die from tobacco-related causes, up sharply from about 1 in 6 (17 percent) in the early 1960s. In 1987 lung cancer passed breast cancer as the leading cause of cancer mortality among women. The ACS in *Cancer Facts and Figures*

2001 estimated that there would be about 172,000 female cancer deaths in 2001 that were related to tobacco use. In addition to lung cancers, smoking increases the risks of pancreatic, oral, esophageal, laryngeal, urinary, and cervical cancers. Smoking can cause chronic lung disease and increases a woman's risk of lower respiratory infections, CVD, osteoporosis, and other debilitating diseases.

Alcohol

In 1999, 56.1 percent of women over 18 drank alcohol, 38.8 percent regularly. (See Table 11.8.) In addition, 14.5 percent of women were former drinkers and 29.4 percent were lifelong abstainers from alcohol, up from 27.7 percent in 1997. Only 14.7 percent of men were lifelong abstainers in 1999. The highest percentages of drinkers were between the ages of 25 and 44 (65.6 percent of women and 77.6 percent of men). Among all age groups higher percentages of non-Hispanic white women were current drinkers, compared to non-Hispanic black women and Hispanic women.

Among current drinkers, 80.7 percent of women and 58.9 percent of men were light drinkers; only 6.7 percent of women were heavy drinkers. (See Table 11.8.) According to the 2000 NHIS, far more men than women in every age group drank excessively (defined as five or more drinks on at least 12 occasions in the past 12 months.) Younger women and men were more likely than older adults to drink excessively. Among women aged 18 to 24, 8.4 percent drank excessively, compared to 23 percent of males. Among women aged 25 to 44, 4.2 percent drank excessively, compared to 1.8 percent of women aged 45 to 64 and 0.4 percent of women aged 65 and over.

According to the NCHS, in 1998 among teenagers aged 12 to 17, about 19 percent each of males and females had used alcohol in the past month, down from 47 percent of teenage girls in 1979. In 1998, about 7 percent of girls aged 12 to 17 had had at least five drinks on at least one occasion in the past month, compared to 14 percent in 1985.

Women are at greater risk for developing chronic alcohol-related diseases than men because of their greater sensitivity to alcohol and their smaller body size. As a result, women are more subject to the side effects of heavy drinking, such as vomiting, slurred speech, hangovers, and depression. Women are at risk for developing cirrhosis of the liver with lower levels of alcohol consumption and at earlier ages than men. According to the ACS, alcohol can cause cancers of the oral cavity, esophagus, and larynx, particularly in combination with smoking. Alcohol consumption also increases the risk of breast cancer.

Other Substance Abuse

According to the Substance Abuse and Mental Health Services Administration's (SAMHSA) National Household Survey on Drug Abuse for 1999 and 2000, 7.5 percent of females aged 15 to 44 had used an illicit drug within the past month, including 5.6 percent who had used marijuana or hashish. Among women aged 15 to 44, 3.3 percent had used illicit drugs other than marijuana, including 0.7 percent who had used cocaine, 0.1 percent who had used crack cocaine, and 0.1 percent who had used heroin. Hallucinogens had been used by 0.6 percent of females aged 15 to 44. LSD had been used by 0.2 percent of the women, and 0.2 percent had used inhalants. Prescription-type psychotherapeutics had been used for other than medical purposes by 2.3 percent of the women, including 1.6 percent who had used pain relievers, 0.7 percent who had used tranquilizers, and 0.6 percent who had used stimulants, including 0.3 percent who had used methamphetamine.

According to *Health. United States. 2001*, in 1998, 8 percent of females aged 12 to 17 had used marijuana in the past month, compared to 12 percent in 1979. Among females aged 18 to 25, 10 percent had used marijuana in the past month. In 1998, 1.0 percent of females aged 12 to 17 had used cocaine in the past month, compared to 0.8 percent in 1979. Among females aged 18 to 25, 1.3 percent had used cocaine in the past month, compared to 0.6 percent in 1994. Drug use was slightly higher among males in each of those age groups.

According to the Census Bureau, in 1998 there were 322,899 female clients of substance abuse treatment facilities, 31.1 percent of the total clientele.

Obesity

After smoking, obesity is the second leading cause of preventable death in the United States, according to the ACS. Obesity is estimated to cause about 300,000 premature deaths each year and is associated with increased mortality rates for most causes of death, particularly CVD. According to the ACS, obesity in women is correlated with cancers of the breast, uterus and cervix, ovaries, and gallbladder. The risk of breast cancer is 50 percent higher for obese postmenopausal women.

According to the 2000 NHIS, the age-adjusted prevalence of obesity was 35.8 percent for non-Hispanic African American women, 25.9 percent for Hispanic women, and 19.3 percent for non-Hispanic white women. There was very little difference in the prevalence of obesity among men and women aged 20 to 59; however, 22.1 percent of women aged 60 and over were obese, compared to 18.8 percent of men. Among women aged 20 to 39, 18.8 percent were obese, as were 25.3 percent of women aged 40 to 59.

Between 1994 and 1998 the prevalence of obesity increased among both males and females in all demographic groups. (See Table 11.9.) In 1998, 18.5 percent of females aged 18 and over were obese, an increase of 3.9 percent since 1994. Among all age groups of women aged 40 and over, the prevalence of obesity increased 3.9

TABLE 11.8

Alcohol consumption by females aged 18 years and older, according to race, Hispanic origin, and age, 1997–99

[Data are based on household interviews of a sample of the civilian noninstitutionalized population]

Alcohol consumption, race, Hispanic origin, and age	Female		
	1997	1998	1999
Drinking status[1]	Percent distribution		
All	100.0	100.0	100.0
Lifetime abstainer	27.7	28.6	29.4
Former drinker	15.4	15.7	14.5
Infrequent	10.1	10.5	9.3
Regular	5.2	5.1	5.2
Current drinker	57.0	55.8	56.1
Infrequent	18.1	17.8	17.3
Regular	38.8	37.9	38.8
Race, Hispanic origin, and age[2]	Percent current drinkers among all persons		
All persons:			
18–44 years	64.2	63.1	63.6
18–24 years	57.7	53.5	57.1
25–44 years	66.1	65.9	65.6
45 years and over	48.5	47.4	47.7
45–64 years	56.2	55.4	56.1
65 years and over	36.6	35.0	34.2
White, non-Hispanic:			
18–44 years	71.4	70.8	71.2
18–24 years	66.5	62.5	66.5
25–44 years	72.8	73.1	72.6
45 years and over	52.2	51.3	51.6
45–64 years	61.2	60.4	61.3
65 years and over	39.5	38.0	37.0
Black, non-Hispanic:			
18–44 years	49.8	47.9	50.2
18–24 years	42.1	31.6	41.6
25–44 years	52.4	53.5	53.2
45 years and over	30.8	32.3	30.7
45–64 years	38.3	38.5	38.3
65 years and over	16.4	19.6	15.0
Hispanic:[2]			
18–44 years	46.5	44.1	43.9
18–24 years	40.1	40.5	35.4
25–44 years	48.9	45.5	47.2
45 years and over	37.8	32.9	35.2
45–64 years	43.2	39.4	38.0
65 years and over	25.7	18.0	28.8
Level of alcohol consumption in past year for current drinkers[3]	Percent distribution of current drinkers		
All drinking levels	100.0	100.0	100.0
Light	81.4	81.4	80.7
Moderate	11.7	12.0	12.5
Heavier	6.9	6.6	6.7
Number of days in the past year with 5 or more drinks	Percent distribution of current drinkers		
All current drinkers	100.0	100.0	100.0
No days	78.6	79.3	78.9
At least 1 day	21.4	20.6	21.1
1–11 days	14.6	14.2	13.6
12 or more days	6.8	6.4	7.5

TABLE 11.8

Alcohol consumption by females aged 18 years and older, according to race, Hispanic origin, and age, 1997–99 [CONTINUED]

[Data are based on household interviews of a sample of the civilian noninstitutionalized population]

Alcohol consumption, race, Hispanic origin, and age	Female		
	1997	1998	1999
Race, Hispanic origin, and age[2]	Percent of persons with 5 or more drinks on at least one day in the past year among current drinkers		
All persons:			
18–44 years	28.7	27.9	28.5
18–24 years	40.2	42.3	42.0
25–44 years	25.7	24.5	24.8
45 years and over	10.3	9.6	10.0
45–64 years	12.9	12.0	12.5
65 years and over	4.4	3.6	3.5
White, non-Hispanic:			
18–44 years	30.8	30.2	30.8
18–24 years	44.2	47.4	46.4
25–44 years	27.5	26.2	26.7
45 years and over	9.4	9.2	9.7
45–64 years	12.0	11.7	12.4
65 years and over	3.8	3.3	3.2
Black, non-Hispanic:			
18–44 years	15.8	17.8	15.9
45 years and over	15.2	13.4	14.7
Hispanic:[2]			
18–44 years	27.2	21.5	23.0
45 years and over	17.8	14.3	*8.7

*Estimates are considered unreliable. Data preceded by an asterisk have a relative standard error of 20–30 percent.

[1] Drinking status categories are based on self-reported responses to questions about alcohol consumption. Lifetime abstainers had fewer than 12 drinks in their lifetime. Former drinkers had at least 12 drinks in their lifetime and none in the past year. Former infrequent drinkers are former drinkers who had fewer than 12 drinks in any one year. Former regular drinkers are former drinkers who had at least 12 drinks in any one year. Current drinkers had 12 drinks in their lifetime and at least one drink in the past year. Current infrequent drinkers are current drinkers who had fewer than 12 drinks in the past year. Current regular drinkers are current drinkers who had at least 12 drinks in the past year.

[2] Persons of Hispanic origin may be of any race.

[3] Level of alcohol consumption categories are based on self-reported responses to questions about average alcohol consumption and defined as follows: light drinkers: up to 3 drinks per week; moderate drinkers: 4–7 drinks per week; heavier drinkers: more than 14 drinks per week for men and more than 7 drinks per week for women.

SOURCE: Adapted from "Table 66. Alcohol Consumption by Persons 18 Years of Age and Over, according to Sex, Race, Hispanic Origin, and Age: United States, 1997–99," in *Health, United States, 2001*, National Center for Health Statistics, Hyattsville, MD, 2001

to 4.0 percent between 1994 and 1998. Black women were most likely to be obese (31.5 percent in 1998, compared to 16.3 percent of white women). However, the percentage of obese Hispanic women increased 7.6 percent between 1994 and 1998, to 23.8 percent.

Separated women were most likely to be obese, and never-married women or women in unmarried couples were least likely. Women without a high school degree were most likely to be obese (28.1 percent), and women with a college degree were least likely (12.2 percent). Former smokers were more likely to be obese than current smokers (20.9 percent versus 15.5 percent). Inactive women were far more likely to be obese than those who exercised regularly (25.5 percent versus 13.9 percent). Obesity rates among males followed similar trends as those among females.

Fat Intake

Nutritionists generally recommend that diets should contain less than 30 percent of total calories from fat. Diets high in saturated fats (animal fats present in meat and dairy products) contribute to cardiovascular diseases. Excess saturated fats can raise blood cholesterol and fat levels, clogging arteries and leading to heart disease. However,

TABLE 11.9

Prevalence of obesity by gender and demographic and behavioral characteristics, 1994 and 1998

	Males					Females				
	1994	Weighted Prevalence (%) 95% CI*	1998	95% CI*	Increase, %†	1994	Weighted Prevalence (%) 95% CI*	1998	95% CI*	Increase, %†
Overall	15.1	(14.6, 15.6)	18.2	(17.7, 18.7)	3.1	14.6	(14.2, 15.0)	18.5	(18.1, 19.0)	3.9
Age in years										
18-29	10.1	(9.1, 11.2)	12.6	(11.6, 13.6)	2.5	9.2	(8.4, 10.0)	12.3	(11.5, 13.1)	3.1
30-39	15.5	(14.4, 16.6)	18.3	(17.3, 19.3)	2.8	13.3	(12.4, 14.2)	16.5	(15.6, 17.3)	3.2
40-49	18.6	(17.3, 19.9)	21.6	(20.5, 22.8)	3.0	18.2	(17.0, 19.4)	22.2	(21.0, 23.3)	4.0
50-59	20.6	(18.9, 22.3)	23.7	(22.3, 25.1)	3.1	21.0	(19.6, 22.4)	24.9	(23.5, 26.2)	3.9
60-69	17.1	(15.5, 18.7)	21.9	(20.3, 23.5)	4.8	18.2	(16.8, 19.6)	22.2	(20.9, 23.6)	4.0
70+	10.7	(9.2, 12.2)	12.6	(11.4, 13.8)	1.9	12.5	(11.5, 13.6)	16.4	(15.3, 17.5)	3.9
Race										
White	14.8	(14.2, 15.4)	18.1	(17.5, 18.6)	3.3	13.0	(12.5, 13.5)	16.3	(15.9, 16.8)	3.3
Black	19.5	(17.5, 21.4)	22.8	(21.0, 24.5)	3.3	27.8	(26.2, 29.5)	31.5	(29.9, 33.1)	3.7
Hispanic	17.1	(14.6, 19.6)	18.9	(17.0, 20.8)	1.8	16.2	(14.0, 18.4)	23.8	(21.7, 25.9)	7.6
Other	8.6	(6.9, 10.4)	11.0	(8.8, 13.3)	2.4	11.0	(9.0, 12.9)	13.4	(10.9, 15.8)	2.4
Marital status										
Married	16.4	(15.7, 17.1)	20.3	(19.6, 20.9)	3.9	14.2	(13.6, 14.8)	18.0	(17.4, 18.7)	3.8
Divorced	14.7	(13.0, 16.4)	17.7	(16.3, 19.0)	3.0	17.1	(15.7, 18.4)	22.1	(20.8, 23.4)	5.0
Widowed	16.4	(13.5, 19.3)	17.3	(15.1, 19.6)	0.9	17.2	(16.0, 18.4)	19.8	(18.7, 21.0)	2.6
Separated	14.5	(10.9, 18.1)	18.9	(15.3, 22.6)	4.4	23.1	(19.8, 26.5)	25.2	(22.2, 28.2)	2.1
Never married	11.6	(10.5, 12.8)	13.2	(12.3, 14.2)	1.6	11.9	(10.8, 12.9)	16.2	(15.1, 17.3)	4.3
Unmarried couple	14.0	(10.0, 18.1)	14.7	(11.9, 17.5)	0.7	10.4	(7.8, 13.0)	16.8	(13.7, 20.0)	6.4
Education										
<High school degree	18.9	(17.2, 20.5)	20.9	(19.4, 22.4)	2.0	22.6	(21.2, 24.0)	28.1	(26.6, 29.7)	5.5
High school degree	16.1	(15.1, 17.1)	19.8	(18.9, 20.7)	3.7	16.0	(15.2, 16.7)	20.0	(19.2, 20.7)	4.0
Some college	15.6	(14.5, 16.7)	19.0	(18.0, 19.9)	3.4	13.0	(12.2, 13.8)	17.8	(16.9, 18.6)	4.8
College degree	11.5	(10.6, 12.4)	14.7	(14.0, 15.5)	3.2	8.8	(8.1, 9.5)	12.2	(11.5, 13.0)	3.4
Smoking status										
Never	13.8	(13.1, 14.6)	17.8	(17.1, 18.5)	4.0	15.0	(14.4, 15.6)	18.8	(18.2, 19.4)	3.8
Former	18.5	(17.5, 19.6)	21.9	(20.9, 22.9)	3.4	15.5	(14.6, 16.5)	20.9	(19.9, 21.9)	5.4
Current	13.3	(12.3, 14.3)	14.9	(14.0, 15.8)	1.6	12.5	(11.6, 13.4)	15.5	(14.7, 16.4)	3.0
Leisure-time activity										
Inactive	20.1	(18.9, 21.3)	22.6	(21.6, 23.6)	2.5	20.2	(19.3, 21.1)	25.5	(24.5, 26.4)	5.3
Irregular	14.1	(13.2, 15.0)	18.1	(17.2, 18.9)	4.0	14.6	(13.7, 15.5)	18.2	(17.4, 19.0)	3.6
Regular	12.6	(11.9, 13.3)	15.7	(15.0, 16.4)	3.1	10.4	(9.8, 11.0)	13.9	(13.3, 14.5)	3.5

*95% CI = 95% Confidence interval of the prevalence estimate.
†All increases are statistically significant at $P < 0.05$.

SOURCE: "Table 1. Prevalence of Obesity by Gender and Demographic and Behavioral Characteristics, 1994 and 1998," in *Cancer Facts and Figures 2001*, American Cancer Society, Inc., Atlanta, GA, 2001

polyunsaturated and monounsaturated fats can be beneficial, and some of these fats are essential to the diet. Vegetable oils, as well as green vegetables, nuts, many types of seeds, and cold-water fish, are high in these types of fats.

According to the ACS, fruits and vegetables, especially green and dark yellow vegetables, legumes, soy, and vegetables in the cabbage family, help protect against a variety of cancers. These foods are rich in substances, including weak estrogens, that protect against cancer in general and particularly those such as breast cancer that are affected by hormones. Furthermore, vegetables that are high in antioxidants can help protect against biochemical events that can lead to cancer.

Exercise

Only a minority of Americans, and fewer females than males, participate in even light to moderate leisure-time physical activity (defined as at least 30 minutes of physical activity at least five times per week). (See Figure 11.10.) Only 15.1 percent of women aged 18 to 24 and only 15.2 percent of women aged 25 to 64 participated in physical activity in 2000. Among women aged 65 to 74, 16.5 percent did physical exercise, but among women aged 75 or older, the percentage dropped to 9.9. In contrast, 17.8 percent of men 75 and over exercised regularly.

The AHA found that in 1998, 63.5 percent of overweight white adult women, 62.6 percent of overweight African American women, and 52.7 percent of overweight Hispanic females were using physical activity to lose weight. However, only 20.1 percent of the white women, 16.9 percent of the African American women, and 14.3 percent of the Hispanic women were meeting physical activity guidelines.

FIGURE 11.10

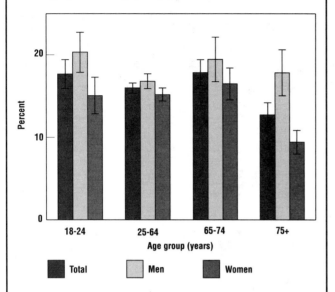

Percentage of adults aged 18 or over who regularly participated in light or moderate leisure-time physical activity, by sex and age groups, 2000

Note: Regular participation in light or moderate leisure-time physical activity was defined as engaging in such activities for ≥30 minutes ≥5 times per week. The analysis excluded 1,730 people with unknown physical activity participation. Brackets indicate 95% confidence intervals (CI).

SOURCE: "Figure 7.2. Percentage of Adults Aged 18 and Older who Regularly Participated in Light or Moderate Leisure-Time Physical Activity, by Sex and Age Group: United States, 2000," in *National Health Interview Survey*, [Online] http://www.cdc.gov/nchs/data/nhis/measure07.pdf [accessed October 8, 2001]

IMPORTANT NAMES AND ADDRESSES

AARP (formerly American Association of Retired Persons)
601 E St. NW
Washington, DC 20049
(800) 424-3410
member@aarp.org
http://www.aarp.org

The Alan Guttmacher Institute
120 Wall St.
New York, NY 10005
(212) 248-1111
FAX (212) 248-1951
http://www.agi-usa.org

American Association of University Women
1111 16th St. NW
Washington, DC 20036
FAX (202) 872-1425
(800) 326-AAUW
info@aauw.org
http://www.aauw.org

American Cancer Society
1599 Clifton Rd. NE
Atlanta, GA 30329-4251
(404) 320-3333
FAX (404) 329-7530
(800) ACS-2345
http://www.cancer.org

American Heart Association
7272 Greenville Ave.
Dallas, TX 75231
(800) 242-8721
http://www.americanheart.org

Amnesty International USA
322 8th Ave.
New York, NY 10001
(212) 807-8400
FAX (212) 627-1451
http://www.amnesty-usa.org

Association for Women in Science
1200 New York Ave. NW
Suite 650
Washington, DC 20005
(202) 326-8940
awis@awis.org
http://www.awis.org

Catalyst
120 Wall St., 5th Floor
New York, NY 10005
(212) 514-7600
FAX (212) 514-8470
info@catalystwomen.org
http://www.catalystwomen.org

Center for American Women and Politics Eagleton Institute of Politics Rutgers, The State University of New Jersey
191 Ryders Lane
New Brunswick, NJ 08901-8557
(732) 932-9384
FAX (732) 932-0014
http://www.cawp.rutgers.edu

Center on Budget and Policy Priorities
820 First St. NE
Suite 510
Washington, DC 20002
(202) 408-1080
FAX (202) 408-1056
bazie@cbpp.org
http://www.cbpp.org

EMILY's List
805 15th St., NW
Suite 400
Washington, DC 20005
(202) 326-1400
FAX (202) 326-1415
emilyslist@emilyslist.org
http://www.emilyslist.org

Families and Work Institute
267 5th Ave.
Floor 2
New York, NY 10016
(212) 465-2044
FAX (212) 465-8637
http://www.familiesandwork.org

Institute for Women's Policy Research
1707 L St. NW
Suite 750
Washington, DC 20036
(202) 785-5100
FAX (202) 833-4362
iwpr@iwpr.org
http://www.iwpr.org

National Abortion Federation
1755 Massachusetts Ave. NW
Suite 600
Washington, DC 20036
(202) 667-5881
Hotline: (800) 772-9100
http://www.prochoice.org

National Association of Anorexia Nervosa and Associated Disorders (ANAD)
PO Box 7
Highland Park, IL 60035
(847) 831-3438
FAX (847) 433-4632
info@anad.org
http://www.anad.org

National Coalition Against Domestic Violence
1201 East Colfax Ave.
Suite 385
PO Box 18749
Denver, CO 80218-0749
(303) 839-1852
FAX (303) 831-9251
Hotline: (800) 799-7233
http://www.ncadv.org

National Coalition of Girls' Schools
57 Main St.
Concord, MA 01742
(978) 287-4485
FAX (978) 287-6014
http://www.ncgs.org

National Gay and Lesbian Task Force
1700 Kalorama Rd. NW
Washington, DC 20009-2624
(202) 332-6483
FAX (202) 332-0207
ngltf@ngltf.org
http://www.ngltf.org

National Organization for Women (NOW)
733 15th St. NW
2nd Floor
Washington, DC 20005
(202) 628-8669
FAX (202) 785-8576
now@now.org
http://www.now.org

National Older Women's League (OWL)
666 11th St. NW
Suite 700
Washington, DC 20001
(202) 783-6686
FAX (202) 638-2356
(800) 825-3695
http://www.owl-national.org

National Osteoporosis Foundation
1232 22nd St. NW
Washington, DC 20037-1292
(202) 223-2226
http://www.nof.org

Planned Parenthood Federation of America
810 7th Ave.
New York, NY 10019
(212) 541-7800
FAX (212) 245-1845
(800) 230-PLAN
communications@ppfa.org
http://www.plannedparenthood.org

U.S. Department of Commerce
U.S. Census Bureau
Washington, DC 20233
(301) 763-INFO
http://www.census.gov

U.S. Department of Health and Human Services
Centers for Disease Control and Prevention
National Center for Health Statistics
Division of Data Services
Hyattsville, MD 20782-2003
(301) 458-4636
http://www.cdc.gov/nchs

U.S. Department of Labor
U.S. Bureau of Labor Statistics
Postal Square Building
2 Massachusetts Ave. NE
Washington, DC 20212-0001
(202) 691-5200
FAX (202) 691-6325
http://www.bls.gov

U.S. General Accounting Office
441 G St. NW
Washington, DC 20548
(202) 512-6000
FAX (202) 512-6061
info@www.gao.gov
http://www.gao.gov

The Urban Institute
2100 M St. NW
Washington, DC 20037
(202) 833-7200
FAX (202) 331-9747
paffairs@ui.urban.org
http://www.urban.org

Women's Research and Education Institute
1750 New York Ave. NW
Suite 350
Washington, DC 20006
(202) 628-0444
FAX (202) 628-0458
wrei@wrei.org
http://www.wrei.org

RESOURCES

The U.S. Census Bureau (Washington, D.C.) is publishing the data from Census 2000 as it becomes available. Census 2000 Briefs used in the preparation of this publication include *Gender: 2000* (September 2001) and *Households and Families: 2000* (September 2001). The Census Bureau publishes the findings of its annual surveys in a variety of publications. *Current Population Reports* used in the preparation of this publication include *Money Income in the United States: 2000* (September 2001), *Poverty in the United States: 2000* (September 2001), *America's Families and Living Arrangements: March 2000* (June 2001), *Population Profile of the United States: 1999* (March 2001), *Women in the United States: March 2000* (March 15, 2001), *Fertility of American Women: June 1998* (September 2000), *Money Income in the United States: 1999* (September 2000), *Voting and Registration in the Election of November 1998* (August 2000), and *Marital Status and Living Arrangements: March 1998 (Update)* (1998). The *Statistical Abstract of the United States: 2000*, published by the Census Bureau, is an important source of statistics on all facets of American life.

The National Center for Education Statistics of the U.S. Department of Education (Washington, D.C.) provides detailed information in its annual *Digest of Education Statistics 2000* (January 2001) and in *The Condition of Education 2001* (September 12, 2001).

The U.S. General Accounting Office (GAO) investigates all areas of government activity. Valuable publications from the GAO include *Intercollegiate Athletics: Four-Year Colleges' Experiences Adding and Discontinuing Teams* (March 2001) and *Child Care: States Increased Spending on Low-Income Families* (February 2001).

The Bureau of Labor Statistics (BLS; Washington, D.C.) of the U.S. Department of Labor (DOL) is the major source of statistical information on the nation's labor force. The monthly publication *Employment and Earnings* provides complete statistics on employment, unemployment, earnings, and occupations. The *BLS News* is an important source for the most recent labor force statistics. The *Monthly Labor Review* is also an important source for labor force statistics. Other BLS publications used in the preparation of this work include *Highlights of Women's Earnings in 2000* (August 2001) and *Occupational Outlook Handbook* (2000–01). The DOL published *Meeting the Needs of Today's Workforce: Best Child Care Practices* (1998). The Women's Bureau of the DOL is a good source of information on women in the workforce.

The National Science Foundation (Arlington, VA) published *Women, Minorities, and Persons with Disabilities in Science and Engineering: 2000* (2000) and *Land of Plenty: Diversity as America's Competitive Edge in Science, Engineering and Technology* (September 2000). The latter was prepared by the Congressional Commission on the Advancement of Women and Minorities in Science, Engineering and Technology Development.

The U.S. Department of Agriculture (USDA) publishes economic information in its *FoodReview*.

The Office on Women's Health of the U.S. Department of Health and Human Services (DHHS) published *HHS Blueprint for Action on Breastfeeding* (Washington, D.C., Fall 2000). The National Adoption Information Clearinghouse (NAIC), a service of the Children's Bureau of the DHHS, and the Child Care Bureau of the DHHS provided useful information. Information on Early Head Start came from the Administration of Children, Youth, and Families of the DHHS.

The Federal Interagency Forum on Child and Family Statistics publishes an annual report, *America's Children: Key National Indicators of Well-Being* (Washington, D.C., July 2001), a collaborative effort of 20 federal agencies.

Within the U.S. Department of Justice, the Bureau of Justice Statistics (BJS) (Washington, D.C.) conducts an annual National Crime Victimization Survey (NCVS) and publishes statistics about victims and crimes. Its publications include *Hate Crimes Reported in NIBRS, 1997–99* (September 2001), *Census of Jails, 1999* (August 2001), *Prisoners in 2000* (August 2001), *Criminal Victimization 2000: Changes 1999–2000 with Trends 1993–2000* (June 2001), *Prison and Jail Inmates at Midyear 2000* (March 2001), *Capital Punishment 1999* (December 2000), *Intimate Partner Violence* (May 2000), and *Women Offenders* (1999). The BJS and the National Institute of Justice (NIJ) published *The Sexual Victimization of College Women* (December 2000). The Federal Bureau of Investigation published *Crime in the United States 1999* (Washington, D.C., October 15, 2000). In July 2000 the NIJ and the Centers for Disease Control and Prevention (CDC) published *Extent, Nature, and Consequences of Intimate Partner Violence.*

The National Center for Health Statistics (NCHS) of the CDC publishes the *National Vital Statistics Reports* and the annual overview of the health of the nation, *Health, United States, 2001* (2001). The NCHS's 2000 National Health Interview Survey provided data on women and health. The CDC also published *Sexually Transmitted Disease Surveillance 1999* and *HIV/AIDS Surveillance in Women.*

The National Institute of Mental Health (Bethesda, MD) publishes information about women's mental health, including *Depression* (2000) and *Facts about Eating Disorders and the Search for Solutions* (2001). The Substance Abuse and Mental Health Services Administration published the *National Household Survey on Drug Abuse* (1999, 2000).

The Human Rights Campaign published *Gay and Lesbian Families in the United States: Same-Sex Unmarried Partner Households: A Preliminary Analysis of 2000 United States Census Data* (Washington, D.C., August 22, 2001). The U.S. Conference of Mayors provided important information in *A Status Report on Hunger and Homelessness in America's Cities: 2000* (Washington, D.C., December 2000).

The American Association of University Women (AAUW) Education Foundation and the National Coalition of Girls' Schools provided information on single-sex education. The College Entrance Examination Board (Princeton, NJ) provided information on college-bound high school seniors and the SATs.

The American Association for the Advancement of Science published its *Survey of Life Scientists* in 2001. Catalyst, a nonprofit research and advocacy organization concerned with women in business, published *Women in Financial Services: The Word on the Street* (2001), *Women in Law: Making the Case* (2001), and the *2000 Catalyst Census of Women Corporate Officers and Top*

Earners of the Fortune 500. The National Foundation for Women Business Owners provided research summaries that included *Women of All Races Share Entrepreneurial Spirit, Access to Credit Continues to Improve for Women Business Owners, Women-Owned Businesses Top 9 Million in 1999,* and *Women-Owned Businesses Thrive in the Nation's top 50 Metropolitan Areas.* The Women's Research and Education Institute (Washington, D.C.) published *The American Woman 2001–2002: Getting to the Top* (2001) and *Women in the Military: Where They Stand* (3rd ed., 2000). They also published *Midlife Women: Insurance Coverage and Access.*

The AFL-CIO publishes information on working women. With the Institute for Women's Policy Research they published *Equal Pay for Working Families: National and State Data on the Pay Gap and Its Costs* (Washington, D.C., 1999). The IWPR also published *How Much Can Child Support Provide? Welfare, Family Income, and Child Support* (1999) and *The Gender Gap in Pension Coverage: What Does the Future Hold?* (May 2001). The Center on Budget and Policy Priorities (Washington, D.C.) publishes information on low income women including *Poverty Trends for Families Headed by Working Single Mothers: 1993 to 1999* (August 2001) and *The Initial Impacts of Welfare Reform on the Incomes of Single-Mother Families* (1999).

The Alan Guttmacher Institute (New York and Washington, D.C.) publishes a wide variety of materials on human sexuality and reproduction including *The Guttmacher Report on Public Policy* and *Facts in Brief.*

AARP (formerly known as the American Association of Retired Persons) published a study in July 2001 on the child- and elder-care responsibilities of the "sandwich generation." The Center for Law and Social Policy published *Child Care after Leaving Welfare: Early Evidence from State Studies* (October 1999). Useful publications from the Families and Work Institute include the *1998 Business Work-Life Study: A Sourcebook* (New York, 1998). The Foundation for Child Development published a working paper entitled *Child Care Employment: Implications for Women's Self Sufficiency and for Child Development* (January 1999). The National Center for Children in Poverty published *Better Strategies for Babies: Strengthening the Caregivers and Families of Infants and Toddlers* (2000). OWL (National Older Women's League) is a good source for information on older women. The Urban Institute (Washington, D.C.), a nonpartisan economic and social policy research organization, publishes a wealth of research on a variety of subjects. Among the publications used in the preparation of this work were *Who's Caring for Our Youngest Children? Child Care Patterns of Infants and Toddlers* (Occasional Paper Number 42, January 2001) and *Parental Care at Midlife: Balancing Work and Family Responsibilities Near Retirement* (March 2000).

Child Trends is a nonprofit, nonpartisan, Washington, D.C.–based research organization that conducts studies on children, youth, and families and publishes an annual statistical study of teen childbearing.

The Center for American Women and Politics is an excellent source of on-line information on women and American politics. EMILY's List conducted the survey *The Women's Vote and the 2000 Elections* (December 14, 2000). GenderGap.com is an informative Web site devoted to women in government, politics, and the military.

The American Medical Association and the National Coalition Against Domestic Violence (NCADV) publish information on domestic violence. Amnesty International USA publishes information about prisoners and the death penalty in the United States. They published the 1999 report *"Not part of my sentence": Violations of the Human Rights of Women in Custody* and a follow-up 2001 study, *Abuse of Women in Custody: Sexual Misconduct and Shackling of Pregnant Women.*

The American Cancer Society's *Cancer Facts and Figures 2001* (Atlanta, GA, 2001) was an important source on women and cancer. The American Heart Association's *2001 Heart and Stroke Statistical Update* (Dallas, TX, 2000) was an important source of information on cardiovascular and other diseases. The American Social Health Association publishes information about women's health and sexually transmitted diseases.

INDEX